Books by MacKinlay Kantor

Fiction

BEAUTY BEAST (1968)
STORY TELLER (1967)
SPIRIT LAKE (1961)
IF THE SOUTH HAD WON THE CIVIL WAR (1961)
THE WORK OF SAINT FRANCIS (1958)
ANDERSONVILLE (1955)
Pulitzer Prize Novel, 1956
GOD AND MY COUNTRY (1954)
THE DAUGHTER OF BUGLE ANN (1953)
WARWHOOP (1952)
DON'T TOUCH ME (1951)
SIGNAL THIRTY-TWO (1950)
ONE WILD OAT (1950)
THE GOOD FAMILY (1949)
WICKED WATER (1949)
MIDNIGHT LACE (1948)
GLORY FOR ME (1945)
On which the motion picture *The Best Years of Our Lives* was based
AUTHOR'S CHOICE (1944)
HAPPY LAND (1943)
GENTLE ANNIE (1942)
CUBA LIBRE (1940)
VALEDICTORY (1939)
HERE LIES HOLLY SPRINGS (1938)
THE NOISE OF THEIR WINGS (1938)
THE ROMANCE OF ROSY RIDGE (1937)
AROUSE AND BEWARE (1936)
THE VOICE OF BUGLE ANN (1935)
LONG REMEMBER (1934)
THE JAYBIRD (1932)
EL GOES SOUTH (1930)
DIVERSEY (1928)

Juvenile

GETTYSBURG (1952)
LEE AND GRANT AT APPOMATTOX (1950)
ANGLEWORMS ON TOAST (1942)

Personalia

MISSOURI BITTERSWEET (1969)
THE DAY I MET A LION (1968)
MISSION WITH LEMAY (1965)
(With General Curtis E. LeMay)
LOBO (1957)
BUT LOOK, THE MORN (1947)

Verse

TURKEY IN THE STRAW (1935)

MISSOURI BITTERSWEET

Missouri Bittersweet

MacKinlay Kantor

Doubleday & Company, Inc., Garden City, New York

Grateful acknowledgment is made to the following for material included in this book:

Holt, Rinehart and Winston Inc. and The Society of Authors for "Hell Gate" from *The Collected Poems of A. E. Housman.* Copyright 1922 by Holt, Rinehart and Winston, Inc. Copyright 1950 by Barclays Bank Ltd. Reprinted by permission; Hastings House, Publishers, Inc. for excerpts from *Missouri, A Guidebook to the Show-Me State*, 1941. Reprinted by permission; Jonathan Daniels for excerpts from an editorial from *The News and Observer*, Raleigh, N.C. Reprinted by permission; Savannah Evening Press for the October 21, 1954 editorial. Reprinted by permission; William A. Settle, Jr. and the University of Missouri Press, Columbia, Missouri, for excerpts from *Jesse James Was His Name*, by William A. Settle, Jr. Copyright 1966 by the Curators of the University of Missouri. Reprinted by permission.

Library of Congress Catalog Card Number 69–15182

To the memory of Daniel Longwell

Contents

Representation by the Author

When, some forty-nine years ago, as a barefoot youth I left my home to venture amid the thorny thickets of journalism, letters, novelistics—call them what you list—my agéd great-grandmother stood upon the cabin stoop, took her corncob pipe out of her mouth, and called after me as I ran down the path:

"Don't git sued!"

This adjuration I have borne in mind constantly, even unto the construction of this present book. Historical fact of the past remains untampered-with (except by meddling hands which preceded me) but some contemporary persons and, in rare cases, towns or regions— Some of these are made up out of homespun fabric. Usually I call attention to such cowardice on the author's part. Not always.

There is no chronology. Sometimes I witness this Missouri of 1969 through the lens of nigh-onto-half-a-century of acquaintanceship. Sometimes the Missouri of the young 1920s takes command; but, in other portions of the book, Interstates and Holiday Inns fill the foreground.

As a cantankerous Conservative it has pleasured me to discover an increased leaning in that direction, in Missouri, through the past few years. Except where architecture is concerned! Even then, healthy minorities express alarm and resentment in those towns which have had computer-designed monstrosities foisted upon them.

Cities? A few nights in a St. Louis suburb, a couple of nights in Kansas City, and we'd had it. Kansas City and St. Louis aren't Missouri, any more than New York City and Washington, D.C., are America. Thus we were spared contact with those numerous elements of society—mainly urban—who embrace the delusion that recent Administrations have advanced our National welfare, instead of plunging us into chaos.

There was a time when bittersweet vines (*Celastrus scandens*) tangled bountifully over leafless trees in chillier months, a beckoning blaze of orange pods splitting apart to exhibit their red-wrapped seeds. Birds fed happily on this painted treasure; so did squirrels, before they'd cuddled for a wintry doze.

Florists' shops were all too eager to sell such wild decoration, and it came to them by the truckload. Now bittersweet is rarer, as is the original essence of a haunted hundred-and-fifteen counties. But still it can be found.

Lord knows that there is bitterness within this book, but the author prays that readers will taste a sweetness too. May they believe that I looked upon the storied landscape and its inhabitants with concentrated and consecrated sentiment, nostalgia, severe prejudice, and affection for elder days, and distrust of those days newly come. God Bless Missouri, and I love an old tick hound more than a Japanese motorcycle, and a boarded-up crossroads store better than W. T. Grant's, Katz', or Sears'.

MacKinlay Kantor

1. It Takes a Long Time for an Old House to Burn Down

A little after one o'clock in the morning the fire-whistle woke us up. The air-conditioning appliance in this heart-of-a-village motel had thumped and grumbled until I pulled out its plug (switch wouldn't work). Then I forced open three reluctant windows and achieved some decent cross-ventilation. Rains had been general all around, the air drifted with a fragrance of fresh-cut alfalfa and the odor of fried onions from a drive-in across the way.

Fire-whistle sounded something like a mechanical tomcat whose voice was changing: it gave blat after blat. Perhaps there was a code but I couldn't figure it out. While the whistle was still groaning we heard a siren, and the local fire-truck roared up the town's main street and away.

Through our north window I saw pulsating blossoms of Chinese-red among low clouds rimming the ridges.

. . . Fire, fire. *Fireman, save my child.* Fire buffs running, Dalmatians barking. Two-alarm fire, three-alarm fire: that's Big City stuff. Get out of bed, and pull on your clothes, and go to the fire. It's not always merely a taut and giddy spectacle. In Sarasota our friends Pris and Charley Walpole arrived home from a vacation trip, but they had to stop where their driveway curved—a barricade had been put up by the police and firemen when they left the scene an hour before. Pris and Charley got out and walked to the bed of cooling cinders where their home had been.

(I recollect the time when I was working with the New York Police Department in the 23rd Precinct, and we had a job on the Late Tour: one of those stables where decrepit horses used to be rented out to peddlers and such. *House* fires can be pretty rocky, but don't ever go to a *horse* fire if you can help it.)

Reflected flames were brighter by the time we headed down the same road where the fire-truck had gone. From a valley in front we heard the mourning of still another siren. Different tone: another company responding from some nearby town. As we crossed the Interstate on a viaduct we saw red lights of the truck vanishing up a road which wound among tree-clad hills.

Like Hebrew children in the wilderness we followed our pillar of fire. Ripples of brightness came weaving to guide us, pulsing like Northern Lights; then smoke would sweep across to obscure the reflection. We could hear other cars. Headlights were fanning behind, and no doubt many had gone on before.

We came to a driveway with brick gateposts: this was the place . . . curved up a hill through parklike trees. Almost you expected to see a herd of fallow deer go scampering. But there were only Hampshire hogs in a wooded lot where our headlights washed them. Then on into glare, into glowering heat which marked the end of a house and of an age.

Crews were toiling to save other buildings on the place. They had hose lines laid from a lake downhill at the back where a stream had been dammed, and that must have been a nice pond for the young folks to go swimming in. I doubt not that the family kept it stocked with fish—perhaps small ones, but still fish. Another batch of men squirted chemicals over a smaller building which probably housed electric pumps and such.

Cars and pick-ups were parked all over the place, stuck heedlessly between trees. There were two girls who had ridden over on their horses and stood with reins in their hands, watching. There must have been a hundred folks present, besides the family, maybe more. A pair of collie dogs ran around, yelping aimlessly, and one was a female whose pink teats showed that she was suckling puppies. We hoped that they'd got the puppies out all right.

Yes, it was a tall house, a long house, and there were mighty chimneys at each end. It had been built about 1850, folks said. It blazed solemnly, end to end, front to back. It seemed to be on fire all at once, although half the roof was already crumpled in. Still flames erupted from that crater.

Ranged round about, removed to varying distances, were as many pieces of furniture as family and neighbors had been able to lug before they had to abandon any effort in that direction. Sofas, some of them upholstered in ancient haircloth. And several mirrors leaned against trees; one had been broken, and that would be seven years' bad luck for somebody. There were a number of pretty tables, one chest-of-drawers, two primitive portraits of somebody's ancestors.

It was possible to identify members of the family by the way neighbors talked to them. There was a tall thin young fellow called Randy; he might have been the original *Randall, My Son*, of ballad fame; he looked like a thin handsome ballad himself. Two younger boys, and a married daughter and her husband. Daughter I say, because she looked a lot like Randy. There was a baby on a table, in one of those semi-lie-down things they have nowadays, to carry babies in. The baby slept blissfully, firelight flickering across his contented sleeping face when we went over to peek. Not a care in the world. Plump lips parted naturally in slumber, a little sigh coming up; you could hear it if you bent close, even with those flames burbling.

Most of all we will remember the old lady. Grandma she was, maybe great-great-grandma to the baby who lay locked in his sleeping.

Grandma did not cry. She sat motionless, staring. You could tell easily that this was her very special chair which they had rescued and brought out and placed far enough away so the heat wouldn't abuse her, and yet where she could have a clear view of everything. There existed no compelling reason why she should have had a clear view of the destruction; but there it was, she had it. She never stirred. Afghan over her shoulders: a pretty thing with varicolored squares of bright yarn, draped against night weather and the ague which might come stalking. (At least old folks were always talking about the ague. Some of them believed that night air was bad, and wouldn't open their windows because of it.)

By morning there would be only four blackened chimneys standing, with frizzled wads of burned equipment in between. Nothing looks worse than modern laundry devices—a modern Frigidaire and electric stove, or butane gas stove—when they have been crucified and squelched in fire. Cast-iron stoves of elder house fires—they simply weren't in it with these. A burned-up hair-dryer looks like nothing ever seen on land or sea. Maybe you could salvage a cast-iron stove which had had a house shot out from under it; but you weren't going to reclaim a deep-freeze or a dish-washer.

They'd rescued the television set. It rested forlornly upon its rack, with ruddy light flashing across the screen as if there were presented a program especially dedicated to Vulcan.

Nearby stood the farmer, the householder, a broad-shouldered round-shouldered man in his fifties. He wore a black felt hat in the style of Missouri tradition, and an incongruous sports shirt. We knew he was the owner, because people asked, "Dave, how much insurance did you carry?" and then his low voice would tell, but I can't recall how much insurance he said.

"How'd she start, Dave?"

"We just don't know."

His wife was with him. Those who will remember that excellent actress and excellent lady, Margaret Wycherly, will know what she looked like. Except younger. Except perhaps a little happier. But how could she be happy now?

She wore a jaunty blue suede jacket which might have belonged to one of her daughters. We heard her voice rise and tell that Pauline had been after her for she didn't know how long, to give up the old place and move in to town. She supposed that now they'd have to do it, less everybody wanted to live in a trailer. She was an especially heroic woman, because she could join with the neighbors—One woman was a dear friend and had an arm around her much of the time. They all laughed obligingly, felt that they were supposed to laugh, so they did laugh, and then her laugh came up along with theirs, but oh so thin and wiry.

You'd watch these other people, but always your eyes would go back to Grandma in her deep chair. It was a substantial chair, bright with chintz, colors falsified by tossing flames.

She moved for the first time. She'd grown weary of sitting in one position, so she twisted herself around, shifting one thin little hip, then resting her weight on the other; and thus turning her feet in a different direction on the ottoman where they rested. As always, she didn't look anywhere else—just at the fire.

So much was happening within those flames and all around them and alongside them and above and under and again within them. Grandpa had brought her there to live with his family and to help inherit their Earth, when she was only seventeen. His grandfather, Captain Avery, was still very much alive; and there echoed lots of talk about the War, talk about bushwhackers and the James boys. In this fire burned the very porch chair (long since broken) where Cole

Younger roosted, the one time he was there. He told the children how he got *wownded* by a shotgun blast whilst trying to rob the bank at Northfield, Minnesota. Later a doctor laid him out on a cellar door, face down; Cole Younger said it hurt like the dickens, or maybe he said it hurt like something else. Doctors were picking the shot out of his back—buckshot maybe. With forceps. One shot at a time.

But Grandma had been on that porch long before, because she was a neighbor, and used to come over to play with Cousin Floss when they were both just little things. They played Lady, they lived at opposite ends of the porch, carrying doll-children back and forth, to call. And also (Floss's mother made them stop this) they played Going to Funerals, and had their hats and gloves and smelling-salts and everything.

Here were represented the treasures of many lifetimes and many different opinions and emotional reactions and influences, because frequently things that are treasures to some are junk to others. Crown Derby can be food for the soul, to one person; and but a teacup to another; and but an encumbrance to a third. So someone had carried out from rural catastrophe a bushel-basket of bottles which contained originally horse-medicines and cow-medicines and hog-medicines, many of them manfactured by the same company. Yet the bottles—I looked closely—all the bottles were empty. Someone had surely wanted these things. I suppose the basket of bottles stood handy to a door, and thus was borne to safety while better articles went up in smoke.

I did speak of primitive portraits leaning against trees, but don't think I mentioned an enlarged photograph of a young man in a beret. It was one of those hand-colored jobs. The color of his beret was green, and I don't think that we had green berets until the Vietnamese war, so he must have died out there. Dead he was: the frame bore one of those little vases where flowers can be placed, to honor The Departed. There was an artificial rose (some purplish color. I only made out the green beret by standing between it and the fire, and then bending near).

Naturally we didn't know Grandma's age. But if Monty—(I considered Monty to be the soldier's name. He looked like a boy who would be called Monty, and cut quite a swathe with the babes over at Central Consolidated High School, and tear the opposing team's secondary defense to shreds when he was toting the ball. I'm only in my sixty-fifth year as I write these lines, but I've got a grandson taller than I; and I'm a little stooped, but still around six feet tall)—

Grandma looked to be eighty-five or ninety. Maybe Monty was her great-grandson, maybe just a grandson. Maybe great-great.

O.K. So some people collect empty medicine bottles, some collect Spode. If there was any Spode which had been carried out from that farmhouse, we didn't see it. We did see a walnut chest-of-drawers, beautifully kept, oiled and waxed. There was a hand-painted china vase of rather large size, which had contained some dried plants —cat-tails and stuff—but most of them had fallen out. A parakeet jerked and shuddered in its cage, being toted around tenderly by one of the little girls. We saw a cedar chest. Some will remember: girls had them for hope-chests, and they looked rather like small coffins. But—

Soft linens and living hopes instead of those now dead and ready to be buried.

Still the billowing licking flames. How could they feed on any house so long? Feed they did. The building was good and solid, rafters and walls thick and solid.

Another fire-truck came rattling and clanging uphill among the trees. The firemen's welcome was mostly in wisecracks. "Where *you* been, Eddie? Was you to the firemen's ball?" A lot of mild jeering. "You folks over there in Something-ville must sleep with cotton in your ears." Then Dave, the man of the house, approached the newcomers. Wisecracks ceased, hand-shaking ensued, a little talk, a little pointing. The fire reached some stored ammunition, we heard a great volley of exploding cartridges, and folks moved back from the blaze. Since the ammunition wasn't contained in barrels of weapons it couldn't do much harm. True, the farmer started toward Grandma, and a couple of others too, as if to carry her back. Then the explosions stopped.

. . . Basket of delicious-looking new potatoes which must have been dug only the day before. Marble-topped table with a lot of little things on it: I moved over and saw where someone had won a prize or citation from the 4-H Club. A pile of books, old and new, also rescued; you could observe the titles as flames still rippled and stung. Damndest assortment: must have been the residue of birthdays and Christmases, sent by cousins in Kansas City. *Sorrell and Son;* and *The Royal Road to Romance* by the long-vanished Richard Halliburton. Another Richard, name of Tregaskis, represented by *Guadalcanal Diary*. And here were Viña Delmar's *Bad Girl* which I hadn't heard mentioned in nigh onto forty years; and a travel book by those Johnsons who used to go exploring and taking pictures in Darkest Africa . . . *Cold Comfort Farm.* I wondered how they ever got aholt of that one. This place should have been called Warm Comfort Farm.

We shall linger amid red shadows lashed this way and that among tall sycamores, and observe Grandma again.

She has readjusted her position. But she shook her head when a girl approached with some more covering for her. No, she was comfortable, wanted nothing else over her. She did accept a plastic cup— It seemed to be coffee; several big Thermos jars were circulating around, and women stirred in sugar and poured milk from a Pet can. (What? No cows?) Thus Grandma had her ration of coffee but it took her awhile to drink it.

Because not only the ghosts mentioned before were going up in that blaze (lower, lower, all the roof fallen in, bulk of the walls fallen or burned off. There persisted those minor crashings and seethings which you hear when you stand close to a conflagration: canned goods exploding, hair-tonic bottles bursting, a sack of garden fertilizer boiling and bubbling as the fire gets to it)— A liberal assemblage of family phantasmagoria vanished as well.

Everything gone. Including Edna's room. That was on the second floor, over at the northeast. They called it Edna's room long after she had lain sick for those eleven years before she died, and long after she was dead. Then it was Dave's room, then Grace's room; but the funny thing was they still called it Edna's room.

A bed in another room, the very bed in which Grandma had given birth to five of her children. In modern years it had been arranged with good box-springs and a fine modern mattress; but they'd retained the pegs where bed-ropes used to be tied. There'd been that dented half-broken knob on the headboard at the right, where Vance marred it the day he got in a fight with Charley. They were about thirteen or so in age. Vance chased Charley into the house after Charley said that he was going to get his gun and kill Vance. Vance had a metal try-square and he said he'd beat out Charley's brains with that. He chased him all the way upstairs while the girls were squealing. Just outside the doorway of the room he let fly with his try-square, aiming to hit Charley on the head; but Charley ducked, or maybe Vance wasn't a very good shot with such an implement. Anyway it sailed through the door and hit that knob. You could see the mark for fifty years. Right up until a couple of hours ago.

It takes a long time for an old house to burn down.

Galleries gone, front and rear. Hammock-hooks tumbled into the embers, they must have turned red-hot or white-hot before they fell. Those hooks had held up the hammock in which she used to sit with her husband, times he'd bring her over here to this house when they were courting. Course, there was a hammock at her house too. But her first home was torn down many years ago.

Now she would wake up in the morning, over at the Popes' or the Shannons', wherever they took her to sleep. She'd wake up, and first she'd think, "Where am I?" and then she'd think, "Why am I not at home?" Then she'd know why she was not at home; but still she'd see home just as it was, just as it had been through the decades—age-defying, tender, the cat still washing herself by the front door, breakfast muffins just coming out of the oven. Edith saying, "Ma, you know what? I think we've got another mouse in the pantry. Why, that cornmeal was—"

House and mouse, both were gone. And the cornmeal or malt or whatever it was that lay in the house that Jack built. Except it wasn't Jack who built the house. It was her long-dead husband's grandfather, Captain Avery. Avery was his first name, not his last. And people said that, before he was a captain, everyone used to call him *Mr.* Avery. You'd call him *Mr.* Avery even if you were working alongside him in the fields, in the earliest days.

I don't know how long we'd been at the fire. We rather lost track of time, because the Present and the Past were being so mixed up for Grandma and for those of us who watched and felt.

Irene looked at me and yawned and said, "Well?" questioningly. I guessed the fire was about over. We looked back at Grandma a time or two as we went toward our car through thickening shadows, with no high rocketing flames to light our way any longer. Indeed, when we had driven to the foot of the hill, we could gaze above trees and barely catch a faint shimmer of color every now and then—the embers had burned so low.

We drove back more slowly than we'd come, enjoying the odors of late summer milkweed blossoms. Thick, blooming heavily with that richness of smell into which you can very nearly bite, especially on a humid night, and this night had been humid.

. . . It was difficult to sleep, once we were again in bed at the motel, because of Grandma and those paper-doll memories (some crueler and not so paper-dollish). I kept wondering whether Grandma would be taken over to spend the rest of the night at the Keithley house or the Johns house, and whether she'd be plagued by the recognition that hallway and stair were now expunged. It was the stair on which she'd sat in 1912, on upper steps around the corner above the landing, when she heard her father-in-law and the Honorable Mr. J. Bingham Peel have their famous quarrel. They disagreed over William Jennings Bryan's allegations about Champ Clark as voiced at the Democratic Convention. She'd almost walked in on the scene, so she took refuge on the stair.

She heard Mr. Peel say, in a strange tone, interrupting her father-in-law, "Excuse me, sir—" Then he must have picked up his hat. "I'm leaving your house for good."

Her father-in-law was silent a moment. Then he said in a low firm tone, "Bing, you can't go soon enough to suit me."

There came sound of the screen door's shutting, and footsteps going across the porch and down the steps; away went the Honorable Mr. J. Bingham Peel; you listened to him cranking his Ford, and off he drove. In the hallway she heard her father-in-law give one great sob, because truly he had loved his friend, and now they would be friends no longer.

They never were. Never even spoke when they met on the street.

. . . Generations of girls giving parties. And Christmases, and illnesses. The time Kenny got so painfully burned when he tried to reach for hot cocoa at Florence's birthday party, and his little hand upset the pitcher of boiling stuff all over his arm. And Monty, sitting at the table on Sunday morning, grinning at the news that he'd made the All-State team . . . well, at least the All-State *second* team. But that wasn't too long back, not too long ago. That one furlough he had, just before he went out to Vietnam. He brought along a girl whom nobody really liked, and everybody feared that perhaps they were secretly married, but it turned out No.

You'd never believe that so many tears and so much laughter could be destroyed when a single house dissolved. But so they were, they were.

Along toward daybreak I went to sleep. I guessed that Grandma would be all right. A great many other things must have happened to her and to the house now ash. Missouri trees had died for reasons other than scorchings and singeings, and fragrant Missouri air and night clouds had witnessed smoke from other fires.

2. What's Missouri Really Like?

You can fall in love with a place sight unseen. Much as a young man may have a Dream Dolores whom he's never touched, an Imagined Ingrid whose perfume he's never scented; yet he's heard of her, formed his opinion. He feels his pulse beginning to pound when her name is mentioned.

I fell in love with Missouri long before I ever walked Missouri ground; though I was born a far hundred-and-thirty-five miles north of that line which one time marked the difference between Slave Soil and Free. Soon as I was able, I went down and slept under mystic hedgerows where the osage oranges loomed in their inedible beauty. Another boy came along with me, and when it rained we sought out alfalfa for our lodging. It was recommended that cut alfalfa be stored in barns, but few farmers had enough haymow capacity available. Hence they used to build tight roofs over the tall stacks to prevent their being soaked (and sometime later going up in smoke following spontaneous combustion). Enough space could be found between the rick and the wooden roof to stretch our blankets and our bodies, and the night was solid with smell of the drying crop and its once-purple flowers. The aroma was heady, a narcotic (as if our weary young frames needed to be drugged).

We'd walked long, but now we were in Missouri, and the chop-chop of hound-dogs rang in woodlands beyond the clipped acres.

> Jesse's up from thunder,
> Which is near to County Clay—
> Jesse and the Younger boys
> Are galloping this way.

This was neither east nor west, north nor south. Kansas and Nebraska and Oklahoma were West; Arkansas and Tennessee and Kentucky we reckoned as the South, sir; and Illinois had always seemed soundly Eastern in our Iowa belief.

But Missouri was the true keystone of Central States. Funny, though: should you pull it out of the map, all those other regions would remain intact. Only the Show-Me State—Old Mizzou, a puzzling commonwealth which partook of the characteristics of all adjacent areas and still resembled none of them in essence—only Missouri would be vanished. Yet surely we'd still listen to the hounds giving voice wherever they had gone.

And Mark Twain on one river, and Daniel Boone on the other, and mules braying back and forth. Woodsy darkness prevailing, always tantalizing in valleys, yet mournful also—

What's that?

Mockingbird.

Golly. We don't have em up in Iowa.

Oh, they're said to flit over into our southern counties once in a while. The ornithologists say, "Irregularly," or "Sporadically."

But they don't utter such songs. I never heard em.

No. These are Missouri mockers. Different.

Why, they speak with the tongues of angels!

Mother asked me, when I got back home after that first trip, forty-odd years ago, "Mack. What's Missouri really like?"

I thought for a long time. "Summed up in one word?"

"If you can."

I said slowly, "Missouri is—spooky."

It still is.

3. Boot Heel and Verna

Most Americans are as familiar with the Missouri Boot Heel as with the Texas Panhandle. A.–They've heard of it. B.–Maybe they've even flown over the place or driven through it. Yet–C.–They don't know much about it.

The area, consisting of most of Dunklin County and all of Pemiscot County, and the lower portion of New Madrid County, would make a more efficient Boot Heel than Italy's, because it's flat across the bottom.

Sometimes people talk about the Iowa Boot Heel sticking into Missouri on the north, but actually that's a triangle. If the long Iowa-Missouri line had continued due east, it would strike the Mississippi at Fort Madison. There ensued a lot of fuss and fume concerning this in the 1830s, and once I wrote a story about the occurrence. It was called *Honey on the Border* (appears in *Story Teller*). Disagreement about the Brown Line and the Sullivan Line; challenges thrown back and forth between Governor Lucas of Iowa Territory and Governor Boggs of Missouri State; ripsnorting "armies" of volunteers who swore to invade each other's territory, and ended up by rioting among themselves. The triangle still lies parceled off from northeast Missouri, with the Des Moines River washing Iowa soil all the way to its juncture with the Mississippi.

The Missouri Boot Heel came into being with less strife, and no armies or battle cries. A man named John H. Walker had moved into that portion of the country before the War of 1812, and he wished to remain a Missourian. The suggested southern boundary for the new State did not include Walker's plantation to begin with; but, as a Missouri guide book says, Walker "began a vigorous campaign to include all land south to the thirty-sixth parallel, between the Mississippi and the St. Francis Rivers. To Walker, Missouri thus owes its 'boot heel'."

Incidentally, the book referred to in the preceding paragraph is one of those WPA products of the 1930s and early 1940s. I think they did a guide book for every State, and many are dull, perfunctory—the inevitable product of modest freeloaders who were trying to be writers and historians and needed to be severely disenchanted. Queer things happened. For instance, the Iowa book has a map of Iowa printed on the front end-papers, and bang in the middle of it is established the town of Blainsbury, a place which doesn't exist and never did. On the other hand, *Missouri. A Guide to the "Show me" State* is mainly a persuasive and valid performance. It was published in 1941 by Duell, Sloan and Pearce, a credit to all who contributed to the enterprise. When I have occasion to refer to the book again I'll think of *Missouri. A Guide*—and refer to it simply as *MAG*.

Hello. Official Missouri welcome sign beside the road. How does the region look today? Same old cotton, very like Mississippi, very like Tennessee, very like Arkansas. It's flat low country, the Mississippi alluvial plain.

The day says rich rich, green green. This is late July and a few venturesome cotton bolls are beginning to burst. Very little white cotton open, mostly it's just the rich rich green green of maple-shaped leaves. The plants look so flavorable that you'd like to cook em for greens. Minus the bolls and squares, please.

Day says, I'm a bowl, myself. Look, I'm a beautiful blue bowl, empty and hot, with cumulus clouds spaced brokenly all the way around the horizon. I'm a Wedgwood bowl, fairytale Wedgwood blue and white. But I'm not baked enough yet, so the sun keeps baking me.

We've just come up, on Interstate 55, from Blytheville, Arkansas. I'm a marvelous driver, but all the other drivers drive like dingbats.

(What is a dingbat? The Oxford Dictionary quotes from Michael Drayton's Moon Calf Poems, 1748. "They drive at him as fast as they could ding." And that was long before vicious men invented nasty little cars which make more noise than a KC-135.)

Please, please, *don't*, people. It isn't that important. It isn't important that you gain eight minutes in getting up to Portageville in order to sell that policy. Not so essential that you stop three minutes earlier in Concord to say hello to Aunt Dora. No, no, little Volkswagen, don't try it, please, not on that curve. . . . But you did, you did. And you stayed upright. And who ever thought that you could? . . . Maximum is seventy mph, according to the signs. Minimum is forty. And you're not In unless you're doing eighty-five or ninety.

Do you know northeast France, up in the old battle zones along the Belgian frontier? That's a canal-strewn area too, though mainly industrial. Otherwise this landscape is similar. Also it might remind some people of the extremity of North Wales. Or the northern portions of Indiana—if you saw metal mills and chimneys looming up, you wouldn't be surprised, but they don't loom: cotton rules, but not yet ready for its own particular looms.

We shall venture into the town of Steele and see what Steele is like. . . . Well, Steele has mimosas, a little past their freshest flowering but still dainty. Well-kept phlox aplenty. Missouri is and always has been more tidy in its rural areas (excepting the true hill country) than the nearby southern States. The outskirts of Steele are less cluttered and dirty than most of the small towns we've been going through in Mississippi and Arkansas.

We pass a new house, built carefully according to Southern colonial pattern: gallery, columns, the works. Many smaller modern houses—flat-roofed, some of them, but not too disastrously ranch-styled. Still a generous leavening of old-fashioned houses with paint flaking off them; nevertheless they spell a comfort with their kitchen gardens and nasturtium beds. You know that good smells will be coming from the oven long before you're ready to sit down to midday dinner.

. . . Utley Lumber Company. Wonder if they're related to Uldine Utley. Who, you ask, was Uldine Utley? Why, she was a child evangelist; I guess it must have been fifty years ago. *A little child shall lead them.* Let us old folks speculate on how many or how few people have been competently led by guileless child evangelists. There used to be a great whoop and halloo about that business. One way or another those child evangelists seemed to make a pretty good living for their parents.

There was a flaxen-haired character named Marjo Gortley who came along much later. We attended one of Marjo's revivals, and he wore a white suit and white boots with gold tassels on them. His father announced that if you gave a love gift of five dollars, you would get a kiss from Marjo. I didn't want to be kissed by Marjo, so

I didn't give five dollars. Soon, with the five-dollar crop being very scanty and hastily reaped, the price went down to one dollar. Still I didn't buy any kisses from Marjo even at that dollar rate. I had only to go home and I could get kisses from Irene for free.

But why go home? Irene was sitting beside me, and she looked especially entrancing. I inquired, "You charge a buck for a kiss?"

She said, "For you I won't charge."

Thus she ran competition to Marjo Gortley. I leaned over and kissed Irene, and then we looked at each other again, and little Marjo bounced back up on the platform and started to blow celestial music. He had a pint-sized cornet or maybe it was a pint-sized saxophone. Irene and I rose and walked out of there. When we got outside, any of those worshipers looking in at the door would have thought that we were still worshiping, because we both said, "Jesus Christ."

Utley, subtlely, Gortley, portly. In Florida we have a vast corporation–Arvida–which is generously improving our bays through the simple expedient of filling them in. The Sarasota branch of this noble institution is headed by a man named Whatley. Utley, Whatley, motley, Gortley. Why the innocent Utley Lumber Company of Steele, Missouri, should cause me to think on these things, I don't know. But it does.

An old restaurant or bank building at the corner of the main business street. In great big letters: *YOUTH CENTER*. That's something they never had the last time I was in the Boot Heel. Youths were not important enough, then, to have a center; now even the smallest towns seem to have them. Because otherwise the youths might come around with their long hair and guitars, and spray paint on your house. For kicks.

At home they blew up our mail-box, twice, for kicks. But the postal inspectors couldn't do anything about it, because they said we didn't have any mail in the box, so that made it a private matter. If we had had mail in the box, it would have been a U. S. Government matter. Now we keep mail in the box consistently–try to keep it there night and day (but it's usually unimportant mail, in case the youths blow up the box again. Jimmy Cagney says that they've destroyed his box on Martha's Vineyard he doesn't know how many times. Finally he had to quit having a mail-box, and his man goes in to Vineyard Haven and gets the mail).

Steele has a generous percentage of pretty girls with shining hair. They are so lovely to look at that I drive very slowly. Can't quite believe that they'd go along with it, if the local boys set out to destroy mail-boxes for kicks. But– Maybe so, maybe so.

Here's an extremely dirty black-and-white dog, trotting in business-like fashion down the left side of the street. He's no stray, he sports a stylish collar, and probably got dirty just through choice, like our hound Maury at home.

Lots of colored folks . . . girls in mini-skirts chattering together. Here are three old black men in faded work clothes, but working no longer. They're squatting next to a wall on the downtown sidewalk, away down on their heels on a low curb against the building. It isn't a Sit-In either. That's the way they always sat in ancient days; that's the way they will always sit, until there are no old black men to squat on their heels. Nor white ones. Just old brown men.

Now we're out north of town on County D (the county roads are lettered: A, B, C, D and so forth, all over Missouri. And sometimes DD and EE and such. This same day we saw Road PP, down which Irene definitely refused to drive).

On the porch of a tiny house are hunched an elderly woman and a fat elderly man. They are coming slowly blankly–still perhaps reluctantly–to the end of their days. There exists a particular and peculiar dignity surrounding even poor and tired and sickly people who have lived long in a single environment. It is this environmental quality which gives them their distinction. They seem indigenous to the place; and, as indigenous things, they demonstrate a calmness and detachment which very nearly approach pride. That same property is inherent in all natural growths, in animals and placid vegetation.

Blue car went past mighty slow.

You can see better'n I can. You reckon it was Mr. Dennison?

No, twasn't Mr. Dennison. Man and woman. Strangers–I don't know who. Don't think they even had a Missouri license plate.

Wonder what they're doing over here, way off the Interstate?

Aw, Addie, lots of folks from other States drive through Steele. I heard that Mr. and Mrs. Triggs had some relatives a-visiting.

Well now, that could be.

What time we going to have dinner?

Don't you get to be such an old greedy-gut. I got the green beans on already.

You put pork in em, didn't you?

Of course, Henry.

Well, last week you forgot.
Anyway, the doctor says you ain't supposed to eat pork.
Man's got to live, *hain't he?*

Most of the folks down here pronounce it New *Mad*rid, accent on the first syllable.

Twas on a cold December night in 1811 that the earth began to rampage. Not only did the earth rampage, the Mississippi did too. The Mississippi started flowing backward. Streams turned into gaseous lakes, bayous went dry, lakes appeared where sere grass had lain before. The ground split open, closed, split again—

A few explorers and traders and rivermen who roved the area in the late eighteenth century said there'd been previous thunderings and shakings, away back in the time of the American Revolution and after. But this had not happened for years, and came as a hideous novelty to most of the 1811–12 residents of New Madrid. . . . *Oh, God Almighty, what's a-happening? What's a-happening?*

Children wailed, the dogs put their tails between their legs, and kitty-cats yowled and tried to climb trees or climb house walls or climb people's backs. The inhabitants came staggering out-of-doors, the world about them quivering and groaning. It went on for weeks . . . people caught colds, huddled in the open and wet as they were compelled to be . . . many fell sick, many died.

When the earth insists on antics directly beneath your feet, it isn't your earth any more. Suddenly hills erect themselves where before there were no hills, and landslides sweep the forests before them, and portions of the territory sink beneath water and stay there. And new land comes belching up out of roily floods.

As you approach New Madrid, there is a large marker alongside the road with the story of earthquakes blazoned in metal. You pull off, and read that this was one of the greatest seismic disturbances of all time. True, it didn't kill as many people as many other earthquakes have killed. That's simple: there weren't enough people in that frontier region to form an impressive casualty list. But it was a moment in history when Jehovah (on whom most of those people believed implicitly) deliberately turned His back. Or—worse—transformed Himself into a spiteful demon who could twist terrain and rivers as He willed. He treated New Madrid and its surroundings like a mud puddle in which He was privileged to wash His hooves. His humors allowed Him to tear the baby out of its mother's arms, suspend it in a floating tree . . . Baby would be found quite safe, though the mother was drowned and gone.

He shook the patriarch out of his bed and put the cottonmouths into it.

Folks who survived ran away, most of them; but the moment those tremblings and explosions and floods had ceased, inhabitants returned stubbornly to their old haunts, or at least settled near them. (When the first King of Cave Men ordered his tribe to move out because rocks threatened to tumble down on them, they probably scurried back into that same cavern the moment their King's hairy back was turned.)

New Madrid, yielding before quakes and inundations, may have been shunted here and there—a mile west, another mile north—half a dozen times. Or maybe more times, or maybe fewer. Historians do not agree, which is the habit and refuge of historians. A fatherly Government pitied the innocent victims of Nature's ungallant behavior, and presented them with land warrants calling for their resettlement in safer climes. The majority sold the land patents. There ensued a lot of crooked buying and selling. Most of the dispossessed never profited to any extent. Professional land speculators were the ones who profited in the end.

No one then seeking for the Garden of Eden would have located it in the Boot Heel of Missouri. Too much malaria, too much flooding, too many snakes, too many savage critters lurking. The whole devil's dictionary of diseases— They called them by various names. Called them galloping consumption, febrile shakes, summer complaint, sinking chills, or just plain plague. This was no ideal spot for a health sanitarium, and to the best of our knowledge none was ever built.

The majority of towns which you approach in the modern age—little places with Youth Centers in wornout buildings, places where most Negroes have moved off the land, and range on the outskirts of villages— These towns were platted much later than other places to the north. Truly it was a new country in this twentieth century, and has grown tidier and less sodden as decades progressed. Drainage systems have been established whereby swollen waters are diverted directly into the Mississippi from other streams, and do not commonly make swill of the land as they did before. Enormous levees contain them (usually).

Cotton is still dominant, but there is more diversification of crops than was the case forty years ago. The miracle of the soy bean has done wonders for this countryside. Machinery whirs its promise. A little farmer cannot afford machinery, a little planter can't either. Better economics if a huge company possesses its own machinery, own gin, own compressor for cotton, own apparatus for the soy beans. The honest story, sad or glad, of American agriculture of our time. Nowhere is this more evident than here.

We see one new beauty. Forty years ago we stared at an empty landscape; but today as one progresses north and east from Steele he rests his gaze on the gentility of trees. Trees should have been here all the time, and yet could not flourish until the country was drained.

Hear, hear! Here, here: bright white-painted rural houses. Mostly used to be shacks. Shack or not, you can always recognize the home where a woman has taken pride in her petunias. Such a woman feels that she holds a stewardship. Her satisfaction in the benevolent color-riot becomes your own joy as you go past.

Most of the citizens, Negroes and whites, are working for the big outfits. They have only a few rows of sweet corn in their own gardens, and miniature patches of potatoes, onions, lettuce and other truck, to keep them in green-groceries. We still observe chinaberry trees as we'd see them in the deeper South. Some of the other trees appear to be studying to be chinaberries. A couple of willows attempt to assume that same bulbiform Grant Woodish shape in which the chinaberry grows. . . .

Hurrah for the names of Missouri towns. Peculiar, Romance, Zebra, Wisdom, Venus. Hurrah for the town of Braggadocio. Road Z joins in for a moment with Road J; but Z still runs north, so we'll go on our way through Braggadocio without even bragging. North of town is a red-brick church of recent vintage, with a bell hung out in the front yard on a low open belfry. Looks like a ship's bell off one of the river-boats, and probably is—just about the right size. I'd like to go over and give the thing a tap and see what the tone is like, but fear it might fetch all the village. And might be interpreted as a sacrilegious act as well as an impish prank practiced by one too old and gray to be an imp. "I did it for kicks." The permissive litany of the 1960s. . . . Reverend George H. Sumner announces on his bulletin board: "We preach the Book. Blood. Blessed hope." Blood or blessed hope or not, I wish that we might hear the tone of that bell. Let's drive off before I do ring it, and get arrested for being a Flower Child on LSD.

Lunch at Cora's Cafe. Roadside heraldry informed us that the Lions prided themselves there one day each week, the Rotarians another day; but neither club was in session this noon. Cora's looked spick-and-span and smelled like pungent potato salad. There were two low-ceiled rather dark rooms, with a lunch counter along one side of the first. We sat in the second room, close to the window so that we might study maps. The menu told of Mississippi River catfish. That was a pleasant item to contemplate . . . here was the Mississippi washing brown on the other side of a levee not five hundred feet away.

Catfish came in due course and in main course. The portions were bleached of any individuality . . . none of that troutish flavor reminiscent of sizzling iron skillets and fires beside shaded pools. A huge fish had been filleted and cut into oblong chunks; we were awarded each a slice off one of those slabs, long since compressed and frozen. Edible? Dismally so. But the taste buds didn't quiver ecstatically, they turned over and went to sleep. It might have been frozen shark for all our palates told us.

"Don't you ever have any *fresh* catfish, miss? Here we are, right on the Mississippi, and—"

"It's gainst the law," she said quietly. "In Missouri we're not allowed to sell fish unless it's frozen. Course, if you caught your cats and brought em to us, Cora'd be happy to cook em for you."

Potatoes were machine-cut french fries—same french fries you get at that little place on the road near Ventura, Bangor, Fort Wayne, Albany, Richmond, Oklahoma City. French fries conceived in grease and dedicated to the proposition that all people are created equal in their desire for a lot of salt. . . . The cole slaw had been made in heaven by beaming angels in golden aprons. Stewed tomatoes tasted like something that darling old Aunt Mary Lou fixed when you stayed for supper at the farm: just the right amount of onion, right amount of brown sugar, wit and delight of just enough pepper.

Sodden sepulchral rolls, coyly flavored with embalming fluid. Must have come from the same supermarket the catfish came from.

Irene had an idea. "Let's live all over and across Missouri on stewed tomatoes and cole slaw."

I thought that we could do worse.

"Oh dear. Maybe it'll be chain store biscuits all the way along. With calcium propionate on the side."

"Wait till we get to the Ozarks. To Galena. Wait till we get to Bill and Addis Rogers'—"

The waitress returned to find out whether we'd have any pie. Being sweet kindly folk, we praised cole slaw and stewed tomatoes to the skies, and said nothing about uneaten fish or unmunched potatoes and rolls. Irene told the waitress that she'd been longing to do a portrait of her, and the girl brightened as ladies do whenever anyone tells them this. I guess men would brighten as well, but I can't really speak from experience. Only two people ever said that they wanted to paint a portrait of me: one was Francis Beaugureau, an Eighth Air Force pal, the other was my wife. They both did paint the portraits. I had to sit still for five hundred hours, and it hurt my back and neck, and bored the hell out of me.

We asked the waitress her name. Let's say it was Verna. Irene asked Verna if she would mind having her picture taken. When we are on trips, my wife always carries along a Nikon camera loaded with color film, and she picks up a lot of interesting slides for reference later on. Verna said, Goodness, she guessed she was an awful sight this day. She hadn't slept much the night before. One of the children was sick; she had to keep getting up to take care of her little girl. But— Oh, sure. If you really *want* to take my picture. . . .

"Will you folks have pie? That's all we've got for dessert today, cept ice cream."

"Does the pie originate in the same place those rolls come from?"

She grinned sheepishly. "No. We don't make any bread or rolls or anything like that, or even biscuits any more. Haven't got time. But we do bake our own pies. Cora's real good when it comes to pies. Try the banana cream."

My calorie-conscious spouse would not indulge. I ate the best piece of banana cream pie I'd eaten in Lord knows how many years. Savoring it slowly . . . luxurious mouthfuls of pale yellow custard, tan sweet banana, delicate light crust. Irene sipped her Sanka, and we watched Verna, looking through the wide doorway that gave on the lunch counter in the other room.

So soft the shining red-brown hair. Neither of us knew whether it had been touched up or not; we argued a little about that. Anglo-Saxon bones sticking out of her face, faint hollows in the cheeks, faint dark shadows under her eyes. Several upper teeth were missing at the front of her mouth. When she kept her full rich lips compressed as she usually did except when speaking, you couldn't see the ugliness of missing teeth. She seemed actually to bear a saintly tragic already-resigned quality in her very skin, and the great brown eyes emphasized this.

I said, "Ozark type."

"Are you sure?"

"Yes. Look at those high cheekbones, look at that chin, those deep-set eyes. She comes from the hills, or her folks did."

"What would she be doing here next to the Mississippi?"

I thought of *MAG* and its statistics, circa 1940. "Of the 15,000,000 acres of forest in Missouri, only 250,000 of virgin timber remain. . . . Toward the end of the nineteenth century, large lumber companies began operations in the Missouri forests on the 'cut and get out' policy. When the best of the timber was gone, these companies moved on."

I told Irene, "The yellow pine people came down, a great many of them did. They were lumbermen, they lived throughout the Ozarks. Yellow pine went out of there in the shape of posts and poles and shingles and railroad ties. For years the rivers were crammed with lumber rafts. Then one day the yellow pine was gone. Many of those 'tie-whackers,' as they were called, didn't want to live off a small garden patch and a hillside cornfield and what they could hunt and fish for. They drifted to towns, larger river ports, cement plants. They're scattered now. You see them in Jefferson City and Hannibal, the same way down in Arkansas. You see them in St. Louis suburbs. But they're still Ozark types. So's our Verna."

Cora, the proprietress, came a-visiting. Was everything all right? We declared that it was—we just weren't quite hungry enough to eat such a big meal. Cora was nearsighted, and looked like a grim old maid. But before we'd talked for three minutes she opened a gold locket to display pictures of her grandchildren. "That's Jerry. That's Hayley. They live in Pensacola. But their daddy's overseas right now."

We did lament again about No Fresh Catfish. Cora said, Too bad, but it was the law.

"You know, sometimes I think there's too much law around these days. You got to keep books for the Government and everything. If it isn't some damn form you got to fill out for the Government, why then you got to do something for the State. And now they've come up with this Zip Code business. There's one man over here at our post office— He's kind of mean. Yesterday I was mailing a package to my sister, and he said he couldn't take the package less I had the Zip Code on it. I said, 'How would I know Lucy's Zip Code number, away over in Columbus, Ohio? She never puts it on her letters.' 'Cora,' he says, 'it ain't my fault. It's the rule. Here's a book, and you got to look it up.' Zip Code, huh. I don't even know what my *own* is."

After Cora went back to her kitchen we both sat and watched Verna. She was wiping coffee stains, cleaning the counter. Every now and then she'd stop and gaze out of the front window, and sun would come in and kiss her hair. By this time we were confident that her hair hadn't been touched up—at least, not much. The sunlight was gentle in caressing it. But oh so sad her face.

I told Irene the story of Verna's life. She was only fifteen or sixteen when she got married. It was a had-to thing. Because by the second month she knew for a certainty that she *was* pregnant, and she went wanly along with Lee Courant to the movies as before and to the roller skating rink on the main highway north of town. But when they were together and alone, she'd cry and cry. Said she couldn't help it. Finally Lee yelled, one night, "Oh, hell, if you're going to howl like that, and if you're scairt to go to Dr. Koenig— I suppose we'll *have to get married*." He took her in his arms (they were parked on that road which led to the dump, but it was the only good place to park anywhere around there). "Now, honey girl, you quit crying. We'll buy a license and just lie about your age. We'll get married, then we'll tell the folks." They sneaked over to the county seat several times—had to fuss around with blood tests and that legally required three-day waiting period. It was all a real headache, but at last they were truly married. A little later on, when it began to show on Verna, and her mother started getting suspicious, why— They waved their wedding certificate around in a big way. Though it said in the paper that they had been married a good while before they actually were married. The headline (rather small headline) in the Breezy Hill items said, *Local Young Couple Steal a March on Their Friends*. They moved into a house on Lee's father's place (Mr. Jean Courant raised mostly soy beans; one of his tenants had vacated the house recently) but it was awfully dirty. Verna had the worst time in the world, trying to clean it up, and then having morning sickness too. Still she got the house prettied after a fashion. For a while Lee was real good to her. He was crazy about the first child, Lee, Jr. Always taking him off with him in the truck to go fishing, soon as the kid could hold a tiny pole. Verna had two miscarriages. Then the next baby came: it was a little girl. By that time Lee was bored with family cares. He liked to go out with men friends, and they did quite a lot of gambling, and drank a lot of beer. He was always carrying six-packs in the car, even drinking while he was at work. Finally– He got sick and tired of family life. Said he guessed he didn't make a very good husband and father. That was the God's own truth, because he'd be gone every evening, soon as supper was over. Verna had to put the kids to bed alone, and just sit there. Then Lee got in an accident one night. He claimed he wasn't driving, but other people said that he was. Anyway, it was in Charlie Warsdale's Chevrolet. The Chev was a real wreck. How those three men got out of it alive no one ever knew. Lee Courant was in the hospital almost five weeks, and even the cheapest hospital accommodation really set them back. His father said, "I'm not going to pay any hospital bill for you. You were drunk, that's what. I brought you up to be a God-fearing man. I brought you up to hate alcohol in any form, but now look what you go and do. You pay your own hospital bill." Lee didn't pay it. He couldn't. Hospital bill had never been paid, or the doctor bills either. . . . Next thing Lee was gone, and they were all worried to death. Finally Verna got a letter: Lee had gone back into the Army. She received a modest allotment every month, that was all. Lee very seldom wrote to her. Occasionally he got drunk and called up on Long Distance, and wanted to talk to the kids. A year or two ago he was killed down in Georgia during some kind of war games. With the Government insurance that came to her, Verna paid off the mortgage on her mother's house. Now she and her mother lived together. Her mother got eighty-three dollars Social Security each month and a considerably smaller pension as the widow of a WW I veteran. But, even with Verna's working there in Cora's Cafe, it was hard to get along. Kids do cost a lot of money. Every time you turn around it's this or that.

While I was opening our stifling closed car (had to lock doors and shut windows because the car was full of stuff, and we had to park away down the street)– While I was trying to cool it off with the air-conditioning, Verna stood on the sidewalk outside the cafe, and Irene took several snaps. The waitress kept her face set firmly and self-consciously, and was annoyed and embarrassed because some men friends drove past and yelled that she'd break the camera.

We said goodbye and thanked her, and Irene promised that she'd have a copy made of one of the slides if it was any good. (So she did, and already she's sent it to Verna.)

I do think it perked the gal up a little to have a customer come in, a stranger, and mention that she was a painter and wished that she could paint Verna's portrait. Bet she told her mother about it, and Cora too. I like to think of her telling them. We remember how she looked after we were in the car and driving slowly past Cora's Cafe, and how she looked out at us, through all those posters and ads in the window, and how her face lit up. She waved violently. We waved back. Irene reached over and honked the horn twice.

Goodbye. 'Bye, Verna.

4. An Old Square in Cape

Seems good to be back in Cape.

That's what they call it, the natives. They don't bother to say Cape Girardeau—just Cape. You see a sign on a garbage truck: HELP KEEP CAPE CLEAN. Thank the Lord they don't say HELP KEEP KAPE KLEEN.

I hold this truth to be self-evident: that a Cozy Camp makes better sense than a Kozy Kamp. If after my demise I discover that, contrary to previous belief— Discover that there is indeed a Hell, and I am sent there— I aim to volunteer for duty on the Devil's staff, in order to carry out one particular assignment if Old Nick will give it to me. That is the exclusive privilege of torturing those persons responsible for this distortion of our language in the field of visual advertising. And, while we're on the subject—

Forget it. Cape Girardeau, here we come.

There were some errands which needed to be done downtown. I left the motel and drove over to Sprigg Street. Along Sprigg a great many elderly French and German brick houses were built so substantially that they've never been torn down. Some are still maintained for residential purposes but the majority have been converted to business or public usage. Everything from cafes to fire companies are housed in these. They've been repainted—white, in most cases—but still you see the original copings, and ornamentation up around the eaves. On many you can estimate where windows were closed up and doorways bricked in.

In this neighborhood you may encounter some of the most courteous and obliging people you'll ever meet. Missouri must have a training school for them. This would offset what has come to be known in our family as the Howard Johnson Training School. I don't say that such an institution actually exists, but my son-in-law and I pretend that it does. We declare that young women attending the Howard Johnson Training School take special courses in: (a) yakking in a huddle near the kitchen doors while hungry customers are waiting for menus; (b) being certain to look in the other direction whenever a customer signals them; (c) writing hard-scrambled eggs on the breakfast check when clearly you asked for soft-scrambled eggs; (d)— There's no limit.

Also we envision a special training school for hostesses or head-waitresses. One and all, we hold that they are taught to act as if they were having their menstrual periods every day of the year, and suffering the most miserable effects which any gynecologist could identify. Their dispositions deteriorate accordingly.

My son-in-law and I may not even be poisoned in a Howard Johnson restaurant (such eateries we enter only when no others are available) after these words appear in print. Look at Shelley Berman. He coined that inspired airplane stewardess phrase about *Coffee, tea or milk?* which has passed into the language. Despite scurrilous epithets which stewardesses apply to Mr. Berman, he is still flying. Or was, the last I heard.

In this era of scant courtesy, dedicated selfishness, and hostile treatment on the part of salespeople, and store and office and hotel staffs in general, I recommend that the bruised and the ill-treated hasten to Cape Girardeau. If they're driving on Goodyear Double Eagles and have tire trouble, they can go into the Goodyear place just off Sprigg Street. Their faith in human nature will be revivified.

I'd been bumping around on one squarish wheel for some driving hours previously, but supposed only that a balancing weight had been tossed off from the rim.

"You haven't thrown any weights," said a smiling bespectacled young man. "You've got a punctured tire, that's what. In a Double Eagle there's a huge cushion which enables you to drive three or four hundred miles on a flat tire, and still not damage it."

"What do we do now?"

"I take off the tire and patch it."

"Patch?" I asked doubtfully. I had a vision of old-fashioned tire patches which always worked loose.

"Not the way you think," he said. "We use—" He named it,

and for the life of me I can't remember what the substance is. But it's some kind of liquid material which replaces original fiber and fabric.

"How long will it last?"

"The life of your tire. Just the same as if it weren't there."

I've been in some tire stations where they acted as if you were trying to foreclose their mortgage by coming in and requesting assistance. Here, in Cape, I was treated as if I were a long-anticipated Uncle Sugar whose coming might bring about the declaration of a public holiday. Mind you, they didn't ask whether my name was Charlie or Brown or Schroeder or Snoopy. They knew only that I was a Double Eagle customer. As Goodyear purveyors and servicemen they were expected to offer the best service they could give, and for free. You pay for that in advance when you buy a set of Double Eagles.

During an earlier experience with these remarkable but fiendishly expensive tires, I went into a place in upstate Florida, and waited fifteen minutes without any attention being bestowed. I sought out the manager (that took a little doing), at least ten minutes being invested in that research. He kept me waiting another half-hour before anyone came near my car. So being in the Double Eagle business isn't any guarantee that you will appear to your customer as friendly, courteous, kind, obedient and cheerful. I'm only saying that in Cape Girardeau all the personnel on duty that day were as obliging and efficient as Santa Claus's Little Helpers up at the North Pole.

Was there time for me to do a few errands and maybe grab a quick bite of lunch while they took off the wheel, performed what surgery they had to do, and checked inflation in the other tires? Sure there was. "If we have to move it before you come back, we'll put it right over there. O.K.?"

I walked around the corner onto Sprigg Street, and in the 200 block stopped to gaze at a yard crammed with phlox, zinnias, nasturtiums, salvia, hollyhocks, spirea, roses. You stood and looked, and you had a hunch that there was some old darling on the place to whom those flowers were the breath of life. Also she or he or they had gimcracky flower-pots of various sizes and shapes, stuffed in all over the premises, along with those horrendous jars you see for sale at ceramics places on the highways. The plantings took your breath away if the containers didn't. Quickly my breath was taken away by quite another spectacle. An intruder appeared, only a few feet distant. He was majestically black, wide of wing, slow fluttering, slow sailing. A spicebush swallowtail butterfly, *Papilio Troilus*, an old friend from boyhood days. It was as if he knew how the silver-blue of his after-wings glimmered like changeable satin in the sun, how the Chinese-red dots stood out (or were they raspberry?) as he contented himself with a sip from the corollas of the nearest phlox. It would have been a pleasure to follow him in his slow-moving tour of the yard. He was so fresh, so newly emerged and unblemished—one of the largest and rarest of North American butterflies. But it was the sort of yard you didn't walk into casually without an invitation. I thought a goodbye to Mr. Spicebush and went on down the street.

That morning I'd observed to myself, while dressing at the Holiday Inn, "You're doing right well about losing weight. Down from a hundred and ninety pounds to the hundred-and-sixties. But your belts have become pretty loose. This one you're wearing should have a hole or two punched in it."

Here was a shoe repair shop, and surely the man would have a punch. I went inside, and he turned from his machinery, shoe in hand. Anything he could do for me?

"Yes, please. I'd like to have a hole—maybe two—punched in this belt."

"Same spacing as the other holes?"

"That ought to be fine."

The punch went snap-snap, the belt was passed back to me. "Try that."

I put it through the trouser loops, and now it was tight in the first hole he'd punched. (Later: Glad to say I'm using the second hole whenever I wear that belt now, and am maybe a little past it. Could be that I'd need a third. Let's all lose weight in our old age. It's easier on that timer which kicked up in 1963.)

"So I owe you—?"

"Mister, I wouldn't think of charging you for a little thing like that."

"Well, thank you very much. By the way, I see you've got a stock of new belts here, and I could use one. May I look them over?" Thus I acquired a new belt, and I like that one, too. But it would have been all the same with this plump-faced man with the cordial grin. He would have been agreeable to anyone who came in his shop.

They grow them like that on the commendable trees of Cape.

Went on down to the next main cross-thoroughfare, and found a little cafe with a bar. I went in and ordered lunch, and treated myself to a beer in celebration over those new holes in the belt. My waitress was a woman with twinkling eyes and all the poise and pose of the late Margaret Dumont who used to play those Mrs. Van Rich Bitch roles with the Marx Brothers.

Everything good, from cold sliced meat to cottage cheese to lettuce.

"Where you from?"

"Florida."

"That's my favorite place on all this earth. Except– Well, I just love Cape too."

"So do I."

"Now, you come back again."

"Sure will."

Stood looking around when I got outside. Wanted to get some manila envelopes–heavy ones of a certain size, so I could ship back to my secretary, Phyllis Gossling, the Dictaphone bands on which I'd made notes along the way.

Try that drugstore on the corner. . . .

No, they sold only ordinary envelopes for ordinary correspondence. No manilas.

"Mister, see that tobacco and candy shop across the street? They have magazines and stuff, and I guess they do carry some stationery also."

I went over there. The folks were sorry . . . they didn't have any manila envelopes . . . just stuff for school kids. The proprietor led the way out to the sidewalk. "I'll show you right where to go. I'm positive you can get them there," and he pointed out a junior department store, and he was right.

Back to the Goodyear place. Car ready and waiting. "Just the normal loss of air in one or two tires, sir. None of them required much inflation. And that bad one's all fixed up. I'm sure it won't give you any more trouble."

I had a hell of a time getting the young man to take a tip "for a drink," but in the end he accepted. I think he did it just to make me feel good—not because he was expecting tips from everybody who came in there. He liked making people feel good.

Well now, I've got satisfactory envelopes so I can send home eight or ten bands previously dictated. Don't want to send more than that at once, for fear of loss in the mail. We did lose an important manuscript, one time. One: that was all. Never have lost any of the Dictaphone belts or bands, but— I'm not through writing yet, nor through dictating, nor through sending manuscripts and plastic bands in the mail. (Anyway it turned out that I wouldn't lose any of the Missouri bands, and that I would send back to Florida exactly one hundred and sixty-six of those.)

So write the address on the envelope, and stop at the post office to have it registered. There's only about half a parking space in front of the post office . . . hold on. That young woman ahead is moving up. She was back farther than she needed to be, and she saw me trying to come in—

"I do thank you, miss," as I walk past her car. She's pretty, and offers an absolutely radiant smile. Beautiful women, fast horses? No, no, this is not Kentucky, it's Missouri. . . . Beautiful women, fast mules perhaps? Certainly fast cars on the highways, and too-fast cars on some of the roads which ain't even highways.

At the registry window a middle-aged clerk takes the envelope and weighs it. The transaction is completed, money paid, registry receipt stamped. I ask the clerk if he has a spare moment. "Need a little guidance to a certain spot in town."

"Of course. Where is it that you want to go?"

"Up to that little park, at the point where Ensign Girardeau was reputed to have established himself, away back in the early eighteenth century. I think there's a marker or monument—"

"Let me draw you a map."

He went over the details painstakingly . . . where was I parked now? "Why, you're headed just right. Continue on north till you get to this street here, then turn right, then follow over till you strike—" So on, so on. He even told me how long it should take, not driving too rapidly.

"I'm indebted to you."

"Not at all. It's pretty up there. Wish I wasn't working—I'd like to go along myself."

. . . Here's where the young French officer settled. He had been stationed at Kaskaskia, Illinois, and came over here to found a trading post. (His name is spelled *Girordoo* and *Girardo* and in other ways, in some of the old records.) It isn't a very high hill, and they've set a boulder to mark the point where his fort was situated.

Eighty-five degrees in the shade. Muggy. You exert yourself a little, and you're a mass of perspiration. No rain last night . . . once again the leaves turn their backs upon the world, praying for moisture. "Where's that rain you promised us?" . . . Little stone steps have been arranged, leading up to the top of Girardeau's mound, but— It is preferable to sit in oaken shade and bless the trees yonder. Girardeau won't mind a mite if I don't climb those steps.

Over here on the other side, the Mississippi River is creeping in false docility. Near the opposite shore appear some green flat islands with channels flowing lazily between them. The river wears its tawny peaceable midsummer aspect, riffled occasionally by minor breezes, with not an ounce of barge traffic in sight.

. . . A mutter as of thunder, but it turns out to be a jet airplane on high. Semi-overcast, misty, the air filled with dusty vapor from the cement plant. People in Cape say that on certain days, and when the wind's just right—or *wrong*—the cement dust falls, drifting, covering yards, streets, sidewalks, lying thin on freshly washed automobiles. Then, if rain comes, the stuff turns to concrete and is very hard to get off.

Maybe we shan't buy that little house with the zinnias and the spicebush swallowtail, down there on benign Sprigg Street, after all.

A newly developed district out northeast, with medium-sized homes sprouting over the hills. Children enjoying vacation even in these hottest days. Boys stripped to the waist, girls more or less bikini clad, revelling with puppies or at indiscriminate games on small sloping lawns. Two little boys and two little girls stand on opposite sides of the road, busily engaged in warring with handfuls of sand and gravel. Fearful lest they assault the car from both angles of fire, I slow down, wave my hand. "Hey, you're not supposed to be doing that."

"Huh?"

"You shouldn't throw gravel at those girls, nor they at you. You all live in Cape Girardeau, therefore you're supposed to be *friendly*. Haven't you heard?"

The older boy scorns to pay any attention. The smaller boy motions imperatively for me to move out of the way so they can resume their battle with the babes. I know right well what's going to happen. Pretty soon someone's going to get hit in the eye with a pebble, and go howling for Mommy, and then both sets of neighbors will come out, and–

Park idly for a few minutes on Broadway, principal east-west street through Cape. Some distance away, now, from Sprigg Street and from Main Street down by the river, and any other areas which reflect certain vanished tranquillities and are replete with the few remaining ones. There isn't a thing to distinguish this Broadway from the Broadways in a hundred other medium-sized American towns. Same signs, same awnings, same new telephone building or new this or that . . . a few remodeled older buildings, an attempt at *Vogue*-styled chi-chi in a jewelry shop thrusting out from the front of a grandmotherly red-brick house–

But if one protests a sameness about Cape, a sameness to confuse it with other good-sized towns such as Columbia or Joplin or Hannibal– This sameness is not a sadness observed only in Missouri. It claims the entire Nation. Speedily we are losing–have very nearly lost, in fact–the regional characteristics which made one section of the country differ from another. Helena turns into Hackensack, Grand Junction and Uniontown wear the same face, neither Enid nor Elmira desires to be out of uniform.

Years ago I was working as a technical consultant to the Chief of Staff of the USAF, and was compelled to do a good deal of traveling. I had an aide, a fine young major of Hungarian extraction. I observed, as our acquaintanceship progressed, that this man was keenly sensitive to whatever regional variations we might discover in the course of our travels; but we both kept shaking our heads over the wearying conformity. (Land of Mercy, that was in 1952, and how could I be talking about conformity then, or even tolerate the recollection of it, when I think how cities look *today?*)

While standing on a corner–we were out in Boise–I said to the major, "Let's play a game. We can't use automobile licenses: they're out. But if we don't use auto licenses, and make allowance also for the fact that this is summer all over the United States, how do we tell just where we *are?* Suppose that we've been dropped here, perhaps unconscious and/or blindfolded. And the blindfolds are removed, consciousness and awareness return. How are you going to tell whether you're in Boise, Fayetteville, Norwalk, Cedar Rapids, Bakersfield—? Go on, name em. Name a lot of small cities. How are we to know where we're *at?* The girls wear the same sort of dresses in Eugene, Oregon, that they wear in Baton Rouge. Same signs, same drugstores, same notion stores, same movies, same cacophony blatting from the TV shop—"

Neither of us could come up with any simple solution. We guessed that we'd have to keep wandering around and talking to people until perhaps we ran into enough of them with similar accent and idiom which *might* still be peculiar to a certain portion of our country.

But give people here in Cape the credit they deserve. They fought an ardent little civil war against the soulless robots in our Nation's capital. (Invariably I imagine those officials as looking exactly alike, cut out of a common sheet of metal, a long row of miniature Robert S. McNamaras.) This rebellion was conducted with intelligence and spirit, but in the end the Government won out (usually does). There was to be erected in Cape Girardeau a new Government building—not a post office, but for other facilities: the Social Security office, maybe veterans' stuff— For all I know, Health, Wealth, Education, Welfare, Fanfare, Head Starts, Rear Starts, and other components of the Great Society. Hopefully the locals persuaded an architect to draw plans for a traditionally styled building. It would, in fancy, be a piece of dignified serenity amid the new façade of Cape Girardeau, with historic German or French gentility (both of which flourished here). Well, their flight of fancy got shot down in flames over Washington, D.C. There were too many computer-brained characters sitting in authority. Nay, the United States Government could have no truck with the *Past.* This had to be a *modern* building, reflecting the excellence of this immediate decade. Prayers of the citizenry fell on deaf ears.

By the time this book is in print, they will probably have chiseled out a chunk of masonry about as graceful as a carton of ScotTissue.

Come one, come all, and cruise down a Miracle Mile. It is Route 61, creasing and curving along the western edge of Cape. It is known also as Business 55, the deviation from Interstate 55. Here is Tampa, Florida; here is northern New Jersey; here are the outskirts of Phoenix, Arizona, and Durham, North Carolina. Here is our aggressive, cheap, imitative, clap-trap supermarket civilization.

It bruises like a neon sore across the face of the Nation and is promptly imitated eagerly by other inhabitants of this planet. Tokyo copies it, so does England. So does Montego Bay, Jamaica; so has Madrid done, so have endless German towns.

In the June 1968 *Reader's Digest* there appeared a page of back-patting attributed to one Reuben L. Perin, Chairman of the Board of an organization called (no, I'm not kidding) Keep America Beautiful, Inc. According to *Who's Who* (again I'm not kidding) Mr. Perin is a can manufacturer. It doesn't tell what sort of cans. "The *Digest*," said Mr. Perin, "has shown what communities and individuals have done to preserve beauty in such diverse places as Cape Girardeau–"

Wowski. Next time I go back to Cape, I'm going to invite Mr. Perin to come along, and we shall coast blissfully and admiringly along Business 55.

. . . Japanese motorcycles in phalanx. Ah yes, SUZUKI CITY. I can remember being in Cape when no one–repeat, no one–had a Japanese motorcycle. They had Indians and Harley-Davidsons. The only thing of Japanese origin might have been silk stockings in the ladies' stores downtown. . . . One begins to meditate . . . silk stockings, ah. Think of them in comparison to nylons. . . . Well, an old man can dream, can't he?

WIMPY'S DRIVE-IN.

If Elzie Segar hadn't invented that character Wimpy in his *Popeye the Sailor* cartoon strip, what would all the folks who run hamburger cafes have done? Wimpy's in London, Mexico City, Duluth, Torremolinos. Not one in a thousand customers has an idea what a Wimpy is or was, or who the original Wimpy was, or who dreamed him up.

BIG STAR.

COMMERCIAL CREDIT PLAN.

CUT RATE LIQUORS.

BLANKENSHIP'S MOBIL OIL–

A descendant of Tom Blankenship of Sam Clemens' fame? Could be.

Here's the MOON DISTRIBUTING COMPANY. I didn't realize we'd got quite that far in our dealings with the moon, and were now actually distributing it–

COUSIN FRED'S. One of those factory outlet places. It says that they have 48,467 ITEMS FOR LESS. Less than what? . . .

And where is the elephant? Last Saturday when we drove past, Cousin Fred had a big live elephant chained out in front of the place, merrily tossing hay on its back. There was a herd of ponies, too.

BINGO BARBECUE.

CAPE MACHINE WORKS.

CAPE READY-MIX. Cement mixers drive in and fill up with the ready-mix and carry it off to be stuffed into the composition of Sonny's San-Witch Shoppe or the Forty Winx Motor Lodge.

By golly, here's an old red barn with a pig painted on one end. It's a bar now, so what do they call it? The Lido? Riviera? Trader Vic's? Hell, no. THE BARN.

THE GIRLS GIRL-WATCHERS WATCH DRINK DIET PEPSI.

Why must Standard Oil drape an entire station in red-white-and-blue— I suppose it's plastic, but it looks something like the tinsel you put on Christmas trees; except it's not silvery, it's red-white-and-blue. Are they proving to the public that the Standard Oil Company is patriotic? Do they sell more gas because they have that stuff on there? Do customers come driving in who might have considered stopping at some other service station, but are simply queer for red-white-and-blue tinsel?

Hard to figure out. Hard to figure out anything in our uncanny 1960s.

Not too long ago this conglomeration did not exist, and the barn which has the pig painted on it was a real barn instead of a bar. There was a frog chorus instead of an elephant, down there by Cousin Fred's. Red-winged blackbirds pitched their wet camp where W. T. Grant's store now glares, stark and demanding.

Those of us who walk nostalgic, and who find allurance in a tumbledown cabin but never in a Laundromat— We are apt, with emotional and unreflective persistence, to declare that the net result of such changes are an unmitigated wickedness . . . that, in the words of a venerable British Army song, "The Good have all gone before us, and only The Dull are here."

Conscience compels me to quote from a faded clipping. Listen to this:

There was no concrete or asphalt on the roads, and they were alternately powder dry or grease-slippery. . . . Motive power was a mule or pair of them, and the weekly trip on Saturdays was the crowning event of a week of farm life. Necessities like plough points, salt, meal or tobacco had to be purchased—on credit as a rule—and sometimes there would be a few cash coins to be spent on movies or a bit of ribbon. In town all the wagons gathered at one central lot where about half the countryfolk were found to be congregated. . . . One poignant picture of these days that shall ever remain with us is that of a gangling, red-necked and overalled farmer with a group of towheaded, undernourished children grouped eagerly around him. In one hand was a nickel ice cream cone. In the other was a pocket knife with which he meticulously peeled off slivers of cream for deposit on the waiting tongues of his youngsters—for all the world like a parent mockingbird feeding its young. That ice cream cone represented a week's hopes, a week's ambitions for an entire family. . . .

Recently we had occasion to visit that same . . . town, and out of curiosity we had a look at the old wagon lot. It wasn't a lot any longer. On one corner of it was a supermarket; another corner was the site of a modern hardware store. There was a parking lot filled to the last place almost entirely with shiny late model automobiles. . . . Gone was the romance of the old days, but in its place was something a lot more substantial. For these shiny new autos belonged to the same farmers of yesterday who used to drive the mules to town.

Likewise we recalled a creek bank pasture where we used to hunt Indian arrow points or shoot birds. Now it is a subdivision replete with fire hydrants, paved streets and filling stations. . . . The spreading pasturelands, the grazing cows and the creek bank thickets have all been displaced in favor of spruce new houses, well-tended lawns and cement driveways.

. . . The blue-jeaned farmer who yesterday doled out slivers of ice cream to his brood is a different man today. Now he's sitting in a new auto, auditing his bank account to see if he can afford a television set.

That could have been Missouri. It wasn't. That editorial appeared in the Savannah (Ga.) *Morning News* in 1954. The present managing editor, Tom Coffey, believes that more than likely it was written by the late William J. Robertson. Well, Georgia has been altered too; so have the rest of the States. But dire revisions of economics and mores, not even imagined by editorial writers of 1954, have come about during the succeeding fifteen years.

Nor have all of them been for the best, no matter how shiny those compact cars and pick-up trucks, or how extensive the wide-screen television sets.

Are the customers who force their way down crowded aisles of jalopies or the mules which preceded them . . . and had battery-powered radios at home . . . or lived in Dark Ages—pre-TV, pre-radio—when folks had to make their own music or else listen to the whip-poor-wills?

The Kreem-Ee-Dare-Ee-Drive-Inn sells more ice cream to children and parents alike than was sold over a drugstore fountain in the early banana split days. Probably there are fewer undernourished family broods on farms than there were then.

Also there are a lot fewer farmers.

. . . More ice cream, more leisure. So many youths especially seem to be surfeited with leisure. They loll in new Sunbeams, in third-hand souped-up Mustangs and fifth-hand Corvettes with absurd tachometers attached, and their faces are blank with unresponding boredom. Why should it be surprising to discover that hallucinatory Cousin Fred's— Are they happier than those who drove the old drugs find favor and custom among such unfortunates? They hold no ambition to labor, serve, build, invent or excel. The fat of a too-permissive, too-benevolent civilization has grown like a carcinoma within their souls.

Edgar Lee Masters' stately lines come echoing from those libraries and attics where bound volumes of *Reedy's Mirror* gather dust, and where the voices of fabled Spoon River inhabitants first spoke in St. Louis type and ink.

> What is this I hear of sorrow and weariness,
> Anger, discontent and drooping hopes?
> Degenerate sons and daughters,
> Life is too strong for you—
> It takes life to love Life.

We preen ourselves because of inventive and technological achievement. But the jet aircraft is a better vehicle than the rattling wagon only insofar as it conveys its human burden to a better destination. The most modern mechanics of communication are an improvement on the ancient smoke signal, lusty halloo, or waved apron, only insofar as they bring a wiser understanding between individuals and Nations alike, and sound a more inspiring message.

An excellent writer and editor, Jonathan Daniels, reminded us in a recent editorial which appeared in his Raleigh (N.C.) *News and Observer* that certain physical elements of dignity and sublime importance are being eradicated on a wholesale basis.

> In almost every town . . . landmark homes are gobbled up swiftly to make room for parking lots and the like. Of course, many of these ancient dwellings are bereft of human habitation.
>
> Sometimes the windows are sockets without eyes. The floors have severe mumps, the chimneys have DT's, and rats riot in the library. A few stand with militant square-jawed and two-fisted gables, fighting time for every corroded inch and hour. But if the incessant demands of expanding society must be met, the truth is that the bulldozer pushes down in two days the last physical symbol of all that love, tears, and labor wrought across a century or two centuries. . . .
>
> Today, unknowing motorists park where the white roses grew, where oaks once seemed tangible lessons in immortality. People park and stomp cigarette butts and toss gum wrappers where vanished men planned the town's future and good grace. Engines stutter where pianos played and poetry was read. Well, such may be historically inevitable. But someone should cherish and tell these sagas so that his son may know tomorrow that the moon once shone on something more than a big piece of concrete.

Increasingly unpopular is the author who would "cherish and tell these sagas." Tell them, and you will be sneered down, derided by a prevailing cult who mock every elderly beauty, and seek to spray them with the DDT of their juvenile disapproval. If you found more charm and reassurance in silver quarter-dollars bearing Miss Liberty than in copper alloy quarter-dollars bearing the likeness of a Kennedy, you are either a member of the John Birch Society or the Ku Klux Klan. At the best they will scream, "Incurable sentimentalist!" If you hold that men of the Past displayed more honesty, vigor, decency and courage than the college Sit-Inners and draft-card burners of today, then you've probably been brainwashed by the *Reader's Digest.*

These people find anything in the Past offensive simply because it was *in the Past.* The Past to them was a miserable failure, and no one who even contemplates it will be forgiven. The Past did not bring a perfection to mankind at large, the Nation at large, or even to your individual Pocatello or Pikesville. Therefore the practice or even the teaching of the Past's virtues is not to be tolerated. Honesty failed, vigor failed, courage failed, cleanliness failed.

Failed to do what?

To erase every cruelty and every inequity from the pattern of living.

Aye, they failed. Therefore— Away with them all.

That's not a dirigible hangar over there—it's a church. That's not a crematorium—it's a medical arts building. Dig that groovy new drive-in. Dig that DOG N' SUDS place across the road. Television masts sprout where orioles used to weave their nests. (Excuse me. Their *pads.*) And Miss Joan Baez croons an anti-anti-song for the ears of the appreciative young; and someone named Updike (or Upchuck?) is their literary priest; and Miss Vanessa Redgrave is their Florence Nightingale, their Molly Pitcher, their St. Joan.

Sorry about that.

5. Love Apples

Early morning. In our room a starved pair of Missouri explorers were dressing as fast as they could.

Irene said, "Damn. We forgot to buy any fruit juice, to have here before breakfast."

"I know something that would be much better."

"Tell me."

"'A semivinelike annual herb of the family Solanaceae, native to South America in the region of the Andes.'" Quoting from some botanical source or other.

"Have you seen any of those semivinelike annual herbs around lately?"

"Yes, I saw *Lycopersicum esculentum.* In quantities. So did you, and we neglected to buy any. We even have salt handy: you know how both Frank Dawson and Harold Shaffer have always recommended salt water as an alternate dentifrice. So we must not let another day pass without acquiring plenty of *Lycopersicum esculentum.*"

"Are specimens of Missouri *Lycopersicum esculentum* especially desirable?"

"Not so utterly delicious as *Lycopersicum esculentum* grown in Iowa. But second *only* to the Iowa variety. Now, you take the Florida product: they haven't one-tenth the flavor of the Midwest kind, or even of those grown in New England. But California ones are the worst. Their effulgence and enormous size are sheer fraud. Remember how we used to become excited by them in the markets out there? And had them turn to ashes in our mouths?"

Irene said, "Somebody ought to shoot these modern tomato growers who rob them of moisture, fill them with pulp, and thicken their skins just to make them easier to handle in marketing. Some have hides as tough as plastic Baggies! With a fraction of the juice they used to contain—"

That day we watched and sniffed and listened, but didn't discover a single roadside stand along any route where we drove. As the afternoon lengthened I tried supermarkets . . . nay, these tomatoes were from Georgia . . . those came from Texas. Had little stickers on them. . . . It took four tries to find the home-grown variety. They lasted for a couple of days, then I was on the prowl again.

By that time we were ensconced in an inn adjacent to the Three Flags Restaurant at an Interstate 70 intersection south of St. Charles. Packing up every morning and unpacking every night had become a nuisance. Much easier on the nerves if we spent three or four nights at a selected motel without moving. We could branch out each day, drive anywhere we wished. Whenever Irene felt in a working mood she'd stay home and paint all day, while I was off Missouri waltzing.

Our first pleasure on rising was in the tomatoes we could enjoy for a fruit course long before we reached the dining room. Irene likes hers chilled unless she can pick them right off the vine; I prefer tomatoes at room temperature, like many good wines. They lay waiting, freshly washed, on one of the long tables built against the wall, or else frosty in our portable ice chest. Not once, from then on, did we miss morning tomatoes while we were in Missouri on that particular trip.

The very best ones we found were on Route 94, going down from St. Charles toward Weldon Spring. Had to admit that their flavor and fragility could match the ultimate in the Iowa product of sixty years ago. . . .

One supermarket manager insisted, "I daren't bother with home-grown stuff. Anyway the company doesn't want me to. Our other arrangements work out a lot better."

"For your *company*."

"Well, that's who we're in business for, isn't it? See, people like to buy tomatoes which look alike and are a standard size. A lot of these home-grown things are twisted around, large, small, wadded up, creased. And if they're truly vine-ripened we just can't handle them. They burst and squirt, and we have a spoilage rate that cuts into our profits. Oh, I agree with you," he added, "from the point of *taste*. Yep, the locals *taste* a lot better. But—"

He glanced around in a manner of conspiracy, then leaned over to whisper, "I grow my own, right in our garden at home. I've been generous with water, and despite the drouth we've got a fine crop right now. The Missis has put up I don't know how many quarts, and she's been making chili sauce too. She and the girls. You going to be around this evening?"

I told him that, unfortunately, we were driving on. Had reservations in Columbia.

"Too bad. If you were going to be here you could drive over to 1214 Cranny Court and I'd give you some. But my wife and the girls aren't home now either—they've gone to a sorority picnic. And I can't suggest that you go by the house and pick em yourself. Our Doberman wouldn't let you in the yard."

. . . When I told Irene what he'd said, she smiled appreciatively. "Isn't that Missouri all over again? There's an admirable race of people hereabouts. Generous, hospitable—"

Huh. We encountered Mr. Sopper a week or so afterward. (Fake name.) This genius was in the insurance as well as the tomato business. His insurance office was a tar-paper shack built on as a projection: a cubic lump fastened to his dwelling in the main street of a pleasant village. Sign painted on the office: *SEE SOPPER FOR INSURANCE*. Naturally we judged that our tomato salesman was Mr. Sopper. He lounged in his deck-chair at the roadside stand where he purveyed corn, melons and—mainly—tomatoes.

"How much are the tomatoes?"

"These here are a dollar a basket. Over here's some that are way too ripe. I'll let you have those for fifty cents a basket."

We wanted only a supply which would last us for two or three days, so we wouldn't have to be stopping all the time. Therefore we didn't fancy overripe ones. "I'll be glad to take half a basket of the others."

"No. Only sell em by the basket. Dollar."

"We can't eat that many."

"Sure you can."

I explained that we were traveling from place to place, and didn't want to have tomato bisque all over the back seat of the car. "Can't you sell us less than a dollar's worth?"

He shrugged, scowled, settled back in his chair, and picked up the children's comic book which he had been reading before we stopped.

Irene said a little later, "You know, we should have bought a basket."

"Couldn't have eaten that many. Just a mess and a waste."

"They wouldn't have been wasted. We could have driven around a couple of miles—then come down that highway, and bombed Mr. Sopper as we drove by."

But we hold memory of crimson treasure along the way . . . perfumed slices, at lunch or dinner in little restaurants. Fresh stewed tomatoes we ate at the homes of friends; salad at clubs in Cape Girardeau, Columbia, Trenton, other towns. Missouri tomatoes at the height of their season. They exuded the scent and benignity of sun-beaten fields and drowsy afternoons . . . hinted of the past when they were called love apples—deadly poisonous, fit only to be set up on the kitchen window ledge as decoration.

We thought, "Let's not call them tomatoes any more. 'Love apples' is a dear designation. Let's revive it."

6. The Inn Thing

First time Irene and I ever stayed at a motel, it was back in the years when they called them cabin camps. This one was north of Moberly, Missouri. We were attempting to dash on to central Iowa non-stop from the Ozarks. We'd had a rough day in the hills and were completely exhausted. Lord knows I was accustomed to driving while my wife slept in the front seat beside me, but this was a little too much. I'd never yet gone to sleep while driving, and didn't want to go to sleep then. (Come to think of it, probably there aren't too many men, comfortably alive and ambulatory, who can say, "Sure. I often go to sleep while driving." Or, "I remember the first time I went to sleep while driving." Reckon not.) We had a tiny daughter at home, and she might not like the idea of being parentless.

I kept slapping my face with one hand, wetting my handkerchief with my tongue, wiping my eyes with it. In regretful recollection there appeared unto me the dismal sign of a cheap hotel, picked out in weak yellow electric bulbs, in the last town we'd gone through.

In those days the best roads in Missouri were two-lane highways, and a good many of those were graveled, not paved. Folks called the concrete pavement *slab.* "Yeh, you might have a moll or two of mud, but then you'll hit the slab, and–"

I was looking for a place where the ditch wasn't too deep, so that I could pull completely off at the side of the road and catch a little sleep. Country schoolhouses and churches used to be good for that: they were tenantless at night. Country graveyards weren't bad either, far as that went: their tenants rested undisturbed, but quite possibly *disturbing* to the superstitious soul of some prowler bent on mischief. Any place close to a farmstead was no good at all. The dogs were full of accusation. "What the hell are you doing down there in that car? *Wow-wow-wow-wow-wow.* We're going to tell the whole county about it," and they did.

On this occasion, before I could find a roadside verge which suited, a few lights and a home-painted sign emerged from brown night on the left. CABINS. The place didn't look exactly like the Drake in Chicago (to us in our young years, and within our limited experience, the Drake was the *ne plus ultra* among hotels). But right then I would have settled for a packing case full of excelsior.

I drove into the yard, got out of the car, found an illuminated night bell. . . . Presently the yawning proprietor appeared in flannel undershirt, and pants with suspenders draped around his middle.

"How many, mister? See, the double cabins are a little bigger, cause they got double beds in em. Cost double, too."

"How much is that?"

"Single cabins one dollar a night, double cabins two dollars."

"O.K. on the double. If it's clean–"

"We scrub em out every week. And my wife puts new sheets on, every day. Take a look."

He flashed his light into an empty double cabin, and it did look clean, smelled clean.

"Where do I go to sign the register?"

"This ain't no hotel, this is a *cabin camp.* You don't have to sign nothing."

He stood waiting amid shadows while I brought the Chevrolet around and squeaked to a stop in front of the door, and while I awakened a seemingly drugged Irene and led her inside. I wondered what the proprietor was waiting for, then suddenly it struck me. Money. You had to pay in advance at such places, or maybe you'd be gone without paying before the boss was up in the morning. I forked over two dollars, and he thanked me.

"Would you like to have a jug of nice fresh water? We got a deep well."

. . . Cup of cold water offered by how many hands, and through how many ages . . . I followed the man to his own cabin, where he fetched out a cracked china pitcher.

"Sure is nice of you."

"And here's a glass. The well's right over yonder, under that there box elder."

Irene and I went to bed by the light of a kerosene lamp. . . . Sheets and pillowcases were of thinnest sleaziest cotton, but they felt fresh. Like the cabin itself, they diffused a kind of hard-worked-for, enforced sense of cleanliness. Windows had screening nailed on the outside, and we slid them open and breathed the cool night air. There was red clover in bloom . . . its perfume came in . . . no more cars troubled the highway. . . . Sound of a calf bawling. That cry ceased, and there lived only the breathing silence which surrounds things growing in fields. Then far off, farms and farms away, the eternal night sound of a dog's challenging, and other dogs taking it up. . . . Had I locked the car? Yes. Had I hooked the door? Yes. I came back from examination of the screen and its fastenings, lay down beside Irene, knew no more.

Next morning.

"Gosh, I hated to spend that money. But if we don't eat *too* much, we've still got enough dough for food and gas until we get home."

Irene frowned in consideration. "Let's see. I've got thirty-seven cents, and I've got my Emergency Money. It's right here in this compartment of my bag."

She referred to a tightly folded dollar bill which we had thought it wise for her to always have with her. As for my own Emergency Money, I was a little puzzled about what to do with that dollar—where to carry it safely. First I'd tried putting it inside my hatband, but then one day I left the hat hanging in a restaurant, and someone else got the dollar as well as the hat. Then I tried carrying it in my watch pocket; but sometimes when I'd pull out the watch to look at it I'd pull out the dollar also, and not be aware of the loss until too late. This didn't seem very economical. Finally I hit on a grand idea, at least when traveling in the car: the knob on the gear-shift lever was a perfect sphere in those 1928 Chevrolets, and you could unscrew the top half of this globe, and there was a little space inside. My dollar bill was then folded tightly, long way to, and wound around the post with the threads on it. Then the upper hemisphere was screwed back tightly. Good deal. It was always there, and I regarded this as a great comfort. Only long after I'd traded the car did I realize that I'd traded in my precious dollar as well. There was money in the car doors, too. We'd found our daughter happily rummaging through her mother's bag, and dropping change down inside the panel which held the window glass. Question: Would it cost more to have the door taken apart, than the money itself amounted to? Probably so, therefore we did nothing about it. Doubtless thousands of other cars have gone to junkyard Valhallas with money in the doors, deposited by thousands of baby hands. We teach babies that it is a fine thing for them to push coins through the slots in their toy banks; so they can't be blamed if they toss an irretrievable fifty-cent piece into an engaging aperture where the coin tinkles nicely as it goes down. They think they're putting money in the bank . . . well, I seem to recall other banks, on a larger adult scale, where depositors placed their riches for safe-keeping. And then what happened.

Told Irene firmly, "No, indeed. Our Emergency Dollars must be kept for that purpose solely: *emergencies*. Of course you might say that an emergency prevailed last night when I was nearly dead for sleep, and afraid that I'd drive off the road. But who knows what other emergency might *emerge* between here and home?"

We munched soft pinkish-yellowish crab apples which we'd picked in the dooryard of an abandoned farmhouse the previous afternoon. Then, when we got to the next town, we had our coffee, and shared one ham-and-egg sandwich. Gad. There was a big man eating breakfast, just down the counter from us, and he was putting away three eggs and a regular woodpile of bacon slices, along with a stack of cakes. We tried to forget that spectacle as soon as possible. . . . Bought the gas we needed, and I only had to buy one more quart of oil. And I was positive—well, almost positive—that there would be a check from *Real Detective Tales* or the *Chicago Daily News Midweek Magazine* waiting in the mail.

Thirty miles south of home we gobbled two reckless hamburgers, and forty minutes later Granny was guiding our excited and jabbering daughter toward us as we turned in at the driveway.

Heard Irene telling my mother later, "Can you imagine where we slept last night? In a *cabin camp*," and witnessed Mother's exclamation of mingled apprehension, amazement, amusement, and downright incredulity.

Not long after that, they started building them in rows, and landscaping the places a bit, and calling them cabin "courts." And soon, "motor courts." That's one name which has stuck. *Motel* didn't come into the language until some time later. Our language seems forever elastic and adaptable, and *motel* is one manufactured word which owns reasonable excuse and purpose.

Just thinking . . . I remember the first motel we ever saw with *wall-to-wall carpeting*. That was something over twenty years ago, and it was out in Wyoming. Far cry from the cabin camps.

In 1929 there could have been no estimate of the extent to which the motel would become an intrinsicate part of America's civilization. (And on its way to becoming, in lesser degree, a worldwide institution.) Despite any memoir I have made concerning abhorrent breakfasts, or churlish treatment by some roustabout staff– And that one in– Not many miles northeast of Columbus, Ohio. I journeyed alone, but at midnight had to take a room with two double beds because there weren't any other rooms. After I'd taken off my clothes I got into one double bed, and it hadn't been made, and it was full of cookie crumbs; and then I got into the other double bed, and it hadn't been made either, and somebody had been making love in that one. "*Someone has been eating cookies and making love in my beds,*" *roared the Big Bear*. So I spent the night on top of a newly blanketed unmade bed with my raincoat over me. And no pillow, Ma. . . . But despite such monstrous memories lurking in caverns of the past, the motel is here, and is substantially a part of us, and I'm glad it is.

Because this institution serves not only the itinerants. It gives villagers a brightness, luxury, gaiety, a social outlet which they never knew before and in which they rejoice.

Cities don't seem right for motels, and motels don't seem right for cities. I deplore a tendency of the big chains, sticking a Holiday Inn and a Howard Johnson's right in the middle of Manhattan and in many other metropolitan centers.

. . . Year or so ago we were in New York, and got a call from our friends Phyllis and Irving Vendig. They were staying at Howard Johnson's, of all places, over on Eighth Avenue.

I repeated, "Howard *John*son's?"

"Yes, they've got one here now. John D. MacDonald recommended it. He said, 'Think how easy it is to come in with your car, and have it right under the same roof with you.'"

Irene and I stopped by for drinks with the Vendigs before we all went out to dinner. But the moment we entered the lobby, even before we pressed the elevator button– Same old fried potatoes.

In 1935 I published a thin volume of verse called *Turkey in the Straw.* Very few people today have ever heard of the book, but it did elicit a rather pleasant critical response. I was hipped on elves in my youth, and Stephen Vincent Benét shook his head over this. He wrote in a newspaper review— Steve wrote, and I can just hear him saying the words in his dry nasal voice: "One must forgive Mr. Kantor his frequent mention of elves in these indigenous poems. Somehow elves never seem to have become thoroughly domesticated in the United States of America." Steve and his Rosemary, Irene and I were warm friends and used to have great times together. But if Steve felt critical, no matter how dear the friendship, he always spoke his mind. He wasn't anybody's back-scratcher.

Next time we met, I said, "You're right. So I've reformed. No more elves."

"That removes a certain load from my mind," says Stephen feelingly.

By the same token, I represent that motels have not been properly domesticated in large American cities, and never will be.

More and more do Interstates and express highways come together at points remote from cities. At such intersections there is crying need and economic excuse for adequate motel space. As anyone can see with half an eye while driving cross-country, there are often three or four specimens of the well-known chain hostelries located at or adjacent to the same intersection. Eccentrics who idle along tertiary roads and cartpaths (like the Kantors) are in a minority of such infinitesimal proportion that it cannot be seen with the naked eye. Most members of the gas-burning public want to get to a specific point, and get there fast, and with the least—to them—effort. I'm positive that it takes a greater toll of physical and nervous energy to drive on an Interstate than on a secondary road where there isn't much traffic, but the majority don't share that opinion. On the other hand, when the day grows toilsome, it's nice to reëxamine the map, and see just where we might turn off in order to reach a principal highway intersection. Grilled steak or roast chicken may have its charms, so might refrigeration. The picturesque small-town hotel is gone, gone, gone. Last year we drove through or past many Missouri towns where once we enjoyed family-style pot roast and Aunt Mamie May's beaten biscuits, and where once we snuggled in four-poster beds. But the hotels have been torn down to make room for

Merchandise Marts. You have to search out that Quality Inn eleven miles west of town.

The old Gaylord House might have done well enough for drummers and for the Velie and Hudson pioneers, but to natives it offered little in the way of facility for entertaining. You could eat there, and that was about it. And after the Gaylord gave up the ghost, if a resident of the town of Juneberry wanted to take his tired appreciative wife out for dinner, they either went to Buster's Sandwich Place down by the railroad tracks, or else they had to drive forty miles to the nearest city and forty miles back.

Now vast motels ramble over ridges and plains, flashing their charms every evening like winking bulbs on an operational chart adorning the wall of some military establishment.

. . . When Luella got married in 1962, she wanted a fancy wedding. Friends and relatives were invited by the score. There had to be food and drink provided for exactly one hundred and thirty-three guests following the ceremony at First Christian, and Luella's mother wasn't the same for two months afterward.

But last summer Luella's younger sister, Allene, got married, and what a change. They had the ceremony right on the edge of town, there where Interstate This meets Route Number That. The Reverend Mr. John Wesley or the Reverend Mr. Adoniram Judson or whoever he was, spoke sacred words amid flowers in one of the convention rooms, and bridesmaids looked like they had sprung from the pages of *The Bride's Magazine*. Afterward, with the kissing and giggling and gushing going on, folks had only to make their way down a hall into a private dining room, and there was the buffet set up for them. Better than all that cooking and baking for days beforehand, in the house over on Azalea Street, eh, Mom? . . . Little niceties could be observed just the way they would have been at home. Allene and Toby were going to feel very much married, when they started off in their car.

(They wouldn't tell anyone where they were going on the wedding trip, but they might as well have advertised it over the local radio station. Allene had been dying to visit New Orleans, and she was always talking about it, and going to movies about New Orleans, and reading books about New Orleans. . . . Out at the side porte-cochère, incoming and outgoing tourists stood around and chuckled. The boys had really done a job on that Ford Galaxie. Had it all painted up. . . . *The Pill Express*. . . . *Silent Night? No!* . . .

Ouch, honey! All in huge letters, and painted everywhere they could possibly paint. Some of the guys were still stretched out on the pavement, reaching up under the Galaxie, working with chains and garbage-can lids, cow-bells, wash-tubs. Toby wasn't going to be able to halt at the first available place and get that junk off of there by himself. He'd have to stop at a filling station, and get somebody to put the thing up on a hoist and cut the assortment loose, while a whole new set of people stood around. . . . Back inside the motel, in the closed-off dining room, guests were mobbed around, eating and drinking and laughing and talking their heads off. Also take note of the bride's room and the bridegroom's room, where the young folks could change before they started off on their trip . . . welter of banging and clanking, storm of rice, and friends cheering them on their way.)

One recent summer, in driving around Missouri, we tried to keep track of the wedding parties we ran into. Or honeymoon couples whose cars, still bedight with signs, happened to be pulled up near ours when we came out in the morning. We'd see the Just Marrieds afterward occasionally, in cafes. They could be classified as glum or confused or quietly ecstatic, as the case might be . . . counted a dozen or so. So multiply that by the number of motels in the State.

Certainly it was something of an annoyance to worm your way through crowds in the hall at times. But it was nice to think of Mom being emancipated from her kitchen on Azalea Street.

Which brings to mind the notion that a lot of babies must have been born—as well as conceived—in motels already. And a lot more will be born in the future. My own niece came into the world in a roadside bedroom at Cameron, Missouri; but that was back in the cabin camp days. Still, you can't put a population on wheels and have them bowling all over the place, and not have a lot of young women who think they're going to make it to Poplar Bluff or Buffalo perfectly all right, but don't manage to do so.

There is an imagined litany ringing from Present and Future—one perhaps perfectly acceptable to those who voice it, but rather poignant to ancient ears.

"Oh, darling, remember the first night we spent together at that Western Lodge? It was called the Cape Codder. And the ice machine was just opposite our door, and it was a hot night, and people kept coming for ice, and digging it out and putting it in their containers, until the ice was all gone, and we could hear them cussing about it."

"Gee, sweetheart, remember the first night after our marriage? It was in that Ramada Inn, over on Route 69. I remember we were scared, and thought we'd have bad luck or something, because the room they gave us was One-Thirteen."

"Honey, whenever I think of our wedding night, I think of Joey Bishop. Because the man in the next room at our Shamrock Motel had the TV turned up so high that we could hear the whole thing right through the wall. And then– Well, later we wondered if they could hear *us*. And then, in the morning, he turned up the news real loud again, until it sounded like the announcer was practically there in bed with us. But, being newlyweds, we were too embarrassed to call up the office and complain."

And what about children now growing up, many of whose first memories must necessarily be associated with the Helpy-Selfy Market? The first thing they'll be able to recall will be the hour when they rode upon that grocery cart, gazing in wonder at packages and people . . . rising and stretching dangerously to try to reach oranges or a shelf of peanut butter jars . . . little feet struggling among the cart's contents. Duz, Dreft, Dash, Kleenex, Tampax, Tays-Tee franks, Tays-Tee pizza, Tays-Tee mix, six-packs of Tab, and a hundred other things their great-great-grandmothers never heard of.

(I was about to add to the last line in the preceding paragraph: "Or wanted to." Then I went over the list again, and promptly wiped out those three final words. . . . Kleenex? Tampax? The great-great-grandmothers, poor souls, would have been ecstatic.)

We were domiciled momentarily at a maverick privately owned place which had what our grandchildren call a *loverly* view, but with no restaurant or bar attached. So we drove for fifteen minutes, and halted at a Holiday Inn Junior. Hadn't realized that Holiday Inns were old enough to have offspring in the business, but family resemblance proved this to be a fact. Holiday Junior resembled scores of Holiday Seniors where we'd been guests through years and States—a resemblance in countenance if not in stature. But they had a dining room and they had a bar, or so the Mobil Travel Guide proclaimed.

The liquor situation in Missouri is one of those crazyquilts where, according to local option, rules vary not only from county to county, but also from town to town, with discrepancies between a town's law and the law of the county in which that town is located. Back in Cape they had a satisfyingly grandiose bar in the New Orleans Restaurant downtown; but out at our hostel adjacent to Interstate 55 you had to drink in your room, unless you wanted to consume beer in an inhospitable chamber which had the aura of a rumpus room in a YMCA. But we can recall frosty gibsons at the Three Flags, mentioned earlier; or at a place in Joplin named the Embers or the Rafters or the Shingles or something like that. Anyway, they had lively live lobsters just begging to be dip-netted out of their tank—as hearty lobsters as you'd find at The Pier in Damariscotta, Maine.

On a green-hilled shore of the Lake of the Ozarks we sought out the Lodge of the Four Seasons, alleged to possess a *loverly* restaurant and bar. We didn't have sense enough to tote along our own bottles. It was the law of the land in that particular region: you must be escorted arm-in-arm by your own bottles, in order to be served. Maybe they had a package store handy . . . if they did, our sourpuss dumb-bunny of a waitress didn't know where it was.

. . . Same deal in a different location, now, at this Holiday Junior. Once again I felt tricked.

But wait a minute— What was that waitress telling us?

". . . You say you have a liquor store right here? Is it open?"

"No, but I've sure got the key," and she patted the pocket of her crisp uniform.

We walked down to a hole-in-the-wall crammed with an astonishing collection of brands. I picked up a quart of Hudson's Bay scotch, and one of Smirnoff's white label, and some dry vermouth. Didn't matter, we'd use these all up in time. Back at the bar, our very jolly little blonde brought us glasses, ice, water. Even some olives.

"You can keep your bottles right on the table, too."

"No can do in Texas."

"Then that's another reason why Missouri has it all over Texas, sir."

"What about those ten million bottles lined up over there behind your bar?"

"Those belong to various people who are drinking here right now, were drinking here, or will be drinking here again. We keep the bottles safe for em. All marked, and everything." She beamed and asked, "Wouldn't you like to order dinner? You can be served right here."

. . . Home-made vegetable soup came along at the exact moment when we were ready for it. Irene declared it to be the best vegetable soup she'd had in months—better than her own, she said, which I denied staunchly. But it was damn good. We confined ourselves to soup and salad and crackers and iced tea. We'd had a head-on collision with a rib roast that noon.

The room was a tiny place; they couldn't get more than six or seven tables in there. It was almost full at the early hour when we arrived, and jam-packed when we left; also several groups came and went in the meantime. We overheard no conversation which didn't bear a local tinge. Two men at the little bar seemed to be traveling salesmen, but familiar with the area and its people. The rest were *nativos*. You could tell by the way they greeted one another.

A jook-box stood at the end of the room. No, not a *juke*-box. A jook-box. This spelling, with which most of my readers will not be familiar, is the correct spelling. I'll tell you why, when a good opportunity comes along.

Early in the game I'd hastened over there in order to make a lot of selections. That had come to be Standing Operating Procedure. We happen to enjoy the nigh-onto-forgotten tenderness of genial popular music. How the hell one can relish a drink or a meal when held captive, compelled to listen to monotonous headachy drums, snarling phony ballads, the yelling of cannibals— This I cannot see. In most places we visited, a majority of the records were obnoxious. Point was, then, to put in some money and press levers of the *less* obnoxious numbers, before someone else elected that you must listen to The Apes or The Drips or The Pots or The Poops.

But here at Holiday Junior, what a surprise. *Missouri Waltz*, *Tennessee Waltz*, *Lazybones*, *Beautiful Ohio*, *Stardust*. Enduring favorites, many of them played by the same enduring and endearing people: Hoagy Carmichael, Artie Shaw, Nat King Cole. Furthermore the volume wasn't turned up too high.

Showboat music, dreamboat music.

A man at the next table leaned over and made the little circle of thumb and finger which signifies approval and good fortune. (Maybe they still use that in the Air Force when somebody is about to take off.)

He said, "You prefer the old ones, too."

"You folks, as well?"

Soon we had shoved our chairs around and were tabled together, talking together, introducing ourselves.

7. Fetch

That's how we encountered Mr. and Mrs. Leonard Fetchley.

There's a type of somewhat saturnine visage met with among males which will, mysteriously but promptly, inspire confidence and affection. The late Walter Huston had a face like that. So has Congressman James A. Haley. So did the late James D. LeCron, long ago an executive of the Des Moines *Register*, and subsequently an assistant to the late Henry A. Wallace in Washington—

(Hey. Let's lay off this *late* doctrine for good and all. The longer one tarries in existence, the more people is he compelled to refer to as *the late*. So if I do it again in this book, may I be condemned to a solid week of boarding at the nearest Howard Johnson's.)

Be such a man actor, editor, doctor, lawyer, merchant, chief, in his face there is combined somehow the wryness of a legendary rustic storekeeper, together with sharp perceptive vision—the roving discerning glance, eager to seek out whatever humors can be discovered. Overall there is a jauntiness, an unstudied tolerance never engendered by weakness or insipidity.

(Too many weak or insipid people are all too tolerant. That's because they're reluctant to tread upon anybody's toes. They ignore a self-declared evil and run from an obvious danger, and call that being tolerant.)

There was more than a suggestion of physical power in Leonard Fetchley's long-armed long-necked stringy frame. He looked like Middle Fifties, hair thinning, hazel eyes bright beneath reddish brows turning gray. The lines of his face showed that he laughed oftener than he frowned. He wore a brown-and-white-striped seersucker suit

—fitting carelessly, as one could observe when he finally arose and put on the jacket which had been hanging on the back of his chair.

His wife Genevra, called Gen or Genny, was plump but trim of figure, silver-blue crowned, and seeming younger than Fetchley (later they said they'd been married for thirty-three years). She was one of those lucky dames in whose wide pale eyes the reverie of a musing imagining childhood is preserved, and even enhanced, as years progress. When a new record was played on the machine—an acceptable rendition of *Annie Laurie*—Mrs. Fetchley mentioned her Scottish ancestry on both sides. She said that an elder sister had been named Annie, and the next child, a boy, Laurie.

"And when I was little, we did have a pet mule. We named him Maxwelton, for obvious reasons."

Now, then. During the introductions, there was a good reason why we became Irene and Mike Connor. This has occurred before, and is admitted with no great shame. I'm not the best-known author in America, nor am I the least-known. (Plenty of times when I give my true name, some character is apt to smirk and say, "Any relation to Eddie?" I must have heard that first when I was fourteen.) Also, not too many folks remember much about *The Philadelphia Story*, a play written by Philip Barry back in the 1930s. . . . But, in setting forth this confession, I've bunged up the Connor thing for future usage.

For some reason or other, Phil Barry always admitted to being fascinated by my name. He said that he liked the alliteration, the uncommon combination of a Scottish name and a Jewish one.

He told me one night, at the home of our mutual publisher and close friend, Tim Coward, "Mack, I think maybe you've inspired the name of a character I'm struggling with in my new play. How about Macauley Connor? Called 'Mike' instead of 'Mack.' Would you mind?"

"Why should I?"

So when we went to see Phil's play, there was Macauley Connor, called Mike, big as life.

Perhaps it was natural that later I should adopt the name as an alias. I do have several. As one's books pile up, and one's name becomes more familiar to the reading or movie-going or television-watching public— Strangers, when you meet them, are apt to evince a (to them understandable, and to the author an annoying) tendency to build conversation about the writer's works. I don't enjoy talking about my work. I have to talk about it enough with agents and editors and publishers as it is, and have had to discuss my books with them all these years. When you toil as a writer through so many of your waking hours—and often through your sleeping hours also (the *Andersonville* and *Spirit Lake* dreams were pretty rough) people should understand that you desire a change of pace and scene and subject matter. This author is willing to hold forth on practically any subject in the world, rather than that of his own product.

(Two other topics are also out: the Vietnamese war, and recent administrations of our Government. Therein lie seeds of apoplexy.)

"The world is so full of a number of things," chanted Stevenson. I mean Robert Louis, not Adlai. . . . It's fun to talk about those numbers of things. I don't know anything about breeding race horses, but if I happen to be in Kentucky I'd rather have the inhabitants give me a lecture on Dancer's Image and Reigh Count and Regret and Whirlaway, than to engage in discussion of a book which has cost me the ultimate in mental, physical and spiritual coin. Or in attempting to explain why I didn't quit writing forever when I got that bad review in *Time* or *Newsweek.*

There are a few million other topics. Sex is still interesting, even in the seventh decade of this one's existence, thank God. There are all the stories to be related and shared gleefully, bawdy or otherwise. There's every captivating category of conversation from Catalina to corn to corn-lilies to catastrophes to cats.

Actors are unfortunate. They can't flee from themselves. Men and women of the stage and screen have been selling their bodies and their voices and their physiognomy, as well as whatever interpretative and presentative skills they possess. (N.B. I've got news for them. Actors do not create roles, although steadfastly they are credited with doing so. The author or playwright creates the roles. The actors interpret and present them. N.B. again: This may get me kicked out of the Players Club.)

When actors wish to retreat from the public, or desire to maintain a discreet anonymity, there's not a chance. Example as follows: Dana and Mary Andrews and Irene and I wanted to go down to Sweet's, the delectable but overcrowded seafood restaurant in New York's Fulton Street. There was a mob that night, and we had no reservation. (Matter of fact, I don't believe Sweet's makes reservations.) A double line extended all the way up the ancient stairs from the sidewalk. We went up slowly, one step at a time, then maybe three or four steps at a time, as tables were vacated above.

My guess is that Dana had to sign his autograph at least a dozen times while we were on that stairway, and that meant fresh conversation on each occasion.

"You know, Mr. Andrews, the picture of yours that I liked best was—"

"Mr. Andrews, I've got a very talented nephew who wants to be a movie star. Now, how should he go about it?"

"Mr. Andrews, is it true that your father was a preacher?"

With these people Dana was obliged to appear friendly, simple, sincere, obedient, cheerful and thrifty. . . . Maybe I'm mistaken, at that. Maybe there is one role which actors must needs create as well as interpret. That is the great starring role called *Being Themselves.* Let's not envy them.

Their faces have grown familiar to millions of pairs of eyes which have never looked upon them in the flesh. Therefore there's small chance that they may escape scrutiny and approach. Some go around wearing dark glasses, days and evenings alike, pulling their hats down over their faces, and indulging in other such tricks; but it doesn't work very well. Greta Garbo used to visit a friend who lived in the building where we maintained an apartment, and she wore the dark glasses, the turned-down felt hat and such-like . . . she stood aloof in the elevator, not looking at other people. Just the same, the others looked at her. She was unmistakably Garbo. . . . And it's difficult for a Jimmy Stewart or a Gregory Peck to disguise himself. His stature and stance give him away.

We authors are in an easier position. Our likenesses are seen from time to time in magazines and newspapers, or occasionally on the television screen. But it is a fleeting impression which the public preserves at best. (Except in the case of Carl Sandburg, who created for himself a character part, complete with make-up. The role was known as *Carl Sandburg.*) Only when our names are scrawled in registration at a hotel, or when they appear in print on a ship's passenger list, do we become targets for the sort of overtures which can drag you down and make you feel drowsy, dropsical—in short, dreadful. Actually I have never strangled a little old lady in my life, but there have been times when my hands were itching and tingling . . . the dear flat voice, intoning through the nose: "Well, I don't care how many books you write . . . if you live to be a hundred years old, you'll never write anything as good as *Bugle Ann*." Not what you might call encouraging, when you realize that *The Voice of Bugle Ann* was written more than half my lifetime ago.

. . . After an hour spent in company with the Fetchleys, I was mighty regretful about having gone into the Macauley Connor caper in the beginning. But we were committed, and there was no help for it at the moment.

From a mutual appreciation of the music at hand, our colloquy progressed into regional songs, then into hymns. Irene lived a Methodist childhood and I a Baptist one. Genevra Fetchley had grown up as a Presbyterian and her husband as a Baptist. We talked a little about evangelists (not the child variety). I recalled one man whose forte was in persuading various Protestant denominations to band together and build a wooden edifice for his revival meetings, which would then be attended by all those denominations en masse. If he managed to assemble an aggregate congregation of six or eight sects, resultant benefit to the Glory of Heaven—and to the Reverend's exchequer—was manifest.

Fetchley struck the table with the flat of his hand. "You don't mean Reverend *Bromley?*"

"Certainly."

"Why, I heard him when I was a little kid, when I went to visit my uncle! I'll never forget it. It was the first time I'd ever heard what you might call juvenile delinquency mentioned from the pulpit. Before that, there'd just been Sin in general terms. Or maybe Sins of the Flesh. But in this case Reverend Bromley told about a saucy little girl who came around to him and denied that there was any necessity for her being Saved. He could really take her off, too. You'd see him standing there, trying to Save her, and then you'd see her mincing up to him . . . he'd imitate her smarty little voice to perfection—at least I thought so."

I stared at Fetchley with open mouth. "My God. I remember that routine."

My new friend's eyes were dancing, and his loose scrolled face one vast grin. "Remember what he said?"

I guess our wives thought we'd gone crazy. We leaned across the table in dramatic unison. It was as if we had rehearsed the act as a team, and many times . . . and the good Lord knows we hadn't set eyes on each other until we met that evening.

If there can be such a thing as a whispered roar, it was in such manner that we spoke.

"'And, six months later, that girl and *her child* were kicked down the back stairway of Society!'"

Customers at other tables swung around. They laughed to see a disbelieving Fetchley burying his face in his hands.

"I sang in the Bromley Tabernacle choir," I boasted. "We got points for our high school class if we did that, and there would be a grand prize. Of course the freshman class was the most populous, and that was my class. We freshmen won a bag of peanuts. But that's where I learned to sing *A Volunteer for Jesus, a Soldier True*."

Fetchley told us, "I couldn't sing in the choir. They said I was too little. But my older cousin sang, and she taught me that song."

We began to sing it.

Irene said, in a tone all husbands will understand, "Come on, darling. I think we'd better be going back to our own motel."

"No, no," said Fetchley. "You're not going back to any motel. We'll go over to our house. Look, it's not yet nine o'clock."

"Do come," said Genevra Fetchley. "Please come, Mr. and Mrs. Connor. Please come, Mike and Irene. Irene, you said you painted? Well, I'm no painter, but I do ceramics, and love to show my wares to folks, so let me show them to you. It runs in the family. My father owned the local monument company."

We had our laugh about this; then the Fetchleys' bottles went back behind the bar; we put our own into a paper sack, and strolled to the parking lot.

"It's this T-bird here," said Fetchley. "Note the license number, and Follow Me, Boys. Did you see that movie?"

"Oh yes," we told him, squirming in guilt, since I had written the original story.

"It was too saccharine," said Genevra Fetchley.

"The Disney people are apt to do that. But the original story was a lot better," I added boldly. "Except for that adorable Lillian Gish. Her part didn't appear in the original story. It was written in."

"Well, I never did read the original story," said Fetchley. "Where are you parked? Over there? O.K., we'll wait for you at the exit."

When the traffic situation permitted, he pulled across into the north-bound lanes, and we followed. My wife and I meditated about Missouri hospitality.

"We've only enjoyed it thus far," Irene said, "where we were known."

"But remember that chain store manager who wanted to give us tomatoes. And I had the post office clerk in Cape who said he wished he could go along up to the place where I was driving—"

She said, "The original Killers With Kindness."

Yes, *ma'am.*

Suppose that you know John and Jessie Wescoat only slightly. But you drive to Cape, and you call up the Wescoats, and ask them how's about getting together? Great. You make a date for the next night.

Then, in no time at all, Jessie Wescoat calls back and says, "Are you people doing anything special for dinner tonight? Because we're invited over to Dick and Helen Brown's, and I've just called Helen, and she wants us to bring you along if you can come."

"Oh, my. We shouldn't do that. Not at the last moment—"

"Helen says to tell you it's a good-sized party, all buffet, and two more won't make any difference. But you'll never find their house by yourselves, so we'll pick you up."

. . . Everybody Having Wonderful Time at the Browns'. And while you're there, Harry and Martha Keim announce that they've invited guests for cocktails late the next afternoon, and can't you come? You go to the Keims', and there you meet Bob and Skeeter Lamkin for the second time. Next thing you're over at the Lamkins'.

The following night you find yourself down at Willow Hall, having dinner with Harvey and Mary Drake. . . .

Missouri. Land of the Dangling Luminescent Latchstring.

Leonard Fetchley led us through a maze of circling drives on the edge of town, past new low-spread houses, identified as the homes of people in upper brackets of the local economy. But when we came to the Fetchley place it was not one with these. That house had sat in importance for a long time at the summit of a hill; the straight driveway leading up to it was lined on both sides with thick-bodied sycamores. The white house, with old-style gallery across the front, blazed with so many lights that I thought a dozen people must be there already. As it turned out, there was no one present except us chickens. And a dog. The three Fetchley children were gone away into lives and homes of their own.

Gen informed Irene during the evening that their maid who came in by the day was a demon laundress and a demon cleaner-upper, but could scarcely squeeze a glass of orange juice. "I do my own cooking. If too many people are coming in, why then I send for a woman who can cook, and another to serve. That's the way most folks do, here in town. The day of the wonderful family cook, Living In, seems to have vanished."

Fetchley explained, "All these lights. People are burning lights all over town. There's been a hell of a lot of break-ins and general thievery around here. Cars plundered, signs stolen. We keep the house doors locked, and our golden retriever raises the roof when unaccompanied strangers approach the door."

"He's not barking now."

"No, he knows the sound of our car, and he knows that we usually come in through the back, down here below. So he'll be the reception committee, right inside the door. Doesn't matter how many people come with us, he's friendly to all of them. Trouble is, I'll have to shut him up as soon as he's said Hello to you. He jumps on people, and we just can't break him of it. He's a school drop-out. It's a great disgrace."

"Drop-out?"

"They had one of those canine obedience clinics downtown at the Armory, and Sun—that's the dog's name—was duly entered. But he got nowhere fast. He just wanted to run around and kiss all the other dogs, and try to leap up to kiss the people, and no amount of stepping on his hind feet would do any good, either. First school drop-out we ever had in the family, except my oldest brother Gus. Gus ran away to join the Army when he was only fourteen, in World War I, and never did get back in school again."

At our host's direction, we had followed the Thunderbird down an incline into a parking area in front of the garage. To the east, a garden yielded up its munificence of tender odors in the night.

Genevra said, "Fetch, take a look. Someone has backed or driven directly into my golden cannas."

"Well, twasn't me," said Fetchley. "Though actually I'm not too keen on cannas, especially the red ones. Their leaves always look something like carp," and he looked down from his slouching superior height and jabbed me with his elbow.

His wife had conducted Irene among the flower beds, and already their voices were vying in that intimate exchange with which women demonstrate their enthusiasm on a given theme. It weaves in and out, a fugue of conversation, question and answer intermingled and recurring. . . .

Gen called, "Turn on the garden lights as soon as you get inside."

Fetchley unlocked the door, and we pushed in amid the gambolings of one of the largest golden retrievers in captivity.

"At least he's dry at the moment," said our host. "I hope his paws don't bruise you too much. *Get down!*" he roared. Then, while dragging the slobbering beautiful creature off to imprisonment. "Christ sake, I don't know how we happened to end up with something like this. But he's such a darling doggie. Yes, yes, yes," and he talked baby talk to the writhing lumbering critter, all the way into remote distances.

Out in the garden Gen was crying, "Turn the lights on!" Irene joined her. "Light, light! 'Let there be light. . . .'"

I went to a panel of switches, experimented, managed to find the right one. Yelled out through the screen, "'And there *was* light.'"

"Thank you, God."

Telephones burst into simultaneous ringing throughout the house above and at the end of the bar (this was a combination library and playroom). Fetchley returned, and picked up a phone receiver. I watched his responsive expressive face, and recalled that he had been summoned to the telephone twice while we were at Holiday Junior.

This time he said, "Well, I don't consider myself on call tonight. Talk to Roy, and he'll go out there right away." Then he was silent for a full minute, listening while something was explained. His face seemed to have grown incredibly sad, whether it bore so many lines etched by laughter or not.

He spoke gently. "Very well, that will be quite all right. Tell the woman to come in to see me late tomorrow morning if she can. I'll be in my office."

He hung up, shook his head, blinked. "Now let's get busy and do a little drinking. Maybe you and I can grab an extra one before the girls come in. How about some good pure flavorable corn? Do you switch from vodka after eating?"

"I'll stay with the vodka, but it'll be sweet this time. By any chance do you have Tab?"

He bent down and rummaged in cupboards. "Got plenty of Pepsi."

"That'll be fine."

"Want to make your own?"

I came over and joined him at the bar.

"You know," he said, "it's a wonder we're not haunted in this place here."

"Why should you be haunted?"

"On account of Judge Colverston's wife. This house was built by the old Colverston, way back when, and we bought it from the Judge's estate many years ago, and then remodeled it. Don't you believe that this bar was here at the time. It sure as hell wasn't. This was partly storage place and partly laundry, down here on the hillside."

"You've made it into a wonderfully attractive room."

"Well, we just call it the downstairs sitting room, and I guess we spend the bulk of our time here socially when we're at home. Upstairs is slightly more formal, and I like this a lot better. But what I was going to tell you–"

Our drinks were made, and we could just lean there comfortably and talk.

"The late Mrs. Colverston–that was the Judge's wife–was in the Women's Christian Temperance Union up to her ears. I think she would have made even poor old Carrie Nation jealous, and you know Carrie used to live here in Missouri. Stuffy Maguire–that was our local newspaper editor– He couldn't even mention a cocktail or highball or anything like that in print, but what Mrs. Judge Colverston would be right down there in his office to bawl him out, and demand that he apologize publicly for putting such words in the paper. Oh, she was hell on wheels! So just imagine her being identified with this house for maybe forty years, and then her ghost comes back and finds us with all this nice booze– *Ugh!*"

"Ever seen her?"

"No, Mike, I have not. What's more, I don't want to."

Our wives came in, but didn't tarry. Genevra was all set to show the house to Irene, and Irene would rather look at houses than eat. They went upstairs, and I turned to find Fetchley searching the bookshelves at the other end of the room.

"It ought to be right along here," he said. "There were two or three of them. Oh, here's one–"

He offered a battered copy of a novel entitled *The Man from Glengarry*.

"Just remembered that there used to be an author named Ralph Connor. Any relative of yours?"

I told him No . . . Ralph Connor was the pen-name of a Canadian named Charles William Gordon. "He was a Presbyterian preacher in Winnipeg when our Aunt Florence Bale used to live there."

I was feeling uncomfortably guilty about this Macauley Connor thing, but decided that I could make a better explanation later on, by letter. (And have long since done so.)

"Over at the Holiday Junior I heard your wife call you Lenny. Is that your regular nickname?"

"No, that's what my folks used to call me. About everybody else calls me Fetch—at least after I was grown, and went away to school. And later, in the Army."

"Where were you?" I asked. "Which way?"

"ETO. Third Army. I was picking up the pieces."

He said this with a sigh. I realized that he was a doctor. That was the reason for those several calls, and the sad, detached, but still relaxed expression which came over his face when he was speaking on the phone.

A not-unpleasant silence fell between us for a while, to be broken suddenly by a high-pitched screech. I thought it must indeed be the ghost of the WCTU termagant . . . her soul was being tortured. But Fetch had no sympathy, he merely bellowed, "*Shut up!*"

Silence.

"What on earth was *that?*"

"Sun."

"Is someone pulling out his toenails?"

"No, he just gets overcome with remorse because he's such a dope, and has to be locked up like that whenever visitors come."

I said, "Fetch, I want to quiz you about something that's very important to me."

His quaint lopsided smile. "Well, go ahead."

"In a book I'm writing about Missouri, I would in some way epitomize the typical Missourian. If there is such a thing. Think there is?"

He said with conviction, "I don't think there's a typical anything, anywhere, any time."

"Then let me put it in a different way. I'd like to pick people's brains, all over the State, and learn their ideas on what makes a Missourian different from other people. You're so very articulate—You're a native Missourian; and you live here now, you've spent your life here, except for time out during the war—"

"Right," he said.

We went back to the bar and renewed our drinks. But all the time he seemed pondering, pursing up his wide mouth, awarding every attention to the matter at hand.

Then he roved around, studying various photographs and framed cartoons and souvenirs which hung upon the wall. Once he interrupted his thought to tell me, over his shoulder, "I'm still considering." Strangely he stood longest before a faded map which showed the old fur routes and the course of the Lewis and Clark Expedition. . . . I went browsing myself. Five more minutes must have passed before he called me to attention.

"I've got it," he said. "At least a number of qualities that I'm sure about, though you could ask the man next door, or a citizen of the next county, and he might not agree with me. On the whole, I think most intelligent Missourians *would* agree with me. And I do like to at least pretend that I'm an intelligent Missourian."

He said, "First off, your Missourian is one of the most gregarious people on the face of the Globe. He loves his old friends, but that doesn't mean that he doesn't love to make new ones. All over this State, in places like Columbia and Jeff City and Joplin and Hannibal and right here in this little town, there are gangs of fellows who stick happily together socially, wives and families and all, and they've been friends ever since they played marbles. Went to high school together, went to college together, many of them even went to the war together. You'd think it might be an inbred, exclusive and snobbish organization of themselves which they have contrived, but it doesn't work that way. They love to broaden their horizons. They're eager to accumulate a wealth of what you might call— Yes, human resources. People. That's a man's true human resource, at least a Missouri man's. It's people."

Before this I had not realized how deep-set were Fetchley's eyes, and now they seemed to blaze with interest in the caverns under his bushy brows.

"Folks will tell you that Ozark folks are regular mountaineers—withdrawn, shy of strangers, reluctant to accept newcomers. That's true only up to the point where the newcomer makes it perfectly plain that he is not one who wants to alter their lives, or change their ways, or take a selfish advantage. In other words, a person with whom they feel a basic lack of harmony. But if you have an interest which an Ozark-dweller can respond to, or share with you mutually, you've quite possibly got a friend for life. And if you demonstrate a sincere interest in him—in them—that's all that's needed. They'll do anything for you.

"I remember one time some of us went on a fishing trip down there, and one of our guides lost his teeth. Yes, he really did. He'd had bad teeth when young, like so many of those hill people, and although he was only in his early twenties he had a complete upper denture. Well, what do you know? One morning he waded out into the little rapids of the river alongside our sandbar, where we performed our ablutions. Jack was rinsing this denture when it slipped out of his hand and rolled away among the submerged gravel. Did he really let out a howl! And actually it was a tragedy. That denture represented a lot of scraping and saving, and now where was the money going to come from, to get a new one? Naturally the rest of us—guides and visiting fishermen alike— We all waded out there, and searched and sifted around under the water for a long time. It was only a few inches deep, but the river ran fast, and there were a lot of bright-colored little rocks. A dozen times one or the other of us thought he'd found the cussed thing, but he hadn't. So finally we gave up and went back to have breakfast. Poor Jack was reduced to a diet of coffee and soup and tomato juice and stuff like that.

"When we came back from fishing in the late afternoon, there was another try. No good. From then on it was Jack against the river. We couldn't spend our whole vacation in hunting for his lost denture. But every spare moment he had, Jack was wading around on that gravel bar or squatted down, sifting with his fingers. Most of us agreed that the false teeth were probably miles downstream by that time. But he didn't give up hope.

"Then came Sunday morning. I remember that well enough, because one of the men in our party was quite religious, and he'd brought along a little transistor radio, so he could be sure to hear his favorite preacher, come Sunday. Also there had ensued one hell of a thunderstorm, and the river went up at least a foot. Not wishing to be drowned in the open boats, we were all lolling around under the tent flies, except Jack. He was out there on that sandbar. And the rest of us didn't care much about the Sunday sermon, but we listened to it, along with Wilbur Stake, because there wasn't anything else to do.

"Right in the middle of the sermon we hear the most God-awful shriek you ever heard, and it comes from Jack. He was out there in the middle of that rapids, waving his arms like he'd gone crazy.

Yes, siree, he'd *found* the denture. Stepped right on it with his bare foot. But it went down, kind of, in soft stuff under the pressure, and wasn't even bent. He put it back in his mouth and came grinning to shore.

"Well, both Vernon Kirkstone and I were on the wagon. We'd been drinking a little too much of late, and we'd made a bet, and decided to go on the wagon together. But I said, 'Vernon, this does it. Every blesséd one of us is going to have a drink right now, in honor of Jack's recovered denture.' We broke out some jugs and we all had some glorious drinks. That was good corn, too, that they made down there in those parts in those days.

"Now, here's the interesting thing. We'd all got along with our guide Jack ably enough, just the way we got along with the other guides and the cook. But the fact that we were willing to make a ceremony in honor of his finding his teeth– And two of us breaking our non-alcoholic oath just to signalize the event– That went deep with him. It showed that we realized the importance of his loss, and the double importance of this miraculous recovery. He'd been a kind of sober boy before that, but he wasn't sober any longer. I mean, not so taciturn and kind of remotely polite as he'd been previously. He was all smiles all the time. Not only because he'd found his denture–"

He hesitated, then inquired, "You think you know what I mean?"

"I think I know what you mean."

Fetch declared, "When it comes to independent thinking and performance, the Missourian yields to no one. Once Gen and I took a little vacation trip to Spain, and noted how all the guide books talked about the independent thinking nature of the Spaniard. Well, when the Spanish controlled Missouri long ago, they must have left a good deal of that attitude behind them. The true Missourian inherits it, right up to this very minute. He's not going to be persuaded to do anything which he *as an individual* doesn't think he ought to do. I remember Grandpa talking when I was a kid, and telling about old families in this town, time of the Civil War. The town was all split up, just as the county was, just as the whole blame State was. Actually the preponderance of sympathy as a whole was for the Union, but there were die-hard Rebs in every community just the same. Locally the Colverstons and the Ricksons and the Webbs went with the North; but the MacBaynes and the Dowders and the Fetchleys were all Secesh. My own great-grandfather got shot dead at Wilson's Creek. He'd left a wife with five small children, to go to war. Plenty of Yankee sympathizers did the same thing. There was never anything settled or solid about Missouri during that war. And matters didn't calm down for a long time afterward."

He thought for a moment, and then added, "Guess it was the same way with Kentucky. And Maryland. I mean, about neighborhoods and families being split up. So that doesn't show anything unique about Missouri."

It doesn't? wailed the retriever. *Owooooo.*

"Sun, shut up!" Fetchley groaned, rolled up his eyes, and then continued: "Therefore I'm not referring especially to national political problems or things so far-reaching. I mean the Missourian is that way in *little* things: an independent thinker. He wants to be his own boss. And there's one big stumbling block *there*. I'll tell you what it is, pretty soon. . . . At the same time we are probably the greatest collection of extremists you'll find anywhere in the United States. When a Missourian goes all out for something– Golly, does he go. He may step on a lot of toes, and it's too bad. But he's going where he wants to go, or he's voicing the beliefs he wants to voice, and that's that. Except–for that same stumbling block.

"Then– What you might refer to as culture. The Missourian has what I consider an instinctive admiration for culture. This leads to some pretty gruesome things sometimes."

He lowered his voice and glanced toward the staircase. He whispered, "Gen is not a dabbler. She's really a hard worker. She has taste and talent, and she sells a lot of those ceramics. But– I know a woman in another town–I won't identify her any further– But, my God, does she come up with the most repulsive abstract *sculpture!* Big tangles of meshed wire, tin cans and I-don't-know-what-all hanging around them, prongs sticking out. . . . And we've got our local finger-painters. Or maybe they tie a paint-brush to the hound-dog's tail, and let him take over.

"But here's the point I want to emphasize: the Missourian admires people who climb to importance in the world of culture, and that includes the professions. For instance, they're rightfully proud of the attainments chalked up in the Missouri medical profession. And some of those same medical men branch out into other fields. I'm thinking of one doctor from St. Louis–he lives elsewhere now–who is truly an authority on both orchids and archaeology, as well as being one of the best surgeons who ever held a knife. We're proud to think that Mark Twain was born here, but we're also proud of Thomas Hart Benton. Just as early Missourians in their time were admirers of—or haters of—his great-uncle Thomas Hart Benton. Course, the elder Benton was born in North Carolina, just as Kit Carson was born in Kentucky. But Missouri likes to claim them both.

"To get back to the little people. You'd be surprised how many Missourians have something they fancy to do, whether it's painting or music or journalism or— You go to a new town, and make some new acquaintances there— Maybe you will have been talking with the local orchestra leader, or a sociology professor from the college; then you'll turn to the next man and try to find out what *he* does, how does he spend *his* life? He'll say most apologetically, 'Oh, I'm just a businessman. Just run the old family store.' Or else, 'Oh, I'm just a builder,' or, 'I'm just a real estate man.' See, they're kind of apologizing for not being in the arts or education or something. But you talk with them further, and you find out that one of them is maybe a coin collector, and has written some monographs on old American silver coinage. And then the next one may play the violin. And that real estate man is maybe a kind of graduate gunsmith and an authority on old rifles. . . . I guess you wouldn't call gunsmithing *culture*. But I'm trying to get across that it's nothing unusual for people out here to have a lot of vital interests besides the one with which and in which they earn their livings."

Genevra Fetchley called from the upper hallway, "Who's orating down there? Oh, I should know. Fetch is on a soap-box again."

"Well, by God," said Fetch, "Mike Connor put me there."

"Would you boys like to have some cheese dreams? Irene and I have decided that cheese dreams might be a good idea."

"Of course we'd like some cheese dreams. Are you going to put bacon on, and tomato, when you grill them?"

"Anything you want," and she went off to the kitchen, and distantly we could hear her and Irene laughing together.

Fetch nodded wisely and pointed his thumb. "That's another thing, just demonstrated. Missourians love informality, although they can do honor to all in the strictest formal sense. They have a good notion of protocol, just instinctively. But at practically every gathering in the homes, men still gravitate together in one room, and women in another. Kind of like when they 'forted up' during the war with the Sauks. We all know it's silly and outmoded, but we still do it."

He said, "Guess I've mentioned mostly the praiseworthy characteristics. I can think of some less enviable traits too. Now, in most cases, it's a very strong paternal civilization. *Too damn strong.* That's the stumbling block I referred to before. It was planted in antiquity. All too many fathers have dominated their sons, here in this region. I happen to know, because I was one of those who was dominated."

He had hurt himself in this admission, and made a face about it. Then he shrugged, but in the manner of accepting a familiar burden. If he had a drinking problem in his life, I now knew why.

"I can smell those cheese dreams already. You know what they are, don't you, Mike?"

"Sure. We each like to make our own at home, because we belong to different schools. Irene doesn't like meat grilled on hers, and I do. We both like onion and tomato—"

"Golly, I'm getting hungry," said Fetch. "Can you tell me more about your book? . . . No? Not yet? Well, as you go around the State, you'll probably ask other people the same question you've asked me. You're going to get a lot of answers."

"I already have a lot of answers. But most Missourians would agree with you in the things you've said. I'm sorry to hear about this parental domination. Are you certain that your views in general aren't colored too much by your personal experience?"

He said firmly, "I'm absolutely certain. I've seen it on every hand. But no more about that at the moment. Let me say only that the Missourian has an enormous love for his State. He's born with it, it's there, it's deep. But strangest of all is the depth of this affection among people who have *adopted* Missouri. They become— What's the word? Proselytes. It's like a religion."

With fervor I told him, "I'm very near to being a Missouri proselyte myself, though I wouldn't live here on a bet because of the savage weather in winter. But I've got a friend named Dan Longwell: former Doubleday editor, former editor of *Time*, former just-about-everything at *Life*—executive editor, managing editor, chairman of the board of editors. Dan was born in Nebraska, but he happened to spend one year of his youth in Neosho—"

"That's where Benton was born," said Fetchley. "I mean the younger Benton. Course, he's old now. The painter."

"Yes, I know Tommy. Well, when Dan retired from *Life*—that was quite some years ago—there was only one place where he wanted to settle. Not in Omaha where he was born. Not in New York, where he'd spent so much of his life. No, sir. He wanted to go to Neosho, Missouri, and that's just where he went. He and Mary are living down there right this minute, and they love Missouri with a passion as undiluted as it is sincere. And the people in Neosho love *them*."

Then the idea hit me hard—so hard that I saw a splintering of silver in front of my eyes, the way you do when you are struck physically. *Seeing stars*, we used to call it.

"I'll tell you something, Fetch, that even Irene doesn't know, because I never knew it myself until just this minute. When and if I ever get my Missouri book finished, I'm going to dedicate it to Dan Longwell."

[Author's note, 1969: Daniel Longwell died at Neosho, November, 1968.]

Up in the kitchen our wives began calling, "Cheese dreams, cheese dreams! Who's ready to undergo some cheese dreams?" In varying accents and intonations, the way women do when they're truly having fun. (Also I've noticed this: they won't do it in front of each other unless they like each other very much indeed. No woman of strength will lower her normal dignity unless she feels completely at ease; nor will she do it in the presence of one whom she considers either inferior, or so palpably superior that she is frightened to death.)

Irene came running down into the bar-library. She carried two small paper boxes. "Look at these! This one I bought, and Genevra has given me the other. I was afraid I'd forget them if they weren't put in the car right away—"

She lifted a plate from its nest of shredded paper, and I exclaimed involuntarily. Recollection flashed: a day at Segovia when we were taken through a drafty room where a small quantity of Zuolaga's works reposed . . . works still unsold. But Zuolaga had been dead for some years at that time; the few remainders were going fast. We bought two plates: one for a gift, and one to keep for ourselves. . . . It's on the wall near our dining table at home now. There's a little feeling of Corot about it.

On the plate which Irene had purchased from Genny Fetchley, a flight of migrating bluebirds shafted through a grove of dogwoods in full flower. It was and is a radiant thing.

Fetchley explained, "You see, she likes to work with traditional

Missouri material. The dogwoods are our State tree, and the bluebird's our State bird."

Irene said, "I won't open up the darling ashtray she gave me. You can see it later, darling. But I want to put these safely in the car—"

I told her that she had darlinged me into doing that little task for her.

"Don't *drop* them—"

After I'd packed the two little boxes in our car trunk, I returned to the playroom and turned off the garden lights which we had left on. For the first time I saw a poem, under glass in a small frame, on the wall next to electric switches and thermostat. I bent closer. It was entitled *The Blind Priest*, and at the bottom was the author's name. Leonard Fetchley. Seemed to be a page cut from some magazine, but there was no further identification. . . . Heard voices of the others upstairs, and scented the richness of melted cheese and grilled ham or bacon. But I was impelled to linger another minute to read the verse.

> I walked your streets when I was blind
> But now so many things I find. . . .
>
> * * *
>
> A Man mixed colors of the day
> To paint my sightlessness away.
>
> He took an unseen cloth of gold
> To show the new beneath the old. . . .

There were ten couplets in all.

We ate at a rounded table at the end of a high-ceiled kitchen.

"The kitchen wasn't as large as this until we remodeled," explained Genny. "We included an old porch, and even built on some more construction beyond."

On wall space between windows of the semicircular breakfast nook were pictures of three Fetchley children—two with their wives, one with her husband, along with photos of grandchildren.

"Little Len," said Fetch, pointing him out, "he's the eldest. He's in the banking business in Chicago. Naturally we called him Little Len when he *was* little, but it just stuck. He was quite a basketball star. Stands two or three inches taller than I do."

"And tell about Lindsay," Genevra directed him. "She's our daughter, Connors. I named her after a favorite grandfather of mine. We had Lindsays and Roses and Murrays and Buchanans all mixed up together. I told you about that Annie-Laurie-Maxwelton business, didn't I? Well, anyway–"

Fetch said, "Go ahead, woman. You tell about Lindsay. My mouth's too full."

"Oh, her husband was also a basketball player, and he got acquainted with Little Len in a tournament, so that's how Lindsay got to meet Blondie Norquist. They're celebrating their tin wedding this very month. Oh no, couldn't wait to get married! Nineteen years old . . . had to get married right out of school. Well, I don't mean that actually they *had to get married*," as we all laughed.

"Maybe they did," said Fetch.

"Fetch, behave youself. To talk that way about your own daughter–!"

"Plenty of girls have to get married. It's no disgrace. Why, you yourself– You were just lucky–"

"*Fetch!* Anyway, they live in a new place, kind of a new suburb out northwest of Chicago. But it's close to O'Hare Airport, which makes it easy for Blondie, because he's with a big airline. And Jamie –our youngest, over here–he's in the Army."

"Already done two tours out yonder," said Fetchley. "We're keeping our fingers crossed against his going out for a third tour. Real career boy. Complains that he's just about the oldest captain in the Army. But I think he may make major pretty soon."

Fetch and Gen and Irene were drinking the last of their Sanka, and I had finished my glass of milk. "Fetch, there was something you were going to tell me."

"What's that?"

"About so many Missourians having other things that they like to do or want to do, away from their regular workaday lives. I guess I've discovered what yours is."

He stared for a moment almost stonily, and then began to smile. "You mean–" He nodded toward the hall which led to the stairway.

"Framed on the wall down there. What was that from?"

"Oh, Fetch's poetry they're talking about," cried Genny. "He published– Why, it was five or six, wasn't it?"

"Just four," he said quietly. "Little magazines. The kind of magazines that get started at some college by an English professor and his students."

I told him that I had read only the one framed on the wall near the switches. It was called *The Blind Priest.* Why?

"Well, it's like this. We used to have a blind piano tuner in town, name of Priest, and he was always talking about how he wished that he could see pictures. He said that he saw pictures in his mind, anyway. He'd been blind from birth. He used to chatter and chatter if there was anybody around, when he was tuning a piano. And he knew his way all over town. This was long before the days of Seeing-Eye Dogs; but Mr. Priest went out by himself, pounding the sidewalk ahead of him with a cane, and he never hesitated to ask directions if he thought he was lost. He'd hear someone walking close to him, and he'd lift his head and seem to gaze in the direction of the person who was approaching, with those squinted-up eyes . . . the congenitally blind usually have eyes like that. You know."

Fetch squinted his own.

"Then he'd raise his head and his voice all at once, as I said, and he'd ask, like this: 'I believe that I'm at the corner of Hawthorn and Third. Is that right, please? Am I at the southwest corner?' Then whoever was there would reassure him, or else tell him No, he had one more block to go. . . . Well. This business of seeing pictures in his blind eyes—I mean inside them— It kind of haunted me. I took care of him at the end. It was shortly after my father died, and I was in sole charge by that time. I think it was only a day or so after he was buried, that I wrote that poem."

Fetchley had another set of verses, also framed. He showed this poem to me, at the opposite end of the downstairs room, before we left. It was called *Klan.*

Into the devilish paleness of the wind
They went. And someone heard a sighing
Of black men trampled in the heat,
And Jewish women crying, far through silence
Of an old, old agony in barren cities
And a barren street. . . .

"I didn't frame my others which were published. They weren't good enough. But I like these. Oh," he continued, "my father was probably right when he tromped on my poetic aspirations. I did get on the staff of the literary magazine when I was at college, and had all sorts of notions about running away and leaving everything, leaving Father and telling him to go jump in the lake, I wasn't going to live his life over for him and do just what he had done. But I never had the nerve to cut loose after he once laid down the law. That's the great Missouri weakness. Bossy Pappy.

"I'll say this: I didn't tromp on my own sons' aspirations. If Little Len got interested in economics and finance and business administration—if that was the thing he wanted to do, why O.K. for him. He started working right here in the local bank, summers, when he was home from school. He knew what he wanted to be, and I didn't interfere.

"And as for Jamie— Hell, it was apparent that he was destined for the military, from the time he was in his teens. . . . No, my sons are not providing any third generation extension of the Fetchley career. And I'm glad I never put any pressure on them."

It was almost twelve o'clock. Irene was carrying on about how we'd abused their hospitality by staying so late, and Genevra was saying she couldn't imagine where the time had gone to. And then both were ordering us, "Break it up, boys. Break it *up*. Tomorrow's another day."

Fetch went to bring the beautiful retriever out into the garden as we made our farewells. ("Once outside, he's O.K. He won't jump on anybody there.") Then telephones pealing their impatience once again. Gen had opened the screen door. Fetch let go of Sun's collar and the dog rushed outside. Phone kept ringing. Fetch went over and picked it up. Again his face was imbued with that same stain of melancholy I'd noticed before.

"Yes . . . yes. Well . . . what time? Just a few minutes ago? Thanks for calling me." He hung up the receiver and came out from behind the bar, and back to the door. He and I walked outside to join the women.

Fetchley said, "Genny, that was Lucas on the phone. Prof Brockett has just died."

"Oh," cried Gen with feeling, "poor, *poor* old man. How glad I am! It was *so* hard on his daughter—"

Fetch explained, "Prof Brockett was ninety-two. He served as high school principal for many years. It was all right, being old, when he could see people and go places, because that was what he loved to do. But he's been in bed the last eighteen months. For several days he was just drowning miserably with edema."

I asked, "Do you have to go over there now, to sign a death certificate or anything?"

He was staring through the gloom in some surprise. "No, I don't have to sign any death certificate. Dr. Steinhauer will do that."

Irene. "Darling, come *on.*"

Then we were standing beside our car, and Sun galloped amid terraced flower beds, we could hear the jingling collar-tags as he loped the paths. The women kissed each other, and Fetch kissed Irene, and I kissed Genevra. We were in a huddle, squeezing hands and saying, Wasn't it lucky that we'd met. Irene got into our car, and I went around to the driver's side, with Fetch following along, and insisting that I let him know when the Missouri book was published.

I said, "You'll be in it, and I'll send you a copy. But there's a letter I need to write you, long before that. In the meantime—"

Now I sat behind the wheel, but the door was still open and Fetchley was standing, angular and stooped against lights of the house and fragrant paleness of the night behind him.

"I'm puzzled, Fetch. You got that call, but you talked about Dr. Steinhauer. Wasn't the elderly professor who died—? Wasn't he your patient?"

He said, "Jesus." Then, after a pause, in a resigned tone, "You must think I'm an awful fool. I thought I told you about our family business, real early in the game. But guess I didn't. . . . I'm not a doctor, I'm an undertaker. We own the local funeral home."

8. Sing May, Queen May, Sing Mary

When mentioning savage winters to Leonard Fetchley, I was flying in the face of sentiment, if not abusing statistics. In every corner of Missouri, boosters declare that their annual climate is the best ever. (This may not have been true of the Boot Heel before drainage was established, but I can't quote chapter and verse.)

Anywhere you go amid perfection of a single day, they brag as wickedly as Californians. "Oh yes, this is the kind of weather we have at this time of year." In winter, should subterranean temperatures prevail, or should a vicious ice storm disrupt transportation and communication– Or should there ensue a doleful period of comparative warmth which harbors a raw and paralyzing sogginess– Heads are shaken, and identical time-worn testimony is ready on the lips of all. "This is very unusual."

Temperatures of forty below zero have been recorded. Definitely I remember trotting miserably on an airfield, stiff with cold, when the mercury hovered in the neighborhood of twenty below.

Frequently the pavement grows treacherous beneath a meager but durable film of ice. It isn't there when you start out, it develops while you're driving; yet you're not aware, in your car, that the temperature has lowered. Then something happens, and you hit your brakes, and you're floating like a fancy figure skater. All you can do is pray.

In January, at about 2 A.M. a generation ago, I watched a car coming toward me, bright head lamps shafting from side to side like twin searchlights. I didn't know what agony had befallen that onrushing vehicle . . . thought the driver must be drunk . . . I swerved to the west shoulder of the road . . . stopped, sat there. When the other car was almost opposite me it leaped out into space, fortunately on the east side. Twin headlights rolled up and over. There sounded a splintering crash amid black bushes, down in a ditch. Headlights out. Silence.

I grabbed a flashlight and jumped out of my car. The next second the back of my head hit the pavement. Ice: sheer thin ice. You couldn't know it was there. When finally I'd tottered over across the glaze, there was revealed a hand fumbling upward, trying to open the door on the driver's side, which in that position was like the lid of a box. Appeared a sad face, with voice beseeching, "Please, mister, you've got a flashlight. Help me to get out and see what the damage is."

There was damage, all right. That driver, together with his wife and little son, occupied the car of the man's employer. The boss's family were moving, and these servants had charge of a whole cargo of treasures: glass, pictures, china, silver—articles not easily packed to be freighted.

. . . Got a fire started for them, the miraculously uninjured, to huddle over; then I drove at about ten mph to the next town. The night policeman said he would send out a wrecker. Glad he didn't have to dispatch an ambulance.

Certainly such an accident could occur in any State where you find freezing conditions. Might even happen in northern Florida. (Years ago our Governor's children had the joy of building a snowman in their Tallahassee yard.) All I'm trying to dispute is the assumption, which has somehow crept abroad, that Missouri is a perfectly grand summer resort all year long. No, sir. Snow fences sprout at points where they are believed essential, and after a violent storm the plows go out to plow.

Ah, there occur benefits: white scintillating stars, evergreens resplendent with crusty decoration. Still in the Ozarks may be heard the howling of small cold wolves in a night made to order for wolf howls. Among narrow gorges, icicles are dependent from the ledges, and you may listen to a faint melancholy soprano of water running under ice. Or perhaps the hollow silence which proclaims no water to be running . . . only ice bent upward at its margins. Bittersweet vines on trees have turned into black wire, there seems no life left in the vines, desolation walks the woods where May-apples and bloodroots flowered in their time . . . they'll rise again in months to come, although it seems unthinkable in this bleakness. But unmoving air has a tonic quality. Although it hurts to breathe it in, it inculcates vigor if you don't stay outside too long.

Rounded bald hills say, *Cold, cold, cold*. So does the forest, when a limb snaps under squeezing of frost. The sky is inhospitable and far. Let us find the fire.

Betty Love is a brisk woman with a smiling pink face and graying windblown hair. She's a photographer for Springfield's newspapers, all issued by the same company: *News* in the morning, *Leader and Press* in an afternoon edition; and, Sunday, a combination *News and Leader*.

We sat at lunch with Betty Love and a perfectly grand gentleman who rejoices in the Horatio Alger-ish name of Frank Farmer. Frank is a feature writer for those same newspapers, and I guess several kinds of other writer as well. In his non-professional hours he turns cattleman, feeding Herefords in pens and pastures he owns. I believe he has a notion of one day giving up journalism and devoting himself to the beloved White-Faces.

We weren't discussing cattle at the moment, though in an odd way they were shortly to enter the conversation. We were talking about mules; or, more correctly, I was complaining about mules' absence from the contemporary scene.

"Never believed the day would come when you could drive for hundreds of miles through Missouri countryside, and not see a single mule. It's still unbelievable, but we've just done it. Eventually we glimpsed one single solitary mule, or maybe it was a jack, standing far off in a pasture. . . . What's the answer? Mechanization?"

That was it: mechanization of farms and of the huge plantations farther south. Missouri mules used to be bred as sugar mules or cotton mules (depending on whether they were going to work in cane or cotton) and also as all-purpose draft animals. But machines have taken over. Farms lie bereft of inhabitants, where once a couple of mules spelled the difference between being able to get a crop out of the land, or not.

Betty wondered whether we'd like to hear a story concerning an old mule barn?

Of course we would.

"We had in our family a farm we liked to go back to. Don't you think it would be nice if everyone had an old family farm like that?"

The moment and the particle of Missouri which she described bore neither the lush plush of summer, nor the drowsy smoke of autumn, nor yet spring's medicinal incitement. Betty was talking about what they termed a White Christmas long before Irving Berlin wrote his song. The pioneers used to utter a dreadful but pertinent statement . . . it was more than credulous superstition. *A black Christmas makes fat graveyards.* These words were repeated with a shudder. Blowy weather, dry earth, dust and germs mingling, respiratory infections coming on. Complications in the cases of the weak or the old . . . infants, too.

But our friend delineated a hard icy-gleamy-full-moonlight Christmas, a Charles-Dickens-Washington-Irving-Bracebridge-Hall Christmas carpentered to Missouri terms. There had been much anticipation before people reached the farm, much jollity after they got there.

"There were eleven of us grandchildren. All the way from little tykes around four or five, up to teen-agers—at least early teen-agers. We had a kind of dormitory at one end of the house: boys sleeping on beds and cots in one room, girls in the other. But on Christmas Eve, when it was time for children to go to bed, and while parents and other relatives were still celebrating downstairs, we kids gathered in one room and huddled together . . . told stories, and discussed things. Of course we'd fetched up apples and popcorn. Oh yes, there'd been a taffy-pull, so we had molasses taffy too. Just full of hickory nutmeats. I wish I had some now."

"So do I," mourned Irene.

"Not for me," I said. "It would pull my partials out of my jaws. Go on, Betty. You said this story had to do with a mule barn—?"

"Our grandfather was a livestock dealer. Sometimes he assembled for market a big herd of mules, but there were times when they needed to be housed away from the weather. So he'd built this enormous barn, years before."

But, she said, the mules were gone, long gone, in that winter. Instead a herd of cattle occupied the barn, walled away from stinging breathlessness of low temperatures outside.

And there the oxen do bow down—
Sing May, Queen May, sing Mary!—
To praise the Babe who wears a crown. . . .
Sing, all good men,
For the newborn Baby.

Betty said that it started with carols. They'd joined in such songs before and after supper, downstairs, and the children continued singing gently in the bedroom.

> Lo, in a stall with humble beast. . . .
>
> All meanly wrapped in swathing bands,
> And in a manger laid. . . .

Wise Men and Shepherds came in for recognition, and Friendly Beasts of course—all the way up to "the dove in the rafters so high, who cooed Him to sleep so He should not cry." But a most consequential discussion began to evolve, concerning oxen.

The children knew well enough that there were oxen active even in their time. They saw them often, on back-country trails, plodding along, dragging carts or—in the rougher Ozarks—sledges.

But would Missouri oxen, or any other cattle, know that they must bow down, must get down on their knees, at midnight, on Christmas Eve, to honor the Christ Child? Maybe this was all something which happened too long ago and too far away. Like the First Noel, or the children who sang from door to door.

One of the early teen-agers was emphatic in her belief that cattle must still indulge in such quaint ceremony. But others of her age, or a bit older, were trying to laugh her out of countenance. The littlest ones listened with round eyes, happy in the fact that they had been permitted to join their elders in this surreptitious nighttime revel.

"Well, *I* don't believe that any cows, down here in that old mule barn, would bow down at midnight."

"Pshaw. They wouldn't know when midnight *came.*"

"I believe that they'd know by instinct, and do it, just the way cattle always have—"

"You talk like a *loony*-tick!"

"What you want to bet that *all* cattle do it?"

"Even *calves?*"

An idea struck them almost simultaneously. When twelve o'clock came, why not go and *see?*

"What if The Folks found out?"

"We'll keep real quiet. Be just as still as mice, and then they wouldn't hear us a-tall. We can go down the back stairs, right out here at the end of the hall. All the grown-ups are sleeping clean at the other end of the house—"

There was a half-pint size Big Ben ticking away on the dresser, and one of the eldest girls said she'd put it under her pillow. Then she'd be sure to hear it go off.

"Everybody go to bed right now. Then, when the alarm goes off at a quarter to twelve–"

. . . A few minutes before midnight a weird procession emerged from the kitchen door of the farmhouse. Eleven figures, muffled in shawls, blankets, comforters. (Their outer wraps had been put away in closets downstairs, and The Folks might hear them if they tried to find coats and mittens and overshoes.) They'd pulled on their shoes and stockings . . . took quilts off the beds, and extra covers from shelves or out of old skirt-boxes where they were kept.

". . . Bundled up like eleven little Indians," said Betty. "By that time it seemed terribly serious. There wasn't any laughing or raillery or joshing with each other. But even the littlest ones had been waked up, and they came along too."

The night was not only deathly cold, it was deathly still. Moon hung aloft, burnished, silvery, austere. Every shadow across the snow lay hard and pointed. The investigators filed timidly toward the venerable bulk of the mule barn, now tenanted by cattle who might or might not be at Worship.

"We were an odd collection. Looked like a troop of gnomes or gypsies. . . . There'd been two snowfalls that week, with a thaw in between. So the eaves were loaded with icicles."

And moonlight stung against them, and metal of the icicles seemed almost to sputter . . . *polished daggers*, a child might have thought, and yet never dared to speak the words. Light smoke of breath went aloft from each Indian, each gnome, each gypsy. A glowing smoke to freeze against their eyelashes. And on such a night, if you were very young, you could look in awe at blue-black patches of forest along the sides of hills, and in creases between naked hills where snow was so white. And imagine that somewhere, hidden in the most sacred of antiquities, shepherds were still keeping their flocks by night.

Or perhaps King Wenceslaus and his page walked toward St. Agnes' Fountain . . . .

Brightly shone the moon that night,
Though the frost was cruél,
When a poor man came in sight,
Gathering winter fuél.

Feeding pens stood fenced at both ends of the structure, so the main path led up to one of two doors on the south face of the barn. This was the easternmost door; it was tightly closed, but not locked. A flange clung against a big staple, with a whittled peg to hold the flange in place.

Elder boys were now taking command, and one of them had fetched an old kerosene lantern. Rays from this would reveal whether or not the cattle subscribed to Holy tradition, and wished to play their part in the Holy myth.

Already some of the smaller children fell a-whimpering, complaining that they were cold, they wanted to go back to the house.

"I remember that that peg seemed to make an awful noise coming out of the flange. The door banged slightly as we opened it, and we were sure The Folks would hear us up at the house. But they didn't."

Interior blackness of the barn was musky with smell of cattle, warmth of their bodies, pungency of their droppings, grassy richness of the very cuds they chewed. It would have been a good place wherein to be born, as the tiny Christ was born. There was no longer any terror of the unknown . . . this stable was a friendly place, the cows would be comforting.

Then soft yellowish beams of lantern light swept across stalls and mangers. They hadn't realized before–none of the children had realized–that there were so many cattle in that barn. But there were. It was filled completely.

Sing May, Queen May, sing Mary!
To praise the Babe who wears a crown. . . .

"They were all down on their knees," said Betty. "Every last one of them. They were all down on their *knees*."

Not one word was spoken by any of the children. (She's as sure of that today as she was at the time.)

"We were too stricken to talk about it. We fled to the house in utter silence. Even those kindergartners–not wrapped up well enough, and chilly and shivering– Even they didn't cry. We had seen something which might not be believed. Not a one of us wished to talk about it."

Nor did they tell their parents when morning came, when sun was bright and they could look down and see cattle in the feeding pens, munching lazily at fodder put down for them. They just seemed like cows by that time—not as part of a mystery and a revelation to startle the soul and torment the brain.

"And you didn't mention it at all? Not divulge anything about the midnight trip, or what you saw?"

"None of us did. Not until years afterward."

When the girls had gone ladies'-rooming, and Frank and I sat alone, I asked him, "What about ruminants?"

"Well," he told me, "of course they do prefer to lie down. It contributes to their process of digestion. I take it that you're referring especially to *Bovinae?*"

By all means *Bovinae,* and especially the ones shacked up in a certain ex-mule barn a good many years ago, on an extremely cold Christmas Eve. "Of course, you often see cattle chewing their cuds while standing up."

"Oh, sure. But as a rule, after feeding, they do it lying down."

"But— On their knees?"

He laughed. "You heard her. It was Christmas Eve."

Betty and Irene came back to the table, and both were smiling as if they shared some interesting secret.

Frank explained. "We've been ruminating."

"About what?"

"About ruminants. And cuds and things. You know: that peristaltic motion of the cow's esophagus—"

Betty asked Irene, "Shall we let them off the hook?"

Irene nodded.

"Very well, gentlemen. Here's my theory, evolved after long consideration. Those cattle were startled by the noise, however slight, which we kids made when opening the door and stepping inside. They had all been lying down contentedly, but on an instant they were triggered into getting up. Then the lantern's rays held them transfixed—frozen on their knees. As in an old-fashioned movie, where the film is stopped, and everyone remains motionless."

I said, "And the custard pie hangs suspended, halfway between Charlie Chaplin and Mack Swain."

"Exactly. You must remember, too, that we children got out of there *fast.* The cattle didn't have time to either lie down or stand up. We saw them on their knees . . . a moment later we were running to the house."

That's Betty's anecdote, with its accompanying explanation. Her answer may be the correct one.

But I'm not so certain. Seems that, if good Christians hold sincere belief that Jesus was the Son of God– If "in Bethlehem, in Jewry, this blessed Babe was born–" If they accept this, then why should they refuse to countenance the idea that those cattle were at worship when children saw them there?

Maybe eleven little bundled-up investigators can't be wrong, then or now.

Especially when a memory of carols is like frosty breath in moonlit air.

9. Jesse's up from Thunder

"Jesse James was a lad who killed many a man—"

Jesse didn't really want to kill nobody. The murders attributed to him were committed by bandits other than Jesse. He was kind of like Lancelot or Galahad or Jolly Robin—real nice. When he slew at all, he slew as a knightly duty whilst riding in support of the Lost Cause, suh.

Jesse was the brains of the James gang. His brother Frank was the strong-arm boy, the goon, the gunner.

Frank James dreamed up all the plots about who and what to rob, and where; but Frank was wishy-washy at heart, and it took a real tough guy like Jesse to command.

The Younger brothers—Cole, Jim, Bob, et al—persuaded those decent forthright honest James brothers into banditry.

It was the James boys who were the original Bad Company, and the Youngers were bedazzled by them into a life of crime.

"Jesse robbéd from the rich, and he gave unto the poor—"

He never gave away a nickel in his life. He was tough and mean, but stupid. If he hadn't been plain born stupid he wouldn't have taken off his guns on April 3rd, 1882, and thus permitted Bobby Ford to take a crack at him.

Jesse James was smart as tacks.

"He was a great big tall man. Oh, taller than— Taller than—"

"My grandpa knew Jesse real well. He said he was just about ordinary-sized."

"Jesse was kind of on the small side. What my Granmaw always said. And she had good reason to remember him. Cause one time the mortgage on her place was due, and she didn't have no money, and she was crying. Then along come a band of men riding right up this here lane, and they says, 'Lady, we ain't gonna harm you, but we're right hungry, and need something to eat. So will you please trot us out some dinner.' Well, Granmaw give em what she had, and they et, and then, when they was about to leave, Jesse—for it was him, in person—he asked Granmaw what she had been crying about. She up and tolt him, and he left a pile of gold pieces right there on the kitchen table, for her to pay the mortgage with. Long towards evening here comes Mr. Caleb Sniggs from the bank in town, and he says, 'Drucie—' He'd knowed Granmaw all her young life, so he called her by name— 'Drucie,' he says, 'I know you hain't got the money, so I'm gonna have to foreclose.' She says, calm and firm, 'I have too got the money, every cent of it. Here tis, and you kindly hand over that mortgage paper.' Well, was old Sniggs mad and angry, for he'd planned to get this here farm for his own self, see? But by that time Granpaw had come in from plowing corn, and he cast an eye towards his Forty-four-forty— There tis, same gun, right up there on them brackets. So there wasn't nothing for Caleb Sniggs to do but hand over them mortgage papers, and Granmaw and Granpaw burnt em, right there in the fireplace, before his very eyes. Old Sniggs started off towards town in his buggy. Pretty soon there's an almighty row down the road, with shots and yelling, and, fore you could say Uncle-Speck-go-spit-on-the-stove, old Caleb Sniggs come running up the lane, fast as he could pelt. You know what? Jesse James and his outlaws had laid in wait for that there banker, and they'd stole *back* all them twenty-dollar gold pieces that Jesse'd give to my Granmaw. They took along his horse and buggy, too. I tell you, that's the kind of man Jesse James really *was*. And that's all the pure truth, and it happened just like that, right here on this place."

Jesse's father was a preacher, and Jesse learned to read and write when very young; and when falsely accused of crimes later on, he wrote voluminous letters to the Kansas City *Times*, extenuating himself.

Those Kansas City *Times* letters were written by an alcoholic newspaperman, John Newman Edwards. Jesse himself was illiterate.

Jesse had a *mother* whose name was Zerelda, but she was known as Zee.

Jesse's *wife* was named Zerelda. Commonly called Zee.

(Pshaw. Both were Zereldas.)

Jesse wore a full beard, most times.

Jesse usually sported a mustache.

Jesse was always clean-shaven, except when he went disguised as "Mr. Howard."

From one end of Missouri to the other there exist multiple caverns, and many of the caves are open to the public on payment of a fee. (Once in a while you find a free cave off the beaten track, but those farmers are beginning to get the word.) In a good half of the caves a wide rock will be pointed out to you; and behind that rock the James boys lay in ambush, and shot the Pinkerton detectives when they came in. In the other half the Pinkerton men lay in ambush, and shot it out with the Jameses. But, either way, it was the Pinkerton men who got killed in the end.

(Thus far no serious student of the Jesse James saga has found a record of any such cave or any such encounter.)

But the legends keep growing, like grainy brainy tan mushrooms which rise in moist woodland every spring. They are old, they are new, they shrink, they expand, they can be dried for future use. And, like those same April morels or like autumn thorn-apples, they taste good when you bite into them, be they fanciful myths or no.

Along about fifty-five years ago a hard-faced man with pale tobacco-stained handlebar mustachios came driving his van into our little prairie town, and parked it alongside John Richardson's jewelry store at the corner of Second Street and Willson Avenue. Carefully he set brakes against all four wheels of the van, which was bedizened with exciting signs. The largest of these read: *See Jesse James. In Person. Admission 25¢, Children 10¢.* We boys followed along, after Mr. Handlebar had unhitched his team, and by bicycle we escorted him to Filloon's livery barn where his fine black Percherons became star boarders for the next couple of days. We used to sneak in there and watch the team munching their dinner. It was a thrill just to observe them; they were a *foreign* team— "Missouri bred and foaled," their owner declared between expectorations.

So was Jesse James. In that glorious pink-painted van he reposed in an absolutely terrifying coffin, clad in the exact costume which Jesse wore the day when the Dirty Little Coward shot him (so said the proprietor). Also displayed were Bobby Ford's gun; Jesse's own revolvers; ropes used to hang the Bald Knobbers in 1889; Daniel Boone's rifle—"Old Tick-Licker"; Daniel Boone's very own coonskin cap; an alleged two-headed calf in alcohol; an alleged three-headed colt; copperheads, rattlesnakes, "the only hoopsnake ever captured alive in the Ozark Mountains"–but by now it too was dead and all tangled and twisted in a five-gallon jar. There were front and rear steps, and you came in at the rear and went out at the front. (Reluctantly.) I wasted my substance on Mr. Handlebar's portable museum. I collected the regular weekly dollar for carrying my *Freeman-Tribune* paper route, gave Mother the prescribed twenty-five cents which was Mackie's token contribution to our family budget, and spent *sixty cents* in worshiping beside Jesse James' bier. I would have spent seventy cents, except that the curfew blew and I had to go home.

I wasn't the only one, either. At seven o'clock Saturday night the line extended around a corner and all the way up to Alfred Rasmussen's shoe store. The old Missourian–the live one–had a way of saying, "Show's over. Lecture's over. Next show starts in five minutes," and shooing the public out the front door, no matter how much we longed to linger. It cost another dime to get back in, when our turns finally came again. . . . Truly, I have visited many museums over the world which afforded less macabre satisfaction. Take catacombs and crypts, whether in Paris or Rome or Naples . . . Jesse James had them beat by a mile. He wasn't just a wad of bones or a dummy, not by a dang sight. He was a man–real, dead, dried up, kind of mummified. Mr. Handlebar Mustache would open Jesse's coat, pull up his shirt, and show you the cross-hatched stitching on that brown parchment hide where the *viscera* had been removed. "They took out his–" (lowered voice)–"guts; yes, them doctors did. Claimed they wanted to find out what made him so mean. But I reckon they never did find out." Jesse's face had been reconstructed with wax, so the boss was forced to admit that the beard was false as well.

Fearful and wonderful the moment wherein a large key was produced . . . the proprietor would reach into the coffin, twist the key through a powerful amount of clicking, and set in motion some cranial clockworks whereby the staring glass eyes of Jesse James began to open . . . shut . . . open . . . shut . . . until the mechanism ran down.

"Folks'll try to tell you that after Jesse was kilt, they put his body on a train, and tuck it over to Mrs. Samuel's place–that was his Ma–and buried it in her front yard. They had a real bang-up funeral, and I reckon even Governor Crittenden come to pay his respects. But twasn't Jesse who was lying in that grave. Twas a poor tramp who got knifed in a fight down by the railroad tracks in St. Jo, same day that Bobby Ford come a-sneaking and a-murdering. Some friends of Jesse's—my own brother Claiborne was one of em—was fearful that maybe the enemies of Jesse James would dig up his corpse in the dark of the moon, and cut it up, and sell the pieces for souvenirs. So they carried his body to a place of safety, and nobody else knew any different. That's how come that I am now enabled to exhibit before your very eyes the positively genuine body of the one and only Jesse Woodson James, treacherously slain by Robert Judas Iscariot Ford for the sake of thirty pieces of silver. . . . Speaking of silver—Come on now. Everybody out! Lecture's over! Next show begins in five minutes."

He drove his brawny Percherons and the lumbering van west on a long road toward Fort Dodge, come Sunday morning. A posse of small boys rode herd on him for a way—then we turned back: too many mud-holes. An hour afterward I put in my required appearance at the Baptist Sunday School, where our teacher talked endearingly about *David, the son of Jesse*. You can imagine just which Jesse that conjured up . . . an annoyed ghost on a phantom horse, stalking that pink portable museum all the way to Fort Dodge and farther. Even at such early age I recognized that the Jesse James corpse, relics and tales were all a lot of rubbish, fascinating though they might have been. I didn't think that any man who robbed the Gallatin bank, stopped the Glendale train, shot Captain Sheets to the ground, and went to his rest with his hand on his breast—"the Devil will be upon his knee"— No such man would take all that hogwash lying down. In eerie dreams I saw him spurring his horse alongside Mr. Handlebar with menace and profanity; but still I doubted that the old rapscallion might see or feel Jesse James in the wind.

For some bizarre reason difficult to assay, there is a healthy but still disturbed segment of humanity who are reluctant to accept the obvious, the sound, the apparent, the established. They go shopping instead among marts of those who profit by selling The Whole Truth under the counter.

H. L. Mencken spoke with his usual incisiveness in *Melancholy Reflections:* "The truth, indeed, is something that mankind . . . instinctively dislikes. Every man who tries to tell it is unpopular, and even when, by the sheer strength of his case, he prevails, he is put down as a scoundrel."

Kidnappings, assassinations, mysterious disappearances, and the cold fact—no matter how solid the audience, how keen-eyed the witnesses—are never accepted as gospel. . . . No, no, do not believe what you read or what you are told by those who were there. *Someone* is tricking you, is trying to trick *all* of us.

History books will tell you that Marshal Ney died in front of a firing squad in 1815. Aha. This they try to make you believe! But do you not know that for a fact Marshal Ney fell before muskets loaded with dough instead of leaden musket-balls? Certainly: his body was placed in a box, and carried away to be buried—supposedly. And then, later, a very-much-alive Marshal Ney was smuggled, in disguise, aboard a sailing vessel. He disembarked in North Carolina (South Carolina, Georgia, Virginia) where he spent the balance of his contented lifetime as a schoolmaster. *Pardon, Monsieur le Maréchal, ou est votre plaque d'identité?*

History books declare that John Wilkes Booth fired his derringer at Abraham Lincoln, and then fled down into Maryland, and eventually to Virginia. Pursuing Federal troops caught up with him, and surrounded a barn where he had taken refuge. There he was shot to death by one Sergeant Boston Corbett (this man had been an Andersonville inmate, and wasn't any too fond of Southern sympathizers, especially one who had murdered the President of the United States). Following this, there was manifested a female disposition to remove locks of hair from the corpse. So the officers lugged Booth's body to the Old Penitentiary at Washington and buried it in well-tamped-down dirt. But . . . poppycock! As the old Scots said, *Tits! Havers!* As modern slang still has it: Balogny! Do you not know the correct story? John Wilkes Booth never died on that Virginia farm. High-level influence had its way, and in fact he escaped to Kansas (Missouri, Nebraska, Texas, Colorado, and what is now Oklahoma). The rest of his attenuated life was lived in a new identity, as a veterinarian (doctor, photographer, lawyer, peace officer). Mean to say you never heard this version? It's the *real low-down* on the case!

A contingent of John Wilkes Booths kept bobbing up—and dying, after appropriate deathbed confessions—in their dotage, all through the Nineteens and the Nineteen-Twenties. One, I seem to recollect, as late as the Nineteen-Thirties. There was a newspaper photograph in circulation which showed a cadaver said to be that of the late one-time actor-assassin. To me it looked for all the world like the mummified trunk of Jesse James as exhibited by the peripatetic Missourian circa 1912–14. Same old fancy embroidery on the dried-up tummy.

Hitler dwells incognito in the Argentine. Maybe Lee Harvey Oswald has moved in with him by this time (that TV scene, wherein Jack Ruby deleted him, was deliberately faked at the behest of the Secret Service, the Dallas cops, the FBI, and maybe even Jackie, Bobby, Teddy and LBJ).

. . . Some bushy-haired old gal is going to emerge from limbo one of these days, and swear by her false teeth that she is Amelia Earhart. And who wants to bet that she won't find a multitude of credulous customers?

A superannuated wretch came rambling through the scenery some years ago, and gave his oath that he was the original 24-karat Jesse James. Previously his name seems to have been J. Frank Dalton, but he had finally decided to make a clean breast of the matter before being gathered to his Reward, whatever that might be. This rattlepate, complete with hoary locks and a well-oiled tongue, was wined, dined, moonshined, interviewed, photographed, broadcast, listened to, gaped at, and generally groveled before and marveled over, by whole brigades of native gudgeons. His crowning achievement may have been posthumous: his True Life Story printed on paper place-mats and distributed liberally by canny restaurant proprietors, even unto this very year. I quote now from such an item of makeshift napery, which lay under my plate in the Meramec Caverns Motor Cafe, near the village of Stanton, Missouri, and bears only a few smudges of strawberry jelly and bacon grease to deface what we might designate as History in the Over-ripe rather than History in the Raw.

Jesse James, as a member of Quantrill's Guerrillas, gained knowledge of the Meramec Caverns back in 1864. In the early 1870's, he and his band used the cavern on numerous occasions because it afforded a complete hideout for men and horses. In 1874, after a train robbery at Gadshill [*sic.* It's Gad's Hill], Mo., the gang was tracked to the cavern by a posse; and after a siege of three days, they escaped by an unknown route which remained a mystery until the rediscovery of this huge passage with its underground river in 1940. At that time, a number of articles were found around, what we now have named, 'The Loot Rock.'

Controversy over the identity of an aged man, revealed Jesse James to still be living in 1948. Jesse James, alias J. Frank Dalton, caused tremendous furor and consternation as months went by during 1948 through 1951, and no agency could disprove his claim to being Jesse James. He and the last living members of the James gang held a reunion at Meramec Caverns on September 5, 1949, Jesse James' 102nd birthday.

Jesse Woodson James, alias J. Frank Dalton, died in Granbury, Texas, August 16, 1951, at the age of 103 years, 11 months, and 10 days.

In musing over this choice sample of bamboozled Americana, I am haunted by the realization that Place-Mat History now plays a vital role in shaping the regional appreciation of our past. It starts in New England tea-rooms with witches who never were burned, and mythical girls named Candace and Purity who never were carried off by the Naragansett or the Iroquois. Such phenomena continue down the Atlantic Coast into the Deep South, with silver chalices which never were buried to protect them from invading hordes, and Rebel belles who never did drive away invading Yankees with Great-Grandaddy's dueling pistols. The mats yell their wild assertions along the Natchez Trace, in the Panhandles, in the Dakota country, the Blackfeet country, the Modoc country, the Apache country, the Gold Rush country. In the face of this, how dare the waltzing traveler decry a patriarchal Jesse James who was lunched-over by the local Kiwanians? Forgive Governor Bradford and Minnehaha and Cynthia Ann Parker their trespasses, say I. And long may New Hampshire sawmills slice the sequoias, and Tennessee guerrillas massacre the Mormons.

Fumbling through those draperies of J.J. nonsense—still adorning the Missouri landscape, as brashly and palpably manufactured as plastic banners snapping in a gas station breeze—we seem to find but one item missing. That is the candy. Becky Thatcher candy, Mark Twain candy? Yes—they are available when the sweet-tooth yearns, no matter how ominous the caloric count. In distant shrines we have discovered as well Martha Washington chocolates and Dolly Madison bonbons, and the assorted Barbara Frietchie sweets retailed in Frederick, Maryland. (Munch one of her caramels, and try to forgive the Quaker Poet for putting that look of sadness and blush of shame on the face of Stonewall Jackson, as devoted and dedicated a Rebel as ever drew breath. We can still respect Maud Muller and the Barefoot Boy with Cheeks of Tan—as we respect a tender little New England buttercup, for instance. But the United Daughters of the Confederacy would be in better business picketing the grave of John Greenleaf Whittier at Amesbury, Massachusetts, than in putting up monuments in honor of Henry Wirz.)

Going to Harpers Ferry? Buy some John Brown candies, with his picture on the box yet.

A few months back we traveled thirty-four hundred miles along Missouri highways and byways, and not one Jesse James gumdrop did we see. Somebody seems to be passing up a mighty good bet.

My boyhood friend Robert Richardson was the companion with whom I first walked Missouri soil. We grew up in an intimacy like brotherhood: Doctor E. E. Richardson had brought me into the world, and Bob and I were (are) but a month apart in age. It was natural that I should, in venturing on my initial pilgrimage, ask Bob if he wanted to come along.

He welcomed the proposal with enthusiasm. "But why Missouri? We could go up to northern Minnesota, or maybe even to the Black Hills."

"Well, the whole idea of Missouri has always fascinated me. You know . . . Jesse James. . . ."

He gave the long tinkling laugh which was so typical of him (still is). "I guess we won't meet *him*."

"But Jesse's ghost will be among the prickly orange rows."

We started out, laboring under our packs, two skinny minstrels who harmonized melodiously (we thought) on *Doodle-Dee-Doo* and *I Wonder How the Old Folks Are At Home.*

"Remember that old galoot who had the dime museum on wheels? With Jesse James in a casket? I must have gone in there three or four times—"

"Gosh, I spent *sixty cents*."

The first native Missourian we encountered, on his native heath, was insane. It happened south of a village called Coatsville and northwest of the little town of Lancaster. Bob and I had crossed the State line about an hour previously, and we were looking for a comfortable place to spend the night.

It comes back clearly and in detail, even after the lapse of nigh-onto-half-a-century.

Rain clouds puffed, towered like dark Alps in the western sky.

An occasional shimmer of distant lightning put power and speed into our feet as we strode the road. But still our celerity was not as swift as that of the team and wagon which came rumbling from the north and gradually overtook us.

One man in the wagon, standing up, driving. He swayed to keep his balance as the wheels banged over ruts and holes. He slowed the team, then stopped altogether.

"Want a ride?"

"Thanks." We climbed into the rough-planked vehicle. It didn't have any manufactured box—only boards for the bottom and sides—mainly a home-made article. And it wasn't a team of horses: he had a horse and a mule hitched together with sorry-looking harness.

We were grateful for transportation of any sort. We'd been marching under weight of pup-tent, blanket rolls and knapsacks, all day long. There wasn't any such thing as hitchhiking in that era—at least we'd never heard of it. Boys didn't stand on the edges of towns, holding up their hands, trying to thumb their way. If your finances were meager and you wished to go on a trip of this sort, you went out and walked. Whenever somebody wanted to pick you up they'd do it. Sometimes, in lonely regions, you'd walk all morning and all afternoon. We'd secured only one ride that day. It was with a bootlegger. He told us that he had five gallons of moonshine in his car right then, and he bet we could never guess where it was hidden. We tried to guess, and couldn't. But the bootlegger had to visit some customers on ahead, and he let us out, politely and firmly, before he reached the target area. We were strangers, he said, and he didn't mind confessing his vocation to us, a couple of harmless kids; but he wasn't going to have any outsiders identifying his customers. So we thanked him, and he gave us each a foil-wrapped cigar.

(Chancellors. Anybody remember those?)

Now aboard the rattling wagon Bob sat on the end of the planks at the rear and let his legs hang down, while I went up front and stood with the driver. He must have been six-feet-five or -six—extremely tall, with sagging shoulders and a narrow sickly-looking chest, scrawny arms, scrawny face covered with a week's tangle of black beard. His hair was long for the style of that time, matted and dirty over the collar of his stained flannel shirt. Incongruously for summertime he wore what we used to call a Scotch cap: a felt thing with a bill and high crown. (I don't know why it was called a Scotch cap. I've spent quite a little time in Scotland, and never saw anyone wearing headgear like that.)

Well, the combined team of horse and mule was enchanting to consider, and I thought of a story about a hillbilly. Indeed we had such people in Iowa then, and some of them used to live right in our county, and we did speak of them as hillbillies. The hillbilly in the story is driving his mixed team, horse and mule, down a precipitous road at a furious pace, quaking along the edge of chasms, narrowly missing destruction at each hairpin bend.

Finally he gets to the bottom of the hill, and is hailed by a neighbor who has stood gazing up at him throughout the wild descent. "Jake, I've always heard you were a crazy driver, but I don't see how on earth your team stands for it. It's a wonder they don't balk on you, and refuse to haul you a step farther."

Hillbilly says, "Tell you something. That horse, he's blind. The mule– He just don't give a damn."

It isn't an excruciatingly funny story, but I have affection for it, as one does for something he's owned for a long time–something of no intrinsic value, yet familiar through the decades, loved accordingly. Right now, in a drawer, here in the oversized library desk which Irene gave me when we rebuilt the house– There's a little tin box with a faded battered lid. It contains hooks, pins, paper-clips, similar junk. My mother used to have it in her own desk. But I gave it to her long before that, when I was a little boy. She had a passion for preserved ginger (a vile confection, in my opinion). It was a luxury, and seldom did she permit herself to buy any. So it was my birthday present to her, maybe about 1912, when I saved five nickels from my pay as paper-boy to buy this thing. It was crammed with the sugary goodies which she adored . . . printing is still there on the lid, and so is a lion, the trademark of Reid, Murdoch & Co., Distributors, Chicago. "Monarch Brand Crystallized Ginger." It is in my desk now, and it will be there when I die (if the house hasn't burned down first). And the old story about the horse being blind, and the mule just not giving a damn– That is still in my mind, and always will be.

Perhaps human beings are the only creatures who deliberately clog and clutter their lives with trivia of no worth? . . . Well, just what use might a brushy-tailed wood rat make of the whetstone he's carried from your tent? And a crow will steal your thimble . . . but can he sew? Or your quarter . . . but can he spend it?

My hillbilly tale was duly related to the gangling hairy-faced driver. He didn't laugh, didn't snort, didn't sneer. Just stood looking down at me with a plaintive stare which seemed to say, "I have suffered all my life, am suffering now, and will suffer through Eternity. There's nothing in it for me but suffering."

It fairly broke my heart to gaze up into a face like that, into eyes like those.

He said, "Tell me. Where you come from?"

I told him that we were from Hamilton County, Iowa, and he shook his head almost in disbelief. "That must be a long ways off. I never been so far away. Not in all my life. Born and bred right here in Schuyler County, and I reckon I'll be buried here. Never been anywhere else, except—" I thought he then said, "To the asylum."

Then I knew that he couldn't have said *to the asylum*—no one would say a thing like that. By chance I'd heard of a tiny place down in the Ozarks called Siloam Springs. Likely enough that was what he had said. *Siloam.*

We rumbled and crunched . . . dusk began to settle. The landscape assumed that uncanny appearance any prairie country wears when it's threatened by a tempest. You observe such ominous quality in John Steuart Curry's *The Line Storm,* and you find it in David Cox, Mauve, Rousseau as well. You find it in Missouri in summer when storms approach at twilight. I kept wondering where we were going to sleep. I hoped that the tall man would tell us that he had a barn with a tin roof. Or maybe he had a nice grove where we might put up our pup-tent and dig a ditch around it—on a knoll, with ground sloping away in all directions. And not under any big trees. Oh, no big trees. Because the lightning was growing sharper, and we caught a grunting of thunder above the clangor of our wagon and eight hooves drumming the hard road.

The driver cleared his throat and asked, yelling, "Any work up there where you come from?"

"What kind of work do you mean?"

"Work for a laboring man."

. . . Couldn't recollect that any large number of outside laborers were being employed in Webster City. "I guess there's farm work."

"Farm work." He seemed to think about farm work for a spell. Then he said clearly, "That's what I been doing ever since I got out of the insane asylum."

There it was, he'd said it. It was the truth this time . . . no wonder he looked so mournful about everything.

"How long were you in the insane asylum?"

"Long time."

"How long have you been out?"

"Not very long."

Instant recollection of a certain old man at home. He used to sashay over the sidewalk, stepping on ants, and counting aloud the ones he squashed. Then he'd call happily across the street to anyone coming along, "I just got sixteen!" That was all right, up to a point. But he did muse aloud one day, and say that he always figured he'd been put on earth for the purpose of killing somebody. They lugged him off to the State hospital at Cherokee. . . . I thought of August Hoff. He was walking down Willson Avenue one day, carrying a coil of rope, and just starting to turn at an alleyway halfway between Boone Street and Walnut Street. A neighbor came driving along in a buggy, and he yelled, "Hey, August, what you going to do with all that rope?" Mr. Hoff turned around and, with his free hand, ran his finger across his throat, and smiled and nodded. The man in the buggy laughed and drove on. August went on down the hill and into the first barn he came to. He used the rope to hang himself.

Now through thickening portentous darkness there was the sight of a side road going off to the west. Narrow road, not even graveled —dirt road, ridged and rutted, ten times worse than the one we were traveling on. But it was a corner.

I yelled *Whoa* at the top of my lungs. Horse and mule stopped so promptly that the driver and I were nearly pitched over the front end.

Bob Richardson had been singing to himself there at the tailboard. He was flung backward against his big knapsack, and stared in amazement as I scooted past with my own luggage and dropped to the ground. Bob told me later that no matter how loud we talked, he hadn't made out a word of our conversation.

I crowed to the driver, "Thanks a lot, mister. This is where we turn off."

Bob protested, "No, no! This other way is more of a main road—"

I screamed, "Don't you remember where we have to *go?* Come on." In bewilderment he picked up his belongings and followed me into the lane. I turned once more and cried, "Thanks again." Then, in an undertone to Bob, "That guy just got out of the insane asylum." Bob swore, and we both made time through the shelter of thickening darkness. In a minute or two we heard the wagon starting up again, heard the rattle-rattle-rattle as it went south and faded finally from our hearing. Just about that time— Here it was, on the left, lightning revealed it plainly: our dearly desired alfalfa stack, neatly roofed against rain. We slid between fence wires. Soon we'd climbed the stack, hoisted up our gear, spread our blankets, were comfortably ensconced.

"Do you think he knows where we are?"

"Well, he didn't see us climb up here, because he was gone—gone with that mixed team, away off yonder."

"Yes," said Bob doubtfully, "unless he jumped out of the wagon and followed us, and the team went off by themselves."

I thought that Bob might have something there. We worried briefly, even while we ate crackers and apples. Then the storm hit hard, and we knew only gratitude.

"Boy. If we were out in *that*."

"Mighty lucky to find this stack."

Bob began to chuckle. "I was just imagining. Suppose that queer wagon-driver was a descendant of Jesse James. . . ."

I said, "Well, it's contended by some folks that there was a *streak* in the James family. You know: mental aberration."

"How many children did he have?"

"In that Billy Gashade song—the Lomax version—it says, 'Three children, they were brave.' But I think there were only two, a boy and a girl. Probably should have been, '*Two* children, they were brave—' or '*The* children, they were brave—'"

We sang about Jesse for a while, and fell into slumber while puzzling aloud on, What is sanity? What constitutes being sane? How far can you wander amid eccentricities before you become *in*sane? Weren't some of our greatest geniuses insane? Also the majority of our worst monsters?

And why are we, who term ourselves sane, commonly so terrified by The Insane? Often we fear them more than we do death itself, and not alone because death may walk with them. How widely unhinged, how deeply deranged must a person be before . . . ?

Soporific of the thick alfalfa scent had its way, so had physical exhaustion. That night we slept placidly under our first Missouri roof. Jesse James never came round to bother us no way.

He's been dead going on ninety years. Yet you can sniff him in surviving hedgerows and wild crabapple trees, and see him running with lies or loot above the fields of hybrid corn—say Pioneer, Single Cross, 3306. (Conforming corn, never imagined by people who cultivated the ragged fields of Jesse's time.)

Clay County, where he was born, is today mostly a squeezed carton of ranchhouses, swimming pools, parking lots, motels, filling stations, supermarkets . . . Kansas City suburbs, with Interstate 35 booming off toward the north; and U.S. 69, nearly as swollen with traffic, fired like a string of noisy bullets toward Excelsior Springs and back again.

Jackson County, immediately to the south, is more of the same. It retains only a few tiny corners where there's room enough for a bird to perch or silence enough for him to sing in. Farther south, in the old guerrilla country of Cass, Bates, Vernon and adjoining counties, there are still extant the farms and villages which one time knew the pressure of Jesse James' feet or the squeak of his stirrups. Also up north of the Big Muddy in Carroll, Ray, Caldwell, and over across Daviess and De Kalb into Andrew County and Buchanan, where he died . . . there stand certain deserted farmhouses which were packed with busy breathing humans when Jesse was a-riding and a-robbing . . . now tenanted only by bats, and swallows and wasps building their own odd cottages in corners of the sagging porches and privies.

Dr. Robert Collier Page, in his *Occupational Health and Mantalent Development*, says, "Since World War II, about 900,000 individuals per year have been leaving the farms to enter the ranks of industry." Since Dr. Page's book was published in 1963 there is every reason to believe that the figure is higher now. Probably more than a million people leave the farms every year. The dried dwellings in which a rural tribe once flourished lie along the roads of pastoral Missouri today, empty as the hulls of fallen hickory nuts. In driving past you're apt at first to experience a wonder and excitement because in many cases the houses are so charming—or were. Then you begin to be annoyed at seeing so many idle and neglected; you say, "What a waste!" Finally you are close to tears. Mile after mile, hour after hour, here, there, two or three in a row; then a few busy farms; then another empty house; then another tenanted farm, then two more untenanted.

Jesse, it sure was different in the olden days.

But the mere fact that a murderous outlaw trotted these roads in his own season is certainly no excuse for sentimental ostentation. There's no valid reason for this perpetual attention paid to Jesse James . . . except that somehow the man grew into a suit of clothes which antiquity tailored for him; and then the seams had to be let out and the trousers lengthened as years went past.

A recent book on the subject was written by William A. Settle, Jr., Professor of History at the University of Tulsa—published by the University of Missouri Press in 1966, reprinted in 1967. Seemingly Dr. Settle, a native of Wayne County, has been imbrued and imbued with the Jesse James fever throughout his life. (No shots have yet been devised to cope with this tantalizing febrile complaint. It yields neither to penicillin nor antibiotics.) *Jesse James Was His Name* is definitely a scholarly work, conceivably a bit too statistical for general public consumption. But any J.J. addict will take this book to his heart and find the familiar characters weighed, measured, balanced with the keenness of a Bertillon.

"How did these cold-eyed bandits who gunned down unarmed men and terrorized the countryside become heroes? How did their robbing and murdering become the stuff of legend?" Dr. Settle asks. "The answers lie in the motives and attitudes of Americans who . . . find Jesse James fascinating because, through reliving his exploits, they release vicariously something of their own outlaw spirit and their suppressed rebellion against the restrictions of modern society."

I think that makes damn good sense. Same way with Bonnie Parker and Clyde Barrow in their own Tom-gun generation, and in their resurrection via the motion picture of 1967. I don't know how many prints of the latter were in circulation among exhibitors, but for a while it seemed as if Bonnie and Clyde were banging away at the Law in every other movie theatre and drive-in throughout the Nation. And the world. (Last year in England we observed that they were organizing Bonnie and Clyde clubs.) Nasty characters on the whole. They put their mark on Joplin, Springfield, Neosho, and a batch of other places in Missouri, but I hold no reverence for them. Clyde was some five years younger than I, and we didn't resemble each other; still I was hauled out of my car one time in 1932 by a bunch of cops who were looking for Clyde Barrow. Reportedly at that moment he was driving a stolen car with an Iowa license, and here was Poor Me with an Iowa license. Actually it was not the first time I'd had guns aimed at my middle while I stood with upraised hands, but the experience is never enviable. Also those characters went shooting down a street in an Oklahoma town, one fine day, while my baby nephew regarded them solemnly over the rail of his playpen on the porch. . . .

Jesse James, if you review his record candidly, was every bit as contemptuous of human life. The only place where I will quarrel with Dr. Settle, in his statement back yonder, is in his use of the word *modern*. The "suppressed rebellion against the restrictions" is not limited to any single time. There were earlier Robin Hoods and Jack Sheppards and Willie Brennans; and our own bad men of the East and West who came before the J.J. time and after; and France's and Spain's and Germany's robbers, and Turkey's and China's; and all have had their sycophants.

Not long ago I happened to see an advertisement for some play pants for little boys. What did they call em? *Billy the Kid* pants. Gol damn. Why not Gyp the Blood pants, or Al Capone pants, or John Dillinger pants? Or maybe name some boys' pants after those Harpe brothers who terrorized the Southern Traces before Jesse James ever breathed, or Billy the Kid either. The Harpes had a habit of robbing innocent travelers, slaying them, cutting open their bodies, filling the abdominal cavities with rocks, and sinking the bodies in rivers and ponds. How's about some Harpe Brothers cough drops instead of those tired old Smiths?

William Bonney (no relation to Bonnie Parker), known as Billy the Kid, was a buck-toothed brat—a stabber-in-the-back, a sadistic and greedy killer dedicated to the gentle Art of Ambuscade. When Pat Garrett finally disposed of Billy it was the best day's work—or night's—of that sheriff's life.

People are silly damn fools about bandits and they always have been. Look at Myself When Young, explaining to Bob Richardson when he asked, "Why Missouri?" that J.J. was a stellar attraction. Or at least the *notion* of Jesse James—

We're getting nowhere fast. We humans tote along our silly devotions and delusions from one era to the next. There is nothing unique about this day and age, except for a frantic application of scientific skills disproportionate to man's ability to reason and to achieve a beneficent (and a relaxed but stimulating) morality.

In the St. Joseph Museum, Bobby Ford stares at you as he sits, gun in hand, apparently posed on some ornate bench in a photographer's studio: round-headed, round-faced, with round eyes, delicate chin, pouty mouth. His countenance betrays him as the infernal white-livered yellow-bellied rat of all time. To those with any knowledge of the human race and its often inhuman representatives, discernment announces that Bobby was spoiled to death by his mother in earliest years, and spoiled by other silly women who followed.

MAG, Page 292:

The Jesse James house . . . is a small, one-story frame cottage, recently moved to its present location from 1318 LaFayette Street and operated as a tourist attraction. . . . Here the outlaw . . . lived quietly with his family as a respected, mild-mannered citizen known as "Mr. Howard." And here, on April 5, 1882, [*Sic.* This would seem to be a misprint. The correct date, April 3, is given on page 514] he was killed by a former lieutenant, Bob Ford, assisted by his brother Charles, who wanted the $10,000 reward. Mrs. James swore out a warrant charging them with the murder of her husband. The men were sentenced to be hanged but were pardoned by Governor T. T. Crittenden. They were subsequently released from another charge of murder in Ray County. According to early accounts, after receiving the reward, they lived in debauchery until Charles committed suicide and Robert was shot in a Colorado dance hall.

I have had neither time nor inclination to pursue Bobby's post-J.J.-murder career down the byways of Evil Americana. But anecdote relates that, when Ford was murdered, the killer offered his motive for the crime. "He wanted to kill the man who killed Jesse James." The anecdote progresses: Bobby Ford's killer was in turn killed by a man who wanted to be the man who killed the man who killed Jesse James. As I say, this is unsupported anecdote. Just how long might that domino-soldier technique have continued?

The Howard cottage is little more than a shack, but in 1938 there came an attempt to move it to the World's Fair which would open the next year in New York. Mr. Walter Meierhoffer, Sr., then president of the Chamber of Commerce, did not wish to see the house taken away from St. Jo. He bought it himself, and hauled the cottage down to the Belt Highway. I hear as how a Mr. George Miller owns it now.

Maybe he owns also the place next door. JESSE JAMES ULTRA-

MODERN MOTEL. WELCOME SALESMEN AND TRUCKERS. There are a couple of antique buggies out in the yard, and some handsome locust trees grow beside the house itself. MUSEUM OPEN DAILY. WHERE JESSE JAMES WAS KILLED. SEE THE BULLET HOLE.

The attendant is charming—Edna Martin, a widow of middle years with a calm manner and an honest Missouri accent. If you want to buy any of the tourist junk which is for sale in a room alongside the death chamber, Mrs. Martin will be glad to wait on you. I suspect that she enjoys much more the business of discussing the death of Jesse James, and in authentic language.

I told her that I remembered the old wallpaper from years ago. Tan, with a little blue splotching on it—

"It's the same. So are all these pictures of Jesse, both alive and dead, hanging around the room. And that's the same 'God Bless Our Home' motto up there on the wall—"

"Some say that he was hanging up the motto when Ford shot him, others say that he was taking it down. Which is correct?"

"Neither one. He was straightening it. It was crooked, and he wanted to set it right. The Ford brothers had come here, and he trusted them, although Bobby was a new recruit in the gang, and hadn't yet participated in anything big. They were out for that ten-thousand-dollar reward, pure and simple, but Jesse never had a notion about it. His guns were heavy and uncomfortable, so he took off his guns and put them on that sofa over there. When he climbed up on a chair to reach for the motto, Bobby shot him in the back of the head. The bullet came out near his left eye and went into the wall."

"That's where they've got the glass over the old bullet hole?"

"Yes, people were always digging out chunks of the plaster, or cutting off tiny bits of wallpaper. That's how it got to be such a big hole. So finally the glass was put over it so's they couldn't work any more ruination. . . . We don't have too many personal items that were actually in the house in 1882. There's some old lamps, and those pictures of Jesse's children. And here's some marbles that the children used to play with—at least the marbles were found in the house after Jesse's wife and children were gone. And here's the frame of his mother's spectacles . . . this is an old platter which came from his mother's house. . . ."

I looked into the back bedroom allegedly occupied by the pretended Mr. Howard and his wife the night before he died. Nothing in there but a cheap bed with a blue-and-white comforter over it. I wondered whether the Jameses made love in that bed, or on one like it, during the early morning of April 3rd. Many J.J. buffs insist that Zee was beautiful, and that Jesse loved her with devotion.

The whole place seemed pathetic, lower-rustic-middle-class, shop-worn, trivial—a let-down after fierce gunfights and front-page banditry. If there should exist any survival of the human entity (Uncle Mack hain't witnessed no evidence of such survival to date) it is difficult to believe that Jesse would be hanging around there, with Belt Highway traffic howling its head off a few rods away, and a gas station promising JESSE JAMES SUPER SERVICE. REGULAR 22 CENTS.

Well, they may have had some J.J. candy for sale in that next room, along with the souvenirs, but I couldn't force myself to go in there.

You can feel more of Jesse James when you look at an abandoned right-of-way where a train groaned through prairie night until the bandits stopped it. Or in riding the same ravines where their horses whickered. Or in listening to a banjo or a guitar strummed beside a fire, and hearing Billy Gashade's song sung as it should be sung. Or in wondering what ancient revolver shots go echoing still, far through other space and other dimensions, even though neon signs now glow in all too many dark places previously sacred to the katydids.

10. Ram and Poddy and the Uncanny Nineteen-sixties

The sign above the filling station read RAMEAU'S SUPER SERVICE. None of those nervous flapping plastic pennants offending the eye, or I wouldn't have driven in there. Two employees were busy with other tasks—one changing the oil of a compact sedan, the other putting a new tire on a pick-up—so the proprietor himself waited on me. I knew him to be the boss because people called him Ram. He filled the tank, looked under the hood, made the windshield shine.

"Can I do you any more harm, mister?"

I held up the microphone of my dictating machine. "This thing is coming apart, and I wanted to take a little screwdriver out of my glove compartment and try to tighten it properly. Do you mind if I pull over here in the shade?"

He pointed out a space behind the pick-up truck. "Back right in there. If you can manage. I'll guide you."

Carefully he waved me into position. There wasn't much room, with the pebble-dashed wall of the station only a few inches away on one side, and a temporarily dismantled gas pump only a few inches distant on the other.

"There you are. All right?"

"Fine. And I do appreciate the shade. I won't be long."

"Stay as long as you want to. We're not using this pump now. Waiting for some new parts."

Rameau was in his middle forties, burly, bald-headed, with mighty arms almost solidly tattooed in dark blues and scarlets. He had everything on those arms—a complete record of his life, he'd confided while washing the windshield, and when I mentioned the tattooing.

He spoke in quick jerky sentences.

"Started getting tattooed when I was a kid. My old man sure raised hell. Didn't do any good, though. I just liked to be tattooed. Got everything on here. Names of old girl friends. And the Big Mo, too. Had it done ashore. Places all over everywhere."

"Ever regret having it done, now that you're older?"

"Hell's bells, no. Doesn't bother me. Don't ever have trouble getting a conversation started. Folks are always asking me about it. I see you're from Sarasota. Dealer's name on your front bumper. Some of this tattooing was done in Key West. Some in Tampa. That's right close to you. My wife's gotten used to it. But the night we first met—"

His fat sunburned sweaty face broke open in a wide smile.

"She says to her friend, 'Who's that tattooed man from the circus?' How you like that?"

. . . I had just finished tightening the screws on the microphone (in an attempt at temporary repair, until I reached some city large enough to boast a Dictaphone agency) when a yellow convertible moved into the lane directly across.

I heard Mr. Rameau exclaim, "Poddy!" and saw him stride over to shake hands with a man who opened the door and got out of the driver's seat.

"What you say, Ram?" The fellow called Poddy slapped his other hand on Ram's shoulder. The two appeared to be about the same age. Poddy was dressed in sports attire, a trifle on the gaudy side: pea-green slacks, orchid-striped shirt. His slim tanned face was half hidden by enormous sunglasses. He was round-shouldered, not tall, but he moved with the muscular grace of the born athlete. (Paul Waner came to mind as I looked—old friend and neighbor—"Big Poison" in the National League for twenty years, with a lifetime average of .334.) Poddy strolled leisurely alongside or stood behind Rameau as the big fellow serviced the convertible. From their conversation I learned that they had shared high school days there in town, but Poddy now lived in St. Louis.

"Playing much golf this year, Poddy?"

"Much as I have time for, and that's not a lot."

"Saw your name in the paper. In that Open tournament."

"You saw where I ended up, too. I was three-putting all over the place."

"Can't win any tournaments that way, Poddy. Well—" Ram's

voice rose higher. "What you going to tell everybody tonight? What you going to say to the kids?"

"Tell them to do as I *say*, and not do as I *do*."

"Aw, go on. You'll be better'n that."

"Are you coming to the exercises, Ram?"

"Couldn't miss, could I? Eloise is graduating in that class."

"Eloise? My God, is *she* old enough to graduate?"

"She sure is. Also she won some kind of an honor. I think it was an essay. From the DAR or something."

"Good enough." Poddy got back into his car.

Ram yelled after him, "You're sure not going to wear that *shirt*, are you?"

"I'll put on a very sober one, just to please you," and Poddy waved, and then turned out into the street and drove away.

I was very close to going away myself, but thought I'd ask Ram a couple of questions first.

"I couldn't help overhearing your conversation. Your friend Poddy sounds as if he'd been a local boy."

"Born and raised right here in town. His mother still lives here. He's come back to give the commencement address. That's tonight. Eight o'clock."

"And you've got a daughter graduating?"

"I'll say so. Got three daughters in all. Two of em married." Ram reached into his hip pocket, pulled out a thick wallet, displayed pictures. "These are the two oldest girls. With their husbands."

"Any grandchildren yet?"

"Not yet. And this one—here with the cat—that's Eloise. She's our baby. Graduating tonight."

"Perfectly darling girl. Tell me: What does Poddy do in the world, besides play golf?"

"He's quite a big shot. Lawyer. He was in the State Government a while. Had some really important jobs. But he left to go with a private firm in St. Louis. Said he couldn't resist the opportunity. . . . Played quarterback here at high school. Same three years when I played tackle. Then he went away to college. I never went to college."

I told him that I'd never gone to college.

"I guess it's good for some people. Maybe good for a lot of people. Way everybody goes to college nowadays."

"Is Eloise going to college?"

"She's going to take nurses' training. Wants to be a nurse. . . . I sure am looking forward to Poddy's speech. He's a real good talker. He came back and talked to us. At the local Kiwanis. Real good speaker. But I wouldn't have an idea— How to advise kids today. Maybe Poddy's got some ideas. Hope so. . . . So long. Nice talking to you."

I waved back as he lifted his brawny greasy illustrated arm.

That evening, eighty miles away, I thought frequently of Ram and Poddy, and commencement exercises, and the speech. At length I challenged myself. . . . Pretend you've got to give a high school commencement address in this month of June, 1968.

I took a phrase from earlier notes to be used in this book, and called the speech, *These Uncanny Nineteen-sixties.*

Why term the 1960s to be uncanny?

Let us do a little exploring of the word. The unabridged Oxford Dictionary informs us that the origin is Scottish and North English. Back in 1596 we find synonyms such as *mischievous* and *malicious.* Then we read of a source from 1638, using *uncanny* in the sense of *careless, incautious.* A North Country Glossary, published in 1825, deemed the meaning to be *giddy, careless, imprudent.* There is also the sense of *unreliable, not to be trusted.*

Inference relating to the supernatural first appeared in 1773, and later Sir Walter Scott used the word with such connotation. The supernatural essence became common from 1850 on.

There are other meanings, employed variously at different times: *unpleasantly severe or hard, dangerous, unsafe.* Or possibly one may fancy best the final summing up in the Shorter Oxford Dictionary: "*Mysteriously suggestive of evil or danger.*"

The 1960s have been and are being—and I fear will be for their remainder—an irksome presentation of all the above meanings: *mischievous, malicious, careless, incautious, giddy, imprudent, unreliable, not to be trusted, mysteriously suggestive of evil or danger.*

It was during this decade that you, the members of the 1968 graduating class of this high school, attained the greater portion of your physical maturity. And, we hope and pray, at least the glimmerings of mental maturity.

As for spiritual maturity: all Mankind is still engaged in seeking that enraptured state. And few are those who attain it.

. . . Emotional maturity? That also is very hard to come by.

You may own it; some of you may be emotionally mature in this very moment and will remain so throughout your lives. The only difficulty is that rarely will you find other folks willing to testify to the fact. Your humble speaker is at present in his sixty-fifth year of life; but his detractors, especially among literary critics—and they number more than a few—are still ready, at the drop of a typewriter, to typify him as *emotionally immature*.

In fact, I have made up a new definition for the word *immature*, and trust that it will be included in future editions of a dictionary to be prepared by some wise and receptive philologist.

Definition: *An immature man is one who consistently voices opinions with which you do not agree.*

On May 29th, the President of the United States patted the young of the United States on the back when he went all out in demanding that the voting age throughout the entire Nation be lowered from twenty-one years to eighteen. He went so far as to say, "This generation of college people is the best I have ever seen." He is alleged to have pronounced this same college generation to be *better trained*.

Better trained in what? In breaking windows, locking up the trustees, wrecking the office of a university president, setting fire to a dormitory, sniping at passersby with rifles? If our Chief Executive had reference to such liberal arts, then he was most certainly right; and it will be the first time that many millions of Americans have considered him to be right about anything.

There is nothing new in this business of campaigning for a voting age of eighteen years. The most casual research will reveal the fact that the subject was raised frequently during the Civil War—or what you may prefer to call the War for Southern Independence. It is an old old argument, and has never been settled to anyone's complete satisfaction.

If a person is old enough to be a soldier, then is he old enough to vote, and old enough to enter into connubial bliss, and old enough to drink liquor? The great trouble is: these things are responsibilities. Some people discharge their responsibilities better than others, and some people never can learn, and never will learn, to discharge them capably.

It is natural for young people to be experimentalists. Your bold six-year-old filches one of Grandpa's pipes and some of his tobacco, and sneaks out behind the garage with his cronies to see what smoking a pipe is all about. An eight-year-old girl is apt to borrow Mommy's lipstick or Mommy's cigarettes. . . . What's it like to be a lady and wear lipstick? What's it like to be a full-grown lady and smoke cigarettes?

When I pick up the paper and read that some high school students got into trouble because *they* were picked up—by the police—while parked in a car behind a hamburger joint, in illegal possession of beer, or maybe whiskey or vodka—I do not, frankly, hold this to be another proof that the world is coming to an end.

Certainly it is a naughty thing and an illegal thing and a somewhat perilous thing for high school students to be in possession of liquor, and obviously to be consuming it. But this isn't exactly a new milestone in human conduct.

My recollection strays back over a crowded and complex forty-five or fifty years to the moment when we boys, preparing to take some girls out on a picnic in a secluded region where we would unfortunately be bereft of immediate parental supervision or any other sort of chaperonage— We would break our little necks to procure any sort of liquor we could get hold of, for this big event.

I remember one season when a local grocer provided us with hard cider. And I mean *hard*. Trouble was, it was so bitter and acrid that the girls wouldn't drink it, and we had to baby it up with grape juice. Thereupon ensued an epidemic of stomach agitation which sadly nullified whatever romantic pleasures we sought to pursue.

Another time I recall helping one of the boys to steal cherry syrup from the soda fountain, and straight grain alcohol from the back room, of a drugstore where this youth worked after school hours. I wonder just how many laws we were sundering besides the liquor law? Larceny and illegal entry, certainly.

Also, as churchgoers—which most of us were—we were not heeding the adjuration of Our Savior, when we considered the young ladies who were to be partners in our projected revelry.

"But I say unto you, That whosoever looketh on a woman to lust after her hath committed adultery with her already in his heart."

Well, we were certainly looking upon those girls with lust. But, strangely enough, several permanent and pleasing domestic relationships were established by members of that same group later on.

It would be absurd to suggest that every marriage founded on a teen-age infatuation can be an enduring and rewarding union. Unhappily, statistics do not bear this out. But I contend that when most young men gaze for the first time upon the females who are destined to be their future brides—and eventually the mothers of their children, and their companions through the struggle for existence—they do not think in any individual case, "Will this girl be a good homemaker? Will she nag me because I don't make as much money as the man across the street? Will she be active and resourceful in community affairs? Will she perform to perfection her role of motherhood?"

Nonsense. The young man looks at her and he thinks, "Boy oh boy oh boy!" Translate that into the slang of whatever generation and whatever century, and it still goes. And it *will* prevail, up until that excruciating epoch when it is found more efficient and more conforming to make babies in test-tubes, instead of making them in bed.

I'll offer an extremely personal revelation. My wife and I are now only eight years short of our golden wedding anniversary. But the first time I ever set eyes on her, I was sent down five flights of stairs in an old Chicago apartment building, to answer the doorbell when she rang, replying to an ad for *talented people to join drama group.*

"Looking for the Graeme Players?"

"Yes," she said, and her voice sounded like divinity fudge or whipped cream or Chanel Number Five— I couldn't decide which.

"O.K. Right up these stairs. We don't have any elevator—"

And what did I do? Did I lead her, did I precede her up the stairs? No. I motioned for her to go ahead, and I followed behind, so I could decide whether or not I liked her legs.

And I did like them.

Back to this business about the vote. I know a sixteen-year-old boy and a fourteen-year-old boy to whom I would willingly entrust the ballot. I know a sixteen-year-old girl whom I would be happy to see ushered into a voting booth.

And I have met some people in their twenties and thirties and forties and fifties and sixties and seventies who are utter damn fools, and should be barred from suffrage purely because of sheer native stupidity.

Age is no guarantee as to the acquisition of reason, discernment, understanding. Nor are all the members of your immediate generation, or probably all the members of your class, to be typified in glowing terms as our revered President Johnson typified them. There are some congenital idiots among you, too. You wouldn't be a typical graduating class if there weren't. Every one of those elderly ignoramuses whom I just mentioned, graduated from some school—some time, somewhere.

And please accept this thought: If you wander the world widely, you will find some downright illiterates who demonstrate a keen sagacity where other human beings are concerned.

Not many days ago, a person (I shan't call him a man) sat before a group of senators in a Washington chamber. Calmly and dispassionately he testified that it was the intent and ambition of himself and of others with whom he worked and whom he admired, to destroy the entire structure of our Nation: civil, economic, military.

In Red China, or in Yellow China, any critter making such a remark would be beheaded. In Russia, guns of a firing squad would stammer in salute to his departure.

In our spongy America of the 1960s, was this man sentenced to be executed for treason?

Certainly not.

Was he locked up for life in a Federal penitentiary?

Don't be silly.

Was he sentenced to even *a month in jail?*

You keep on, man, and I'll blow my cool.

. . . Don't wash your face and hands. Live *dirty*. Don't comb your hair. Live *tangled*. Don't work: demand a hand-out. Burn your draft card in public, tear down the yard signs, destroy the *Stop* signs, blow up the mailboxes with cherry-bombs. If indeed you are apprehended, you have the perfect explanation, easily acceptable nowadays: you did it *for kicks*.

Do you wish to dream dreams, wish to see visions? Want a lift, want to be *sent?* Apply at the nearest LSD station, and take a trip, man, take a trip.

Duly-recorded lunacies are hammered into our heads in endless repetition through the public media. Not at all singular among such phenomena was the performance and utterance of five psychiatrists immediately after the slaying of Senator Bobby Kennedy.

It seems that they have a center for the Study of Violence, at Brandeis University, headed by one Dr. John Spiegel. The learnéd *Herr Doktor* speaks of "America's gun fetish, and the notion that a gun can be used to solve conflict. It begins with children, acting out with guns."

I tried to look up Dr. Spiegel in the 1967 edition of *Who's Who in*

America. He wasn't listed, so I don't know from what culture he sprang. He speaks with quite an accent. Only one of the five psychiatrists seemed to be of sufficient importance to be listed in *Who's Who.* That was Dr. David Abrahamsen, who came forth with the following: "We are still living under the legend of the Wild West, where action was the easiest solution. On the frontier, settlers solved their problems with the gun."

They certainly did, Dr. Abrahamsen. And you must have heard all about it over in Norway, where you were born and educated. As for Dr. Thaddeus Kostrubala and Dr. Jacob Chwast, they don't sound like they hailed originally from Kansas City or Kearney or King City, either.

I am not sneering at these illustrious practitioners because they were born elsewhere. Every American ancestor of every person here tonight came from another country to begin with (unless there are some Cherokee or Osage or Shawnee among you). What I deplore is our spinelessness in permitting immigrants to accept our hospitality and to become naturalized citizens; and then granting them audience while they rave about what's wrong with *us.* And that applies to naturalized citizens all the way from Stokely Carmichael *up.*

Still, there are many pundits of *indigenous* stock who join wholeheartedly in the great liberal sport of this moment: cursing out the Nation which gave them birth. Mr. Ralph McGill, Tennessee-born, said in his syndicated column: "We have an environment of violence in America. We always have had."

Germany, to offer but one example, only a quarter-century ago generated an environment of violence unparalled in the history of the World. The Nazis killed more men, women and children than have died at the hands of Americans since two-footed beings first walked this Continent.

Who shot Senator Kennedy? A Jordanian, an Arab extremist. People keep citing the murders of Presidents Kennedy, Lincoln, Garfield, McKinley. By the way, who shot William McKinley? Fellow named Leon Czolgosz. And no one mentions the fact that the same year Garfield was assassinated, Czar Alexander of Russia was assassinated as well, and not by any American.

During the past century not only czars have been struck down. (In the case of Nicholas II, his entire family was butchered at the same time.) A king of Yugoslavia, a king of Serbia, a king of Iraq, a king of Italy, a king of Greece– And it would take a computer to tell you how many presidents of Mexico, Guatemala, Panama, Nicaragua, Venezuela, et al, have been riddled while in office. And when you start counting Lumumbas and Mpolos and Okitos and Olympios and Ngendandums perforated in what President John F. Kennedy called the "peacefully emergent nations" of the Dark Continent, the map of Africa looks like a sieve.

Twenty years ago, before the members of this graduating class were alive, the original mild soft-spoken prophet of anti-violence–Mohandas K. Gandhi–was mortally wounded by a gun in the hand of a fellow Indian. And I don't mean a fellow-Wild-West-American-Indian.

Last Friday's newspapers informed us that the officials in Los Angeles who plan to prosecute the killer of Senator Bobby Kennedy were very much disturbed because Mayor Samuel Yorty had divulged to the press the contents of a notebook which belonged to Sirhan Sirhan. They cried alarm, it is said, because they thought their case against the perpetrator might be imperiled by a Supreme Court decision relating to the rights of the criminal.

This, in a case where the act was performed in the middle of a crowd, before the eyes of dozens of people. A man stood in cold blood–or hot blood–and mortally wounded another man, and wounded a number of innocent bystanders, and was observed and caught in the act. And then the prosecutors say their case against him might be imperiled because the mayor divulged the contents of that notebook to the press!

If this isn't a concentrated sample of the uncanniness of these Nineteen-sixties, then my name is Juliet Jones, and you're a bunch of Blondies and Beetle Baileys.

Somewhere–oh dear God, somewhere–among the millions who troop forth from high schools and colleges during this month of graduation, there may be men and women who will do their part in bringing back some elemental sanity to a Democracy now quivering with every derangement ever chronicled previously–and a few never chronicled before. Maybe such a man or such a woman is sitting here tonight. If so, I genuflect with sincerity and passion.

Our confused permissive unrealistic society has gone a long way toward fouling things up for you graduates. But soon you will have an opportunity to help improve matters, *if you can.*

I wish you well, whether you go immediately into a madhouse

university, or to one that is by no means a madhouse; whether you go directly from high school into the business or profession of your choice; whether you do it alone or in some vine-covered trailerette built for two. To those of you who will enter the Armed Forces, let an old man, who has been shot at in two wars, offer his melancholy congratulations.

Incidentally, you're one of the very nicest-looking gangs of narcotic addicts I've seen in a long time.

I was pleased with my commencement address to the high school graduates of 1968, and wondered whether Poddy had done better. . . . Bet you he didn't. Bet you he talked sanctimoniously, as so many commencement speakers do. I hate sanctimony, which is probably one of the reasons for my being *immature.*

And *uncanny.*

11. Mark Twain and Other Lost Children

Mark Twain Cave . . . discovered in the winter of 1819–20 by Jack Sims, a hunter. At first it was called Big Saltpetre Cave, because a large quantity of saltpetre was manufactured from the bat guano found in it. Later it was called McDowell's Cave for Dr. E. D. McDowell of St. Louis, who unsuccessfully experimented with placing the body of a child in the cave to see if it would petrify.

That's from *MAG*. I love the gruesome implication of the term "unsuccessfully experimented." The good doctor shouldn't have done that. Should have telephoned for Leonard Fetchley instead.

Oh yes, and the author named it McDougal's Cave when he wrote *The Adventures of Tom Sawyer*. And the first guide I ever had there called it the Douglas Cave.

Forty or fifty years ago you entered upon elaborate alluring blackness, toting your own light in your hand—a flashlight or lantern. Just as in Mark Twain's boyhood, when visitors carried lanterns or candles. Now the cavern is illuminated like a city street—at least those main-traveled tunnels are, through which sightseers are escorted in parties by guides of student age.

To be sure, there is nothing *mod* in wiring caverns for electricity. Proprietors have done that with popular caves throughout the world. Even the inscrutable beauty of Lascaux was thus invaded. But I cannot but feel that such systems constitute an evil intrusion upon the dignity and menace of beckoning crannies which the true speleologist, amateur or professional, worships in his heart.

Innate crassness of Man begs to be let out in order to perform, the moment he meets up with the unfathomable and the untouchable.

Once I went into a cave where a Hammond organ was huffing and puffing—*Souvenir* by Drdla being the *pièce de résistance*—and was counseled to take note of the magnificent acoustics.

In another such grotto our conductor played on their Color Organ. "Just watch," he said, as slyly he pressed switch after switch, and pulled green shadows down into purple, rosy highlights into gold. In mellifluous accents he recited something which he called a prose poem, and which I fear he had written himself. Like unto this:

"Day dawns. . . . See the beautiful color of dawn stealing above the horizon. . . . It is growing brighter now . . . the sun climbs higher. . . . All Nature shows her delight in the sun's beauty. . . . Noon, now . . . and afternoon to follow. . . . Comes the evening when man, weary from his toil, seeks the shelter of his humble cottage. . . . Twilight. And night to follow—"

At that moment we were plunged into stygian blackness. But not for long: tinted electric stars began to twinkle prettily on the cavern's roof. An orange moon arose. "The world sleeps," intoned our poet. "But somewhere far beyond the oceans another day is dawning." Back came those sunrise colors again, to yield in grand finale to a fireworks display.

All you have to do is to spend your boyhood somewhere, and later become famous; future generations will enrich themselves in your name. MARK TWAIN, MARK TWAIN, MARK TWAIN. Signs line the highways as you approach Hannibal. MARK TWAIN MARINE, INCORPORATED. TOM AND HUCK MOTEL. No, by golly, it's the TOM *N'* HUCK MOTEL.

Oh, good Lord— THE INJUN JOE TV MOTEL. (Readers dear, I am *not* making this up.) Have those imbeciles got Injun Joe interfused with Nigger Jim, who was Huck's beloved traveling companion? Injun Joe was thieving, treacherous, murderous, sadistic. Remember what he planned for the Widow Douglas?

> When you want to get revenge on a woman you don't kill her—bosh! you go for her looks. You slit her nostrils—you notch her ears like a sow!

So let's all go to Hannibal, and stay at the Injun Joe TV Motel, and get our ears notched and our nostrils slit.

On the edge of town you find, not much to your surprise, the Mark Twain Mobile Home Park. Long ago, too, Mark Twain tires and Mark Twain cigars made their bid for national recognition, but Akron and Tampa triumphed in these respective categories. Down in Ste. Genevieve there's a little factory where Mark Twain Boys' Shirts and Mark Twain Boys' Shoes are still manufactured, if one may judge from huge painted signs on the exterior. How the devil did they ever get that enterprise away from Hannibal?

Finally you reach the Clemens house, to discover that Hill Street has been blocked off and the whole area turned into a Mark Twain esplanade, complete with Mark Twain Gift Shop and Weavers, and the Becky Thatcher Book Shop. A plaque on the door of the boyhood home announces that this house was designated as a registered National Historic Landmark with the U. S. Department of the Interior, National Park Service, in 1963. The white frame house looks much the same as it always did; but there has risen a stone-brick museum next door which wasn't there in the old days. . . . Again the National Historic Landmark folks have done themselves proud. Everything is in good taste. Furniture and clothing and dishes of the 1840s appear in a reconstruction of mundane home life, though admittedly few of these objects were the actual ones employed by the Clemenses. The adjoining repository resembles a corner of the Vatican Museum: everything from Confederate money to Norman Rockwell and Dan Beard—holograph manuscripts, old editions, new editions. Visitors jam the narrow aisles and grope in bewilderment . . . there's so much to see that no one knows exactly what he's looking at. . . . Outside, and on a lot to the east, a section of the original high board fence still stands, about twelve feet long, where the whitewashing episode took place. Beyond that you may walk into a tiny park, among coxcomb and other old-fashioned garden flowers. But there's a crying need for shade. You'd think that the Government could afford to set out some fast-growing cottonwoods or box-elders for the benefit of future delvers into Twainiana.

On the whole, all is serene enough, as long as the Department of the Interior is in command. But directly across the street, the Lewd and the Crude run rampant. I refer to the Mark Twain Gift Shop. Indian arrows, Indian war-clubs, and those same beaded belts which are hawked to tourists in Florida. Maybe these Great Minds think such junk has something to do with Injun Joe? . . . Want a nasty little rabbit who says, "Of all my relations, I like sex the best?" (This is jotted down from memory; could be that the legend on the miniature rabbit reads, "Sex *is* the best," or something similar. Comes the nagging notion that Samuel Langhorne Clemens might have laughed long and loud over that. If his wife Livy wasn't anywhere around.)

The Becky Thatcher Restaurant is a block or so away. We went in there briefly, but they seemed to be having bus-boy trouble. Tables which weren't occupied were piled with dirty dishes. A harassed-looking woman sought to clean up and make way for new customers. The whole deal didn't look (or smell) too promising, so we strolled east and south toward the old Mark Twain Hotel.

Irene said, "Last time we lunched at the Mark Twain Hotel in Hannibal– What year was that?"

"It was just after World War Two. Forty-six or Forty-seven."

"Do you recall who was sitting at the table next to us? There were two men lunching, and the one behind you–"

"Yes, dear. John L. Lewis. I kept wanting to turn around and stick him with a fork, but my better nature prevailed. Or maybe it was fear of that-there jail-house."

Irene said, "You wrote about him in *Glory for Me.*"

"Sure did."

Soon Derry found his voice released;
He said the things that crowded in his mind,
The angry residue of war.
He told of empty beds left by the boys
Who took their last cold bath off Beachy Head;
And other boys who argued, wrangled, rolled the dice
To see who got the radios and Kodaks left behind,
The brand new flying-jackets. . . .
(What the hell? The guy can't use them now!)
Who spoke with tough tone of the Messerschmitts
That danced in to the kill, like eager bees–
The hard guys, seldom crying tears,
Who went away to cover up their heads on cots
Sometimes, and never speak when people
Knocked upon the door.

"And coal strikes, rail strikes back at home–
The workers making parts for fighter planes–
If we'd had John L. Lewis over there
In 1943, we'd dropped him through the bomb-bay. . . .
Used to lie in bed and talk about it;
We wondered if he was too big to go!
And I'm not kidding. Plenty fellows

Would have pushed him off the edge.
We thought that men like that
Were killing us, and killing better men than us,
Because we didn't have the fighter-cover
That we should have had."

My wife asked, "For Heaven's sake, why have you got that twisted grin on your face?"

"Just remembering."

"Remembering what?"

"Remembering that twenty-one years after those things were happening, our noble President Lyndon B. Johnson smilingly awarded, to that same John L. Lewis, the Medal of Freedom."

Irene decided on chicken salad. I asked our neat-but-not-gaudy waitress, "Please, what is a Mark Twain sandwich? You've got it listed on the menu. What does it consist of?"

"They take some sliced turkey and put it on some sliced tomatoes, with lettuce and thousand island dressing."

"But, my dear child, why do they call it a Mark Twain sandwich? Was Mr. Clemens particularly given to feasting on that combination?"

The waitress smiled. "No use asking here in the Mark Twain Hotel. The question has been asked plenty of times, and nobody knows the answer. Maybe," she said brightly, "they'd know at the Mark Twain Apparel Shop, on up the street. Or down at the Mark Twain Cave."

Road-building was in progress along the Mississippi. (Like all over everywhere. Well, the engineers and the construction companies and the heavy equipment people have to live, don't they?) We were compelled to proceed part of the way to the cave by means of a detour. Dust whipped high and thick. We blamed ourselves for coming on Sunday. Cars were more numerous, dust more blinding, than would have been the case on a weekday. I had visions of parking out in the blazing sun on some baked field of concrete.

But no. Benign trees still stood thick, even near the cave's main entrance with its ticket-sellers, guides, snack bar.

My bride informed me, "I don't care what you say about electric lights. I want to go in. I've never been in this cave before."

"Enjoy it in good health. And take along that heavy jacket of yours: it'll be chilly in there. Fifty-two degrees. I'll just drowse here, and maybe dictate a little. And recollect how it was in the old days."

She went to join the next detachment. Parties were being escorted inside at ten- or fifteen-minute intervals.

Whoever is running this deal (it's a private enterprise) must be given a lot of credit. They could have ruined the whole area and they haven't. As noted, there's a splendid stand of trees throughout that valley and over the westerly hillside, still. Even on Sunday afternoon I had found parking space beneath an august sycamore and was able—since adjacent cars were deserted by people gone expeditioning into the cavern—to dictate a few notes.

By craning my neck I could see, to the northeast, the exact spot where Bob Richardson and I camped during our long-ago footslogging tour. We had a pup-tent, complete with flaps which could be tied shut. We'd leave all our stuff in there—blankets, a few cooking utensils, spare clothing—and saunter blithely to town. That two or three miles was child's play. So were the three miles back from town, after we'd visited Mark Twain spots or played pool in our favorite eating place. It was the lowest-priced cafe we had found where food was any good. Located somewhere on Main Street on the east side, several blocks north of the Mark Twain Hotel. Maybe there are still pool parlors in combination with cafes around the State of Missouri, but I haven't seen any in years. Thirty-five cents each we paid for dinner or supper, back in those halcyon early 1920s. Breaded pork chops in tomato sauce, mashed potatoes, steamed onions, lettuce, biscuits and butter, coffee or milk. Nothing cheap about us. If we still had room, we'd go whole hog and order a big slice of cherry or apple or chocolate pie for an extra dime. Not a care in the world.

You couldn't leave a pup-tent full of your belongings near any busy public facility today, and expect to come back and find it intact. Thieving bastards—big or little, black or white—would have that stuff out of there, tent and all, before you'd been gone two hours.

Oh, indeed there was a caretaker at the cave. He lived in a farmhouse nearby, and he was the one who got his keys, unlocked the padlock of the big wooden door, collected fifty cents from each of you, and personally conducted you underground. He had volunteered to keep an eye on our tent when we were gone, but there was scarcely ever anyone else in the vicinity. Half the time, too, the man was busy with his chickens or his hogs, back behind his house, and he couldn't see the tent from there.

I would guess that his spiel was slightly different from whatever discourse Irene might now be listening to, deep in the earth, with the weight of that young mountain above her, and minor excitements of Aladdin's Palace or the Fat Men's Misery already part of her experience. (And the recurrent Jesse James rock where bandits and detectives had their shoot-out.) Some of those guides waiting for new parties around the entrance looked downright scholarly. But I doubt that they could have matched our elderly conductor of yore, in color or in imagination.

We tagged along on several occasions when he was shepherding other visitors, and he always came forth with the same story.

"Now, you know in this here Douglas Cave, there was a very famous boy used to come here. Yep, Mark Twain, the great author. I seen him once when he come back to town. Cause he lived up there in Hannibal, and he and Tom Blankenship—he was the original Huck Finn—and a lot of other kids— They use to come down here, for to explore and play around. Then one time Mark Twain, he got lost in here, and he weren't with no boys that trip. No, sir, he was with his girl friend by the name of Becky Thatcher. And you know where they hid from the Sunday school picnic that fetched them here in the first place? Well, I'll show you. Now look way up there, past them rocks. Note where I'm pointing. See that row of stalactites? For that's what the learnèd scientists call em. Yep, stalactites hang *down*, and stalagmites, they grow *up* from the floor. And that's how you tell the difference. But right in there— You see that dark place, little kind of hole, all by itself? Well, right in there is where Mark Twain and Becky Thatcher hid out. And, you know—"

Then he would bend close as in utmost confidence, and speak in a stage whisper. "Folks say they was in there a-*diddling*."

One rainy day Bob and I didn't want to walk up to Hannibal through the drizzle; the cave seemed the best place for us. You might have thought that the grizzled caretaker would be reluctant to escort us again . . . just two boys at fifty cents apiece. But he declared himself to be "a natural born cave cricket," and admitted to having done quite a little exploring off the main routes. "Nobody ever found the complete end. I got a notion it maybe hooks up with what they call Mammoth Cave, way down in Kentucky." This was the belief held by some during the period of Clemens' boyhood. Even today certain natives declare that a complete survey has never been made. Others in the neighborhood say, Nonsense, the cave has been thoroughly explored, long since. I wonder.

Anyway, in we went. The guide (wish I could remember his name, but can't) no longer uttered extravagances concerning Mark Twain or detectives or bank robbers or guerrilla bands. By this time, too, he would take us a little way off the main routes. He himself was thin of body, and Lord knows neither of us boys was much thicker than a stalk of celery. We could worm our way through all sorts of crevices. This was a great lark: wondering what was on the other side. Maybe we would find an Indian maiden . . . The guide said it had been done in the long ago.

"Yep, she was really beautiful. Had kind of red hair. And she was all dressed up, laying there where she had been put away, maybe a hundred thousand years agone. Had on her beads, and some kind of woven stuff around her. And you know what? The air in this here cave never gets above fifty-two, winter or summer. Well, there was something in the air that had kept her *preserved* in all her original beauty. No sir, boys, I never *seen* her; but I heard about her, and they say she was as beautiful as any girl alive. So the folks that found her, they picked her up. Naturally they wanted to lug her off and have her kind of examined by some of them fellers from a college somewheres, who knowed about such things, and could tell em maybe who she'd been, and all about it. They started carrying her outside, and you know what? They got her outside and she just fell apart. Yep, that's what she done. When they tried to pick her up, there wasn't nothing but just a pile of plain old dust. That was all. She'd stayed whole and beautiful while she was in here. But outside– She kind of *exploded.*"

A Dr. McDowell-child-petrifaction in reverse, it would seem.

This day I succumbed to a desire which had been afflicting me since the first moment we walked those vaulted passages. I wanted to be alone in there, and in the dark. Actually I wanted to *feel lost. Be* lost, and then find my way back again.

How stupid can some young people get? Answer: Very.

As we passed a corner, I observed a tunnel, hitherto unpenetrated in our tourings, swerving away to the left. I allowed myself to drift farther and farther behind Bob and the guide until they had rounded another corner and I could not even see reflection of the lights they carried. Then back I went to the intersection of the two passages, and made my way down a narrow crease slippery with the excreta of bats.

Now I am alone.
O, what a rogue. . . .

. . . Unexplored solitude and silence, broken only by a rhythmic dripping of water from some stalactite still wet after thousands of years of dripping . . . silence, save for the peeping of some brown-furred *Eptesicus fuscus* hanging high on the seamed limestone ceiling, awaiting only the invigorating impulse which would tell him that night was approaching, and he had best fly with his mates to the secret aperture from which they would issue forth into a darkening world.

I had decided that I knew perfectly well how to lick this business of cave exploration. It was simple: just remember every step you took, and how it looked, and where you were; and remember where you turned left, and where you turned right; or where you climbed, or where you went downhill– That was all. I had it licked to a frazzle.

But I discovered something I'd not realized before, even though I'd probably read it in many books. Maybe, God bless him, in some of Mark Twain's own. Fact: after you've been alone awhile, in mystery unknown and previously unplumbed, you lose all sense of the passage of time. You cannot tell whether five minutes have elapsed since a given event . . . when last you bumped your elbow . . . when last you coughed. You cannot tell whether it's been five minutes, twenty minutes, half an hour. Maybe trained speleologists can. But I was no trained speleologist. I was just a crazy kid seeking sensation.

(What poverty-stricken lives we led in those days! No psychedelic drugs available for the young. Just think: we had to make our own sensations by experiencing an actual *experience*. Couldn't rely on pills. Poor us.)

. . . Didn't know how far I'd traveled, didn't know how long I'd been gone from the others. Knew only that I'd been concentrating prodigiously on remembering each of those landmarks along the way . . . back where double stalagmites joined together, very like the torso and thighs of a female . . . place where the bat was disturbed and planed close to my head. Somebody had carved a huge set of initials and dates on the smooth wall. . . .

But since it was impossible to recognize how long or how far–

Best to go back and rejoin the others.

I turned squarely in my tracks. Certainly I could find the route. Hadn't I *memorized* it?

Yes, right up there.

. . . Now, here's this corner–or a sort of corner– My light shows it. And I came around *here* from the other side– That is, I swung to the right when I passed this place, so now I must swing to the *left*. Ah, that's correct. Yes. Now, it goes downhill *here*. Because I was going *up*hill when I came–

Wait a minute. What's this?

The flashlight showed what it was: a solid wall of rock. The passage squeezed together there and terminated. It wasn't exactly a path that I was on: there was firm stone and some sandiness and some dampness, too, underfoot. But–

Well, all right. Go back now, the way you came, back to that corner, and go down the *other* way.

Ho, ho, here we are! Of course this is right. I remember this. And right up the next slope is the place where that wide stalagmite–

It was nothing of the kind. Because up that slope the ridge broke off abruptly. I swept my light out into space. Yes, space: a steep declivity. If I'd been traveling faster I would have fallen over the edge. This was a high cliff, and down below I could hear water running.

Swinging the light this way and that, an immense chamber was revealed. How large, I did not know. But I hadn't been here before.

Panic was pounding. I crouched down, and kept commanding, "Now, be calm. Be *calm*. It's hysteria that kills people. You wanted to be lost underground, or thought you did. Are you sure now that you really enjoy it?" I did manage to laugh aloud. My mirth went skittering into distances, the hilarity of many echoes seemingly called back by spooks who might have been dancing in the emptiness of that chasm.

Faintly I heard something else. A wailing cry. A shout, the echo of someone's voice, calling? . . . It came again, a little closer. The sound was distorted out of all semblance to human utterance, yet some creature must have been the originator.

Kobold, troll, troglodyte?

The thing *hoo-hoo-hooed* again. Perhaps there were owls in there—horned ones which had lived so long in the fastnesses that their eyes were rendered sightless, and they could exist only by smelling out the bats at their roosts.

Belatedly I felt that it was up to me to yell back. I yelled. A new conglomeration of echoes began their tittering; but a wan scrap of light appeared remotely, moving among limestone growths, and it was followed by another. Yowl of voices arose, nearer and louder. Then there were tiny figures descending a steep path, at what seemed an incredible farness. The black valley lay between us. But on the opposite side the path curved downward among boulders and encrustments. People were carrying lights. . . .

It took considerable floundering and climbing and sliding on my part before I could meet up with them. Bob Richardson and the guide, of course; also two strangers. They were employees of the Atlas Cement Company, and had come from the big plant over near the river, on the opposite side of those wooded hills. A blast was about to be detonated in a quarry. Always they sent emissaries into the cave, in order to bring everyone out before the charge went off.

I confessed to Bob the whole story about my being lost, and the ensuing fright, later that day. But all I said at the time was, "Somehow we got separated. I couldn't see your lights any more, so I tried to come this way."

The guide said, "Mighty lucky that we caught up with you. Or lucky that you caught up with us. When that dynamite goes off, it's liable to shake down big chunks of stone."

Sometimes it shook down so much that whole passages were closed off, and had to be reopened laboriously.

"We been hunting and yelling for you for I don't know how long," he added crossly. No one could have blamed him for being annoyed. His own safety was involved as well as ours.

After we reached the entrance, the guide started toward his house. The cement men went in one direction, and Bob and I in another. We weren't a hundred yards away from the mouth of that cave when the entire hillside shuddered under our feet.

There ensued fresh falls of stone within the cavern. Big chunks. We saw them, next day.

More parties went in, other parties emerged, but Irene's crowd was tardy in reappearing. Then an idea struck me, and I crossed the road, bought a Coke, and talked with the proprietor of the gift shop and snack bar next to the entrance.

Some months before, there had been printed a series of newspaper stories relating to the disappearance of three small boys from the Hannibal neighborhood. It was feared that they might be in the Mark Twain Cave. Had they ever been found?

Bad news.

"No, sir, they never were found. The cave was searched for days and days, but there was absolutely no trace of em. A lot of us, though, had other theories at the time, and I guess most people accept that now."

"What do you mean?"

"I think they're over there under the dirt, where the equipment's working, on that new highway."

"Under the *dirt?*"

"Yes. They had been seen playing around that area the day before; in fact they were over there often. Now, there were a lot of little pockets and holes and things, where the earth was being moved. I think those kids tunneled back in one of those, and it caved in on em, and they were suffocated. Then, when the machinery came along, their bodies were just rolled and packed right into the road embankment. That's what a lot of us think. I wager you they'll never be located in this cave."

I returned to the car, wishing that I hadn't gone over to ask that question, and wondering about the parents of those boys who had disappeared, and then trying very hard not to wonder about the parents of those boys who had disappeared.

The new highway would have the same colossal dimensions and appearance as those thousands of miles which have so recently creased in fabulous pattern—and at fabulous price—across America's marshes and meadows and mountains. If the snack bar proprietor was correct in his assumption, and he could very well be, then the children were pressed in permanent burial directly beneath the throbbing pavement where a billion tires would be moaning through the years.

Sometimes at night, when the air was right, and charges of the Past and the tenor and setting of the percipient were at their keenest, would someone see those little boys? Would a driver feel that he had run them down, and then stop and try to search them out?

In England, persistent stories concern a road which runs west from York to Harrogate, and crosses Marston Moor on the way. They bob up from time to time amid lore of the Society for Psychical Research. Several accounts appear in as many books.

For instance, we have the experience of Mr. Thomas Horner and Mr. Arthur Wright on the York-Harrogate road, on the night of November 5th, 1932. Horner was driving the car, and was about to swerve to pass around several men whom he observed walking ahead. Both he and Wright, his passenger, saw the men turn and glance over their shoulders. But the odd thing was their dress. They wore long hair, big wide hats, cloaks, boots or leggings.

Suddenly the lights of a motor-coach came into view, approaching from the west, and the drivers of both vehicles had to dim their lights.

Wright cried out to Horner with some such expression as, "My God, Tom, you've just run over some people!"

Indeed, the car seemed to be among the men, and then they disappeared. Mr. Horner stopped. There were no injured persons to be seen. Horner and Wright hunted along the grass verge, hunted beside the hedge . . . where had that group of strangely attired men come from? And gone to?

Inquiries were made. No costume balls scheduled for that evening, in any nearby village or in adjacent cities.

The Battle of Marston Moor took place at that same location on July 2nd, 1644.

Peculiar tales of vagrant wanderers compound their interest through the years. There are a hundred different versions of the young girl walking, lonely but prettily gowned, beside a highway at night. A driver comes along and picks her up and asks her where she wishes to be taken. She gives him an address in the next town. Proceeding there, he halts in front of the house which she designated. He turns around to open the car door. No babe. Driver goes up to the porch and rings the bell, and someone comes out, and the traveler says, "I can't understand it," and tells what occurred. Person who came to the door reacts in different ways, according to the different legends. But invariably he or she finishes off with the statement that the description given was an exact description of his daughter or her daughter (niece, wife, sister, cousin, name it) who died in a motor accident a few years (days, weeks, months) before. And the accident occurred at the very spot where the kindly motorist picked up the babe.

So possibly, somewhere around that line which separates Ralls

County from Marion, drivers of the future may pause in their jetting rush along a speedy highway bordering the Mississippi—a highway panoramic with curving scenes of charm—highway which destroyed so many other scenes of charm in its mere building— And they will say, "Why, look at those boys out in the road! Where did they come from?"

Where indeed?

Irene's party emerged into hot sunlight at last, and she came to join me. She admitted that those electric lights had undoubtedly changed the whole aspect. Just the same she was glad she'd gone in. At hearing sad tidings about the three missing boys, Irene shook her head. "You know, if Mark Twain had been a boy of today, it could have happened to him."

We went southeast on Route 79, Irene driving. Traffic was thin, as we'd hoped. Most visitors to Hannibal use the big routes: U.S. 61, 24, 36. But 79 is a State road which edges around hills, and occasionally offers a view of the tawny Mississippi working its stubborn way southward, dotted with islands like little green ships afloat. And then we'd go down into bottomlands where cornfields were drowned out by floods earlier in the season.

I had fetched along copies of *Tom Sawyer* and *Huckleberry Finn.* Wanted to look up something.

What a story teller he was.

"Irene, listen to this."

Judge Thatcher's house was on Tom's way, and he stopped to see Becky. The Judge and some friends set Tom to talking, and some one asked him ironically if he wouldn't like to go to the cave again. Tom said he thought he wouldn't mind it. The Judge said:

"Well, there are others just like you, Tom, I've not the least doubt. But we have taken care of that. Nobody will get lost in that cave any more."

"Why?"

"Because I had its big door sheathed with boiler iron two weeks ago, and triple-locked—and I've got the keys."

Tom turned as white as a sheet.

"What's the matter, boy! Here, run, somebody! Fetch a glass of water!"

The water was brought and thrown into Tom's face.

"Ah, now you're all right. What was the matter with you, Tom?"
"Oh, Judge, Injun Joe's in the cave!"

Irene said, "I remember what came just afterward, when they hastened to the cave and opened it up. Injun Joe was lying dead of starvation and exposure, with his broken knife beside him, where he'd tried to chip his way through the foundation beam."

"Correct. Remember what happened after that?"

"After that? Well, he was buried, wasn't he? . . . Oh, yes! And didn't the townspeople say, after they'd flocked to the funeral—Didn't they declare that they'd had almost as good a time at the funeral as they would have had if Injun Joe had been hanged?"

"In SAC talk again: That Is Correct."

And then:

This funeral stopped the further growth of one thing—the petition to the Governor for Injun Joe's pardon. The petition had been largely signed; many tearful and eloquent meetings had been held, and a committee of sappy women been appointed to go in deep mourning and wail around the Governor, and implore him to be a merciful ass and trample his duty under foot. Injun Joe was believed to have killed five citizens of the village, but what of that? If he had been Satan himself there would have been plenty of weaklings ready to scribble their names to a pardon petition, and drip a tear on it from their permanently impaired and leaky waterworks.

Irene cried, "Are you certain that Mark Twain is *dead?* Sounds exactly like he's writing about people *today*."

"They hain't changed much, hon. So, when you were down in those depths, did you see Injun Joe's hand, holding a candle?"

"No. But I could have seen something else. Didn't you write a story one time entitled *The Boy in the Dark?*"

I had to stretch far back for that one. "Woman, there's nothing wrong with your memory. Just about one-third of a century ago. . . ."

"Did you ever sell it? I can't remember—"

"No such luck. Couldn't find a buyer. Finally I let Cyril Clemens print it, for free, in his little *Mark Twain Quarterly*."

"Have you ever included it in any of your collections?"

"Nay."

"Then why not put *The Boy in the Dark* into this Missouri book?" . . . Well, why not? Here we are, back in 1935.

It is eleven years since my nephew, Benny Fuller, walked into darkness of a cave which falls away beneath hills near the Mississippi River. Yet I cannot tell you exactly what it was that happened, though I have spent much time pondering it.

But the cave still curves its black channels among Missouri highlands, close by the town of Hannibal. A guide lives near its entrance, or did in the time when we parked our car amid afternoon shadows.

The guide was a thin woodsman-farmer with a tangled beard and shrewd pale eyes; his clothing was stained with kerosene and clay and tallow-drippings, and he knew the blind crickets of buried fastnesses much better than he knew the orioles of day.

I paid for myself and for my nephew. Then we went into the cave, with Benny tugging at my hand like a kite jerking its tether. Half an hour later he was lost.

Desperately and unmistakably lost, gone beyond the shrill curses of the guide, and the frantic howlings which I sent echoing through every passageway.

In this record (again I tell you I cannot understand it) you will find no certainty as to why Benny Fuller chose to lose himself. Something strange happens to boys when they venture underground among crannies of limestone. The eerie light of a lantern does things to their faces. Laughter runs away into echoes, the hush of untouched twisting miles steals out to wrap them in its legendry.

They are not frightened, they are lured and invited. Benny was so lured, and he vanished without a sound.

We called, *Hi! Come here!*—at first in amusement, and then in anger, and then in downright terror.

But only reverberations came back at us from every vaulted corridor, and in ten minutes the lantern was shaking like a leaf in the guide's hand. I kept seeing the face of Benny's mother, and wondering how she would look when I talked to her again.

"How many miles . . . ?"

"Don't know. We only know part of the cave. Nobody's found the end. It goes miles and miles. Away down the river—maybe underneath—and on, and on— Just like in the book! Just like it said in—"

I tried to shut out the maddening wails which hooted in return whenever I shouted the boy's name. "How many labyrinths—halls—whatever you call them?" I was crushing the man's arm. "Tell me—"

"Don't know!" he shrieked, his face waxen in the lantern light. "Once there was a girl got lost . . . never found her until too late—"

There was nothing for it now but the front entrance, and already the evening had turned purple when we got there. We cranked a wall-telephone at the guide's house, and before long automobile headlights came pressing up the side road from the river. There arrived constables and farmers, and lean young men with serious faces, and all of them had lanterns or flashlights of some sort.

We went back into the cave before eight o'clock, and came out at ten minutes to ten, and we had Benny with us when he came. He was in my arms, half asleep. We had found him in the main tunnel, not a hundred yards from the front entrance. We had found him only a few minutes before we came out, and he had not been there when we went in.

From some secret hiding-place, he had come in all the mystery which wrapped his departure a few hours before. He told us his story as he sat in the guide's kitchen with a bowl of hot milk before him, and a dozen weary and clay-smeared men listened as he talked.

Benny said that the shadows had seemed to whisper to him. It was the greatest experience in life to glide like a runaway rabbit amid those blacknesses. He had a little flashlight, and like a good Boy Scout he tried to keep track of the devious turnings and windings, so that he would not be lost.

But the maze was too overwhelming. He went wandering between unmarked ledges, and silence talked loudly at him, and he wanted to cry. But he didn't cry at all. He walked far into the gloom which drew back ahead of his flashlight beam . . . cave crickets scuttled from beneath fallen stones, and he found a mouldy three-cent piece, with the date *1853* on its face. He had the three-cent piece, now, clasped in his grimy hand.

There was no telling, he said, how long he might have blundered among the stalagmites, if he had not met the other boy.

The other boy was there ahead of him. Benny's light shone faintly on him.

"Hi," the other boy said.

And Benny Fuller said, "I'm glad I've found somebody. I'm sort of lost. . . ."

"Lost!" repeated the other boy. He was a tanned muscular child about Benny's age, with a shaggy mass of hair, and eyes that twinkled like stars. "You couldn't ever lose *me* in here."

"You know the way?" marveled Benny.

And the boy said, "I know it all."

"My name's Benny. What's yours?"

And the boy said, "Sammy. You can call me Sammy."

So he led Benny Fuller through a great many narrow caverns and wide ones where bats chittered overhead, and past rocks where no one had ever carved any names. Benny had a feeling that no one had ever been in this part of the cave, except that boy. . . . There were silver stalactites like a fairy timberland, and there were glittering frescoes of damp moss, and cliffs where the boy led him and they could sit quietly with underground oceans murmuring far beneath them. And Sammy laughed a great deal. He kept just ahead of Benny's flashlight, a misty figure in torn shirt and ragged trousers.

Finally, Benny thought he ought to go. He said, quite rightfully, that his uncle would be worried.

"Can you find the way?"

"No. I'd be worse lost than ever. I don't see how you'll find the way back, yourself."

Sammy chuckled again—a light happy laugh that echoed itself to death amid farthest closets of darkness. "Nobody ever knew this cave as well as me."

He kept ahead, a guiding beckoning sprite, luring Benny Fuller to the safe width of trodden corridors where the ground was littered with burnt matches and candle drippings, where cliffs were soiled with a thousand names and dates and initials.

And when they were back, undeniably, in the common confines of civilization, Benny raced ahead to thank the boy. But he couldn't find Sammy anywhere. Sammy was gone.

. . . People said that there were clam-diggers dwelling on the river banks nearby. (They made a living by gathering the big freshwater mussels from which so-called pearl buttons are made.) They had children, and some of the children were boys. And, like all boys who have grown up as wild things, those sons of the clammers knew every thicket and foxhole for miles around.

Benny and I went to their colony next morning, after we had spent the night in Hannibal at a hotel with a familiar name. We went because I had not been able to sleep all night, wondering about Benny and what it was that had happened to him.

. . . Yes, the clammers had some boys. Yes, the boys did run wild, and often visited the cave. There were other entrances–far-away, mysterious dens–where they might creep in without a soul's knowing it. . . . It was agreed that one of the boys was named Sam. No, Sam wasn't there now. No telling when he would be. . . .

Benny Fuller and I drove East. And for eleven years we have been wondering about that night and morning.

Benny has suggested that he might take some time off from law school this fall. In November, he declares, he wants to drive to Hannibal with me, to visit again that cave where he met the boy named Sammy.

A hundred years ago a baby was born not far away from Hannibal. The centenary falls on November 30th of this year. There will be speeches, and music, and varieties of celebration. People will take off their hats to the bronze statue of a bushy-haired man, one who used to be enticed by that cave– Long before he grew up to sing the saga of Tom Sawyer and Becky Thatcher, lost in dungeons of darkness– Long before he was Mark Twain, long before he dreamed of Huckleberry Finn– When he was only a boy named Sammy.

So that's *The Boy in the Dark*. He has never adventured his way between hard covers before, but it seems to me that truly he belongs here.

Only one thing–

If I'd known about it, back in those Nineteen-thirties, I wouldn't have had Benny finding any three-cent piece. Instead I would have had him find one of those ancient half-fare tokens issued by the Hannibal Transportation Company. Two barefoot boys are shown in illustration, and their names are stamped as well.

Guess what the names are. Guess hard.

12. Maryville

Mr. Merrill Chilcote is managing editor of the St. Joseph *News-Press*. Any Hollywood director would say that he was typecast for the part. His tired eyes are half-hidden beneath crusty brows; his is a smooth-shaven face with grainy skin. Old pipe sticking out of the corner of his mouth. There are other pipes scattered over his desk, and a mat of galleys and papers and teletype copy and letters strewn about. It's the kind of desk where drawers are jammed solid. You can just imagine him hunting laboriously to find this or that, but always being able to find it.

Merrill Chilcote has a dry terse voice. Nothing he observes happening nowadays can possibly surprise him. Because he seems to feel that he's seen it all, and he probably has.

I asked, "How far are we from Maryville?"

"Oh, a little over forty miles."

I said, trying still to place the year, as I'd been trying for days—Said, "There was something which happened up there in Maryville. Something bad. I can't remember the exact date, and can't even designate the year. But it was a long time ago. I think I was still living in the Middle West at the time. I was running a column for Mike Cowles on the Des Moines *Tribune* in 1930 and 1931."

Merrill knocked the ashes out of his pipe and dropped the pipe into an ash tray. "Monday, January 12th, 1931." He leaned over and pulled out the lower drawer of his desk on the left-hand side. He didn't have to dig around as long as I thought he would. He came up with a scrapbook bulging with headlines, newspaper photographs, clippings.

"How did you know the date, right off the cuff like that?"

Merrill's glance came over to me again, and he reached for a pipe and began to fill it. "I was there. I was in on the thing pretty much from the start. I was on the story when it happened, first, to the girl."

"What was her name?"

"Velma Colter."

"And—the man?"

"Raymond Gunn."

"So you went up to Maryville—"

"Yes, the first night, a few hours after they discovered her body. That was on Tuesday, December 16th, 1930."

"And then. You saw what happened, in finality, on January 12th?"

"I saw it."

Then, slowly, "You figuring on going up there?"

I nodded.

"Possibly the site would be difficult to find. Let me show you a map I sketched at the time, and you can make a rough copy. I'm not the world's greatest cartographer, but maybe this'll make sense."

The day before I drove to Maryville I'd been studying some photographs of Velma Colter, and carried them with me in memory. She was nineteen years old when she died. She was a long-nosed sweet-faced rather plain little country girl of the sort I grew up with and went to high school with, in an earlier decade. That was about one hundred and sixty miles from Maryville, as crows and airplanes and saucers fly.

We may safely assume that the principal photograph displayed in newspapers was a graduation picture—one taken when she was a senior in high school in 1928. She has her hair bound tight to her head. It looks to be brownish hair, or maybe light-brown, and is carefully waved and sculptured around the edges. And her eyebrows are plucked. As a nigh-onto-forgotten Louisa May Alcott says, *Dear me, let us be elegant or die!*

. . . Now, what do they call that thing around her neck? Yoke? No, it's a collar, dripping down below the little chain and locket. Guess they used to call a lace collar like that a bertha.

But your name is Velma, Velma, and not Bertha. You graduated in 1928, and went the next year to Northwest Missouri State Teachers College, which was, appropriately enough, on the northwest side of Maryville. Then you got a job teaching at the Garrett school, out in the country three miles southwest of Maryville.

There used to be a game children played, in those-there parts or these-here parts or however you want to term the region. They called it Black Man. The kids stood on opposite sides of a playground, and whoever was It was roving around out in the middle. He'd start calling out, "Black Man, Black Man, Black Man—" and the third time he said the words that was the signal: everyone started running back and forth, to change sides. It, the Black Man, would try to catch as many as he could. Once caught, a player became a Black Man. He joined the Its.

So that was what happened to you, Velma Colter, in chill darkness, in that schoolhouse with old-fashioned desks and the decorations which you had just been contriving. You'd been printing with colored chalk on the blackboard, and drawing pictures of reindeer and Santa Clauses and Wise Men. Then someone called Black Man on you.

Had it not been for the indescribable manner in which you met your death, probably you'd have married some personable young farmer or storekeeper; and today would be a plump woman of fifty-odd with a lot of grandchildren. You'd be busy with Ladies' Aid, the Sunshine Circle, the Cemetery Association, and the Ladies' Auxiliary of Seth Ray David Post No. 442, V.F.W. Myra's folks would come over, and you'd cook dinner for them on one Sunday; Roy's folks would come over on the next Sunday, and you'd cook dinner for them. You'd smile, and be peering keenly through or over your glasses. But—

Black Man.

Let's drive up to Maryville. This is a fairly bright August day. Sun shines fierce and hard periodically, then slides behind a quilted fabric of clouds. Route 71, leading from Savannah to Maryville, is a two-lane highway crammed with traffic. The countryside spreads in contentment because of last night's rain. Let's hope the excessively parched areas over east and south managed to get a little benefit too.

Idyllic scenery hereabouts, many hayfields which have substantial oaks growing at intervals. They must have been planted by the very first pioneers. But fresh hayseed is sown in repetition, in tradition. Pastures have been mown recently . . . the oaks seem spaced like those in an English park . . . almost you expect to look back through shade and see the distant faded façade of an old Tudor hall.

Loads of fireworks for sale in Missouri any season. FIREWORKS WHOLESALE. FIREWORKS RETAIL. The vending of such merchandise doesn't seem to be permitted in some counties; then in other counties— Galaxies of fireworks signs.

Only a few miles from Maryville. The ads come fast and furious.

INSURE WITH JACKSON. MOST PEOPLE DO.

FIREWORKS.

WELCOME TO THE FIRST CHRISTIAN CHURCH. WORSHIP WITH US.

NODAWAY BANK.

FIREWORKS.

You see, this is Nodaway County, named after the Nodaway River which rises in Iowa. Free Soil up in Iowa. Always has been. They don't lynch colored people on Free Soil. Or do they? Illinois was Free Soil as well, but I seem to recall Chicago race riots during the summer of 1919. And seem to recall—

All of which reminds me that I haven't described Mr. Raymond Gunn at all. His picture was in the paper too. It was in a lot of papers. I'm sorry to report that Raymond Gunn's countenance is not the best character witness which anyone might wish to proffer. In fact, Mr. Raymond Gunn is a dead ringer for what our one-time gardener, Richard Barber (Killed In Action, WW II) used to call "a real bad nigger." Richard got a little scared about one neighbor of his. "He threatens to cut folks. Mr. Kantor, he's *a real bad nigger.*"

FIREWORKS FOR SALE.

That's at Sherlock's Drive-In. (Still ape about fireworks.)

Here's an historical marker beside the road. Let's pull off and take a look at it. . . . Thunderation. It doesn't tell a thing about Velma Colter, or Raymond Gunn, or the schoolhouse, or Sheriff Harvey England, or the mob, or— It does mention Northwest Missouri State Teachers College. That's where Velma had a single year of higher education before she got her job at the Garrett school. In the same college was another girl student whom Gunn attempted to attack. But that was years before, when Velma Colter was still in high school. Gunn was sentenced to a five-year term for that offense. Released after about four years, with time off for good behavior, etc., etc. Still there elapsed an interval sufficient for him to get into trouble in Omaha. Then he returned to Maryville again, where his father was living. Currently in the winter of 1930–31 there was a concealed weapons charge pending against him.

This bronze tablet tells us that Maryville—or rather, a farm right outside town—was where Homer Croy was born. I used to know Homer Croy in New York: he was a shy man, but full of fun. He wrote some good little books about Missouri: *Boone Stop* and *West of the Water Tower* and more.

Guess who else came from this town. You can't guess? All right, I'll tell you. It was Dale Carnegie. You remember—*How to Win Friends and Influence People*. Let me say privately that the way to win friends is not to go prowling around with a club, and using it on a pathetic girl whom you grab in a winter-darkened room.

True, you can *influence people* that way.

In case any pietistic do-gooder is now about to declare that Raymond Gunn was a wingéd angel who couldn't possibly have killed and raped and mutilated this particular victim, and that the local officers ganged up on him and said he was guilty because he already had a police record— *Police brutality*. Or that he was tortured into a confession—

When he was questioned they didn't do any mauling or torturing. I know from Merrill Chilcote. Merrill sat just outside the door and heard every word, every sound. He was the only one, besides that handful of officers, who knew exactly when Raymond Gunn confessed, who knew that he *had* confessed. And that he guided police to a thicket where he'd tossed away the murder weapon two days before. There it was, blood all over it. Nobody'd spied that club, nobody'd been near the place. They didn't know what had been used. They knew only that it was something big and heavy, because of the condition of the girl's body.

They hustled their prisoner, by night and in secrecy, down to St. Joseph. It seemed like a wise idea. They didn't make the news public in Maryville until they knew for a fact that the prisoner was safely incarcerated at St. Jo.

FIREWORKS.

Here we are, actually on the edge of Maryville, so let's go looking for the Garrett school. I mean, for the place where the Garrett school used to stand.

Turn west along Nodaway County Road V, hunting for the country club. On Merrill Chilcote's map a country club is indicated near the northeast corner of a square. I asked Merrill if he thought the square was a mile each way, possibly on section lines, as so many surveys were made long ago on prairie land. Thus, where there is sufficient population to support the necessity, dirt roads or graveled roads are a mile apart. It's what gives that checkerboard appearance to the landscape when you fly over such farmland at medium altitudes.

Merrill thought that perhaps the square was a half mile across. "You know, this is all getting to be nearly forty years ago. Roads around Maryville may be changed now. Perhaps a subdivision occupies the dark and bloody ground."

We go on. Then– *This* might be the road, and maybe the country club is off in a new location somewhere. Turn south. . . . What do we have here? Big modern school strung along a low hilltop. Marvyille R-2 High School. Rural-2, we suppose that means. Some descendants of children who were Velma Colter's pupils at the little white schoolhouse not far away, and so long ago, would be students here. . . . Very trim. Loads and loads of windows–quite unlike the new mausoleum at Trenton. There's silvery metal trim around the windows, and some aqua paint here and there. Not bad at all.

But there aren't any teachers here now. No cars parked, doors all closed. Not even one teacher, in case anyone should want to come a-murdering after dusk has fallen.

We've found the country club, on Missouri 46, running westerly out of the southern suburbs. Here's a dirt road, straight south from the airport, and that's the first road west of the country club. We turn south and stop at an unpeopled corner–no houses nearby. Park on the grass, far removed from traffic which scoots and roars a mile to the north.

And spread Merrill's map again. . . .

This is the place. Here grow, in memorial, purple vervain and fluffy purple horsemint, and the clear gold of brown-eyed susans. A four-strand barbed wire fence fastened to weathered posts, surrounding the field. Spritely meadow butterflies sample flowers which grow where once–

Trees shown in elderly photographs are gone. Ah, that could be a survivor: a scrawny long-dead osage orange against the fence. One slender elm beyond has come up since the catastrophe. This is an innocent unwalked corner of pastureland today.

Is it possible that, somewhere at hand, a phantom choir sings the second verse of *Jerusalem the Golden?*

The pastures of the blesséd
Are decked in glorious sheen. . . .

Huh. Pasture of the damned.

. . . Sound of engines. Two tractors rise over the hill, weed-cutting as they travel. Down goes vervain, down goes horsemint, away flurry butterflies in escape. Maybe those young men operating the tractors know the story? At least, as neighborhood people usually do, they know *at* it?

While they cleave tall weeds, a flat area emerges, one undiscernible when plants grew high. That's where the Garrett schoolhouse stood.

Clyde Martland said, "Being born in 1916, I was just about a month away from my fifteenth birthday when it happened. But I was real tall for my age. Maybe that was why I was allowed to get rather close to the scene of action."

Clyde Martland is still tall, not stooped, in his early fifties. He was in the Marines during the Second World War and got wounded on Guadalcanal. Even after all those insurance-business-years in a city there is something of the old Corpsman about him. His eyes are tan and small and rather sad, he wears his gray hair in a fairly close crew-cut. He has wide big-knuckled hands and, for a man of his height, a thick neck. Clyde used to wrestle (he calls it wrassle) when he was young. Probably he could still make a very good appearance on the mat.

His voice is low, steady.

"Velma Colter was boarding at the Thompson place, just a short distance from our home and real close to the schoolhouse. My folks had known her folks when they lived over at Rockford. That's not a town, it's just a community in the country. But I didn't know Velma except to say Hi to her; though my older brother, Barry, knew her real well. I guess she was a freshman or sophomore about the time Barry was a senior. He never had dates with her or anything like that."

He said, "The Thompsons were kind of worried about her coming home after dark, as she took to doing when days got shorter in winter. Mr. Thompson told her, 'You better get over here to our place before dark, or else stay there at the schoolhouse and I'll come and fetch you.' But you know how some girls are: not a care in the world, nothing to be scairt of. It couldn't happen to them."

We were sitting in the LeBoeuf restaurant in Kansas City, and it was early evening. I didn't know what Clyde planned on ordering for dinner, because it wasn't time to order yet; we sat with drinks. But I'd heard that the LeBoeuf was noted for its steaks, and that was what I planned to have.

It's a quiet place and, if you're back in an alcove as we were, sounds in the rest of the establishment are muted and come as from a distant planet.

Clyde studied the sliced fruit in his old-fashioned and frowned in concentration. I had the notion that this drink was his particular crystal sphere into which he gazed and saw the Past, complete with ragged cornstalks in fields which had been hogged down instead of having the fodder cut.

Winter twilight . . . alone a girl is walking the road. A man watches her. . . .

Martland said, "Gunn was there on Monday afternoon, the day before. Maybe that wasn't the first time. The ground was soft. A hired-man had been plowing in a field pretty close to the scene, and he looked over and saw this man standing behind a big cottonwood tree. The cottonwood tree isn't there any more. Anyway, he observed this Negro just as he was preparing to take his team back to the barn. I think the hired-man started in that direction, to see what was what. But, before he could approach, Velma Colter came along the road, going toward the Thompsons'. Apparently she also saw the man behind the tree. She started to run.

"He didn't take out after her. She ran uphill toward the Thompsons'. Trouble was, when she got home, she failed to complain about any character who had been hanging around. She knew that Mr. Thompson would bawl her out for staying so late at school and not waiting for him to come and escort her home.

"So she didn't say anything. And the next day Gunn was back again."

I asked Clyde if there was any doubt in his mind about Gunn's having been the perpetrator.

"Not the slightest doubt. There were several clues. First, some kids were going home from school after Velma let them out—I guess that was a little before four o'clock, on Tuesday—and they were frightened by what they said was a bad-looking colored man in a duck coat and cap. Well, Raymond Gunn was wearing hunting clothes and heavy overshoes—he wore them every day—and he left his marks in the mud there by that tree. The tracks said *Double Wear*. That was what was stamped on the bottom of the overshoes: kind of a trade name. And the way they were scuffed and worn—It showed just like a fingerprint. What do they call these things—moulages? I guess police officers didn't go in much for that sort of work so early in the game. But someone was thoughtful enough to take up that chunk of mud, when they first started investigating, and they put it in an ice-box. Later, when it was hard and solid, they could make a plaster cast.

"Those same overshoes were standing on the rear stoop of Gunn's father's house, when Gunn was arrested.

"Then also there was the matter of the murder weapon. It hadn't been found, and was certain to have blood on it unless scrubbed thoroughly. Gunn had blood on his coat. He told his father that it was from some rabbits he shot. But, when questioned by the police, he confessed before very long. They went right to the place where he'd thrown the murder weapon. There it was, lying at a lonely point about half a mile diagonally northeast of the schoolhouse, the way he'd traveled when he was going home. He carried the stick along with him—of course it was dark—and threw it in the brush. But he knew about where he'd thrown it, so it was easy enough to discover."

Clyde said, "Oh, yes. He retracted his confession after they took him down to St. Jo and Kansas City for safe-keeping. But lots of murderers do that. He tried to implicate another coon named Shike Smith. He said that he just *held* the girl—held Velma down on the floor—while Shike did the rest of it. Then, another time, he said all he did was stand at the door like a sentinel, and watch to see whether anyone was coming. It seemed to me that that was just as bad as actually doing the job yourself."

Clyde had eaten all the fruit in his old-fashioned except the slice of pineapple, and now he took it out and ate that, and pushed his glass away from him with a maraschino cherry still in it.

"I never eat the cherries. I guess most men don't. Have you noticed that? Most men don't eat the cherry in an old-fashioned. They just leave them. Too sweet."

He clasped his hands together, squeezed them convulsively, then drew his hands apart and looked at them. His patient eyes came up to meet my gaze.

"Look. I think you know how it is. When you're young and impressionable, you get something on your mind, and it stays with you. You keep examining it, trying to learn more about the whys and wherefores, and sometimes you don't get any place, not even years later. This thing truly haunted me because I was a witness. I don't know whether it haunted everyone who saw it or not. I scarcely ever spoke about it with my brother Barry afterward. Course, we were six-seven years apart in age, so we weren't especially thick at the time. We had our own interests, went our separate ways, especially when we were gone from home. With our own age groups, as they say nowadays.

"But this thing—I mean what happened later in January— Hell, the whole business, far as that goes. It stayed with me. I couldn't get it out of my mind, not for months or years. Never did, in fact. I remember one time a lot of Japs got flushed out of a cave. Flame-throwers had been directed down in there, and they came out screaming and on fire. They couldn't make it very far. But, you know, I wanted to scream right along with those Japs. Because it brought the tragedy back to me again."

I prompted him by asking, "You say children were frightened by a man they saw on Tuesday?"

"Yes. They scuttled right home and said, 'Wow, that was a bad-looking man!' I don't know why someone didn't do something about it then and there. I mean, go out and do a little patrolling. If we'd been living close at hand, and children had come into our house with a story like that, why— Pa or Barry or I would have headed right for that school. But nobody did. Except the bad-looking man."

"Clyde, according to the press, she had remained at the school to correct examination papers. Is that right?"

"Undoubtedly. Christmas vacation would be coming along pretty soon, and they were probably having examinations. When I went to that same school—before I entered high school, before Velma was there as teacher—there seemed to be nothing in winter except examination, examination, examination. But, by 1930, it so happened that there weren't many families with small children in the neighborhood. Other kids had grown bigger and were going in to Maryville to high school and— Some families moved away, and so on. There were only, I think, five regular scholars at the school, and already there'd been a lot of talk about closing it.

"It was closed all right. Those little kids who ran up the road that night—Tuesday, December 16th, 1930—were the last students at Garrett. Ever."

He remembered one thing in particular: a Chicago newspaper man named Jake Lingle had been murdered by gangsters a short time before these happenings in Maryville, and the Nation's papers were full of discussions of the Lingle case. People read them avidly, as they'd always done with Chicago gangster details. Then along came Maryville and pushed Lingle completely off the pages.

As the crime became reconstructed, it was believed that Velma Colter corrected examination papers, and later devoted herself to making Christmas decorations on the blackboard. After that she'd started to get some coal, to have it ready for Wednesday morning. Jack Frost was an unpleasant winter companion in those thin wooden schoolhouses. Teacher had to be fire-builder, unless some big boy felt competent to take over the job, and was willing to arrive early.

From an examination of the scene it appeared that Velma took the coal bucket and walked to the front door. Her assailant was waiting for her.

Later one fact emerged from which her friends and surviving relatives might glean a shred of comfort. She was dead before the sexual attack took place. She'd tried to defend herself with a broom, the broom lay with its handle broken off. Then she was bludgeoned to death.

Farmer Thompson became alarmed when Velma didn't show up at the house. It was deep dark by that time. He hurried down to the school, and there she was.

The perpetrator told later—quite calmly, he was said to have related it—that she was moaning and semi-conscious after he'd first lammed her over the head. She begged, as wounded people do, for water. In response the murderer smashed her skull. No more fuss about that drink-a-water business!

The killer, after he'd settled his own necrophilic desires— He'd used his club—

"He used the club for a penis," said Clyde. "She was pretty badly chewed up."

That first night they tried bloodhounds; but since they possessed no article of clothing belonging to the killer, and owing also to the condition of thawed midwinter earth, bloodhounds had nothing to contribute.

Raymond Gunn was a suspect from the start because of his previous record. They began picking up suspects and interviewing them, not many hours after the girl was killed. Gunn's confession came on Thursday. Once the murder weapon had been discovered, it was a case of rushing him down to St. Jo as fast as possible.

"They brought him here to Kansas City a little later on. The NAACP took an active interest in the case, and they were going to hire a lawyer to defend him when he was tried. Having welshed out of his confessions previously given, by that time Gunn was saying that he was only a more or less innocent party to the crime. . . . Yes, somehow he'd got blood upon his clothing. . . . Well, he *was there*, but it was another Negro who really did the job. Yes, he saw it. No, he didn't see it. Yes, he held the girl down. No, he didn't hold her down. All that sort of double-talk.

"A change of venue was sought. But he had to be arraigned in Nodaway County no matter where the trial took place. They were quiet about bringing him back to Maryville; no public announcement was made. Still, the word got around. Saturday night it was believed that he was being held in the vault at the Farmers Trust Company, and then he'd be brought to the courthouse for arraignment on Monday morning. I heard some of the talk that was going around, not all of it. Barry was pretty close-mouthed, though I'd overheard him talking with friends and neighbors. He didn't talk much to Pa. They'd all quit speaking whenever I came to join a group."

Clyde asked, "Mind if I have another drink?"

"I was just about to order. How's your capacity?"

"Right good. Even now that I'm past fifty. I grew up in a Prohibition household, and my mother was a wheel in the WCTU. I never had a drink, actually, until after I joined the Corps. I think, though, this time I'll take bourbon on the rocks."

We ordered, the drinks came, I smoked my pipe. Clyde isn't a smoker. He merely played with the cold ice-filled glass, turning it round and round and watching the bourbon pale gradually as ice melted.

"Church was a queer place on Sunday when we all went, as we always did. Everybody seemed pretty abstracted. The preacher used as his text something about *Whosoever shall kill shall be in danger of the judgment*, but I doubt that the lesson sank very deeply into the congregation's minds. Once again grown folks were muttering among themselves. We kids were eager to hear what was going on, and some of the boys—even some younger than I was—declared that they knew the whole business. Just what had been planned, and everything.

"Monday morning—that was January 12th—Barry and I got up early to start with our chores, and Pa came a little later. He'd had a lot of teeth pulled out that month, and wasn't feeling too spry. He'd been poisoned from the infected teeth, and the doctor warned him to take it easy. Barry and I did the bulk of the chores.

"We had two cars in the family, besides a truck with a homemade body which Barry and I had built onto a chassis and engine we got hold of. A Hudson. Also we had a real old Chalmers touring car, big heavy thing, and it had a cut-out on it. Boy, would that cut-out roar when you opened it! I used to like to open the cut-out when I drove to school and home again. That is, on country roads I'd open it up, and make The Big Noise. In Maryville proper the police said they'd pinch any of us kids who went roaring around, so we had to watch our step.

"I went up and changed to my school clothes, soon as I'd had breakfast, but when I came downstairs Barry was still there. I half believed he might have lit out and gone to town before that. But no, our other car, a brand-new Ford, had to stay at the farm in case Pa got another hemorrhage from his teeth, and had to go to the doctor. He'd already suffered a couple of hemorrhages.

"Barry says, 'I guess I'll ride in to town with you, Clyde.' He came just in his work clothes: overalls and one of those sheepskin jackets, the kind they used to have with a big collar.

"I wore my brand-new mackinaw, practically every color of the rainbow, over my school pants and school sweater. I started driving to town, and about halfway there I said to Barry, 'I'm not going to school. I'm going to flink.' You remember that used to be slang for not going to school? Not to be confused with 'flunk.' My son and daughter tell me nowadays that it's merely 'cutting classes.' But, boy, you didn't cut classes at Maryville High without making a swift trip to the principal's office afterward. Still I thought it would be worth it.

"Barry says, 'Where you going to go?' I says, 'I'm going to come along with you.'

" 'No you're not.'

"We argued about it for a while. Finally he gave in and said, 'O.K. You can came along, but stand away off to one side. Don't you try to mix up in anything.' I promised that I wouldn't.

"When we got down by the courthouse, there were more people around there than I'd ever seen before. You looked at the cars that were jammed in around town: many were from other counties. Seemed to be folks over from Bethany and Albany and Tarkio and Grant City, and up from St. Jo and Mound City, and a lot down from Iowa too.

"I didn't know anything about mobs because I'd never seen a mob before. This looked like an awful quiet one. They spread around in groups, chatting here and there, and watching the courthouse. Once in a while you'd hear some fellow say, 'How long are we going to have to wait for that God damn nigger, anyway?' But if there was anybody up on a soap-box I never happened to witness it.

"We'd heard of course about the National Guard being mobilized. One company was all: our howitzer company. But they weren't deployed, they weren't guarding the courthouse.

"Sheriff England had offered public statements about how no one must try to seize the prisoner, and everybody was entitled to a fair trial, no matter how wicked his crime. Naturally we younger folks had heard about lynchings and read about prisoners being kidnapped from officers who were guarding them. Somehow we didn't believe it could happen in Maryville. Also I'd run into a bunch of friends—they were all flinking school too—and we stooged around in the background. Some of the boys were talking real big, some weren't talking at all. Then one of the guys suggested, 'Nothing's happening right now. Let's go sit in your car, Clyde, and have a smoke.' You see, it wasn't legal for us kids to smoke cigarettes; we were all around fourteen or fifteen. The marshal and teachers and our folks all took a mighty dim view of kids our age smoking cigarettes.

"We figured that the town's attention was centered around that east door of the courthouse, and we'd be safe. My car was parked in a vacant lot about a block off the main drag, and we went over there and sat in it. It was in between two high trucks, and no one could get a good look at us. We got out our Luckies or Bull Durham or whatever. Pretty soon we were all blowing smoke-rings, or trying to.

"All of a sudden we heard a lot of yelling. We were out of that

Chalmers in nothing flat. Threw away our cigarettes and sprinted for the courthouse. The mob had grabbed Gunn before we got there.

"It had been thought by some optimists that the prisoner would be marched to the courthouse surrounded by the MNG's. Rumors said—I guess they were correct—that the State Adjutant, General Adams, had come up from Jeff City on Sunday and had taken charge of the situation, far as the National Guard was concerned. The howitzer company was mobilized early Monday morning—all in uniform and provided with weapons. But they weren't at the courthouse. Governor Caulfield had told General Adams, allegedly, that he must order this company to protect the prisoner the moment the sheriff summoned him.

"Sheriff Harve England apparently thought that no necessity existed for the use of the Guards. He said that he never knew what was in the wind."

Clyde shook his head. "If the sheriff didn't know what was in the wind, then he was just about the only person in Nodaway County who didn't."

In another minute he added, "You know, down in St. Jo there was a sheriff named John Roach. One night, shortly after Gunn's confession and after he had been spirited to Buchanan County, a lynching party showed up at the jail. They were armed. Yelling, 'We want that nigger! Sheriff, open up the door or we'll break it down.' John Roach told them, 'Maybe you will be able to break it down. But the first man who comes through— He gets shot. Dead.'

"Probably you know what happened. Nobody came through that door. They knew that Roach meant business."

Clyde smiled. "Not all Missouri sheriffs were alike. Or *are* alike. Then, or now."

"Well, let's get back to Maryville. Sheriff England had the Negro handcuffed to him when his car drove up to the east door. The car was surrounded instantly, and they hauled Gunn out with the sheriff still attached to him. The sheriff was manhandled a little; he got a sprained back or arm in the fracas.

"They took the key away from Harve England and unlocked those handcuffs. By the time we kids reached the scene, the men had dragged Gunn clear over to the south side of the courthouse, and they were in a thick crowd around him, deciding exactly what they were going to do, and how; and who would do this and that.

Boys kept busting out of the crowd with eager faces, galloping to get to a telephone. 'Gotta call Pa. Gotta call Ma. Gotta call the folks and tell em to hurry up and get over to the Garrett school.'

"I heard Barry speak my name. I turned around, and he looked very tall and gaunt—but menacing, almost as if he might have a knife in his hand, ready to go for you. Actually I was scairt of him in that moment, and he was my own brother. 'Clyde,' he told me, 'you go ahead and take the car. They're going to walk him to the schoolhouse, and I'm going along.'

"There were running-boards on cars in those days. You ought to have seen us when I drove that Chalmers off the vacant lot. There were about ten guys packed in both seats of the car, and several of them holding girls on their laps; then more guys standing on the running-boards and hanging onto the sides of the car. We looked like Keystone Cops in those museum-piece movies they run at the art theatres. Once in a while we see one of them here in K.C. with Fatty Arbuckle and old actors like that. Except we weren't Keystone Cops, we were school kids. Frankly there didn't seem to be any cops around, though the traffic was really ferocious. People driving across fields and yards and gardens, driving like crazy.

"Fortunately I had sense enough to go straight west out of town before I tried to go south. In fact, I went away west of the easiest road I could have taken to get to the Garrett corner. Went way out west, then south, then back east again on a road that came in at the Garrett corner. Even so, wild-acting men and women were all over the place. We went past two-three cars in the ditch. There were a lot of minor accidents: drivers skidding around corners too fast, and hitting other cars. So on.

"The crowd at the schoolhouse was variously estimated at from two to three thousand people. Some said there were that many even before the arrival of the party who fetched Raymond Gunn along with them, walking. There must have been several hundred in that particular little escort party.

"I parked next to a windmill in the barnyard at a friend's farm, maybe half a mile from the school. We ran along a ditch the rest of the way. The kids had wanted me to drive closer, but I wouldn't do it: solid there at the corner, everybody milling around. Already men and boys were carrying stuff out of the schoolhouse itself. They had an awful job getting the piano out, but they managed to do it. Then there were desks and seats. You remember—the old-fashioned kind? Probably had them when you were a kid, if you went to school in a small town or country place."

I told him it was a county seat town, and we had those old desks.

He said, "I mean the ones with the desk part to keep your books in. Usually they had a little ink-well or a place for one, right up in the right-hand corner. Then, in front of *that* desk, and separated by a little ridge, there was a folding seat. And *your* seat was on the front of the desk of the kid who sat behind *you.*"

I said, "And if it was a girl who sat in front of you, and she had her hair in a braid, why then you could watch your chance and dip the tip end of her braid into the ink-well."

"Right," he said. "And if it was a boy who sat in front of you, you could fasten a pin on the front end of your shoe, and stick him through that crack where the seat folded, and still have both hands in plain sight on the desk. Like you were completely innocent."

We chuckled a little together.

"Another drink?"

He said, "Third and last."

"Want to order dinner now, Clyde?"

"Not unless you're in a hurry. I'd rather get it over and done with, first."

I filled my pipe again.

Martland said, "I don't know why I should consider those desks in such detail right now. But I can squint my eyes shut and see the desks being carried out. Fact is, I went inside and became one of the carrier-outers. Cause why? Cause I figured those desks were going to be stolen or lugged away somewhere, and if anyone was going to take my old desk, I wanted it to be *me*. I had things carved on it. After two months in that school—I mean when a new teacher came, after I was completely able to read and write— None of us liked her, and she kept a rubber hose—you know, white tubing like they use for enemas—and she'd double that hose up and beat the hell out of a kid who was bigger than she was. She was dynamite; but she was ornery about it, and didn't take much pity on some of the littler ones. She liked to bat them around. I bet if she'd still lived in Nodaway County in 1931 she would have been in the front rank, you might say, on that January day. But she was gone. I scratched MSIAOB right up at the top of my desk. Not very deep letters, but they were big, and they went down through all the coats of varnish, and would certainly be there even if the top of the desk had been varnished again. It meant, *Miss Sprunton is an old bitch*. Then, another year, when the desks had been moved around some, and I was a class or two ahead of where I'd been before, and by some fluke still sitting behind that same desk– I fell in love. She was a real dish, named Mathilde Frassinet. That was quite a mouthful for an eight- or ten-year-old to fall in love with, but I surely did. She was of French extraction, and had moved out to Maryville with her folks from over along the Mississippi River. She had kind of deep auburn hair that looked brown at times; and her eyelids would be half over her eyes when she looked at you in a certain way. Oh, her legs were rather thick; but her mouth was all pouty and squashy. Ever know a girl like that?" he asked suddenly.

"Yea. Yea."

"So you know what I mean. I couldn't think about anything else except Mathilde Frassinet, day or night. First chance I got, when Teacher was out on what she called a spring botany tour–that meant taking the scholars around the edges of the schoolyard, and everybody picking flowers– Then they'd bring them back inside, and we'd botanize them and hear about pistils and stamens.

"I'd sprained my ankle and had it bound up with tape and stuff, so I had a good excuse not to go on the botany walk. Instead I sat there and carved, very deep down into the wood, a heart. I put Mathilde's initials at the top and mine right underneath. MF and CM, surrounded by a nice heart. Then, with all that fresh cutting showing in the hard wood, I took a pencil and colored up the whole thing with graphite, so it wouldn't be so noticeable to Teacher. But it would be there forever and ever."

He said, "That was the desk I wanted to carry out and claim for my own. I never did find it.

"We got everything out of the schoolhouse, even the waterbucket. Everything. They even took off the metal gratings that were on the windows, so prowlers couldn't get in and steal things: they took those too.

"I went out into the schoolyard and looked around for my desk, and couldn't find it anywhere. There were the remains of some desks which had got broken up one way or another, and it could well have been one of those. In fact that yard was not very well kept up. Somebody should have come around to clean it but they hadn't. You know how it goes: a few kids playing, they'll bring all sorts of junk from here and there, and just let it lay. 'Leave it lay where Jesus flang it,' as the old types of camp meeting preachers were supposed to have said. I often heard Pa tell that one. He said that some woman had been overcome with religious emotion, and she let out an awful whoop, and then spraddled out full length on the ground. People started to pick her up, but the parson held up his hand and hollered, 'No. Leave her lay where Jesus flang her.'"

We thought that this deserved mild laughter, and uttered it, and then were silent.

"O.K. All of a sudden people yelled, 'Here he comes! There they come! They got him! They're bringing him!' Things like that. A young mother—I knew who she was, she didn't live very far from us— She had her little girl, holding her up so the kid could stand on one of those desks out in the yard. She kept calling the child by name. She kept saying, 'Lola Lou, there's that bad, bad man. That bad, bad black man. And those men are bringing him right over here. And you wait and see what they're going to do to *him,* because he was a *bad man.*' The little kid—she was just beginning to talk and repeat things—and she kept saying, 'Bah man?' kind of questioningly.

"Since I couldn't find my desk, I twisted my way through the crowd and got over where I could see farther, and observe the men who were bringing Raymond Gunn. Actually Gunn didn't have a great deal of clothing left on him. It had been torn loose in the process of nipping at him with pincers, like some of those characters had been doing. They'd brought him down cat-a-corner across the fields from town, maybe three miles in all. They picked the route that Gunn confessed to have traveled after he'd attacked Velma. He went diagonally up across that mile square south of the country club and northeast of the schoolhouse, where there were creeks and little bunches of underbrush. It was in one of those places that he'd tossed the blood-stained club that he used for—

"That was the way they brought him along. Some of them wanted to make him crawl the whole distance. There was one fellow who wanted to tear out his tongue. Some others wanted to use the pincers to pull off his balls, and mutilate him generally. But the bigger ones exerted enough discipline, so that they brought him down to the schoolhouse still able to talk, and in one piece.

"He was really running off at the mouth when he got there—babbling and raising his voice above its normal pitch. You know how darkies are apt to do when they get wild. Go up into the treble keys. . . . No, he hadn't committed that crime. Shike Smith did it really, and he—Gunn—was just there. Or he never knew a thing about it. He said he wanted mercy. The men said, 'Yeh, so did Velma. She asked for a drink of water, and what did you do? You brained her.' But it was all such a hubbub of yells and conversation and denials on the part of Gunn— It was just gabble-gabble, mutter-mutter, squeal-squeal, all mingled together.

"Several fellows had marched ahead, smashing down the fences to get through. It was mostly barbed-wire on wooden posts, much the same as we have today. I remembered the word *rabble:* we'd had that in high school in some historical connection, or maybe in Shakespeare, that same season. I thought, 'This is really a rabble. Except it's funny to think of a rabble being composed of so many people you know on sight, and some of whom you know better than that.' Sure—there were a lot whom I didn't know at all, and neither did anybody else. People from out of town, hard-boiled types. You know? Real sadistic. They always gather for a thing like this, and nobody knows quite who they are. But still they go around trying to boss everybody else."

I said to Clyde Martland, "Same thing today. In Newark—in Tampa, Detroit—name any place you want to name— They always say there are strange faces of people from out of town, people they didn't know."

"I know that's what the public is apt to say; but it was certainly true in Maryville."

He'd talked so much by this time that his voice was growing scratchy. He'd been selling insurance all day, too. Probably talking to clients, maybe even making a speech at a luncheon club. Clyde is one of the top fellows in his field. Not long ago he was made an honored member of the Millionaires' Round Table Club (or some such name) because he'd sold a million dollars' worth of life insurance within a year.

He asked, "You believe in hell?"

"In the orthodox manner? No. Do you?"

"I guess I did in 1931. I was pretty orthodox in religious belief up until World War II. Then things happened that changed me around. I became at least what I'd call an agnostic. You may remember how some chaplain used to go around preaching about how there were no atheists in fox-holes. He sure was mistaken about that."

Yes. But why the question about hell? I knew what Clyde was

about to relate, I'd read the newspaper accounts. Already I was trying to think of a quotation from Dante to be used when eventually I came to write this account of what some inelegant people referred to as the Maryville Campfire Girls' Marshmallow Roast. Trouble: I couldn't think of any quotation from Dante. I did think of one from Housman's *Last Poems*. I quoted it to Clyde.

And my dark conductor broke
Silence at my side and spoke,
Saying, 'You conjecture well:
Yonder is the gate of hell.'

Clyde scratched his head. "All right. Except there wasn't any dark fellow doing any conducting. The dark fellow was *conducted*. And how."

He said, "On the west side of the roof, patches of shingles were already being torn off. They had a lot of eager beavers crawling around up there; they wanted to get a draft, and that was the best way to do it. Also tearing shingles from the rafters gave them a place to hang onto, because the roof was built with quite a slant.

"At that school we kids used to play Ante, Ante Over: the old game where two bunches of players are running around on each side of the building. A guy yells *Ante, Ante Over*, and throws a ball over from the other side, clear across the roof. It gets into a game of rough-and-tumble tag.

"You see, it was the same roof where we'd done such innocent things as throwing a ball across. The thought that that roof sheltered whatever had gone on inside, in December, when Mr. Thompson found Velma on the floor, and saw what had been done to her— People were disturbed, there's no doubt about it. I don't think anyone should go around totally condemning any such people—I don't care how long ago it happened or how recently—unless they've endured a more or less similar experience. When a thing like that happens in your community, where nothing like it has ever happened before, you can't say who's going to emerge as— How would you say it?"

I suggested that we say, "You never know who's going to emerge as a saint or a devil," and Clyde agreed.

"In all that multitude there was not one single person wearing a mask. I recognized townspeople and farmers who were tearing off the shingles. One was a real good friend of my father. I recognized men who were tramping around in overshoes and overalls and winter jackets. I knew all sorts of them; and I saw who drove in, forcing a way through the crowd, using the horn on a truck, bringing gasoline. I saw them lifting off those big red cans. Yelling, 'You guys with lighted cigarettes, stay back there, now.'

"They took Raymond Gunn into the schoolhouse for a few minutes. I don't know whether they tried to get him to reënact the crime or not. Somebody said so, but that sounded fantastic. Anyway, he did continue that line about, 'It wasn't me. It was Shike Smith.' Then he said, 'Why don't we have a court of law? I demand one thing: you take me to a court of law.'

"He began to shriek, 'Mercy, mercy, *mercy!*' and this could be heard outside. They came out the door with him, almost on the dead run—I mean several men had hold of him, hustling him along, and they practically knocked over people when they came skooting out of there. They went to the west side of the building, and in no time at all were hauling him up across the roof. He'd quit screaming by that time."

"They chained Raymond Gunn to the ridge-pole. Some participants said those chains were given them by officers in town; also I heard that they used the handcuffs they took away from Sheriff Harve England. But I remember seeing one guy on the step of the schoolhouse, before they brought Gunn. He had a big tire-chain, like from a truck tire, and one of those bolt-cutters; he was chopping off the cross-links, making two big long chains out of it. But there's no way now of knowing if that was actually used to fasten Gunn to the roof.

"The prisoner could move his hands and arms. He was sort of waving to the mob, waving right over the ridge-pole toward the biggest throng which stood on the east. Did I tell you that there were lots of girls and women, and little children and babies? Oh, sure: you remember Lola Lou. Her mother was holding her up in her arms, because those masses of people had been forced back from the schoolhouse to what was thought to be a safe distance; so the kid couldn't stand on a desk any more. The mother was saying, 'Lola Lou, there's that bad, bad man up there. You just wait a minute; you'll see what happens to *him*.' But perhaps the little girl didn't behave too well through the whole rumpus. Later, when the crowd was just standing around waiting for– I mean after it was over; the crowd was still there; I heard that same mother saying to the same child, 'Lola Lou, if you do that again, Mamma's going to *smack* you.' Apparently the kid had gotten restless, or was maybe upset by what she had seen."

I said, "Could be. Could be that she was upset. Clyde, how did they touch it off?"

"They had the inside of the building splashed with gasoline, and a lot more poured on the roof. All over Gunn, too, for all I know. Anyhow he'd torn off his remaining clothing by that time. He must have had some idea that burning clothes would stick to his body and prolong the agony. He could have been right. We received a briefing once in the Marines, when it was thought we were going to proceed somewhere by air, although we didn't go that way–we went by ship. But they told us that if we ever got in a gasoline fire, and it was hopeless–you know: pinned in the wreckage or something–just to breathe real deeply two or three times and it would all be over. I don't know who ever figured that one out; but it did sound like it would work.

" 'Get back, everybody. Get back. You're not back far enough. This thing will go off like a bomb.' They'd thrown lighted matches and more lighted matches, and the matches went out. Then there came a detonator that kept burning all the way–probably a ball of paper. Great big hollow sound of gasoline catching fire. It doesn't go *bang* like ordinary high explosives. It's flash and gasses mingled together, a kind of ringing dishpanny noise. Or like a big dog going *woof*. Biggest dog that ever lived and then some. There was one enormous puff of black smoke and gas and flame. Crowd yelled the way they do when there's a public fireworks display, and those bombs go up; they crack and burst like harmless shrapnel away up high. All the little lights go *rap*, *rap*, *rap*, *puff*, *puff*. There's green stars and yellow stars and red stars, dripping down together in one instant, and the whole crowd says *Ahhhhh*."

I thought, FIREWORKS. NODAWAY COUNTY'S OWN SPECIAL BRAND. PATENTED 1931.

"That's what it sounded like," said Martland. "Except I heard one man crying in an affected falsetto tone, like a girl– 'Good*bye*, Raymond.' Someone else hollered, 'This ought to teach you a lesson.' There were a few halfwits who laughed at that.

"However, by and large, after the first blast of smoke and flame, an impressive thing was the silence, especially among grown men who stood watching. You could see their jaws set and their eyes narrowed down, and they were clenching their fists. There was one neighbor of ours who was supposed to have a weak heart, and I kept looking over at him. Wouldn't have been surprised to see him flop right then and there, because of so much excitement and feeling."

He repeated slowly, "Yes, there was a lot of feeling. Lot of feeling."

"Must have been."

"Yes. Feeling."

After a few minutes the black smoke lifted and they could see the man on the roof.

"Remember how it is when you go to a wienie roast and cook a wienie on a stick? The correct idea is to find some nice little corner above some coals, where you can broil your sausage slowly and not get it too scorched. But there are always a lot of careless cooks who stick the thing right into the flames. Remember how *those* wienies look. They turn white right away; they're not cooked through, still raw underneath; but the surface is pale and pebbled-looking.

"That's the way Gunn was, after that first burst of flame. He had really turned white. He did a little more twisting around than you'd expect. I heard a shriek, but I couldn't make out whether it came from him or somebody in the mob. Maybe he could have screamed if his lungs and throat hadn't suffered too severely as yet. But it didn't take long. His head twisted against what was left of the roof, and then sort of sagged, and he was motionless. The bulk of the gasoline had been consumed in that early explosion, and now there was just wood burning. And a man burning on top of the wood.

"I tried to think about Joan of Arc and how she'd been burned at the stake—we'd had her in high school the year before—but I didn't get very far with that. Nevertheless it would continue to haunt me when I was somewhat older, and after we'd moved to K.C., after Pa had to give up farming. I joined the Order of DeMolay. That's a kind of Masonic organization for boys, sponsored by the Knights Templar. In the DeMolays we have some— Well, it's secret work, as I now recall, so I can't tell you about that.

But at least we do study the life and death of Jacques DeMolay, who was burned at the stake. So when it came to considering Jacques DeMolay, I would always see Raymond Gunn before my eyes instead. That was sure far-fetched, because DeMolay was a good man, and didn't go around butchering little country school teachers."

"How long, Clyde, did it take for the structure to burn?"

"Say fifteen or twenty minutes. He must have remained up there on the skeleton of the roof that long. Then those boards gave way, and down he went kerwhack into the flames below. Certainly he was dead long before that. I guess really that gasoline must have turned out to be one of the kindest things they could have done to him. Because it hastened his death.

"And it was queer: everybody seemed to stand around, feeling there was something they must do, and yet not knowing what it was, or whether it had all been done. I remember one man—I won't mention who he was—who stood right close. He was with a group of— Well, you could say they were rather important people in the town and county—they weren't riffraff by any means. I heard him say, 'It's a terrible, terrible thing. Too bad it had to be done.'

"I went around hunting up the kids who'd ridden out with me, because I didn't want to leave them—especially the girls—high and dry out there in the country several miles, and make them walk into town. I found the girls and a couple of the fellows, but couldn't find the others. Oh, yes indeed—I did find two others, but they said they weren't going to go along with me. They wanted to stay until it was cool enough to get into those ashes and look for souvenirs. I figured that *souvenirs* meant what was left of Raymond Gunn, and I wasn't interested in any such collecting. We said, 'Well, be seeing you. See you tomorrow at school.' Somebody else laughed and said, 'See you in church.' We walked down the road to where I'd left the Chalmers in that barnyard. There were so many cars blocking the driveway, and actually blocking the road in front, that we couldn't get out of there for a good ten minutes.

"One of the girls—she was a real noisy type and always shooting off her mouth— She kept saying, 'Boo-woo-woo! That really gave me the willies. Huh, Clyde? Didn't it give you the willies? Huh?'

"The other girl didn't say anything. She was a more intelligent sort, and she would not speak one single word. I think she was suffering from shell-shock. She just stared straight ahead, and every now and then I'd glance over—those two girls were in the front seat with me—and she was crowded in beyond the talkative one. She stared straight ahead, and seemed very pale.

"On my way back home from Maryville the roads were a lot clearer. I parked again and went over to take another look. People were still ringed around, but the ashes weren't yet cool enough for them to go into them, digging for souvenirs. One guy had a long pole, and he was trying to drag out some pieces of chain which he could see in there. In the schoolyard, people were taking any other kind of souvenirs they wanted, had taken a lot already. They actually pulled that piano to pieces. Oh, it was an old one but— And those desks: they were gone, too. Or going.

"Afterward I did see several of the souvenirs. I saw a couple pieces of bone that the owner swore had been part of Raymond Gunn. There was one fellow had two teeth, and a gold filling had melted and run out of one of the teeth. It must have been in at least some sort of very hot fire, even if it didn't belong to Raymond Gunn. Guy said that he was going to have those teeth fastened on his watch-fob, but I don't know whether he ever did."

Clyde Martland said, after a pause, "Not much more to be told. As you were informed quite correctly, I was there. I made a sort of study about the incident, and it stayed with me through the years. But sometimes you can study and study and you won't get anyplace."

"Tell me something, Clyde. I'd like your considered opinion. If everything had happened the same way, as to the crime and confession—bloody club and all and all— And Raymond Gunn had been a *white* man— Do you think they would have burned him on the roof of the Garrett school?"

Martland made faces and frowned and shut his eyes and rubbed his face with his hand, the way many men do when they're trying to find an answer to the unanswerable. "They would have taken him from the sheriff and lynched him," he said. "But somehow it seemed a worse crime because Gunn was colored."

"You haven't answered my question. Burned him, then? With gasoline? Up on that roof?"

He said, "Mack, I just don't know. Just—don't—know."

The waiter brought us our menus, we studied them seriously.

Clyde lifted his eyes from the menu. "Does a story like I've just been telling— Does it make you sick at your stomach? Take your appetite away?"

"No," I said, "not after a few minutes. There are lot of cruel and wicked things in this world, and sometimes they do make you sick. But you have to toughen yourself and go ahead and keep eating."

"Same as in a war," he said. "You still get hungry."

"Yes, you do. Want to have a steak? LeBoeuf is really noted for them, they tell me."

"Oh, yes," he said. "That's perfectly correct. There are several good steak places in town, and some prefer one and some another. But this place is real good. I think I'd like to have the strip sirloin."

"I will, too."

Clyde instructed the waiter, "Charred on the outside and red inside. But not blue, not super-super-rare."

The waiter nodded. "Yes, sir. Charred and rare to medium-rare." He looked at me and I ordered, "Same way for me, please."

I started questioning Clyde about the Marine Corps, and asking whether by any chance he knew some people I knew who had been on Guadalcanal.

Over in Trenton a little shoeshine man, in his coop just off the main street, gave every impression of having been a community fixture for years. Sometimes his wife came in there and sat, apparently just to keep him company; and other folks would drop in, seemingly not to get shines, only to loaf, and chat about old days.

While he was working on my shoes, I asked the man if he remembered what happened in Maryville. (At that time I was starting an initial check-up and, as told previously, couldn't even identify the year.)

"Oh, yes. I remember that."

"Can you tell me the year in which it occurred?"

They ventured opinion but no one agreed. The guesses went as far back as 1925, and all the way up to World War II. Belatedly the shoeshine man realized that I was a stranger. You could see suspicion oozing into his face as he looked up and asked why I was inquiring about the Maryville affair.

"I'm something of an historian," I told him. "And writing about Missouri."

"Where you from, mister?"

"Sarasota, Florida."

"Had any trouble down there with niggers? I mean—you know—like nowadays? Modern trouble?"

"A little. Windows smashed; looting, fire-bombing, Coke bottles thrown at cars. Some of our colored people insist that out-of-towners came in and stirred up the whole business."

"I read something in the papers about Tampa a while back," he said, and the others nodded knowingly.

"Yes. It was pretty rough in Tampa for a few nights. And in St. Petersburg, later on."

Little old shoeshine man said that he knew how he'd handle it. I asked how he'd handle it.

"Like this." He dropped his brushes and lifted up his hands, and made with sub-machinegun pantomime. He sprayed around the room with imaginary bullets, making machinegun noises with his mouth while he did so.

Boldly. "That's the way I'd handle it."

Well, I said, that was certainly one way of handling it.

"Mister, it's the *only* way, believe me. After that Maryville thing—I tell you, they had the quietest gang of niggers over at Maryville you ever seen. Yes, sir, and all around here. All the niggers was quiet, after that." He bowed to his small audience, and bent his head and continued brushing.

. . . At home my shoes are shined by M. C. Byrd, our present gardener, who's been with us over twenty years. He is a veteran of World War II, and saw service in Mediterranean areas and in France. Sometimes we stand together for a time, talking about World War II. Neither one of us bothers to make machinegun sounds. We've both heard plenty of those.

Maryville is a right pretty town. Oh, naturally you have to put up with the roadside signs.

REAL BROASTED CHICKEN.

(Once upon a time. REAL BROASTED RAYMOND GUNN.)

There are so many attractions that it's difficult to enumerate them. Near the country club there's a gorgeous horse farm named Faustiana. You feel impelled to stop and park, and sit blissfully enjoying mares and colts and the tasty grass which feeds them. Then you drive on over hills into the town itself. Maryville is all hills and valleys, and that makes for charm too.

Alma Mater! Alma Mater!
Tender, fair and true;
Grateful sons with love unfailing
All their vows renew.

Welcome to Northwest Missouri State College Park. They dropped the *Teachers* in 1949. It resembles many other bustling smaller colleges over the Nation: people still living in trailers, some of them even working in trailers. Or so we assume—the trailers are here. Educational enterprise in a state of flux, but still a state of expansion and upbuilding.

Two baby skyscrapers which we take to be residences: Franken Hall is the first, Phillips Hall the second. I don't know why I should be of the opinion that Franken Hall is the women's residence and Phillips the men's, but I am. Probably because there comes recollection of a clever woman playright of a good many years past, name of Rose Franken. [Author's note, months later: Mr. Jack B. Gray, Jr., director of the NWMSC news bureau, says I was correct.]

It might be fitting to go into Franken Hall or Phillips Hall, if time permitted and if such intrusion were allowed, and ride up to the top floor on the elevator, and then look through windows which must provide a view of the countryside west and south of Maryville proper . . . there it is. Old Missouri landscape, groves and meadows dreaming in afternoon sun. A faint bluish haze, and it's hot, and people wish it would rain, maybe it'll rain sometime during the night. Then in the morning you'll hear the mourning doves burbling their contented un-mourning but happy golden morning reassurance, and catbirds will meow in the thickets. Once in a while a stray robin may venture an early yodel, but that's before the sun comes.

In imagination we linger on that high place, and try to identify a certain portion of empty pastureland, murky in southwest mist. Velma Colter was a student at this same college long ago. And then, years before her, there was the other girl student, the first one assaulted by Raymond Gunn. Well, maybe not the first girl he ever assaulted, but at least the first one shown on his record. That's the one he did time for. And got out early because of good behavior.

. . . What's the purpose in young folks coming to NWMSC, anyway? Ah, it's what brings most students to most colleges: they're trying to get ready to work and live. During this period there will become more recognizable a great many questions which might have provoked some of them since first they could think; but which became apparent to others only when the questions were brought up in evening discussions or in the classroom. Or maybe when they really started in to *read* (at college).

In our age many of those problems seem to concern race or violence, or racial violence, or violent racism, however you went to put it. I'm afraid no one will find any of the answers he seeks by merely gazing out of the window, and trying to identify the spot where the Garrett schoolhouse used to stand, and where one winter morning there was a fire. And where, in gloomy dusk twenty-seven days earlier, a girl had found a distinct variety of doom fit only to be whispered.

Savagery begets savagery. There we were, there we still are.

Some atrocious deeds were done in Missouri in centuries past, especially during the reign of Bill Anderson and Quantrill and their ilk, whether the mobs of mounted freebooters professed to Union or to Confederate sympathies. Houses were burned and sometimes people were burned in them. Some people were burned, just plain burned, without being burned up in buildings—or on top of them.

Then, in this decade, we have critters like Bill Coleman. He was the ex-convict—pronounced incorrigible from childhood on—who went into a bar in Moberly on the 16th of February, 1968, and splashed gasoline all over the room. A few of the folks got out, but Bill managed to fry twelve of them.

The Maryville lynching was not the most brutal episode in the world's history by any means. Nor in Missouri's.

Could it happen again? *Oh no*, you try to soothe yourself in question and in answer. And— *Oh yes*, *it could*, your hard-core sense of realism and your experience tell you.

Close your eyes against wistfulness of a countryside with fair blush of lavender weeds, and hybrid corn grown tall, and cattle and horses grazing. Listen again to Clyde Martland's recounting.

Except of course that isn't his real name. Nor is Miss Sprunton's name the true one. Nor Mathilde Frassinet's. Nor Lola Lou's. . . . Remember? "Bah man?"

13. Tales of a .38 Special

Late one amiable afternoon I was driving alone, going south on a back road in Holt County, musing and dreaming and remembering, and being happy that there were so many things pleasurable to remember. Such slow procedure seemed a bliss, and the traffic was minimal. I didn't even have to touch my brake pedal when unexpectedly a car turned out of the driveway leading down from a substantial farmhouse, and crawled along ahead of me.

Regular farm family car, a Pontiac, shiny under its dust. As I came up behind them, I could see that the occupants were two: a young woman driving, a heavy-set man sitting beside her. He appeared to be talking to the lady steadily. He wore a red-and-black checked shirt and a small cap. The gal didn't turn around once, but the man kept looking back at me.

Then red light flashed at the left rear: she was signaling for a left turn, and I slowed accordingly. Down across the roadside ditch she went, and along a barely discernible cart path leading into a field where the gate stood open. No vehicles had traveled there lately, for the Pontiac had to inch along, crushing through masses of weeds. It stopped well down the side of the field near trees and shrubbery beyond the fence. Neither man nor woman got out while I was still in sight of them. Odd.

I drove on, up out of the river valley, winding around among hills, and still thinking, "How odd." Started playing with that little scene in my mind, not knowing what had happened, or how that couple came to be driving through weeds at the boundary of a lowland field. I began to figure out how it *might* have happened.

This is one unpleasant by-product of the fact of experiencing active police duty in your life. Once a cop, always a cop. You think in a cop's terms. Not exactly what *is* happening, but what *might* be happening.

. . . Innocent-looking youth standing in a doorway at a darkened street corner. He could be a high school kid waiting for a late bus after his date; but also he might have a switch-blade knife in his hand, ready to go for the first luckless wayfarer who looked as if he or she couldn't ward off such attack.

. . . Well-dressed woman who moves with staggering gait and soon leans against a wall for support. Yes, could be that she'd had too many martinis in a nearby bar. But also she might be an epileptic, or a diabetic suffering from insulin shock, and in desperate need of immediate medical attention.

. . . That door looks locked, but you'd better go and try it—see if it *is* locked.

. . . A pimply character sidles into an apartment building entrance ahead of you. Yielding to a question, he mumbles that the superintendent sent for him to fix some venetian blinds on the fifth floor. Maybe so. However, let's check with the super and see whether he actually did send for this fellow.

Thus.

Think of a tidy modern Missouri farm kitchen, and the young wife was there alone, checking a roast or loaf in the oven, and wishing that her husband didn't prefer things too well done— Suddenly she heard a step, and looked around. There stood a man in a red-and-black shirt, man she had never seen before. He had a gun in his hand. "Get your car keys, lady. You're coming along with me. Don't yell or I'll kill you."

She didn't want to be shot, neither did she want to be kidnapped; but she feared that if she didn't go with him, he might discover her young daughter asleep with a sick headache on the sofa a room or two beyond. And then— He might take her daughter too. If she went along quietly she might be able to talk him out of it. And—

She took her car keys and went outside. He said, "Get in your car. Get behind the wheel, and drive like I tell you." He had the gun against her side.

When they turned out of the driveway there was a big blue car coming along slowly behind them. The man wondered who that was. That was the reason he kept looking back.

Better to get off the road, even a quiet county road like this. He said, "O.K., sweetie. I see a place ahead leading down there into those weeds. Turn slowly, now . . . real slow . . . don't you yell or try any stunts. . . . That's right, that's a good girl. Take it easy across the ditch. Keep on driving. . . . O.K., that other car's gone past now. We'll just sit here a minute until he's out of sight. Then you and I are going in those woods and—"

They're all over the country, they're all over a lot of countries. You have only to glance at the paper or listen to the news, and you read them Loud and Clear. Same thing happens in France, England, Germany, Italy; happens pretty nearly everywhere, I guess. Happens on *autobahn* and *autostrada*, happens on the big toll roads and Interstates. A psycho, as the cops call him, prowled the Pennsylvania Turnpike and murdered man after man. They were truck drivers who happened to have pulled off at specified rest areas where they could stretch out and sleep. Then would come driving the psycho with his gun, and the truck drivers wouldn't wake up.

There's that fellow who went into the nurses' home in Chicago in 1966. How many of those nurses did he kill, anyway? Eight? . . . And the young man on the Texas water tower, shooting away as if life depended upon it; but it wasn't life, it was only death. Multiple, multiple death.

There seemed nothing absurd in what I was doing now: hunting for a good place to turn around. Found one in a wide gravelly margin at another farm. I headed back north and west, returning to that soy bean field, and shall we say more speedily than I had gone away from it. . . . My .38 Special meant a lot of things to me. I thought of the 23rd Precinct, and thought of Jakey and Bill, and the three thousand hours we rode together . . . streets, roof tops, basements, warehouses, sidewalks, subways, bars, hospital emergency rooms.

I looked at the walnut butt of that S & W again, sticking out of its black holster, and thought of those missions over Korea— Sure, they issued .45s on the hardstand just before we climbed into the airplane, but I can't hit the broad side of a barn with a Colt .45 Automatic. I can shoot with a revolver. So this one went along to Songju, to Wonsan, to Pyongyang, to Chechon and all those other places we went to. It rode so long in that little sweaty corner beneath my left arm where the chute-harness made a convenient pocket to drop the gun in, along with an extra loading of cartridges tied in a black sock– Got rusty, oil or no oil, and our armorer had to re-blue it for me. You've heard, maybe: the crews used to say, "Be sure to save the last bullet for yourself, if we go down." They meant just that. There were some unnice things happening to airmen who found themselves on the ground in North Korea.

. . . Moment I got back to those soy beans and those people, I felt a great warmth of gratitude to God. Everything was all right. The woman backed her car slowly through the weeds, returning to the road; and the man was walking beside the car, the better to guide her because there wasn't much of a track. They needed rain terribly, and the wheels hadn't sunk down into soft earth because the ground was dry and hard. . . . All serene. But I didn't feel a bit foolish, because it could have been the other way, the way I'd thought possible. I would do it over again, same way, if the same thing happened tomorrow.

Naturally they were curious at seeing me back there again. I waited until Mrs. Somebody had backed up to the edge of the road. Then said, "Forgive me, but I didn't know just what was going on. I saw a man and a woman in a car, and then saw you turn off and go down there toward those trees, and I started worrying about it. That's why I came back."

They were both laughing by this time, though they didn't seem annoyed. The woman explained, "We just decided, on the spur of the moment, to come down and have a look at our soy beans."

"How are they doing?"

"Not bad," said the farmer. "Not bad at all, considering how much we need rain."

We surveyed the cloudy horizon, and mentioned hopefully together that rain might come that very night.

Now I should have to drive up to their driveway to turn around and head south again. "Well, I'll get out of your way. Sorry I bothered you."

The woman called after me. It was something I hadn't really expected to hear, and there was sincerity in her tone. She called, "Thank you. Thank you *very much*." The last two words were italicized in emphasis. I said proudly to myself that I had done my Good Deed for the day.

Once a Boy Scout, always a Boy Scout. Troop 2, Webster City, Iowa, 1916.

Wandering on rearmost roads, as Irene and I did so much of the time, we were usually far removed from run-of-the-mill restaurants, or even truck stops, when hunger teased us at midday. As noted previously, the village hotel, with Uncle Jupiter to usher you in and wait table, and Aunt Jemima breading chops in the kitchen, is just about as extinct in Missouri as is the mastodon.

Also vanishing, if not already vanished, is the boarding house which used to satisfy the appetites of a town's loners. Take Mrs. Cuthright, the milliner who lived at the back of her shop, but who couldn't cook there, and didn't want to anyway; and the long-widowed lawyer, Mr. E. Ennis Pashton, who might be termed an ambulance-chaser (if the community had boasted an ambulance); and the Gerry sisters, Chlöe and Florence respectively, but called by all and sundry Klo and Flo. Their old family house was out on the edge of town, but they couldn't walk all that way home for their noon meal. They had the Singer Sewing Machine agency for the area, and also did a lot of hemstitching and such fancy stuff, on orders that came in to their little office-shop. But both were woefully fat; it was quite a task for them even to waddle to their place of business and home again at night. (They could have afforded a Model-T, but were too afraid of automobiles to learn how to drive.) Nor was their tendency toward embonpoint diminished by the fact that the boardinghouse keeper, Mrs. Herschfeld, excelled when it came to potato dumplings with ham hocks, baked sausage *mit* applesauce, pumpkin pies, home-fried doughnuts, crullers—

Oh, go ahead and eat some place else, if you want to keep your weight down!

It was a great moment when you drove into such a hamlet, inquired as to restaurant facilities, and received this answer: "Well, there's the Little Texas Cafe—that's just down there across from the Frisco freight depot. But, honest, it ain't very good. Most folks who want to eat a decent meal, they just go up to Mrs. Herschfeld's. See? It's that yellow house with the long porch, right up there a block from the bank. Go knock on the door, and ask if she's got room for two more at her dinner table. It's about ten after twelve now, and she usually starts serving right on the dot at twelve. You better hurry."

And, oh yes, Mrs. Herschfeld and her lame daughter Alba, and Emmy, the Negress who helped out– They were putting up things, all summer long. There wasn't any such animal as a deep-freeze or a food locker in those days. But, if you were lucky enough to be shown through that treasure-laden Fort Knox, the Herschfeld cellar, you'd see long racks near to bending under the weight of jars. Sliced peaches, pickled peaches, pickled pears, stewed tomatoes; and home-made chili sauce and home-made catsup; and dill pickles and mustard pickles and olive-oil pickles and chow-chow; and grape jelly and crabapple jelly and strawberry preserves; and sweet cherries and salted cherries and–

Enough, enough. The Mrs. Herschfelds have gone their toilworn, nutmeg-smelling way. Instead of alabaster, let us supplicate that the walls which now shelter them are made of sugar cookies, and the steps which lead up to their celestial quarters paved with pancakes. And they have spoons–long wooden spoons with which to stir, stir, stir–instead of the harps which they had supposed awaited them. Adroit angels run their errands. And mince-meat perfumes which issue from bubbling pots upon the golden range–

Cry quarter!

Thus we have knelt down to idolize some of the ancient boarding tables we used to find salted around the country. But have they all been supplanted by tasteful Holiday Juniors serving unbelievably tasty vegetable soup? Well, if there was a Mrs. Herschfeld in Maysville, DeKalb County, Missouri, she has been succeeded by a cafe just across from the courthouse, where we ordered lunch on Monday, 7 August, 1967.

(Maybe the place will have changed hands by the time this book is published. I hope so, for the sake of those residents of Maysville– not to be confused in any way with Maryville–who are compelled by circumstance to try to eat there. I don't think they could *eat* there, that's the reason I say *try to*.)

It may be that we were proffered beef and vegetables. We didn't think so; we thought that they served us buzzard skin and boiled skunk cabbage. It may be that the salad was anointed with French dressing; we thought that the viscous fluid had been drained from the crank-case of a truck. Could be that the dessert was not fabricated by a domestic science class in a home for the feeble-minded, but that was our notion. Oh, probably we're just plain fussy.

"Where is the men's room, please?"

"We don't have none."

"No?"

"If you want a washroom, you got to go over to the courthouse."

My wife said to me, "Proceed, if you wish. I'll open the car and cool it off."

So I walked across to the courthouse. Men's and women's washrooms were both down in the basement, next door to a public library which was functioning or trying to function in a room at the end of the hall. A few people were in there, returning books or checking them out. Will some kindly soul be so good as to call up Andrew Carnegie on the planchette board, and request that he do something about the library situation in Maysville? . . . Stench in the men's room was so overwhelming, and scraps of soggy paper and other filth so deep, that all I could do was turn around and totter out. Marched through the library, and returned to Irene and the car.

"Let's head for the nearest filling station which looks halfway clean."

With reluctance would I recommend that any travelers who wish to go Missouri waltzing should put Maysville down on their list of Musts.

Once more to the .38 Special—

We'd got it through our heads at last that Mrs. Herschfeld and all the Mrs. Cummings and Mrs. Petersons and Mrs. Millers were gone Above. Not desiring to be confronted with any more Maysville fare, we did the obvious thing: bought a few provisions. Also, if there were leftovers on some occasion when we'd been eating an excellent meal, but one much too large for our capacities, we had the bits of meat or chicken or shrimp wrapped up to take along. Bought a supply of plastic bags in which these things could be sealed, and they rode in the portable ice-box on the back seat floor. Fruit, crackers, cheese, olives, milk could be had at almost any crossroads store.

Early one sunny afternoon we drove along a narrow woodland road, and parked in green shade. There was an open glade just ahead where we could have a view of peaceful valleys and still keep our car in sight so we wouldn't need to lock up. We spread a shabby tartan blanket and lunched thereon, then lolled in siesta.

Presently—

Irene's voice, muted but urgent. "Can you hear me?"

"Sure. What is it?"

"Don't move now, or turn your head to look. But there's a man creeping along that dry stream bed just below the hill. He looks up every now and then, to see if he's been discovered. I've been watching him for a couple of minutes. Just now he's behind that largest willow tree which leans over."

Gradually I turned my head and, pretending to study a map held up to my face, soon made out the skulker. He was crawling up a little closer. He crept behind a shelter of elderberry brush, and there he paused.

"Did you see him?"

"Yes. Bare-headed man in overalls. He looks for all the world like a younger edition—and larger—of that fellow who's sneaked up on the lovely nude in Tommy Benton's painting, *Persephone*."

"Do you think he's dangerous?"

"Oh, he could be some sort of woodsy lunatic, but I doubt it. Likely he saw us drive into this timberland. Maybe we're on his land."

"But slinking around like this—"

"There is extant a race of people to whom a man and a woman and a blanket mean just one thing."

"Ah," she whispered. "*Un voyeur!*"

"Reckon so."

"What do we do now?"

"You say, in a voice which will carry to his ears, 'Well, honey, we've got to be going. But you haven't yet done your target practice for today.' "

"Got it."

She demonstrated that she had it by projecting the lines in her best American Academy of Dramatic Arts voice.

I hollered in reply, "Hand me the basket. *My gun* is in there."

She pushed it over. "What are you going to use for a *target*, honey?"

"See that stump, just in front of those elderberry bushes down there? There's a big splinter standing straight up on it, torn off when the tree fell. I'll shoot at that splinter."

"Oh, that'll make a *fine target*. And then the bullets will just go *into the bushes and*—"

Mention of Persephone might bring to mind Pheidippides, the runner who carried to Athens news of the Battle of Marathon in 490 B.C. Certainly it was a modern Pheidippides, clad in faded blue overalls, who bounced to his feet and disappeared down that creek-bed at a speed which would have made him a sensation at the Drake Relays or any other relays.

Goodness sake, my Smith & Wesson wasn't even in that picnic basket. It was in the car, back yonder under those oaks.

Couple of days later, and a couple of hundred miles distant, we heard the squawking signal of an inter-city bus, and witnessed a burly young man in overalls, racing as fast as he could to catch the bus.

Promptly there issued a squeal from Irene. "Look at him go," she cried. "It's Pheidippides! He's still running!"

14. "The Phantom Deer Arise"

Once upon a time there was an Old Man who traipsed out and settled in Missouri and became a syndic.

You ask what is a syndic or what *was* a syndic? Well, he was a man who bossed the area wherein he dwelt. He was sheriff, judge, jury, constable, marshal, and chief magistrate too. . . . Fellow did anything wrong, he was brought before the syndic for trial and sentencing. And punishment.

. . . Old Man loved right well to go into the woods, and trap, and fish for his breakfast, and shoot for his dinner, and gather wild fruit, and live off the land generally. He didn't care how elderly he was—he'd done this since he was a boy, and he intended to keep on doing it to the end of his days.

But don't think he didn't have any domestic life. He'd married a fine brave girl when she was only fifteen. They'd weathered through many a danger and many a jollity together, and had nine children. Two boys were killed by the Indians; but some of the others moved out to Missouri too. They settled round nearby, so there were in-laws and cousins and numerous grandchildren who loved to see Old Man a-coming.

He used to fetch home baby animals he'd found in their dens, and he had a wonderful time taming such little critters, and teaching em tricks. Folks tell how he petted young coons and otter, and beaver also. There's one story which claims he could tame wolves, and oh, but that's a mighty hard thing to do! Must have been a fine sight to see him setting on the grass alongside his cabin, playing with those furry live wild babies. And that was just pie for the grandchildren.

Old Man used to paddle away on long trips, sometimes all by

his lonesome, sometimes with a colored lad to help make camp and clean the peltries and such. He'd say to his wife, "Well, I got to be going now." She'd say, "Take care," and thus they'd part. She might not see him again for months. But I reckon Rebecca didn't worry much. He always turned up again.

There were plenty of Indians in those days, and sometimes a first-class Indian war broke out. Ordinarily, however, twas just small gangs of Indian hunters that he'd run into. Sometimes they were friendly, but other times they'd steal his furs—usually if he wasn't anywhere around. He'd have the furs all hung up careful in bundles, suspended where critters couldn't get at em. So it chanced that he suffered some financial loss if his furs were stolen. Cause those furs were worth money. Take beaver hides: they might average as much as five or six dollars apiece on the St. Louis market. Sometimes more, sometimes less . . . that was about the run of it.

Course, Indians weren't the only hazard Old Man had to contend with. Blizzards came howling in winter. But he waited em out, quite content in his solitary situation, with plenty of firewood, and maybe a snug little half-faced camp he'd made— You know: a kind of slanting roof, thatched with branches and leaves, and filled in on the sides. There was room enough under there to sleep, or to cook at a tiny fire when weather was bad. And right in front of it he could have a larger fire for warmth . . . that slanting roof threw back the heat, so he was warm as toast, front and rear. Old Man liked to live comfortable.

Then, when late winter was beginning to loosen up a bit, people along banks of the Missouri River would look out— Oh, far, far below, down around St. Charles—well past the Femme Osage where Old Man dwelt. And they'd see him a-voyaging downstream in his great big long canoe with a roof built over the center part: a kind of curved shack to cover up those bundles of furs and keep em dry when it stormed. And he might go clean to St. Louis to dispose of his furs.

See, he wanted money, cause he had a lot of debts back where he used to live, and he wanted to pay em off. He'd never seemed to prosper too much, when it came to land. For instance, the Spanish awarded him ten thousand arpents of land at one time, right here in the Missouri country, but the title wasn't very good. Ten thousand arpents—that's somewhere around eighty-five hundred acres, the way we reckon land.

But, see, Spain had to transfer all this Missouri country to France, and then France sold it to the United States, and so on and so on. And what with all those changes and different interpretations of titles, why— Old Man always came off second best, when it was a matter of hanging on to his real estate. There were too many queer stipulations involved, and too many open avenues whereby squatters could take up residence on the territory which had been awarded to him; and thus they might secure, perhaps, a better title than he held.

Nevertheless, Old Man continued stubbornly at his trapping, bringing in otter skins and deer hides, and beaver pelts, and all the others he could catch in his traps. Though beavers were generally the steadiest in demand. Not for ladies' coats . . . no, for men's hats. That's what they made fine gentlemen's hats out of, in those times.

Therefore, what with selling off some of the land which indeed he did own, even to the last— And those furs— He made enough money to go back where he used to live, and pay off his debts. I tell you, he was mighty proud about that. He didn't like to owe anybody anything. . . . Ideas seem to have changed nowadays. Everybody seems to like to owe everybody else. Government owes the people, people owe the Government, the Government is owed by other governments. Twas a different state of affairs then. Debt wasn't stylish nor popular, and nobody seemed to think that the world owed him a living—the Government or anybody else. Fellow just went out and *worked* for his living, as our Old Man did.

But, I tell you, he had a lot of fun along the way. Even through later years when his thick hair had turned to silver and then to white. . . . You know how he wore his hair? All plaited, kind of braided. That's the way he liked to wear it. But he didn't fancy a beard. No. Only times he had a beard was when he was far gone in the wilderness, and couldn't shave. When he was around home, there with his wife— Or, after she died, living alone in his cabin or visiting at homes of his kin— He kept himself shaved clean.

He displayed peculiarities, but doubtless enjoyed doing so. Take that thing about his coffin. He had one, made of black walnut, and he used to keep it under his bed. Yes, sir! And not only that. He wasn't *afraid* of his own coffin, way some of us might be. Every now and then he'd pull it out and lay down in it, just to make sure it fit him all right. . . . One day somebody died, all on a sudden, and there wasn't any coffin handy, so our Old Man let em use his black walnut one. That's how come he had a second coffin constructed, this time of cherrywood. Seemed like he wasn't at ease without such an object under his bed.

He liked children, and much enjoyed telling em tales about the early days—the very *earliest* days, long before George Washington became President of these here States. Oh, they'd listen long; and then grow restless, as children do. "Now you go play your games and sports," he'd say. So the younguns would run and whoop, whilst Old Man sat a-watching with a slight smile on his face and kindness in his eyes . . . and stroking the sleek coat of a baby beaver or otter, or maybe a deer faun he was a taming. . . . I never did hear that he tamed any *skunks*, but I wouldn't put it past him.

Still, going into the forest so frequent— It begun to show on him. He felt especially lonely and bereft after his Rebecca died. She went first, preceding him by several years . . . the country was getting more and more people in it, and Old Man had always claimed he needed plenty of elbow room. So he'd go on long long trips, even when he was upwards of eighty. He'd trap on the Chariton River, and up the Grand, and away out to the River Platte. It is also storied that he even went to the Rocky Mountains, though that's difficult to believe. But he always came back here to the Femme Osage again.

Then, finally, what with falling through the ice and getting immersed in midwinter Missouri water, and having to dry out at a fire on shore— Or what with getting sick abed in his lonely camp, and thinking for sure he was going to die *this* time, and instructing the boy who attended him just how he wanted to be buried— What with exposures to weather, and sinking spells, and rising spells again— It had come time for Old Man to die.

He'd been sick in his own cabin; and then he was sick when over visiting at a son-in-law's place; and then he got better again, so he traveled some miles to visit at his *son's* place. . . . He dearly loved to eat sweet potatoes—twas one of his favorite dishes. And he couldn't have those in the woods, on long hunts and trapping trips, for they would have been too heavy to lug along. But now he could enjoy sweet potatoes. I'll bet those were something, too; cause one of the favorite ways of cooking em was with maple sugar that the folks had manufactured themselves. Usually it was the *only* sugar they had.

You can imagine young girls coming beaming to Old Man, and

saying, "We got just what you want for your supper. Sweet potatoes!"

So he set down, and he et, and he et, and he et some more. He et sweet potatoes until he was nigh onto busting. Well, in fact he *was* a-busting. Cause that did it. He went to bed and he never got up again.

At last they could use that cherrywood coffin for certain, and tote Old Man on a wagon rattling across those autumnal hills. They took him over to Teuque Creek, and bore the coffin up to the knoll where his wife was buried, and there they laid him beside her. And as the sun shone down, it glinted on colored vines and tinted oaks of the region, and made them look like so many Indians in war paint, all in honor of Old Man.

Folks might ask, "Who did he think he was? He certainly wasn't very smart—going out in his old age and doing all those things! Why, he was nearly eighty-six when he died, wasn't he? And— Camping out in the snow, and falling through ice, and exerting himself thataway! Fine way for a man of so many years to be acting. Surely he didn't have much *sense*. What did he think his name was, anyway? Daniel Boone?"

Ah, it was, it was.

My favorite Daniel Boone story is not really a Daniel Boone story at all: it's a Bryan story. Daniel married a Bryan girl. My great-grandfather, Joseph Bone, married a Rachel Bryan. Since both Bryan girls (although nearly a century apart) came from the same neck of the woods, I like to think that the Bone-Bryans were related to the Boone-Bryans. For one thing, there were millers in both tribes. Rebecca Boone's nephew, Jonathan Bryan, ran a water mill. So did my great-great-grandfather, Alanson Bryan. Also several fairly uncommon Christian names keep cropping up in both families. For instance, there was a Willis Bryan, so my great-grandmother Bone named one of her sons Willis. First time I went to that Boone-Bryan burying ground on a little knob of a hill in Warren County near Marthasville, and strolled around, looking at moss-grown gravestones, some of them cracked— I found there Willis Bryan—not big as life, but big as death.

The old tale runs more or less as follows (it is recounted by John Bakeless in his fine biography of Daniel Boone, published by William

Morrow & Company in 1939; and also it bobs up every now and then in various series of anecdotes):

During the Sauk war, Jonathan Bryan had to go away from his house, and leave his wife with nobody but two Negroes—a woman and a little boy—to keep her company. A couple of Sauk warriors came along, and decided that it would be rare sport to have those ladies' scalps for decorations. Mrs. Bryan slammed the door on Raider Number One, but he'd got his head and one arm through. The plucky mistress summoned that prodigous strength which the Almighty sometimes offers in moments of stress, and held the door against the Indian's neck and shoulder, while the colored woman wrenched Mr. Sauk's tomahawk from his hand and considerately buried it in his skull. . . . The Negro boy shrieked a warning. Raider Number Two was plunging toward them across the yard. Mrs. Bryan didn't know whether the rifle belonging to the dead Sauk was loaded or not, but this seemed like the time to find out. She picked up the gun, and dropped the enemy in his tracks. Probably, although the legends don't say, she and her valiant servant then started looking around for more Indians.

Later the menfolks attended to a necessary task of sepulture. They buried both Sauks in a fenced lot nearby.

Folks would come past sometimes and say to the Bryans, nodding toward those mounds, "Some of your kin buried there?"

The Bryans. "Oh, no. Just a couple of strangers who died whilst traveling thisaway."

Shall we say that this family had a *grave* sense of humor?

It all sounds comical at a late date, more than a hundred and fifty years after the incident happened. But that Sauk war was no joke. Along traces running west from the Mississippi, people took to the forts if they were lucky enough to have a fort nearby. Many settlers were murdered in their homes. Children were waylaid, walking along paths . . . farmers killed at work in their fields.

Here's a party of scouts out on the march, looking for signs of Indians—or Indian *sign*, as they said in their parlance.

. . . Fog still clinging to the higher ground. The scouts travelled in a long file. . . . Ben Livingston dropped back to pace beside the tired Dade. He said that the cabin they sought was in the next valley.

"Why wouldn't the Johnsons come to the fort?" asked Scott Dade. The man nearest him chuckled.

"You see," explained Livingston, "they're deep in liquor most of the time. They sell some whiskey to travellers, and they supply the citizens in this region. They trade with the Indians too—Osages, mainly."

Dade said, "I assume they're too friendly with the Indians to have any fear of them."

"These aren't Osages we're looking for today! They're Sauks, mister: that's a cat with another tail. No, all four Johnsons—the girls and their pap and mammy—they never do come forting when they need to. Reckon they're usual too drunk; or maybe they don't want to leave their whiskey still untended."

"How far to their place?"

"Mighty nigh. We'll stop and wet our whistles—find out if they've smelt any paint in the brush."

The ground was sloping rapidly; hazel shrubs grew thinner. High sun scorched the fog away, and at the remote edge of timberland Scott Dade found an odor coming to meet him.

"I smell bacon," he said—they all heard him say it—and at that moment a man squawked in horror and surprise.

All the scouts began to run, as if toward something wonderfully attractive. . . . The men sprang between butternut trees, they crossed an area of stumps. . . . The Johnsons' dog lay dead amid shivered crockery, and it was odd that those who'd killed him had cut off his tail. . . .

The rangers halted, speechless and puffing, around a little limit of ash and rubbish which marked the site of the cabin. They looked with curiosity on the ruins of the still: its worm curled like a stiff dark snake amid the drift of smoke. There were other, more horrid objects to observe; men pushed them with poles from the hot rubble: you couldn't tell whether they had been scalped or not. "Bacon, hell," said old Ben Livingston.

That's from *Missouri Moon*, which I wrote away back one time, before Pearl Harbor. Maybe it offers a little idea of how matters went in those areas immediately west of the Mississippi, and north and south of the Missouri River, during 1815.

Crossed rifles and crossed powder-horns up at the top of the sign.

DANIEL BOONE HOME. SEE THIS STONE MANSION WITH PORTHOLES IN ITS 30-INCH WALL. . . . THE ROOMS WHERE DANIEL BOONE AND HIS WIFE LIVED AND WHERE HE DIED.

A steel fence surrounds the Judgment Tree, praise be. Otherwise visitors would have girdled that priestly relic long ago, by hacking off the bark around its seventeen-foot circumference for souvenirs.

And the sacred spring still bubbles forth at its foot, and goes talking down a slope, beckoning birds to come and drink and bathe. . . . A black-pated catbird skitters up out of the brook, shakes off glistening drops, winks, says *Meeow*. . . .

Arborists inform us that the elm is upwards of three hundred years in age; so it was at least a hundred and fifty years old, back in Daniel's time. Tree surgeons have tended it devotedly: there are supports here and there, rods fastened to keep the huge limbs from tearing off when storms come whirling. You see so many elms in Missouri, after a high wind, split down the middle, muscular branches dangling or torn loose. And how many times has that Judgment Tree been struck by lightning?

. . . Enormous leaves blown free during a gale the previous night. I picked up one of the leaves, and slid it into a famous old book about early Missouri families; and it's still there, between pages describing Daniel.

Let's settle down in the benison of this elm for a moment, and consider the book just mentioned. A century ago an eccentric gregarious gentleman named Robert Rose went riding through the countryside of five counties in the central portion of the State, gathering anecdote and record and Tall Tale from every family who would welcome him in for the night, and give him supper and breakfast. He took voluminous notes. His saddlebags bulged with miscellaneous scraps of paper on which were scribbled the wildness and weirdness of a fast-vanishing frontier.

Daniel Keithley, son of Daniel, Sr., married a Miss Hostetter, and they had a daughter named Kate, who was the largest woman in the world, weighing 675 pounds.

In about twenty years they had twelve children, and Tim surprised the district school master one morning by presenting himself at the door of the school house with nine of them to be placed under his charge. He said he would have brought three more, but their mother hadn't finished their clothes.

He had an old yellow dog that he thought a great deal of, and in order to keep him from running away, he drove a honey locust stake in the yard and tied him fast to it. The stake took root and grew to be a large tree, and its branches cast a grateful shade over the yard and dwelling.

Eventually Robert Rose met up with William S. Bryan, a grandson of the Jonathan mentioned *ante*. A successful newspaper editor and publisher, William Bryan was able to bring Rose's harvest of jottings into some semblance of order, and to write additional historical sketches of his own. The result, a 528 page work, entitled *A History of the Pioneer Families of Missouri*, was printed in St. Louis in 1876. This volume, according to Mr. W. W. Elwang, an antiquarian of later date, "fell still-born from the press. About 200 copies were bound and either sold at $2.50 per copy or given away; the remaining sheets [300] were disposed of as so much waste paper."

Waste paper. Good God!

He was a very absent minded man, and a number of amusing anecdotes are related of him in that connection. On a certain occasion when his wife was about to be confined, he started after the doctor, and did not return until the child was old enough to walk. On another occasion he went to the store to get some salt, and was absent eighteen months. When he came back he was carrying a broadax on his shoulder, but did not remember what he had been doing with it.

At another time Hendricks found some buzzard's eggs, and sold them to Mrs. Felix Scott for a new kind of duck's eggs. She was very proud of her purchase, and took a great deal of pains to hatch the eggs under a favorite hen. But when the "ducks" came, and she saw what they were, she passed into a state of mind that might have been called vexation.

Tilman Agee married a daughter of William Thornton, when she was only thirteen years of age. The next morning after the wedding he left her to get breakfast, while he went out to work. He worked until nine o'clock, without being summoned to his meal, and then having become impatient, he went to the house to see what the matter, and found his wife sitting on the floor playing with her dolls.

He built a house with a very steep roof, and the cone was so sharp that all the birds that lit upon it had their toes cut off.

In 1924 I came across a battered tattered copy of this book in a remote farmhouse. Tried to buy it, but the farmer and his wife weren't a-selling. But in 1935 Mr. Elwang saved the work from oblivion, and the felicitations of all Missouri-lovers should attend his memory forever. He wrote a lively explanatory introduction, together with a lengthy index, and under his aegis *Pioneer Families of Missouri* again came into being, *en facsimile*.

Besides the family histories gleaned higgledy-piggledy from St. Charles, Warren, Montgomery, Callaway and Audrain counties, the book contains a 58-page biography of Daniel Boone, numerous other biographies and sketches, and the autobiography of Chief Black Hawk, as dictated by him to an official interpreter in 1833.

But my own affection still enfolds the bizarre reportage of that mighty Robert Rose, with which this treasury is crammed.

The old gentleman was a great friend of the Indians, and in order to manifest his good feelings, he kept a lot of tobacco with which he would fill their pouches when they stopped at his house. One of his sons, a mischievous lad, poured a pound of gunpowder into the tobacco, and several of the Indians got their faces and noses burnt in attempting to smoke it. This, of course, was taken as a mortal offence, and it was with the greatest difficulty that Mr. Davidson kept the Indians from killing himself and family.

When he got his new wife home, he was so overjoyed that he danced about the room and waved his hat over his head in an excess of delight, when he happened to strike the lamp that was standing on the mantel, and threw it on the floor, where it was dashed to pieces. In a moment the house was on fire. . . .

He built his house under a high bluff that ran parallel with the creek, and cut his fire wood on the top of this bluff, and rolled it down to the door of his house. When the wood gave out he moved his cabin to another place, and when it gave out there he moved it again, preferring to move his house rather than haul his wood.

Mr. Groom and the other members were invited one evening, by Dr. Young, to take tea at his house. Mrs. Young, who was a highly cultivated lady, had a piano and played well upon it. A piano at that time was a great curiosity, for there were none in the country until Mrs. Young brought hers, and people traveled thirty and forty miles just to see the wonderful instrument and hear its music. Mr. Groom possessed an ardent desire to see the piano, and he kept his eyes open from the time he entered the house. They were ushered into a room which contained, among other things, a large, old-fashioned curtained bedstead, which Groom at once concluded must be the much talked of piano. He eyed it curiously, and cautiously felt of the curtains, longing for the appearance of the hostess. He was not kept long in suspense, for she soon entered and welcomed her guests. As soon as an opportunity presented itself, Groom addressed her and said that he was passionately fond of music, that he had heard of her wonderful piano and the elegant manner in which she played upon it; "and now, Madam," said he, "I would like the best in the world to see you *perform on that instrument*," pointing to the bed.

Undoubtedly our old Daniel would have loved these fragments too. He could tell a pretty good story himself when so minded.

Under this rich elm he is alleged to have presided as syndic. The story may or may not be true; nevertheless we know that it was habitual in the past for people to foregather beneath trees for political purposes or for military conferences. Such historic chestnuts, elms and oaks once dotted the Eastern portion of the United States, and Western Europe as well.

Sadly the Dutch elm disease has proved disastrous in Missouri, as elsewhere. It hedge-hops, playing its own dire leap-frog mysteriously from place to place. You go through a region where the cadavers stand like grieving witches, with not a full-leafed elm left in sight. Then again you enter an area where trees are healthy and placid—as graceful, as vase-shaped as well-behaved elms should ever be.

On once more, and—

Lo, more bones, more dry starvelings pleading with stiff hands held mutely against the sky. We've always heard that such should be burned, in order to keep the disease in check, or try to. In some places this must have happened: you don't see the dead trees, only stumps. But some twenty miles east of Columbia, you can stand on any ridge and count the stricken by the score. And no torch has been applied.

When the pestilence first mounted into threat, back in the early 1930s, alarming articles appeared in newspapers and magazines. My agent, Sydney Sanders, a true arborist as so many Englishmen are—I remember his shaking his head as we drove through Deerfield, Massachusetts, and saying, "See these beautiful ancient elms along this principal street. How ghastly!—to think that ten years from now there won't be one of them left standing!"

As I say, it was about thirty-five years ago that Syd spoke those words. I haven't been in Deerfield since 1966; but then the thick-leaved patriarchs still waited whatever judgment Fate might offer them. They stood praying, giving sanction, as if considering that winter dawn of 1704 when the Mohawk struck, and once more *Deerfield* became a terrifying word.

At the Nathan Boone place, we had to march through a large souvenir shop in order to enter the premises and pay our fee. Junk therein displayed would have really curled Daniel Boone's hair. (What am I saying? He wore it plaited, didn't he?) Lances and tomahawks made of rubberoid material, decorated with orange-green-and-blue feathers—no such feathers as any Indian ever put upon his weapon or used for decoration. Ash-trays with alien Sioux or Arapaho embossed . . . pennants stamped in bright colors. "Souvenir of Daniel Boone House." Just what you might expect.

Sure, sure. Tourists will put up with any amount of nonsense, no matter in which century they go a-touring.

Mark Twain, in *The Innocents Abroad:*

We find a piece of the true cross in every old church we go into, and some of the nails that held it together . . . we have seen as much as a keg of these nails.

Irene is reasonably tolerant. She can discard the trivial, overlook such annoyances, and find what satisfaction there may be in a guided tour through any sort of museum or monument. Me— Negative. . . . Our guide was a pest. When we entered Nathan's house, where Daniel happened to die—not where he *lived,* as a silly portfolio describes— I'd had enough of all the fotch-on furniture and of the guide's chitter-chatter within five minutes.

The glorious elm beckoned. . . .

Cars came and went, over a rocky hillside which served as parking lot. Tourists drifted up from snack bar and gift shop, or ambled down to unpack their lunches on picnic tables arranged near the Visitor Center. I couldn't see any provision for the disposal of garbage and trash. Paper and plastic wreckage was trodden or blowing around like crazy. Daniel wouldn't have liked that, any more than he would have liked a sub-machinegun with his name painted on the stock.

After a slow tour of the premises, I returned to the front door just as Irene's party emerged, and I took her down to the Judgment Tree again. She stood rapt, gazing up through abundant leaves, listening to the lyrical rivulet originating in that spring.

She began to sniff, so did I. A delicate sweetness drifted in the air.

"That perfume is heavenly. Where does it come from?"

"Don't know." I tried for wind direction . . . there wasn't much wind . . . a little from the southeast perhaps. We scouted, but could find no blossoming shrubbery of any sort. Still scent existed . . . was it honeysuckle?

Had to go, we were overdue in Franklin County. As we climbed to the parking area, a quarrel broke out at one of the picnic tables below. A small boy named—believe it or not, *Danny*—was being ordered away by his father and mother, in loud voices. "Get out of here, Danny!" they yelled. "You can't have any more lunch, either. You go and get in the car, do you hear?" Danny came, snarling through tears. He was about four or five, and carried an Indian bow-and-arrow adorned with gold and purple trimmings. His face was screwed into a knot, and he gave vent to the eternal *Nyaaaa-nyaaaa* of spoiled or angry children.

The howling followed him. "You're a nasty little *brat*, that's what you are! You climb in that station-wagon, and you *stay* there!"

Nyaaaa-nyaaaa—

What manner of modern discipline was this, which called upon a parent to send his child into a stifling station-wagon, baked in the sun?

"I suppose he'll suffocate in there."

Irene, resignedly. "Might as well. With a father and a mother like those people."

We left the premises. Last thing we could hear were the lamentations of Danny, increasing in volume; and answering roars from his father, who was racing up to the station-wagon to administer some form of torture . . . burn the kid at the stake? Could be.

A shady road, winding gently among Femme Osage hills, lulled us into disregard of the more exasperating phases of Tourist Sites and Sights.

". . . That odor, that wonderful *perfume*. Mack, I can remember it right now, remember how it smelled. Where *did* it come from?" Then, after a few minutes, "Why, I *know*."

She said it was the essence of Daniel Boone . . . the purity of his kind. The simplicity, the courage.

Together we recited a treasured four-line ode, written by Steve Benét so many years before. The one about old Daniel going through a forest in nighttime. *The phantom deer arise. . . .*

15. A Woman of Two Counties

. . . Speaking to my Dictaphone mike.

"If you wanted to be an old lady in a rocking chair, in summer shade . . . or an old man beside the winter stove, and that was all you wanted to be– I should think New Bloomfield would be the ideal place for you to spend your declining years. *If* that was all you wanted out of existence. . . ."

Columbia had proved to be a recurrent satisfaction each evening, including in its composition such pleasant items as Dick and Alice Brownlee, Warren and Ruth Welliver, Bill and Eleanor Beckett, and a lot of other charmers. But we'd played too much. I hadn't gone out to re-explore Boone and Callaway counties in the way conscience demanded.

On this day I was resolved sternly to prowl in earnest. Irene set a courageous example by cutting mats for new watercolors, immediately after breakfast; and I went out and Started Engines . . . taxied, called the tower again . . . they told me to take off on the northeast-southwest runway and do a 90° to the left 60 seconds after I was airborne.

The voice on the band talks back to me now. . . .

"There's an antique shop here in New Bloomfield at the side of familiar Route 54, and the proprietor has left a sign at the front door. *Closed for Lions' Club. Open at 10 a.m. tomorrow.* That's quite a Lions' Club they have in these parts. A man goes to the luncheon, and never gets back to his store until next day."

Here lay a hint of what I sought, but only the faintest hint. I was seeking a Tall Tale or an Eccentricity. Off and on for years I'd been hunting them in rustic corners of the two counties, but without success.

It started with reading the works of a writer (wasn't he a teacher, in the main?) named Raymond Weeks. Back in the days when I was green-young and still emaciated and trying to be a poet, occasionally *The Midland*, a magazine edited by John T. Frederick, accepted some of my verse. Another *Midland* writer was that same Raymond Weeks, with a tale entitled *The Hound Tuner of Callaway*. Also he came forth with *The Fat Women of Boone*, *The Snakes of Boone*—yarns which gave the impression that this region was stuffed with an incredible number of what used to be known in the vernacular as Characters.

. . . Everything was broader or taller or fatter or thinner or meaner or leaner than in any place else. Distinctly, in first scanning Weeks' stories, the reader gains the impression that if a hen was going to lay a square egg, she did it in Callaway; or if a potato grew into the shape of a monkey, that potato emerged from Boone County soil. Villagers and countrymen were manufactured in much the same eerie fashion.

Again and again I roamed Boone and Callaway, and not one Character did I encounter. I stalked along Cedar Creek, which forms most of the boundary between the two. No specimens. One spring day Irene and I did pick some gorgeous misshapen morels alongside Cedar Creek, but that was the limit of our acquisition. . . . We've found strange mushrooms in lots of places and countries. Plucked one of the most grandiose giant puffballs from Thomas Jefferson's own front yard— An alderman, a jolly Falstaff among puffballs— Yet its flesh was firm and white and savory. "Just cook it as you would chicken," we told astounded chefs in restaurants along the way. "Smells good," they'd say. Then I'd quote the line from that dog ballad, *Old Blue*. "You can have some, too." Ah, what a puffball! Raymond Weeks should have been with us, alive and hungry, though the good man has long since strayed from Earthly scenes.

And the Monticello front lawn is in Albermarle County, Virginia. Not in Callaway nor yet in Boone.

On this warm day I traveled from Easley down to Hartsburg, and then up to Ashland and over to Guthrie, and all the way through Mokane to Portland. Not a Character anywhere in sight.

Mentally I scourged Author Weeks. Actually he didn't manage words too well (hadn't written enough through his lifetime to learn how. *The Hound Tuner* was published when he was in his late fifties). Raymond Weeks had a trick of making people take residence in your recollection, however, and that's a good sign. But he labored under the delusion that Somerset Maugham was widely read in America only because he wrote about South Sea Islanders and other furriners; and that Scott Fitzgerald received acclaim and prosperity only because he concerned himself with sleek Long Island types. Weeks said as much in a foreword. He couldn't recognize that his own tales weren't very well put together, and that he was guilty of some of the most dreadful attempts at dialect to be met with on any page.

Just the same, he exerted compulsion. There were times when he'd sent me scouting from Hatton to Hallsville to Harrisburg and down to Hinton. There must have been some elusive power in him.

Then, on that memorable afternoon, skies opened and the drouth was broken. Granaries opened too, and thus the famine ended.

I came up over the top of a hill, and there she was, walking briskly: a woman in a print dress, wearing a wide-brimmed hat of glazed black straw. She dragged a child's wagon of ancient stamp, on which were loaded two bulging zipper bags. Wisely she proceeded on the left-hand side of the road to confront oncoming traffic, though there wasn't any at the moment . . . I hadn't observed a car or a truck in several miles.

I passed her, and pulled off on the right shoulder, listening to a rattle of miniature metal-tired wheels coming along. Then I thought, Idiot! Why don't you back up? . . . I backed up along that shoulder until I was opposite her again.

The woman regarded me with curiosity. Her spectacles were extremely thick, her eyes melted and swam . . . you could scarcely see what color they were. (Later she declared that she had very good vision nevertheless—for *fine* work, as she put it.)

I called, "Can I be of any help? You seem to have quite a load there."

She looked both ways, then hauled her coaster wagon across the road. "I thought maybe you were somebody I knew. But I guess we're not acquainted. You with that Florida license and all."

"How far you going?"

"Fulton."

"Why, that's quite some distance yet. Look, my back seat's empty. We can get those bags *and* the wagon in there."

"Think so?" She was delighted.

"We'll just turn this wagon upside down on the seat. The bags can go on top of it, or on the floor. . . ."

She was skinny of frame but muscular, and rather masculine in the management of her extremities. She could do field work, I thought, and probably had done some; or at least she knew how to use an axe or a spade. Although her dress was not of the cheapest material. Neither was her handbag.

"I'm Mab," she said. "Mab DuBart."

"Well, I'm Mack Kantor."

She laughed. "Hiya, Mack," and we knew we were off to a good start.

Mab said, when she had joined me in the front seat, "I just somehow had a hunch that I wasn't going to pick up any rides—everybody's off doing something somewhere—and now look at me, riding high and handsome. Bet you a dollar to a doughnut you don't know what's in those bags of mine."

"What is in them?"

"Nutmeats. I got a shipment of nutmeats in there. All packed careful, ready to be sent by Railway Express. So I was taking em to the Express office."

"Then I'm glad that I chose this way to return to Columbia."

She shrieked, "Co*lum*bia? You mean to say that you're going to Co*lum*bia, right *now?*"

"Sure am."

"Why— Now, wait a minute, let me think. Wait . . . a . . . minute. Let's see. Got everything locked up? Yes. . . . I keep thinking about my cat, but he got run over last month. Oh, it was just sickening! Well, Mr. Mack, why don't you be so good as to take me right on to Columbia?"

I was a little puzzled, but said of course I'd be glad to.

"You see, it's like this. I'm a kind of practical nurse, among other things. I take folks in to board with me. You know—somebody who hasn't got anybody to look after em, or their folks have to go away: things like that. Now, I had an old lady boarding with me the last three-four weeks. I was looking after her, there at my place, but her nephew came to take her to Jeff City, and that meant that I could have my car worked on. See, I didn't dare do it while she was there—I mean the old lady—because there might be an emergency. She might have a fit and fall in it, and then I'd have to rush her to the doctor or something like that. I don't like to be without transportation. But oh Good Lord Alive, I've been needing to have that engine worked on; and there was something wrong with the transmission, too, that they said they couldn't fix in just an hour or so. And new brake linings necessary. That car had to go to the garage for a few days. So I told that Pryle boy who lives on the next place that I'd be his Dutch uncle if he'd drive it in to town for me. I mean Fulton. So that's what he did: took my car right in, and then he could ride home with his cousin who works in Fulton. Well. And now you come along, and say you're going to Columbia. Well, ain't that just *ducky?* You see, it's like this: my sister Maude lives in Columbia. She's married and got three grown children, and they're all married too, and two of em live in Columbia. I haven't seen Maudie in a coon's age. You know how it is: you both get busy, and have all sorts of cares and worries, and things you got to do, and then you just don't get back and forth the way you want to. Oh, we talk on the telephone sometimes but— That ain't so satisfactory, is it? So it's just *Providential*, you coming by like this. My house is all locked up, everything neat and snug, nothing to worry about cept thinking about poor old Brin, my cat. You see, he was kind of brindled, so I named him Brindle when he first came to me as a stray kitten. Then I just cut that down to Brin. But he was getting on, nearly ten years old, not very spry. But he still liked to hunt a lot, out in the fields. Get mice and things. Even used to bring home garter-snakes and I don't know what all. Brin was probably trying to get across the road— I didn't see it happen. But what traffic there is along this road sometimes travels mighty fast. And so I found him, squashed flat. But anyway I don't have to worry about *him* any more. So I can ride on with you, right to Columbia— You don't suppose you'll be going anywhere near the Express office, will you?"

"You tell me where it is, and we'll go there."

"Oh, ain't that just grand! Then I'll have Maudie or one of the girls pick me up, and I can have a real nice overnight visit with the whole family, and take the bus back to Fulton tomorrow."

I wondered about the little wagon.

"Don't worry about that. It's been on the place since Hec was a pup. Doesn't matter anyway, cause if I still think I need the wagon for anything, why– First time my brother-in-law is driving in my direction in his pick-up, why, he can fetch it right along."

She informed me that her age was forty-nine . . . I'd thought her to be older. She took off the wide-brimmed hat, calmly turned down the sun visor on her side, and examined that hard bony lined face carefully in the mirror. She wore lipstick cannily applied– very bright, of a popular frosty hue. Her gray hair had been tinted with a rinse which showed anything from green to purple, depending on how the light struck it. But there was nothing fancy about her fingernails: they were clipped short, the nails on a worker's hands . . . hands distorted with knots and calluses.

Looking at Mab, and not having heard her speak, you might have thought that her voice would be harsh as a crow's, but it was nothing like that. Her voice was full, rounded. There was a resonance about it, and I should have liked to have heard her singing. She did tell me that she sang often when she worked– "If I haven't got some boarder that it bothers"– But when I asked her to sing something, she laughed and ducked her head and said, Oh, no, she was too shy.

Mab's conversation, mostly about herself, flowed in a perpetual stream. . . . Once again my heart went out to Raymond Weeks and to the counties of Boone and Callaway. For Mab said that she had been born in Boone, and reared in Callaway.

There were about her strength and essential virtue, and that dignity which impresses only when the subject is not trying to be dignified at all and has never even considered the notion.

. . . Hey, Mr. Mack, if you want to get the Interstate, you've got to keep on north here! . . . Oh, I see. You *prefer* back roads. Good enough, suits me. Makes me feel more acquainted with the landscape, somehow.

. . . You'd be surprised if you knew what I receive for these butternut meats. They tell me butternuts are hard to come by in the commercial market. I send em to a candy manufacturer in Chicago, and they're always very generous and prompt with their checks. I been picking up pin-money that way, oh, for years and years. On my place, which has had DuBarts on it now for four generations, there is the most beautiful stand of butternut trees you ever saw in all your born days. There used to be a lot of black walnuts long ago, but those trees of course grow to a much larger size than the butternuts. So they were mostly logged off, way back at the time of the First Great War with Germany. I think they made aer-o-plane propellers out of em. Grandpa got a whole pile of money for that walnut timber.

It was my Grandma that called me Mab. See, actually I was named Mabel, and usually– You know, if somebody's named Mabel, and they want to give you a nickname– Why, then you're maybe called *Mabe*. But I was very little when I was a baby– Actually I was a seven-months' baby– And Grandma was a great reader. She was well educated–better'n I am, by far–and her own father served in the Legislature. Grandma was a great reader of Shakespeare. Always coming up with something out of Shakespeare. So she said, of me, quoting from *Romeo and Juliet*, Act One, Scene Four– She said:

> . . . She comes
> In shape no bigger than an agate-stone.

That's what she said about me, cause I was so little.

And then I was so mis-*chee*-vous when I was a child. Then Grandma would say,

> . . . This is that very Mab
> That plats the manes of horses in the night,
> And bakes the elf-locks in foul sluttish hairs.

Just imagine! What a thing to say about an innocent little child! And you know, they were always calling me *Angry Mab* and things like that. I had to take an awful lot of kidding. But believe me, I could give it back to em, too.

And I could always give it back to a man if he needed to be taken down a peg, believe you me. Men . . . well, I don't need em in my life any more. I tried it three times, and the third time wasn't any charm. I took back my maiden name of DuBart, after that last marriage busted up. Didn't want to be known as Mrs. Gass all the rest of my life.

. . . First one was a drinker, and we had always been a distinctly Prohibition household. I hain't never had a drink in my life and don't intend to begin now. We were Methodists, and the Methodists in those days— Well! But you see *this* man was a *secret* drinker. Always sneaking around about it, and that's what made it so bad. Course I didn't know . . . I was just really a young girl when I got married the first time. Oh, there were stories going around about him, but I didn't believe em. Thought I was *in love,* ha, ha. Well, he actually went away and deserted me; and then he came sneaking back one time, and I literally ran him off the place. Just—like—*that.* I said, "If you ever come back here again, I'll load up Grandpa's shotgun"—Great-grandpa's shotgun, it was—"and give you a good dose of pepper-and-salt!"

Then the next year I had some papers served on me, and you know what? He wanted a *divorce.* Well, that couldn't have suited me better. So then— Well, my second husband was a right nice man, but he was kind of puny, and he didn't last long. He was lazy. But— Oh, I suppose that came from his being kind of sickly. I shouldn't have married him. Maudie said I shouldn't, and everybody else said I shouldn't. But I am a very strong-willed person, and when I once take a notion, why— Anyhow— Well, he died. Yes, died very suddenly. Nobody expecting it, and that left me on the market again. I don't know what it is gets into women to make em think they just got to have a man about the place. But I was a sucker, along with the rest of em.

Now, that sounds like I was born in Illinois, cause you know that's the Sucker State, and of course I was born right here in the Show-Me State. Just the same, I was a sucker when it came to men. When I was considerably younger, I mean.

So along came Number Three, and, oh Good Lord Alive, I don't know how much he cost me. I don't mean necessarily in wear and tear—there was a little of that, too—but I mean in cold hard cash. He was always wheedling a piece of property out of me. We did own some little lots— I mean, I inherited em. And one nice piece of ground right in Fulton. Well, Earl—his name was Earl—he could just tie me around his little finger. He'd wheedle and wheedle, and next thing I knew, I'd sold a piece of property and given him the money. He came up with one scheme after another, and they never did pan out. When he was a boy he'd run away with a carnival first, and then run away with a circus, and I guess he got that kind of carnival-circus idea in his blood. Because he was always going back to it. He actually bought five big pieces of equipment— You know: a merry-go-round, and a Sky-Fly ride, and what they called a motordrome, with motorcycles racing round and round. Oh, he was going to clean up with that stuff. A show had got stranded, and so he could get those at a bargain price. . . . Bargain price! Bah. He couldn't make a go of it. The stuff was all mortgaged, and finally they foreclosed on him, and that was that.

Well, I won't wear you out with all his shortcomings, but they were numerous. Thus came about the second divorce of my life, and by that time I thought, "Young lady, you've been a widow now three times, and you just *stay* a widow. Even if this one is *grass* instead of *sod*." And you may not believe it, but I've been asked several times since then. One was a patient of mine, laid up for a long while after an accident with his tractor, and I nursed him. He was a widower—fairly well off, too—and he did ask me to marry him. He practically insisted, but I said No, by no means, not ever again. So he married a pretty young thing instead, and did *she* lead him a merry life before he got rid of *her*, ha, ha!

You see me as I am. No, I'm not the prettiest thing in the world, I know that. . . . No, you don't have to say anything about my beauty, cause I know I ain't beautiful. Not any more. Oh, I had my looks to some degree when I was younger. My hair used to be considered real pretty but—as you can see—it got thin, and turned gray real early. I must have had gray hair by the time I was thirty. I know it's every color of the rainbow *now*—this week, I mean. Because you just cannot depend on some of these things you get nowadays—like rinses and so on. Course, you wouldn't know anything about *that*. But some of this stuff is just— Well, excuse my French, but it's *devilish*. All sorts of queer drugs . . . I don't know *what* they put in em.

As I said, I had this old lady dumped on me— Well, I suppose I shouldn't say that, because I do have the reputation of running a kind of nursing home. I can't take more than two though. Two is enough for me. You see, I get quite some little income from the property. Mr. George Pryle, he farms part of my land, and I receive an income from that; and then I rent out pastures to Mr. Partley—he wanted to increase his herd. He's got some very fine dairy cattle, but he didn't own the necessary pasturage for em. So he rents land from me, and that helps. I *have* been known to go into other people's homes a-practical nursing; but I much prefer to take folks, if they need to be taken care of, right there at my little place. And then there's this nut business. Course, that requires a great deal of work. Yes, these butternut meats we've got right here in this car are from last autumn's crop; but I keep the nuts stored safe and not dried out too much, and then I only crack em when I'm ready to pick em, and that's the reason my nutmeats are always fresh, and so desired by the manufacturer. Whenever I feel the need of ready cash, I just crack some nuts and get to work picking em out.

Now you probably know– Or do you? That a butternut's very hard to crack. That's because it's real long and slim, not round like a black walnut. A lot of people just smash the meats all to pieces cause they hit em on the side with a hammer, and that just pulverizes the thing. Well, the way to do is to take em–see how I'm holding my fingers?–like this, and hold em *longways.* I mean with the sharpest point down against something. If you've got a rock with a little hole in it, that's very good to use. Then you hit em on the other end–just tap regularly, but not too hard all at once–with your hammer, and if you do it right, that nut will split apart, going down the long way. Just shiver apart. Actually there are numerous occasions when I am able to extract the whole butternut, complete in one piece. That's a very difficult thing to do, but you learn by doing. So when I say nutmeats, I don't mean just little crumbled-up *bits*. These are real sound and solid, and thus appreciated by the candy manufacturers.

But what I was going to say: I had this old woman, and you know what she wanted to do all the time? Course, she's very frail, really frail, but didn't require a great deal of attention. Some nursing cases do, as you can well imagine, but she didn't. I just gave her her meals and helped her with her bath and things like that. And– See, her folks, the ones she *stayed* with– That was another nephew, not the same one that took her to Jeff City. But they had a family emergency arise, and– Well, I hate to tell you what it was, but it had to do with one of their daughters who lived elsewhere, and– Well, she got *arrested*. Oh, she was with a whole gang of youngsters, and they got involved with– Oh, narcotics and I don't know what all. It was pretty bad. Well, anyway, they *had* to go away, so they just took this old lady and dumped her on me, and I took care of her. But you know what she wanted to do all the time? She wanted to watch *TV*. From the moment the program came on until it was turned off. Course, sometimes she'd go to sleep watching it, but she wanted that thing going on, and– Now, I don't care much for television, but– Oh, I like to watch football games, and things like that, and– And *events*. But she– It just drove me out of my mind. So I thought, "Nothing to do, I'm going to have some expenses coming up, like car repairs, and I'd better get busy." So I just fetched up about a ton of nuts from storage, and went to work cracking and picking and cracking and picking. The product is right here in this car, as you can see.

. . . I don't know what your politics are, and I certainly wouldn't want to offend you. But any civilization which permits the things to happen, that we permit to happen in ours– It's due for a change, that's what. . . . You say people talk like that all over the State? Well, that's good to hear.

. . . Yes, yes, I certainly agree with you about Missouri being– What did you call it: ghostly? Oh, spooky. . . . You know, I've often thought that very same thing myself. And I've been right here, my whole life long, cept for one trip to California while I was married to Gass. But the countryside does look like it kind of leaves something– What would you say? . . . Oh, that's just the word. *Unexplained*. Like something was hiding away back beyond that pasture, or down that gully. Specially way late in the afternoon, and early evenings. Like something had happened, maybe, and you didn't know what it was. And couldn't find out.

. . . So you're going to write a book about Missouri. Well, that'll be nice. I mean I *hope* it will be. Now, let me tell you one thing, Mr. Mack, because I'm quite a good historian in my own right, and I want you to get this straight. There's too many *falsehoods* around. Don't you dare make out that the whole State of Missouri was a bunch of Rebels during the Civil War. *By no means*. I had two great-grandfathers in the War of the Rebellion, for that's what they called it among the Union forces. And they were both born in Missouri; and I don't know how many other relatives joined up also. And all of em for the *Union*. Do you know that there were almost three times as many soldiers enlisted from Missouri for the Union, as went for the South? Yes indeed, that is an actual fact. There was something like over a hundred and ten thousand that fought for the North, and only about forty thousand that fought for the South. But, Good Lord Alive, to hear some people carry on, even when it was all finished more than a hundred years ago– I know a woman who calls herself an *Unreconstructed Rebel*. What do you think of that? Yes, after all this time. It's just too silly for words. And always, always, *always* they're telling how the

Yankees took a church and used it for a stable to put their horses in, or how the Yankees burned down the courthouse, or how the Yankees burned down a bunch of people's houses. Huh. The Rebels did plenty of burning, their *own* selves. They did enough and to spare. I learnt this from the lips of actual participants, when I was only a little girl, some forty years ago. . . . Well, I guess I shouldn't say they were *participants*, but they were next door to being so. Next generation. And they *knew*.

And too many folks like to keep spreading falsehoods, just so's they can make money out of it. Oh, don't I know! Did you get over around Defiance yet? . . . You *did?* I mean that place they call the Daniel Boone House. . . . You did go there? Well, what do you think of that? I'll tell you what I think of it. I think it's just about one of the worst *fakes*. That wasn't Daniel Boone's house a-tall. It was his son who built that house—Colonel Nathan Boone—and he was truly an officer in the U. S. Army. Oh, certainly, Daniel and his wife used to come and *stay* with Nathan. And the old man happened to be there when he et too many sweet potatoes, and died, and all that. But it's just sickening the way they have all that *fake*. For instance, those loop-holes. Did you see em? Well, when I went there, there was a little girl—little midget of a girl—and she was showing people around, and Good Lord Alive, if she didn't say that they used to *shoot* through those loop-holes at the *Indians*. Now, I can tell you for a fact that Nathan Boone's house was never attacked by any Indians, at any time. Never, never, *never*. There were a lot of other places attacked, and a lot of people were killed right here in this county during that long-drawn-out Indian war. And I could show you some true sights where—See, I belong to the Missouri State Historical Society. Yes, I do. I can enumerate for you my memberships: I belong also to the Methodist Church, and I belong to the Order of the Eastern Star; and I am a member of the Democratic party, but I don't like Johnson or those dang Kennedys. Hardly anybody does, around here. You wait and see, next election. But everybody *loves* Harry Truman, I tell you that. We all regard him as just our pet. That little man in his old age! We're proud of Uncle Harry. But I have voted Republican on occasion in the past, and have every reason to think that I will again, next Presidential election. But, if I do, it will be the Democrats themselves who compelled me to do so. That's for sure.

I'm glad you took this way. I mean, I'm glad you like to drive on back roads, cause I do, too. . . . You know what? I'm glad I don't have to *live* in Columbia. I think it's just the ugliest place in the world. Oh, I don't mean out where the nice houses are, nor the campus. No, indeed. I mean *downtown.* That's just about as horrid as they come, and people shouldn't put up with it, but I guess they don't care. Holes in the sidewalks, just all over the place. You can really break your neck if you don't walk careful. But the folks in Columbia, they just don't pay any attention.

Right down ahead here now is what they call the Strollway. It doesn't look any different from Ninth Street, and it really *is* Ninth Street, except, if you'll notice, all the signs say *Strollway*. Well, Ninth Street comes from the north, and the way they've got it fixed nowadays, it ends at Broadway, and then from Broadway south they call it Strollway. Well, you can't *stroll* there. You'd get run over. Last time I was here with Maudie, I met one of their neighbors, and he was talking about this very thing, cept he thought it was fine. I said, "How on earth did that ever get started? That Strollway business?" And he said, "Oh, some of the people going down to the campus thought it would be a nice place to stroll." I said to him, "Well, it isn't any different from any other street. You can't go *strolling* in a lot of traffic." He said, "Well, they thought of making a Mall across through the campus, but they haven't ever gotten to it yet. But the Strollway would be part of the Mall." I said, "Frankly, I don't understand it at all." And he said, "Oh, that's because you're a stranger. If you lived here a while you'd see that it makes pretty good sense." Well, I've got my own ideas about *that.* I think it's just stupid. And I'm glad I live in the *country*.

Course, maybe I sound like I'm not grateful to you for hauling me all the way over here, and the coaster wagon, and the nuts and– You know, I've been thinking about that wagon, and it occurred to me: why don't I just give it to my niece's little girl? I think I'll do that. And you know what? I believe I can slip down to the store tomorrow morning, and paint it all a nice pretty color. Maybe a pretty aquamarine, all over. They've got that quick-drying paint nowadays, and it wouldn't take very long, and it would be a surprise. Her name's Sandra, and she's just the *cutest* little thing.

. . . Last time I was here in Columbia, I heard Mr. Richard Brownlee give a lecture. He's the Director of the Missouri State

Historical Society. . . . Why, Good Lord Alive, you say you *know* him? Well, I've met him, but that's just about all. But I did hear him lecture. I think he's wonderful. He's maybe fifty years old—somewhere around my own age—but, oh, he looks so much *younger*. And have you been in our library here, where the Historical Society—? That's it, right over there. . . . See? Just where I'm pointing. . . . Well, if you've been there, course you know how nice it is. They have room after room where you can study up on Missouri things. And that art gallery, with the original painting of Caleb Bingham's *Order Number Eleven*. We had a steel engraving of that, when I was little, and it just used to scare the *socks* off of me. . . . And they have one of the finest microfilm libraries of any historical institution in the United States! I heard Mr. Brownlee explain about that, when he was lecturing. They've got expensive equipment, here in Columbia, which ranks with the best in the world. That is an actual fact. You can go there if you want to—with the greatest of ease, and no danger, no harm to any original thing—and you can photograph any portion of any book you want, and take it right along with you to study. I tell you, we people here in Missouri are mighty proud of our Historical Society. Only trouble is, I keep running into dissension with some of the fellow members over our way. You remember what I told you bout the Civil War, and North and South? Mercy sakes, the only claim they've got for Missouri being a Confederate type of State, is the fact that old Claib Jackson scrabbled together a lot of Confederate sympathizers, and it was an illegal Legislature, and they voted Missouri out of the Union. But then the Conservatives took over and, as I told you, they were in the great majority, and they held a regular session of the *regular* Legislature. And they voted overwhelmingly for Missouri to remain *in* the Union. A lot of people seem to forget that! Or maybe they didn't know about it in the first place!

You know what? If my nutmeats weren't already packed, I'd give you some. But of course they're all wrapped up in boxes and—I tell you what I *will* do. You write out your home address, and when you get back to Florida you let me know. How would you like to have a box of real Callaway County butternut meats? Can your wife make fudge? . . . Oh, you can *both* make fudge! Isn't that wonderful! . . . But you're not supposed to eat it? Not either one of you? . . . Well, a little piece or two isn't going to kill either one of you. So I'm going to send some.

Ha, ha, I was just thinking. You know, I haven't got anything for spending the night. I mean, I haven't even got a toothbrush; so I've certainly got to buy one of those before I go out to Maudie's. Course, she can lend me a nightie and anything else I need, but— Oh yes, I'm very very very particular about dental care. You know what I've got at home? An electric toothbrush *and* an electric Water Pik. You would be surprised how much food debris remains in people's mouths—even after a thorough brushing, even after using *dental floss*. So I consider electricity one of the great blessings of the Age, especially to us who live in rural Missouri. Imagine now, I'm forty-nine, going on fifty, and just *look* at my teeth. . . . See? . . . You can't even see any fillings at the front, and I've got only two fillings in my whole entire mouth. Pretty good for an old girl, isn't it? . . . Well, it sure *is*, and I'm exceptionally proud of my teeth. And a funny thing— You'd be surprised if you knew how many patients of mine, through these years—people I've nursed—are *reluctant* to brush their teeth properly. Well, believe you me, when I'm in charge they *do* have their teeth brushed, and that's all there is to it.

And, speaking of rural electrification, do you know how many kilowatt hours that Bagnell Dam of ours delivers annually? Four hundred *million*. Yes, that's a fact: four hundred million kilowatt hours. And if we didn't have that Bagnell Dam, I bet you I wouldn't have any Water Pik, either. Or any electric toothbrush, or any electric anything.

. . . Here we are, and I just want to offer my thanks. . . . Oh, no, no, no, no, *no*, you're not going to get out of the *car*. . . . Now, here, see? I'll take this bag out *first* and then— No, there's not a good place for you to park, or anything. I'll take these things in myself. . . . Good Lord Alive—that's what I would have had to do if I'd drug this little coaster wagon all the way up to Fulton, isn't it? . . . There, now. And . . . the wagon. . . . Why, I do work like this all the time! I mean, far, far *heavier* work than this. I told you I didn't need a man around the place, and I *don't*.

I addressed her through the window. "Let me make a confession. This morning, while driving along and dictating some notes, I spoke critically about Callaway County and Boone County too. And Raymond Weeks. Let me say that you've made me change my mind.

After meeting up with you, I somehow find the works of Raymond Weeks more believable, and more acceptable."

"Well, I'm glad," she said decisively. "I do like *The Hound Tuner* pretty much, specially the idea of that old man riding along in the night with his hounds, and looking for his lost daughter, and everything. I thought *The Fat Women of Boone* was kind of disgusting. But we folks– Well, we considered Weeks to be a real native, even though he wasn't."

"Mab, one more thing. You said that you had taken back your maiden name. Are you *Miss* DuBart or *Mrs.* DuBart?"

"Either one. It doesn't matter. Thanks again for picking me up."

I said, "Goodbye, Queen Mab."

16. More Shoreline than Lake Superior

Before we arrived at the Bagnell Dam, signs informed drivers that the traffic limit was 25 mph. That was a laugh: we crawled across at 5 mph, like old ladies on an escalator . . . except that a workable escalator wouldn't be stopping from time to time. All cars came to a halt every thirty seconds or so, then started creeping again. . . . Illinois station-wagon ahead of us, jammed with children and camping equipment. Behind was a Wisconsin car—we recognized the driver from an hour back on the road. We'd seen him getting a ticket from a highway patrolman. The driver appeared to be about eighty-five years old—a meek-looking relic, quivery and quavery as he stood talking to the officer. But he'd been cutting in and out of traffic like a juvenile delinquent high on sniffed glue.

Beyond the dam, and when we could discover an unoccupied space alongside the road, we parked to let On Wisconsin get ahead . . . get *very far* ahead. Then we moved on, perforce slowly. With gloom I realized that I'd have to patrol there, north and south, two or three more times, in order to take it all in.

Roadsides adjacent to most summer resorts are obnoxious, but Lake Ozark, which this village is called, wins the pennant if not the World Series title. How come I ever growled about Cape Girardeau? But that is merely another small city with its outskirts defaced in the prevailing commercial fashion. This is a *resort.*

"Now quit gasping and cursing."

"But see what they've gone and done? Brought in those beautiful old weathered silvered saintly lichen-grown fence-rails, and dumped them in front of places like *this.*"

"Hush!"

OZARK MAID CANDIES, FOUR MILES. It didn't say why Ozark candies should be particularly fine candies, any more than candies made in Lake County, llinois, or West Dummerston, Vermont; but so be it. At least they don't call them Ozark Mayd Kandeez.

MISSOURI AQUARIUM. WHERE THE FISH EAT FROM YOUR HAND . . . OZARK WATER SKI THRILL SHOW . . . THE REBEL ARCADE, BIGGEST IN THE OZARKS.

"Exactly what does a 'Rebel Arcade' consist of? I have to keep my eyes on the highway–"

"Oh, pinball machines, bowling machines, shooting machines. And all sorts of–"

"Damn tourist trap."

"Don't you want people to have any *fun?*"

"Do they have to compromise their souls in order to *have* fun?"

. . . Cars are parked solidly on both sides of the road. OZARK GALLERIES. OIL PAINTINGS. WOODEN NOVELTIES . . . ARNOLD REALTY . . . TOWEL SHOP. TOWELS BY THE POUND . . . PEPSI SHAKE SHOP . . . ROYAL CROWN . . . LINGERIE. SAVE UP TO 50% . . . THE DAM CLUB RESTAURANT . . . ADAM'S MARKET . . . TEMPERATURE 77 . . . TASTEE BREAD. . . . Here's an arcade full of bump cars, here's the MOW EM DOWN shooting gallery. And a pancake house that's haunted. It says HAUNTED HOUSE, and they've got a kind of Boris Karloffian face on the front. . . . SKEE-BALL. Skee-Ball? You guess, I can't. . . . BAREFOOT TRADERS. By means of neon they display some barefoot traders in overalls. . . . AL ELAM. REAL ESTATE . . . EDGEWATER BEACH RESORT. NO VACANCY . . . STAR MOTEL. NO VACANCY.

And through all this wander in ambling multitudes the incredible, the credulous, the mad, the wistful, the graceful, the enviable young, the unenviable old, the unenviable young, the enviable old, the stupid, the wide-awake, the gross, the delighted, the bronzed and athletic, and filthy and sloppy, the sad, the glad, the indignant, the pleased, the unpleasant, the very pleasant indeed.

It might not be supposed ordinarily that the Ozarks have anything in common with Greenwich Village and the Everglades. But they do, because you can't find many people in agreement on where any one of these regions begins or ends.

Some New Yorkers insist that Greenwich Village starts at 12th or 14th Street, others say at 8th Street, many say at Washington Square.

In circulation are Florida maps which designate as the Everglades a blue-lined and tinted area with definite boundaries. Yet scrawnily populated Glades County, spread along the west and northwest shore of Lake Okeechobee, and including within its limits a large Seminole reservation, is a full two counties north of the Everglades as shown on those maps.

Lump all the territory between the Missouri and the Arkansas Rivers, say some, and call that the Ozarks. Other Missourians declare that the actual Ozarks don't begin until you get down to Springfield. Or Rolla. Or Mountain Grove. The highest point in the State, Tom Sauk Mountain in Iron County, measures exactly 1771.7 feet above sea level. That ain't very high. Indeed you can observe no mountains as such (until you reach Arkansas). You can call a hill a mountain, and folks do.

The Ozarks are geographically the eldest of our ranges. They have eroded, weathered down through the millennia. Once they might have looked like the Rockies, but that was when this planet was mighty young.

Assuming that Jefferson City marks the exact center of the State—which it very nearly does—then the Lake of the Ozarks sprawls some sixty miles south and west of the center. It amounts to a vast twisted dragon-shaped playground. An old man now squints his eyes, remembering the hour when he first came on the scene, and felt those same eyes smarting in dust raised by squadrons of mules and batteries of old-style two-handled scrapers. They were preparing to build the Bagnell Dam.

The principal rivers to be affected were the Osage and its tributaries. Once upon a time you might have crossed the Osage almost dry-shod, by springing from raft to raft. The stream was practically bridged by railroad ties going down to the Missouri and the Mississippi—lordly pine forests of the past—chopped down, trimmed, squared, borne away to leave their ancient hills denuded until new growth could green the slopes.

Bronze marker recites the story: "Bagnell Dam, costing over $30,000,000, was built by the Union Electric Company of Missouri, 1929–31. The Lake of the Ozarks, impounded by the 148 by 2,543 foot dam, is one of the largest man-made lakes in the United States.

It is one to five miles wide by one hundred and twenty-nine miles long, and has a thirteen-hundred-mile . . . shoreline."

More shoreline than Lake Superior, say the natives. "In northern Ozark counties of Benton, Morgan and Camden, and . . . east to Miller, and west to Henry and St. Clair," farms were erased, buildings torn down, lumber carted away. In town after town the citizens packed their duds, bade goodbye to structures which had housed them, and went up on higher hills to build anew. No one seems to know for a certainty how many graveyards were moved. I heard first that nineteen were to be moved, heard later that twenty-nine had been moved. Maybe some weren't moved at all, and their quiet inhabitants now rest deep beneath a bright surface where young folks go flashing on water-skis.

Those forests which still remained in the area to be inundated were sliced away with care. From an aesthetic standpoint, this was done in a triumph of engineering. One stands on any hill along that thirteen-hundred-mile margin, and he might be looking out at a storied scene in northern Italy, so prettily do woods descend—just to the water's edge, then stop. In the main body of the lake are no wastes where bare skeletons of dead trees rise in gloomy reflection. From the fishermen's viewpoint this is not an unmitigated delight. Bass and crappies would have fed and bred around and among those sodden trunks in profusion. So Izaak Walton might not approve the eventual result, but the postcard people do.

And they do say as how folks catch nice messes of fish, anyways.

In the middle of the night Irene inquired drowsily, "Aren't you asleep? Or are you asleep, and laughing *in* your sleep?"

I said No I Wasn't Asleep, and went on chuckling.

"You ought to stop annoying yourself with such an absurd problem."

"Can't help it. It *is* absurd. That's why I can't stop thinking about it. 'Welcome to a Bit of Denmark.'"

She cried, "Stop it! Or you'll have me lying awake too."

"'The Sherwood Cafe and Restaurant. Welcome to a Bit of Denmark.' For two cents I'd get up right now, and drive down there, and go in, and try to ascertain how and what and why—"

She said that I'd be in fine business doing that. The place must have closed hours before.

"You're probably correct. But let me tell you this: I've taken just about all the anachronisms I can take, in this day and age. My God, woman, do you remember the last time we were in Cleveland? We went into that hotel bar, and they called it The Round-Up Room or Empty Saddles in the Old Corral, or some such. There were branding irons and Colts revolvers and coiled-up lariats and Mexican spurs all over the place. In Ohio yet. Come-a-ti-yi-yippy-yippy-ay! . . . Down in Sarasota we've got the Detroiter Motel on the South Trail, and the Mt. Vernon Motel on the North. In my native town in Iowa, they've got the Flamingo Inn. The only flamingo Iowa ever saw was in a bird book. And I think it's south of Arnold's Park that you find the *Colonial* Chop Suey. . . . Emerson's Smorgasbord up in Maine, on the River Road below Newcastle. *Emerson's* Smorgasbord! Gosh all hemlock! . . . Remember our poor little crippled bookbinder in Florida? He lived and worked in a shabby trailer at the *Aristocrat* Trailer Park. . . . Remember dear dead Werner Christiansen in Copenhagen, and that lovely Thora, his wife? They had an inn down on the southeast coast of Seeland: the Rødvig Kro. Suppose Werner had ever come over here to the Lake of the Ozarks and seen 'Sherwood Cafe and Restaurant. Welcome to a Bit of Denmark–' "

Irene said, "Now, I've heard all I'm going to hear out of you. You remember Werner's restaurant in Copenhagen itself? And what was it called? *Au Coq d'Or*. Isn't there something a trifle anachronistic about *that?* Go to sleep."

Well, I did. But only after extracting from her the promise that under no circumstances would we exist through another day and night of perplexity. We'd lunch at the Sherwood Cafe and Restaurant, come Sunday noon, and learn what the Bit of Denmark was all about.

It's on Route 54 immediately below the Grand Glaize Dam.

Missouri is another State which subscribes to that insufferable notion about No Liquor on Sunday. But I doubt that they would have produced any Tuborg beer; and we didn't own any Aalborg Akvavit to carry along, iced, and pour surreptitiously into our water tumblers. And we didn't have any Cherry Heering to top everything off with.

But we knew that we were confronted with a rather large hunk of Denmark, the moment we met up with their split-pea soup. Time and distance and geography and mysteries and miracles of cuisine had all been turned topsy-turvy. We could easily have been at Oskar Davidsen's in the long-ago days when that place was really good. Irene ordered *Rodspaette Fileter* (Danish flounder) and I ordered *Danske Frikadellar Med Rod Kall* (Danish meat balls with a marvelous sauce, and red cabbage). Mashed potatoes too. (Just about what year did everyone start calling them *whipped?*) And currant jelly and hot biscuits.

Danish glass and china, peasant knick-knacks scattered around, *ja* . . . *Skäl.* . . . Tables and chairs of a style which you might find at Silkeborg, *ja.* Danish apple pie, if you please. In-mouth-melting. *Tak før mad.*

I'd asked a hostess when we came in, What about those weird signs outside? Could she explain, please? . . . Said she didn't know a thing about them. . . . Neither did our waitress, a handsome brunette for whom we promptly invented a background and career: girls' athletic director at a central rural high school in northern Michigan. She was working toward her Master's degree in Phys Ed, and had come down here to wait table for the summer. A sweet and husky lass, about ten cuts above most of the waitresses we'd been encountering, and about ten inches above them in height.

At last a good-looking gray grave man appeared (cashier? manager?)—one sedate enough to be night clerk in a Martha Washington or a Barbizon or an Evangeline or whatever they call those hotels where all the women sleep alone. Sedate or not, he was agreeable.

"Bear with me. I'll give you the story."

"Thanks very much. I've been going crazy on this."

"Then I'm happy to save your sanity. Sunday's the proper day for a good deed, isn't it? Now, then. Originally this place was called something else—I don't know what. It was a tiny restaurant, and there stood a motel right next door, and the motel had no restaurant. The motel guests came here to eat. But the motel, allegedly, turned into— Well, it acquired a bad reputation—"

"One of those hot-pillow joints?"

"I fear. Finally a new owner came along, and he or she changed the motel's name to Sherwood, apparently liking the sound of the name. As the Sherwood Motel it pulled itself up, and was rejuvenated and reformed, and everyone looked at the place with pride rather than suspicion. Later it was bought by a Dane. By that time the Sherwood had acquired the cafe which stood here—about a quarter the size of the present one. The food was— Shall we say undistinguished?

"The Dane went over to spend the winter in Denmark with his

parents. While there he was smitten with the idea of turning his Missouri cafe into a Danish restaurant. Which he did, on coming back. But, you see, it was too late to change the name of the motel. So it had to be 'A Bit of Denmark,' right here at the Sherwood Inn."

I saluted him thankfully. "Now I'll be able to sleep."

Irene said, as we drove on to find our friends the Cullerses at their summer cottage away up toward Gravois Mills, "You'll be able to sleep *if* those Danish meat balls and that red cabbage and the mashed potatoes you ate, and the sauce, and Danish apple pie with nuts on top—"

I used her pet name. "Reno, I wasn't alone in this. It had you standing on your head, too. But now that we know, we both must feel better about it."

"Yes, I do feel better. It's wonderful to *know*. Still—"

"Still what?"

"I can't get over feeling that it's a little like encountering Allan a Dale at Mamma Leone's in New York. Or Maid Marian at the House of Chan."

In late afternoon the surface of the lake, viewed close at hand, was a beef-broth brown . . . shimmered blue in the distance.

Bob and Nancy Cullers had invited friends for a little fresh-water cocktailing aboard their houseboat. We touched at various docks in front of homes where other friends were living, and they came down to climb aboard for a drink, or to urge the ship's company to step ashore and see how the other half lived. And we observed many other vacationers doing the same thing.

The houseboat picked up just enough wind in its leisurely progress to rattle a few pennants up forward. Cottages and resorts moved into view upon the lake's skirt, and receded in easygoing parade. Along the brink around Mill Creek and Cedar Point and Johnson's Bay, and on south toward Horseshoe Bend, there exist infinitely more waterside homes than are apparent when you look the situation over from hills on shore. Then, the cottages—or in some cases more impressive dwellings—are hidden by trees. Thus, from on high, the lake itself appears serenely unpeopled, until all the boats come out on a nice Sunday. And this was indeed a nice Sunday.

I sat aft, talking with a fellow guest who had enlisted my attention—and curiosity—when first we were introduced. He was a pleasant conversationalist: a well-set-up man in his late sixties, dignified but jovial. He had spent most of his life in banking, and was now rounding off a third term as Treasurer of the State of Missouri.

"Would I be out of line, Mr. Morris, in inquiring about your name?"

He laughed. "Everybody asks about that."

I told him, "When I was young, I met Judge Kenesaw Mountain Landis in Chicago. That was in the early days of the Izaak Walton League, to which he was very much devoted. But I never thought I would ever meet another Mountain. 'Mount Etna Morris.' That is truly your name? Not a nickname?"

"Truly my name. I'm a native of Dadeville, about eighty miles over here to the southwest. Most of my friends call me M.E., and a few call me Monty. My lovely new youthful wife—" He indicated a pretty woman sitting forward. "She calls me Etta."

The name had come down from a remote ancestor who was a Welsh fisherman. I don't know what any Welsh fisherman was doing so far away from Wales as to be down in the Mediterranean, but this Welshman was. He had lost his way at sea in a little fishing craft, and the compass was missing— It may have been carried overboard by waves. Anyway, the Welshman didn't know where he was.

Mount Etna Morris couldn't tell me which of the many violent eruptions was going on at the time. There were two disasters in the Seventeenth Century alone when many thousands of Sicilians perished. Might have been one of those. . . .

Through the fog and the smog and the grog, that fisherman managed to espy a towering mass of smoke and lava, which was Mount Etna in eruption, and this sight gave him his bearings. On reaching safety, he swore an oath. "I shall name my first son Mount Etna." It's been a family tradition ever since.

Mount Etna Morris leaned over and whispered, "You know, actually it's not a bad name for anyone to have, in politics. I discovered that when serving in the Missouri Legislature. Although I've never had the opportunity to sentence Standard Oil to pay back twenty-nine million, two hundred and forty thousand dollars, the way Judge Landis did."

"But wasn't that decision reversed, later, by the higher courts?"

"Certainly. Judge Landis's decision was reversed. But think how much fun he must have had *handing it down!*"

Others came to join us. I wanted to learn more about the boating situation, so I went forward and watched Bob Cullers at his steering.

"Want to take the wheel?"

"Thank *you.* Not with all this traffic."

"Oh, it's sporadic, kind of spotty. This is an exceptionally busy evening. Take these areas, where we are now— A kind of bottleneck. Even at this hour we might be in certain places where you couldn't see another boat. Unless maybe a lone outboard, or a canoe."

Bob and his spritely Nancy are two of the many gifts awarded us by the town of Trenton, where we alighted for a while. Bob is ex-Navy. (So is my son-in-law, so we don't fight about that.) He's also a banker by profession, with a keen inquiring awareness of all that goes on in his town and in the world outside.

"You saw me slow down for those water-skiers. And I changed course a little, too. Now, I recall that down there in Florida you have a regulation which decrees that there must be two people in a boat which is towing a water-skier: one to run the boat, one to watch the skier."

"That is correct."

"You may be surprised to learn that we also have such a law, only it isn't enforced. The whole thing is a mess, and I'm perpetually amazed that there aren't more accidents. They've been at swords' points around here, because the Water Commission in Missouri— The whole problem of regulation of this boat traffic got to be a political football. They were denied funds for policing the area; but still they didn't want the Coast Guard in on the act, because it was felt this would constitute Federal interference, and you've seen how most Missourians feel about *that.* The net result is that the regulation of boating activities has more or less gone by the board. Probably no tighter discipline will ensue, or be put into practice, until we have some horrid calamity to dramatize the necessity for regulation."

In turning to a pleasanter subject, Bob pointed out that the fantastic scenery could not be duplicated except at some other artificial lake.

For this reason:

In a natural lake, as along any natural waterway, when the banks are lined by timber it is softwood timber. Willow, cottonwood, soft maple, basswood, and the reeds and grasses to go with them. But here, as mentioned *ante,* when the inundation came about, trees on lower ground had been removed. In result, nearly forty years afterward, hardwood forests adorn the slopes right down to the very edge. White oaks, red oaks, Spanish oaks, shagbark hickories. Walnuts, butternuts, pignuts. This takes a little getting used to. It seems strangely contrived and yet arresting, to those of us who knew an age when there were no man-made lakes embellishing the country– Only swimming ponds above creek dams.

Cullers was still busy avoiding collisions. "You may wonder where all these outboard motorboats come from. Well, I can tell you: right off the farm. The prosperous Ozark farmer these days, on a Sunday morning, loads his Mrs. and the kids into the family car, hitches on a trailer which carries their boat, and off they go to the Lake of the Ozarks. Or, if he lives way down south, say in Stone County or Christian or Douglas, he heads for one of the lakes down there. They spend the day fishing, cruising, swimming, picnicking– Maybe the kids do a little skiing. Then at night the highways are stuffed with these fellows gong back to the old home farm. Lot of accidents too, unfortunately.

"But your farmer can take his pick of a thousand coves and bays. As you may have learned– *More shoreline than Lake Superior.*"

In the middle of the night I heard a screech owl's call, and went out to the screened porch to listen.

We were still at the Cullerses. We'd talked until very late, and then Bob and Nancy flatly refused to let us drive home to our motel on the other side of the lake.

"You'd have two choices," Bob said. "You could go the way you came–all the way down to Camdenton, and then back up on Route 54 almost to the Bagnell Dam. Or you could make your way through these complicated little side roads here, and get over to Route 5, and then try to cut across on county roads immediately north of the lake. You'd be sure to lose your way at night, especially since you've never driven there before. Remember what I said about home-going farmers, pulling their motorboats? Well, they're bound to be all over the roads right now. To say nothing *whatsoever* about people who've had a lot to drink! You're staying here, and that's all there is to it."

. . . Was it James Russell Lowell who said that the cry of the screech owl is the sweetest sound in Nature? Such a pleasant little warble it makes. To me there has always been a note of reassurance, rather than fright or lamentation, in the call. Though another name is the Shivering Owl, which relates by implication to the hypnotic spookiness of Missouri.

Definitely I am a pro-screech owl man. You can identify me as a congenital victim of Muridaephobia, meaning that I hate rats and mice, and have always been scairt to death of em! Well, the screech owls kill rats and mice like crazy; though I wouldn't care to join them in the repast which follows. But that's why screech owls are still in business. They like fish, too, and must scoop plenty of dainties from the lake.

Again and again the tender furry purl came forth. Suddenly I recognized a rare and exquisite moment. Such do come, I trust, to most of us: an instant in which one experiences an upsurgence of appreciation of Nature, of Humanity, of intricate Life at Large—a feeling of belonging, of thankfulness over the mere possession of appetites and ambitions and powers—a gratitude toward all Creation.

And a willingness to let others argue about who the Author might be, or why He Authorized these phenomena.

It is enough, you say selfishly. I am here. Glad to be here. . . .

Then, still hearing the owl, I came down from that momentary eminence, and consorted with the new friends whom our activities had granted to us. It was winning, to listen in recollection to laughter of the previous evening spent with Bob and Nancy and their daughter Sarah, and neighbors.

I had delivered a Philippic concerning a new high school building on the edge of Trenton.

"—There has sprouted, out of the dun dry soil, an edifice, or rather a related series of edifices, more imperishably ugly than anything Missouri ever witnessed before. It is the epitome of solid stolid brick-and-metal disaster."

Nancy saying, "Don't you *dare* put that in your book."

"Certainly I shall dare. Someone must raise his voice against a cubical music building without a window in it. And what about that pernicious pile over there at the rear? One workman told me it was the high school *garage*— Who ever heard of *that?* Another said, No, he thought it was the *agricultural* building. It is constructed of sun-baked left-over mustard—"

Again Nancy. "Don't you *dare* put that in."

"Why not?"

She said, "Because I fought very hard against the perpetration of that monstrosity. So everybody in Trenton will think I put you up to it. *I'll* get the blame."

"No you won't. They must blame *me*, and doubtless they'll feel that they have good right to. Tell them to go ahead and make a public bonfire of my books in front of the courthouse. Or, more appropriately, in front of that new high school. It constitutes a danger to the entire Trenton future. I have a nagging horrid dread that a race schooled amid such surroundings can only go on to something worse than the narcotic conformity and rigidity which now prevail."

A wail. "Oh, *please* don't—"

"My dear girl, your petition falls upon deaf ears. Once more the keen dark-uniformed white-shirted plain-black-necktied designers have had a love affair with their computers. Lord Almighty, I suppose *some* of them were educated right up there at the university in Columbia! Didn't they ever take a look at the breath-taking Columns?"

(Those Attic glories are all that remained after the original Academic Hall burned down in 1892. It is my private theory that the blaze was of incendiary origin, coal-oil and matches having been supplied by ancestors of modern architects. . . . Half the perpetrations of the Nineteen-fifties and Nineteen-sixties are not structures: they are strictures. My dictionary declares that a stricture is "a morbid narrowing of a canal, duct, or passage." Yea. Of the path which leads to the ethereal and eternal.)

"Oh," Nancy was crying, "poor Trenton! How can you *do* this to Trenton?"

"Justice shall be served."

"But it's only *your* interpretation of what constitutes justice!"

Bob Cullers remarked affably, "Well, I guess that's true of any book or any author, isn't it?"

I thanked Bob for this. "Other Trenton friends may be embarrassed, or even annoyed. Bill and Juanita Denslow, for instance. Or Gordon and Claire Blackmore. Or Bob and Louise Redd. Golly, Bob's the mayor, isn't he? But if I'm writing about modern Missouri, as well as the dream Missouri of the past, I must recite what I *see*. Mustn't I? And how I *feel* about it?"

My diatribe was concluded with a bloodthirsty recommendation. "There is only one good use to which some of those blank walls which encase the high school building could be put. That is to place before those walls the architects, and all other individuals responsible for this iniquity, and have them mowed down by a firing-squad."

This declaration was met with groans, as well as with cheers. . . . Huh. You can't get people to agree on anything.

I had felt sublimity and had recalled the ridiculous, all within a few minutes. Time to go back to bed.

. . . Lay there with peeled ears, before returning to slumber, hoping to hear the owl again. He didn't speak. I sensed instead the wide ripple of water, the boats bobbing or rubbing against their wharves, and was contentedly conscious of the joy which this Lake of the Ozarks, man-contrived, is giving to Missourians and others.

Just the same, the Shivering Owl is spooky too. And once upon a time, during a particularly cold and barren winter, a Spectral Owl, *Scotiaptex nebulosa nebulosa*, came down from Canada and died appropriately in Scotland County. And was discovered, frozen solid. Or so I've heard tell.

Boo.

17. The Dark Light-Colonel

The moth wore the angelic decoration of those newly emerged. It quivered on pavement of Howard Johnson's parking lot, dangerously close to an oil puddle which threatened not only to mar the glory of wings but to terminate the moth's life in misery if its body became smeared. This was a Polyphemus, hyaline spots glistening in sun, wild rose colors spreading toward wing margins, great silvery-blue eye in each afterwing daintily brushed . . . large specimen, a good five inches in spread . . . silky-tan realization of the Creator's dream.

But the insect seemed dazed. It might have flown against a car light during late hours of the preceding night. The wings were unbroken, yet there seemed to be present some condition of semi-paralysis. I knelt down, placed my hand in front of the trembling creature, and felt tiny feet walking into my palm. I stood up, holding the moth half-spread.

A bland voice, man's voice. "She is just the prettiest thing, isn't she?"

I turned. The speaker was a burly broad-shouldered Negro in sports shirt and slacks, carrying a shiny tan bag.

I held the moth out for his inspection, and he bent to savor the beauty intimately. "Oh, but she is *so* pretty!"

Although it was not yet nine A.M. by Central Daylight Time, the sun scorched down. We moved over into shadow of the motel.

I told the man, "It's a he, not a she. Notice those antennae, how thickly branched they are. Very fuzzy—that indicates a male. If it were a female the antennae would be slender."

"Do you collect these things?"

"Used to, when I was a kid. Wish I had the time now, and

the energy. I thought that I might become an entomologist, up until I was about fourteen or fifteen."

"What's the name of this butterfly?"

"No butterfly, it's a moth. *Telea polyphemus.*"

"Are they rare?"

"It used to be considered a common moth, years ago. Actually I don't think that many of these big *Saturnidae* are common today. There's been too much spraying, too much weed-killing and general destruction of natural growth along the roadways."

He nodded gravely. "In seeking to control one pest, people carelessly eliminate all sorts of natural beauties."

There was something exceedingly familiar about this man. I tried to reach back . . . the voice . . . I kept trying to make an identification. It turned out that he was doing the same thing.

Abruptly he put down his suitcase and thrust out his right hand. "Sixton here."

"By golly, Captain Edward Sixton! Wait till I get rid of Polly—" I went over to a hedge and deposited the moth thereon. Then Sixton and I shook hands, and I gave him my name.

He asked, "Where did we know each other?"

"You're a flight surgeon, aren't you, Captain?"

He laughed. "Well, I *used* to be Captain Sixton—"

I said, "I'm forgetting that a long time has passed. That your car there?" Cream-colored Olds with a California license and a Travis AF Base plate. Sixton said, "I was just about to get rid of this bag."

While he opened the trunk, I peered through a window. Above the back seat, clothing hung in plastic containers. There were several uniforms and, scrutinizing closely, I identified the silver leaves of a lieutenant colonel. After Sixton had closed the trunk, we both chuckled, and shook hands again.

"Congratulations, Colonel."

"Well," he said, "I guess it comes, if you can manage to hang around long enough. Where was it that we met?"

"Lackland. I used to do little jobs out there for Training Command."

"Oh, yes, yes, yes, I know now. You were always breakfasting late, and so were we. Remember? There was another colored surgeon stationed there—"

I said, "Dental surgeon."

"That is correct. The three of us ate breakfast together a number of times when we were the only ones in the mess. We did a lot of talking."

"Sure did." I told him why we were in Missouri. "My wife is in our room, doing that complicated job which women seem to be doing all the time: washing her hair. I just carried in her portable hair-dryer, and saw that moth on the way. So I hurried back to pick it up before it got squashed."

We returned to the hedge and searched for Polly . . . he had crept into a thicker portion, and that spasmodic shivering of the wings seemed to have stopped.

"I guess he's going to be all right. Probably got hit by something, and he's convalescing now. Colonel, what are you doing at the moment?"

"Not a thing. My wife's upstairs, sound asleep— I bet she sleeps until noon. She underwent surgery not too long ago: tumor, benign. I was finishing TDY in Colorado, and we had some Leave coming up. It's a mercy that Florence recovered sufficiently for us to proceed on our trip."

They were to go to St. Louis for a brief visit with Sixton's father; then to Dayton, Ohio, to see his wife's folks; then they expected to drive to Rhode Island and visit friends.

"It's going to be a real vacation. We'll just vacate and vacate, for the next— What is it? Thirty-three or thirty-four days? I'll have to look at my Orders again."

"Then what comes?"

"Pentagon."

We spoke about having a drink, but agreed that it was far too early in the day.

"Well, we can't talk in my place because my wife's asleep. And we can't talk in your place because your wife's washing her hair. Why don't we go in the cafe and have some coffee or something? You've already breakfasted?"

"Howard Johnson's is strictly for sleeping; not for eating, far as we're concerned. We drove up the road and ate, about an hour ago."

"We had some trays on our little terrace. Pretty bad. Then Flory went back to sleep."

In the cafe we found a table where we could adjust shades against the glaring sunlight. Sixton ordered coffee, and I asked for some orange juice and a bottle of soda. There was a copy of that morning's St. Louis *Globe-Democrat* hanging on the back of a chair at the table, and Sixton picked it up. He glanced at the front page, shook his head, passed the paper over to me. "I had one sent along with our breakfasts. I read all the paper this morning I wanted to read. Just look at that."

Wide headline: U.S. FUNDS USED TO TEACH HATRED OF WHITES. Along with the article was displayed a picture of two witnesses from the Nashville Police Department who had appeared before the Senate Judiciary Committee in Washington. Captain John Sorace, white; Leiutenant Robert Hill, colored. . . .

"Do you have any idea where it's all going to end?" Sixton asked.

I said, Yes, I had a very good idea where it was all going to end. That the United States of America would be up a certain creek without a paddle. I was explicit as to the name of the creek. We laughed grimly.

"What year was that, at Lackland?" he wanted to know.

"In 1948 or 1949. It was before I went out to the Korean War."

"So you got out there too?"

"Flew with the 92nd Bomb Wing. We were stationed at Yokota."

Edward Sixton said, "I was at Yokota also, for quite a while."

We found that we had been there a year apart.

"Let me ask an impertinent question, Colonel. Haven't you put on a lot of weight since those days at Lackland?"

He groaned, and rolled his eyes. "It's a disgrace. My wife's after me all the time about it. Oh, I play tennis, do some swimming, I've got some bar-bells right out there in the trunk of the car this minute. But you know what my wife says to me, MacKinlay? She says, 'Physician, heal thyself.'"

We strolled over to the lip of the hill, and watched a tumultuous job of earth-moving which was going on to the south and east. This was the new Interstate, which would relieve that bumper-to-bumper crawl across the narrow top of the Bagnell Dam.

"Construction, construction, construction," chanted Sixton. "About all you see, wherever you go. And a topic of conversation at all levels."

He asked, "Remember what we used to talk about principally, during those breakfasts we had together?"

"Yes. Racial intergration in the Air Force."

"We did." He stood there, overweight but still brawny, and his big golden-brown eyes seemed to hold a persistent question. "We were the first. The Air Force was first. I believe that the Army followed us, and the Navy came third. But I may be wrong about that."

. . . It didn't matter. The thing that mattered was the smoothness with which the operation occurred.

"On the whole," he said, "it was smooth. But will you please tell me why, if the Armed Forces can make such a transition, we as a Nation can't do it on the Outside?"

I shook my head.

"Well, I'll tell you why. It's because there are too many fools. Fools, fools, fools: colored fools, white fools. The Nation is saturated with them, and that's our self-destructive weakness. We permit the fools to *be* fools."

I asked wryly, "What have you got in mind? A program of euthanasia against fools?"

He doubled up, slapping his knees with his hands. "Dear Lord, I would enjoy very much being a part of such a program! I don't know exactly all of whom I'd put to sleep for a certainty, but I know some of them. Some black ones and some white ones. I mean to say, if I don't know them personally, I know who they *are*. But it isn't likely that I'll draw any such assignment. It would be good Duty, though."

He added earnestly, "There's one man I would not delete, if I were ever to command a Euthanasia Corps. That would be the guy who was our Provost Marshal out there at Lackland. You rememember his name?"

"Negative."

"Well, with this racial integration plan coming into being, everyone knew that we'd be faced with problems outside the Base, in contact between Air Force personnel and civilians. There was a little muttering going on in some of the San Antonio bars, ice cream places, places like that. Hot-dog places and beer places where the kids gathered. You may remember that, at that time, the people in Basic were given their first passes along in the middle of the course somewhere. Was it after five weeks? By that time a lot of friendships had been formed, and a lot of those friendships were inter-racial."

I said, "They certainly were. In addition to which, some of the Training Flight commanders and deputy commanders were colored boys."

"Anyway, the Provost Marshal didn't concern himself in talking with enlistees in Basic. He knew that all of those adjustments would take care of themselves within the structure of Air Force regulations. But there'd been all that gossip going on; so he and his people went into San Antonio and made a personal appearance at various of those joints I mentioned. He went around to the proprietors and said, 'I hear there's been some talk that there'll be trouble, if colored boys from Lackland and white boys from Lackland come in here together. I should like to inform you that if there's *one* incident occurring in your place of business, you will be declared Off Limits. No more Lackland personnel for customers. No more airmen from Kelly, or soldiers from Fort Sam Houston.' Those gentlemen read the message Loud and Clear. The boys said it was comical to see. One colored kid told me that he went into a beer bar with a couple of white friends from his Flight. Some character away down the bar asked in a loud tone, 'What's that damn nigger doing in here?' A squad of waiters converged on him in one split second, and threw him out the back door. No, sir, those places didn't want to be Off Limits."

Sixton pondered for a moment, then shook his head ruefully. "I'm afraid that anecdote emphasizes the real trouble. The Air Force Law could lay down the law in a case like that, but civilian Law can't ever seem to lay down the law. Too many idiots who won't let them do it."

The wind shifted, dry hot dust of the earth-moving operation began to blow toward us. We turned away and strolled to the rear parking lot of the motel. Sixton said that he should be going upstairs soon to see whether his wife was awake. I opined that probably my own wife's hair was getting dry, and she'd be ready to finish packing, and we could take off. But we were both reluctant to break away. Here was a colored man I could talk to, and I was a white man he could talk to . . . we spoke the same language.

"Ed, when you were a kid in St. Louis, did it bother you because you couldn't go to a white high school?"

"Not in the least. It was a case, among us colored, of going to either Sumner or Vashon. One was considered a little more—how should I say it?—elegant than the other. That is, among certain groups. But it would be staunchly denied by others. Anyway, I went to Vashon and was happy to do so. I don't remember ever being presented with any courses called 'The Negro in American History,' but I do know that I became well aware of the exploits of certain members of my race. Especially Missourians. Take people like Dr. Carver. Or Lawrence C. Jones: you know, he founded that remarkable Piney Woods School down in Mississippi. But he was born in St. Jo. . . . I guess the Black Panthers would call them both Uncle Toms, now. They'd call me one, too. But I remember being so thrilled, when I was around Boy Scout age, at reading Booker T. Washington. A teacher introduced us kids to *Up from Slavery* when we were in the eighth grade. I read it again and again, and even memorized certain portions."

"Do you feel that you were handicapped—that you had to crawl over especially cruel Obstructions on Course—in order to obtain your education?"

"Negative. I was aided by people all along the way. Anyone who got the idea that I was sincere in what I wanted to do— As I told you: Daddy was a postman, but he never encouraged me to go after a Civil Service job. Not when I'd once declared my desire to study medicine. He said, 'Sonny, you go ahead and work hard, and I bet you get there.' We've always had a good relationship, Daddy and I. Well, I worked first as a caddy; then I was bus-boy in a restaurant, and in another year or so I got to be a waiter. It meant getting up right early in the morning to get on the job so I could serve breakfast before I went to school, but the proprietor was willing to let me leave in time. Only trouble: there wasn't any time left for athletics. I would have enjoyed that. But that's not a problem peculiar to my race, is it? I know a number of white doctors who had to slug for their preliminary education and eventual training just as hard as I ever did."

He said, "But old Booker Washington went right along with me to Howard. After I'd finished there, I came back to St. Louis for residency. I spent four years at Homer G. That's the Homer G. Phillips Hospital, but everybody just calls it Homer G. Then I got a severe attack of patriotism, and went into the Army Air Force. Now I'm two years away from mandatory retirement. I say *mandatory*— I wish they'd let me stay another ten years. Still, it may be interesting to indulge in private practice somewhere for a while. I wonder whether it's as cold on the Outside as is commonly believed."

I remarked that most people found the temperature a little chilly when they first got Out. But Sixton's manner suggested that he had left something untold. He made a couple of false starts, lifting his hand, opening his mouth, starting to say a word, and then not saying it.

Finally he grasped my arm in a confiding gesture.

"You know, a few minutes ago you mentioned Obstructions on Course. I have been fortunate in not encountering too many of those. But one evil thing did happen."

He told his story.

"My boss's brother operated a garage down the street from the restaurant where I worked. He was a widower, and took his meals at his brother's place, so I got to know him quite well. When I was working there–summers, during college years–he knew that I wanted a car awfully bad. My Daddy enjoyed fishing and so did I, but it was difficult for us to go to a good fishing place without any car. Daddy and I both had bicycles, and rode those to our jobs and home again.

"Well, one day this garage man told me to come down to his place after I got off duty, and I went. Someone had traded in an old Ford roadster on a deal, and Mr. Bantine said he'd let me have it for peanuts. It needed a paint job, but he said I could do that myself, and use his equipment. He even threw in paint for the spray. In no time at all I had that car really looking like something. Got it all shined up, and even painted white sidewalls on the tires.

"Then I met a girl, and got quite interested in her. She was visiting friends in St. Louis, but her home was in Springfield, and she went home all too soon to suit me. So I had myself a little vacation, and drove all the way down to Springfield in short order. Couldn't stay long–couldn't afford to, really–but I did spend two nights in Springfield, and started home late the next evening. I figured I'd drive through the night and get to St. Louis in time for work next day. I was accustomed to going without sleep. Often did that; studied all night. It's not too difficult when you're young.

"In the middle of the night I got into this town. I hate to name the town, because I really ran into some mean people there. But that was long ago, and they've doubtless been supplanted by folks who are decent in heart . . . no, I shan't tell which town.

"I drove through cautiously, observing the speed limit signs. Course, there wasn't much traffic at that hour. Just about the time I reached the north edge, a red police light started flashing behind me. I pulled off at the side of the road. Two white officers got out of their car and said, 'What do you think you're trying to do?' I said, 'I'm not trying to do anything,' and they told me they didn't like fresh talk from any nigger. They said, 'What do you think you're doing, driving around without any tail-lights?' Well, I looked, and sure enough they were correct. Probably a fuse had burned out or something. I apologized, and said I'd get the tail-lights fixed, next time I came to a place which was open. They said, 'Oh no you don't. We can't have people driving around without tail-lights.'

"I argued with them a little, but soon saw that I wasn't going to get very far with any protestation. So I did as they told me to do. They said they'd go ahead, and for me to follow them to a garage, back downtown. It was a mangy little place, and the proprietor had an apartment upstairs. They called out his name, looking up at an open window, and told him to come down and unlock the garage. He came down with his nightshirt stuffed into his pants, and a pair of slippers on. He unlocked the garage, and they made me drive my car inside. I thought all the time that they had called the garage man down in order to fix my lights, but that wasn't the case. 'Oh no,' he said, 'I'm no electrician. I just own the joint,' and he and the cops laughed about that. They said that I'd have to leave my car, and have the lights fixed next day. I was really desperate, but there was no arguing with them. I *had* to get to St. Louis. They said that there was a bus which went through at two-ten A.M. Before I left the garage, I mentioned getting a receipt for my car, but the garage man said it wasn't necessary.

"I took the bus and got to St. Louis in plenty of time for work. I intended to go back down there the following weekend, and pick up my car. So I took the next Saturday off, and had reached that town before noon. I went to the garage, and there was the boss, same man who'd come downstairs in his nightshirt. He said, 'Boy, you're really a crazy nigger. I don't know what car you're talking about. Have you got anything to prove that you left it here? I haven't got your car. You get out of here, fast.' I got out of there, and went to the police station. I told the Chief of Police what had happened, and he said for me to stand there and think it over. 'Making false accusations is a very serious business. You know the names of the officers who stopped you?' No, I said I didn't, but they were night men, and I started to offer a physical description of the pair. He shut me up, and said, 'You're not describing anybody we've got on the police force here. I think you imagined the whole thing. Why don't you just beat it, quietly, and not get locked up for vagrancy?' So I did beat it, back to St. Louis."

Sixton said, "I had murder in my heart for a while, I'll admit it.

But my Daddy, he talked me into some form of submission. He said that there were cruel and wicked people in the world—too many of them—and I had just happened to run into some. He said, 'Sonny, I know some black folks who are every bit as mean as those white cops and that white garage man, down there in—' "

Sixton made a grimace. He'd almost let slip the name of the town.

"He said, 'For every evil garage owner there must be one who is not evil in any way. How about Mr. Jack Bantine, who let you buy that Ford off of him so cheaply? And what about Mr. George Bantine, your boss? How's he treated you, all along? If you had wrecked that car your own self, you would have lost it, and be no poorer than you are now, because you haven't been able to afford any insurance yet. So just pretend like an Act of God took it away from you, and don't go around harboring resentments against all white folks, just because you ran into a few wicked ones.'

"On the whole, it was good advice, and I took it. Otherwise, except for extremely minor incidents—you know what I mean: maybe housing or transportation difficulties— White people have been very good to me."

"And you've been very good to them."

"Yes," he said evenly, "I consider myself to be a dedicated surgeon."

"So you'd go the same route—choose the same life, if you were young again, and yet knew the way it would go?"

"Yes. Oh yes, I would." Sixton added in gaiety, "Naturally I hope the next time that pilot would zig instead of zag. I mean, on the first combat mission I flew, to see how it was with the boys from a psychological standpoint. I got a very lucky Purple Heart out of that one; but there were a few others in the airplane who weren't so favored."

One thing had been bothering me, but I decided to take the bit in my teeth. "Ed, is there any point in our having a mutual introduction of our wives, before we both leave this motel?"

He shrugged. "I don't see any point in it. They'll never be seeing each other again. They don't have any common background, as you and I do. No shared experience, however brief." Then he remarked thoughtfully, "It might be different if we were on the same Base."

"Guess you're right."

Sixton asked, "May I stand up as if I were in a pulpit or some such place, and quote something that is very dear to me? It's a thing that Dr. Washington said, and I learned it when I was a boy; then, through the years, it began to slip from memory. I could recall some phrases, but the rest–"

"I'd admire to hear you quote it, Colonel."

"We went into an antique shop, day after we started on this trip. My wife's crazy about antiques, and also she wanted to buy a nice present for her niece who's getting married. There were some second-hand books. I found *Up from Slavery*, more or less condensed in one of those books. So I bought it, and that night studied out the part I had known before. Maybe this portion is condensed, too, but at least I can say it now."

He said, "I wouldn't say it to everybody. But I like to *think* it."

His bright brown eyes were looking not at me but past me and into space and into distance. He stood at an easy Rest, feet apart, hands clasped behind him.

"'I have always been made sad on hearing members of any race claiming rights and privileges simply on the ground that they are members of this or that race. Mere connection with what is known as a superior race will not permanently carry an individual forward; mere connection with what is regarded as an inferior race will not finally hold an individual back, if he possesses intrinsic merit. Every persecuted individual and race should get much consolation out of the eternal law that merit is, in the long run, recognized and rewarded. This I have said here, not to call attention to myself, but to the race to which I am proud to belong.'"

I whispered, "Hear, hear!" We pressed hands together . . . both of us said, "God bless," and we went away from each other.

18. "Was the Road of Late So Toilsome?"

Susie Billings and her son, "that there boy Watson," lived on the east side of U.S. 65. Watson, a slow-spoken young-middle-aged man with a solemn face, had just finished building a new filling station, and was rightfully proud of it. He had performed the greater share of construction work himself.

Incorporated into plaster which covered the exterior were a collection of interesting stones. Watson Billings said that he had been collecting and saving them for a long time, just for this purpose.

He pointed out certain specimens.

"This here one looks like it could have been something made by the Indians, like enough. See those lines on it, and the way it's kind of chipped? . . . This here one— Now, this is what folks call a mee-tee-or. Can you imagine that one time this thing was red-hot? When it landed here in Benton County, after flying all the way—maybe from the Milky Way? Folks say as how they get hot from traveling through the air so fast."

His mother Susie was purple around the mouth. "Mulberries. Oh, how I love em! Use to pick em all the time when I was a little girl, many many years agone. We had a tree right in our yard. But I haven't had any for years and years. And yesterday I went up to" —somewhere or other—"and first thing I saw: a tree just plain loaded with mulberries. Well, I tell you, I picked and picked, and then picked some more. Brung home a big basketful, and I been piecing on em ever since. Want some?"

Her hair was chopped off in a short bob, almost in what used to be called a boyish bob. A little woman with a persistent but secretive smile, she was given to quick nervous gestures. You thought of a feminine Puck, a grandmother of dryads.

We must have visited with Susie and her son for an hour, but Susie did most of the talking.

"I adore to talk. Oh, my!" and she'd squeeze her darting eyes shut for a moment, and shudder deliciously in pure concentration of enjoyment. "Just adore to talk. Like to talk about *folks*."

She gave us the life histories of half-a-dozen fellow villagers.

". . . And Mr. Gadfry was sick I don't know how long before he died. It was something the matter with his stomach and"—(voice lowered)—"bowels. Poor old thing—you could hear him belch clean down to the corner. . . . Where you folks from? . . . My goodness, you *are?* Well, we do get all kinds past here. Other day we had a car stop from Texas. I spose I oughtn't to be surprised, but we've had em from California, too. Buying gas right here, from that there boy Watson. And come from *California!*"

Watson nodded. "Yep. And we had one carload from Portland, Oregon."

I had given long study to our map at breakfast time, and now I spread the map out and asked advice of the Billingses. U.S. 65 was paved; a road over in the next county to the east, a north and south road like this, also was paved. But in those days there was no U.S. 54 running west from Mack's Creek to Preston. In order to return north by a different paved route, we'd have to go all the way down to Buffalo in Dallas County.

"Still, it looks like it's only about ten or twelve miles from Cross Timbers to Mack's Creek, in a straight line. . . ."

Watson searched his memory. "I think there's a kind of road there. At least it goes part way."

"Do you think that I could get through in this car?"

"Well, now, I don't know. I know folks go through there a-horseback or sometimes in wagons. There just must be some kind of road, way back yonder. . . . That's the Little Niangua River . . . this here blue mark, running in between. . . ."

"If we could make it across from Hickory County into Camden County—from Cross Timbers to Mack's Creek—it might save us a lot of driving. I mean going clear down to Buffalo, and back on the other road."

"Yep, twould. If you could manage to make it. That other road over east is slab, just like this. Least you can do," said Watson, "is to try it."

When he said try, he said *trah*. When he said it, Irene squeezed my hand. We share an abiding partiality to honest idiom and dialect.

"Plumb certain you don't want some mulberries?" Susie asked. "Now you folks come back sometime," and we promised. (Did go back, too, twice through the years.)

We drove south to Cross Timbers and made a few more inquiries there. That side road, leading vaguely in the direction of the Little Niangua, was pointed out. But no one was sure how far it extended.

Irene said, "Best we can do is trah it."

The road had been graveled for a little way but soon gravel ran out. Then came dirt, ungraded; and then, gradually, after we'd passed a few small houses, we were traveling in two ruts with grass growing between. We went down into a creek valley. There was a concrete causeway with merry water running moss-green across it. This seemed like a real lark. I drove through cautiously, not wishing to splash the engine. Climbed a hill, went down another hill . . . twin tracks lured us on, the sparse forest on either side was shady and inviting. Wild weeds blooming . . . a scarlet tanager flashed across in front, his shiny black wings turned to silver.

Irene said blissfully, "The real back-yonder Ozarks. In June! Heaven must be like this. Or should be."

. . . Down another hill, warily. Yes, the ruts led to a new creekside. But here there was no causeway. Only clear water flowing, undisturbed except by a lazy catfish hanging with his head against the current.

"That's a ford, all right," I said a little dubiously. "At least I *think* it is. Aren't those tracks coming out, over there on the opposite bank?"

"Looks like, darling. Are you going to trah it?"

"Yep. Ah'll trah."

(Gad, how many times have I decried phonetic dialect, and insisted that it shouldn't be rendered? But it's sort of fun to trah it again.)

Hadn't forded an un-causewayed stream in a long time, and then it was in a venerable Model-T which had a lot of daylight under it. But here the bottom consisted of several stony shelves: we bumped easily from one to another. And, since there appeared to have been no heavy rains of late, we came out on the farther side without spinning any wheels.

Once across—

"Why are we stopping here?"

"We're stopping because we must decide where the road *is*. Ah jest cain't make out no more road, honey."

We got out for a survey. No longer any ruts or tracks. But were we imagining a wide space, such as a grass-grown leaf-strewn weedless one-time cart-path, opening ahead and curving off toward the east—?

It did seem like the way, after all. We followed this vague sluiceway for another ten minutes, then halted. Bingo. No more route apparent.

I got out for another exploration on foot. We were near the summit of a new ridge. In two or three places through low oaks I could see ground falling away to the east and south. After trudging in circles a while I found, about a city block to the left, a path suggestive of an old road. Tried to recall some misty tracking lore learned in boyhood . . . got down on my knees and examined the earth closely. Sure enough: hoof prints. Horses? Mules? And human feet—bare—had gone through an old mudhole now parched and holding the marks in natural moulage.

I went cheerily back to Irene and told her what I'd found. I didn't however, mention something else. Far ahead, as I lifted my gaze from examination of the path, I saw a figure running rapidly, disappearing amid hazel brush . . . young man, young woman? I couldn't quite decide. I thought it might be a girl. Bare legs flashing and a glimpse of pale blue fabric, that was all. Whoever it was raced with the speed of a weasel.

Picking a way carefully between larger trees, crushing down or scraping through berry vines, we drove to the path and then turned south along it.

"Are you sure this is correct?"

"By this time I'm sure about nothing. But at least it's a clear day. There are a few clouds, but we can see the sun most of the time. We know the time of day, and we know the main direction in which we need to travel. We'll progress through paths and cow pastures until we come out *somewhere*."

"How about our turning around, and going back the way we came?"

"Do you think we'd be able to follow our own tracks?"

Disquieting information was registered by the odometer. We had traveled nearly six miles since leaving Cross Timbers. I could not with assurance embrace the notion that we were already halfway to Mack's Creek. Were we even *on the way* to Mack's Creek? Still, the thought of trying to retrace our passage—a return route over the exact course we'd traveled—was intolerable. Often we'd driven across barren soil—hard-baked stuff which wouldn't offer a clue. Also grass was thin through other distances. On one slope we'd scraped over an expanse of naked rock from which all soil had been eroded.

We agreed that it would be tougher to go back than to forge ahead.

. . . Indeed this must have been a roadway at one time. At least a lane, wide enough for small vehicles. Trees lined the sides but we could always get between them.

Abruptly the path divided, as I'd feared it might.

Once more: examination of the terrain before us and the ground under our feet.

"The major amount of traffic has been on the right, not on the left."

"But don't we want to go southeast? If we go to the right, we'll be turning back *west*."

I said somewhat hopelessly, "Oh, these trails just wander around here and there. And then— Well— We'll probably get back on an eastern course later on."

"You were right," she exclaimed in a few minutes. "We're coming to a house. See? Gray boards—"

Gray boards all right, but they were merely part of a pile of leavings stacked up, some still standing, many fallen amid mounds of long-rotted sawdust.

"Somebody had a sawmill here, and was cutting out planks." I tried to speak in an encouraging tone.

She said, "They look awfully weathered. All twisted and bent and dried. Makes me feel a trifle mournful."

Nothing to do but go on, following the track. We encountered places where the trees were too close . . . had to leave the trace, go out to left or right, circling, backing, filling, in order to return to that vague line of hoofprints and footprints and dehydrated mudholes once more.

Then, rounding a sharp curve, we both exclaimed with satisfaction. Here was a house. Inhabited, too. Thin smoke issued from a tumbledown chimney. A sagging stoop had been built across the front of the shanty, and someone was sitting there.

"We'll be able to get directions. These folks can tell us how to get back to the road!"

A fence surrounded the place, but the gate stood open, and some pales were broken loose. High-backed hogs wandered at will or lay in shadows under the stilt-built house. On that stoop, a woman roosted with her back against smooth once-white-washed logs of the outer wall, and deformed legs were doubled partially under the rest of her body. Nearby were two little crutches—whittled from hardwood, crudely pegged together. But they were child's size crutches. The woman wore a calico gown so faded that she seemed one with dun logs, dun boards on which she huddled, dun stable and sheds beyond. Front door of the cabin stood open. As I walked hesitantly up to the edge of the porch, I could see the glow of fire on a hearth inside the house.

"Good day, ma'am." After a moment, I repeated the words weakly. And once more . . . in a manner of question.

Irene approached, coming behind me slowly, then she stopped. I heard her quick intake of breath as she estimated the quality of the cretin before us. The woman might have been seventy . . . might have been eighty years old. Her face was like a crumpled brown paper sack into which countless creases had been squeezed. Shoe-button eyes peeped out from under pink lids. She held her mouth open and was breathing rapidly. A clawlike hand stole out, trying to grasp one of the crutches. Perhaps she had some notion of using it for a weapon if we came too close.

"Ma'am? Is there anyone at home, please? Anyone else? Any of the folks?"

She spoke no word in reply. Just battled us with those fierce shiny eyes. I thought of a black widow spider. Oh, maybe she was a widow, maybe a spider . . . although she wasn't black. The eyes. . . .

Her creped mouth opened wider. At last she spoke. Two words. "Henry gone," she said.

Then again, to make sure that she was understood, "Hennnry gonnne," and dragging out the n-sounds as if guided by some mysterious instinct toward onomatopoesis.

Irene whispering. "Poor thing. Oh, poor little old *thing!*"

I made bold to ask just where Henry had gone, where we might find him. Convulsively the creature turned her head down against her shoulder and flung one bony arm in front of her face. I turned away quickly. Irene was gone ahead of me, but looking back over her shoulder. "Come *on*. She's utterly terrified. We must get out of here and not frighten her any longer."

Stubbornly I insisted on going around to the back of the house, looking this way and that, to see whether I might discover Henry or some other relative. In desperation I called two or three times. "Hello . . . hello!" Echoes rapped back across the garden patch, echoes came out of boulders and a bulging cliff. *Hello, hello, hello* in quaint flat voices. I scooted for the car.

Irene spoke as we rocked down the trail. "I don't think she moved once. Although your calling probably frightened her even more."

Two or three hundred yards past the shanty. . . . "Hey, Reno! Do you see what I see?"

"What do you see?"

"Tracks. Wagon tracks. They're numerous. This has become a *road* again. I was so upset by such misery that I didn't realize–"

"Oh, God," she said. "And I suppose she's been that way all her life. However long that's been. Sixty, eighty years?"

Grim thought. "Could be forty, as well. Anyhow let's give thanks for ruts and tracks."

They led us down to another stream–or perhaps the same stream, farther along in its meanderings. Another ford . . . we bumped through without trouble. Tracks guided us into a bountiful stand of nut trees.

We were so encouraged that we were singing.

> Flowers I leave you on the grass,
> All the flowers of love and memory,
> You will find them when you pass. . . .

"Wouldn't it be wonderful to come here in the fall, when all those butternuts and hickory trees are loaded?"

"There's more than even the squirrels can use. Look at the old ones from last year, lying thick among the leaves, scattered all over the place–"

Irene cried, "Men ahead!"

"Where?"

"I saw them while you were looking out at the nuts. Just beyond that next patch of brush–"

Honestly at that moment I was near to being uninterested in any men. The thing which we had just witnessed . . . our meeting with the shriveled creature on that stoop . . . kept thinking, *What a scene in a novel!* (Quite some years would elapse before I'd use it. But use it I did, except the specter became a little girl instead of a crone.)

Men indeed: six of them. And a freckled-faced girl, fifteen or sixteen years old, barefoot and dressed in frayed short-legged blue overalls. I thought quickly of the runaway figure I'd seen disappearing along a path. . . .

Six men on the youngish side, ranging perhaps from twenty-five to forty years in age, assorted as to size and dress. Overalls, mostly . . . torn and sweaty cotton shirts. One was in his undershirt, and wearing a pair of obsolete Army pants which flapped around the calves of his legs where once they might have been laced. All wore shoes. One had a lever-action .30-30 Winchester in his hands, another wore a holstered revolver. There was a brand-new (looked like) automatic shotgun leaning against a tree. Several of this party were breaking up clods with shovel blades, spanking the earth down over a ten-foot-square area which had been dug up, and where clayey soil was now replaced. A couple of pick-axes lay tossed aside. The diggers must have had a hard time getting through that topsoil.

I shut off the ignition. The young girl in overalls– She had a sweet face, but pale and studded heavily with freckles. She drifted around behind the men, kept her eyes on the ground.

I said, "Howdy, everybody."

Not one syllable of response.

I nodded again. "Good day."

In the most casual fashion in the world, the man with the .30-30 strolled forward and put one elbow against the roof of the car, leaning in a manner of assurance or deliberate impertinence, we couldn't tell which. We both admitted later to being very much frightened. Then, when he bent down and smiled and nodded, we felt slightly reassured. His face was thin, tough, sallow. He had shaved that morning –and cut himself, too, in a couple of places. He wore a narrow pencil-traced black mustache. I took him to be about my own age. There was inherent mockery in the manner in which he called me *sir.*

"How do do, sir. How do do, ma'am. Where under the sun do you folks think you're a-going to?"

"We *thought* we were going to Mack's Creek."

"You got an Ioway license plate on your vee-hicle. What do you want with Mack's Crick? Got any kin there?"

I brought out my map and explained the whole matter . . . how we had come to be wanderers in remote roadless woodlands. His companions stood mute behind him. He was the admitted leader and spokesman.

"You know, I conclude that you're the first motor vee-hicle that has ever come this way." He turned to the others. "Mack's Crick. You gentlemen think they can get there?"

There was a mumble, I couldn't tell what was said. The girl still skulked around. Idly she was switching at her bare feet and ankles with a green basswood water-sprout.

Every man in the group with one exception wore a black felt hat. The one exception was that individualist who had donned the faded military breeches. He had a plaid cap. The cap was bunchy and bulky, it puffed out beyond the contours of the wearer's head. I had such a cap myself in 1917.

He was the one who now came forward. I judged him to be in his middle thirties—perhaps the father of the freckled girl, since his face was adorned plentifully with the same pigmentation.

In a mildly apologetic voice. "They mought get drownded out, at Tipton's."

There rose a vague murmur of disagreement.

"No," said the tall spokesman. "Water hain't very deep at Dorsey Tipton's ford. I'd be more doubtful about them crossings beyondst. Say, over next to Korthy's."

He looked at us again, and smiled. "Tell you something, sir. You sure must of been traveling through hog lots and I don't know what-all, to get as far as you've got. But from here on, there is a road, of sorts. Man wants to take his folks to Mack's Crick, he can do hit. With a team. I'm just not plumb certain about this here car. What do you call it, anyway?"

"Chevrolet."

"What do you know about that? Chev-roll-ay!"

"Bunce Griffith once't had a Chev-roll-ay," announced one of the others, "fore he come back to live with his folks."

"That's right. I recall his telling of hit."

The leader-spokesman—call him what you will—fellow with sallow face and hairline mustache— He stepped back and bowed almost cordially.

"Wish you a good journey." With that I observed something I hadn't noted before, when he was closer to the car, and his exhalations were directed over the top: the unmistakable odor of corn whiskey delivered secondhand but strongly . . . he had drunk a little more than the others, perhaps? He was comparatively loquacious, and kindly disposed to us strangers.

We burned with curiosity, longing to inquire about the activity they'd been pursuing with pick-axes and shovels. Yet something warned me not to speak of it.

The spokesman took the matter under control in his own manner.

He said distinctly, shaking his head, "Poor old mule."

I had started the engine in response to what seemed an invitation for us to get out of there. Now I paused, and spoke through the open window. "Poor old mule?"

"Yep. A white one. He got smitten by lightning, and killed deader'n a doornail. Poor old white mule. So we had to lay him away."

He broke into quick laughter and, with his free hand, jerked his thumb in the direction in which we should be traveling. Jerked his head, same way.

We stood not upon our going.

Irene kept watching the mirror. "They're still staring after us. Going to watch us out of sight."

"'Poor old mule,'" I quoted, when we were safe amid trees and underbrush. "You know what he had reference to, don't you?"

"What do you mean?"

"White mule. That's one of their names for moonshine whiskey. One of many. Also, that mention of lightning was appropriate as well."

"You mean to say that they bury whiskey in the woods?"

. . . An aging process was involved. And, from what I had read of the region and the little I already knew of it, I was aware that when moonshiners wished to age a batch of their product, they didn't bury it anywhere in the area adjacent to their still. Took it away off somewhere else. The Law might find the still but not its product. . . . These Six Wise Men had chosen a good spot. It was right alongside the main-traveled route, but one good rain would smooth the clay and furrow it—wash a little off the surface. Stones and forest rubbish scattered . . . no indication that there'd been any digging at all.

At last I felt like telling Irene about that vanishing figure far down the path, when I was out exploring an hour before. "She probably watched us when we stopped in those woods, and I got out to look for the trail. Then she took off. So they were warned of our coming. I'm mighty glad that you were with me. If I'd driven down here with— Say, Don Murphy or Tom Duncan— We'd probably have heard a few bullets whining over our heads as a gentle warning. But I doubt that revenue officers bring little blondes along."

Irene's voice was tender. "Do you suppose one of those men was Henry?" She was thinking of that crippled pixie on the stoop of the faded house yonder.

More creeks, more crossings. In one of them, at the deepest part, we heard an ominous crunching. I halted for a moment, then realized that we might bog down entirely. Wheels spun, roaring, then we were out. I looked under the car: everything seemed all right. But that was a close one.

We started up another hillside. Here were two small figures, frozen as statues in front of a tangle of blackberry vines. The little boy was about nine, the girl perhaps six. Their clothing was wornout but had been painstakingly mended in places . . . they were clean. The little boy's hair—we could see it under the rim of his flat felt hat—had been trimmed by loving scissors, and neatly. Each of the children held a tin pail, well filled with berries. But possession of these good things did nothing to ease the stark amazement and dread with which these berry pickers regarded our approach.

We paused, engine still running. The girl shrank completely behind her brother and refused to even peer out again. The boy's pail shook in his hand.

We spoke in the most friendly accents we could muster. "Have you been picking a lot of berries?"

His lips were shivering. "Nnnnno."

"Is this your little sister with you?"

"Nnnnno."

We drove on up the hill. Both youngsters had taken to the brush the moment I put the car into gear.

I lost track of the number of stream crossings, but Irene said that she'd kept careful count. Already we'd forded eleven times, including the causeway near Cross Timbers. We had been roving these ravines and ridges for five hours. It seemed like a week.

"How many miles have we traveled?"

"Sixteen."

"At least the farther we go, the more this road appears to have been used. It's very easy to follow."

"Lady Macbeth," I said. "'Is that a dagger that I see before me?' I mean—another ford?"

. . . Everything went well until we were almost at the opposite shore. Then a terrific thump underneath. The car lurched, we'd struck a rock. I stopped, but water began to push ominously against the wheels, and we were settling lower. The motor was still running, it hadn't been drowned out. I kicked the accelerator, and in seconds we were free of the stream, high but not dry, on the bank beyond. There'd sounded portentous banging and clanking.

I shut off the engine and got out and got under. Those Chevrolets sported a cradle beneath the front floorboards, a bracket in which the battery rested. In striking the rock we had snapped off that U-shaped metal strap. Our battery dangled in space, suspended only by cables. Even as I looked, one cable slipped from its post. The battery dropped, tilted further, swinging a few inches above the ground.

I wanted to cry but couldn't. Hadn't cried since my dog was poisoned when I was fifteen. It would have been easier if we both had shrieked and exploded with tears. *Waaah*—like Snoopy in Charles G. Schulz's inspired cartoon strip, when he, Snoopy, was running for public office. (Many years afterward.)

From the car sounded a forlorn voice. "Is it bad?"

I explained what had happened.

"Is this anything you might be able to fix?"

"I think if we had some rope—which we haven't—I might be able to make a sort of shelf to hold the battery. By the grace of God we'd still get to Mack's Creek: there must be a garage or machine shop there. But we can't move until the battery is properly sustained. So get out, and we'll walk to the next house. Somebody may have some rope."

"I wonder how far that will be."

It was less than the distance of an ordinary city block. We realized, as we rounded a curve and saw that lovely cabin sitting on its hummock above the sketchy road, that we must have been hearing poultry ever since we first emerged from the stream. Chickens went shrieking and streaking off in all directions. A few guineas scattered, emitting staccato cries, their red faces and wattles gleaming like paint.

Another small figure sped away as well. Like most of the hill cabins, this one was built above the ground with open space beneath. As we approached we saw a naked boy under the house. Four-year-old size. He darted up the slope into narrower darkness at the rear . . . went on hands and knees, swift as a rat. We did not see any more of him, nor did the two members of the family with whom we talked mention him at all. (Non-ivory-tower novelists are apt to be rolling stones, but they do gather a generous subsistence of the moss of experiences. If I hadn't glimpsed that infant worming around under the shack there would have been no Zoral Tebbs in *Andersonville.*)

On a sturdy front gallery sat a woman of middle years, ensconced in a splint-bottomed chair, with benches in front of her on which rested several baskets. She was shelling peas, letting them fall into a pan held in her aproned lap. Fingers continued to do their work automatically while we came closer. But she was watching us every step of the way, and smiling in unmistakable pleasure at having visitors, even strangers.

Her greeting chorused with ours. Her face exhibited a record of hard work and exposure to weathers, but the brown eyes were brightening in welcome. She was bare-headed, though a slat sunbonnet hung on the chair behind her. Her hair interested my wife especially . . . Irene talked about it afterward . . . how smoothly the hair was arranged, drawn down and fastened in a thin bun at the nape of her neck; but so clean and smooth, with gray and reddish tones resembling the grain of polished cabinet wood.

Thin clear voice. "Where mought you folks have drapped from?"

"Iowa."

Promptly she upset her pan of peas. Peas went shooting all over the porch. A few of them disappeared through cracks, but they may have been retrieved and gobbled by the child down below. Irene exclaimed sympathetically, and ran up to help in the peas' recovery. I remained down in the yard, for a giant of a young man had just come round the corner of the house.

He was shirtless, a mat of glinting red hair tangled over his wide chest. Bulbous muscles of his arms and shoulders bulged under varnish of sweat. He had on a pair of khaki pants belted around his waist, and they were too small for him . . . one seam had split open along the thigh. His bare feet gripped the ground in prehensile fashion. Once, during the succeeding time we spent there, I saw him idly grasp a sharp stone which had offended him, and pull it from the earth, gripping the thing between his big toe and second toe. Then with a kick he threw the stone away.

Up on the stoop I heard the woman repeating, "Iowa," in wonderment. She asked seriously of Irene, "Did you come by shank's mare all the way?"

The young man was perfectly willing to shake hands, perfectly willing to listen with impassive countenance as I told him our troubles.

"Hit's hard for me to believe that you come here in a car. We'd shore like a car, but hain't never made bold to trah one. Though they do talk about building us a better road, one of these days."

. . . If he could furnish a small quantity of rope—stout clothesline would do—I could probably suspend the battery in a hammock which might enable me to drive all the way to Mack's Creek for more permanent repairs.

"I hain't got no rope of any kind at the moment. But I reckon I could war hit for you." He pronounced *war* not to rhyme with a war in which you fight, but to rhyme with a car you drive, a bar at which you drink.

The giant disappeared for a few minutes, then came back with a length of wire adorned with huge barbs. Looked like the old wire from World War I, which can still be found tangling through French woodlands where signs with skulls on them warn you not to mess around with any *engins de guerre*.

"This here is rusty, but hit's still got a lot of strength in hit. Reckon hit will sarve."

Hit did sarve. Fifteen minutes later the battery was solidly in place, supported by twists of barbed wire. I fumbled around incompetently, trying to assist, but Giant did the lion's share of the work and then the lioness's. I had taken up floorboards and cleaned guck off the battery cables, while he stretched out below, braiding wire and securing it to rods on one side. "Now, whilst I lift up the bat-air-ree, would you be so good as to hold it whilst I fix this war on tother side?"

Gaping, I watched this man put two fingers under that battery and lift it easily on those two fingers as he managed the end of twisted wire with the rest of his hand. (Some readers will think

I'm making this up. I shan't blame them in the least. You had to see this to believe it.)

When I pressed the starter, and heard a rewarding rattle of the engine, I wanted to bow down and worship that young man. But I knew better than to offer him money.

We halted in front of the house, said goodbye to the lady thereof. There was some more hand-shaking.

"You've surely been a friend in need," I told Giant.

He threw back the old saw promptly, with a grin on his streaked round-cheeked face.

"A friend in need is a friend indeed."

They waved us on our way.

In another half-hour we saw our wheel-tracked and foot-printed trail joining with a real road where *cars* could go. Near this juncture stood a house. Once again the front porch was inhabited, this time by a round-shouldered elderly man who had a cane by his side, the traditional broad-brimmed hat jammed down over his forehead, and a beard of dappled black-and-silver flowing to his waist.

"Please, sir, how far to Mack's Creek?"

"Nigh onto four moll." His voice rolled, deep and echoing, a bell speaking in the night.

We wanted to dance in the single street of Mack's Creek when we got there. Yes, here was a garage. You couldn't tell who was the ruling mechanic and who were merely loafers, hangers-on. They all got up off their haunches and came to look at our car, and to approve the fine job which Giant had done.

"If hit wore me," said one, "I'd just continue right on up to Ioway, and not do nothing else about hit."

But welding tools were available, and strips of metal. The garage proprietor nodded, and said he'd fix us up in no time at all, and did we want to buy any gas? We did.

"Any place to eat around here?" and everybody pointed.

It was a dingy cafe, full of flies. Strips of sticky flypaper curled from the ceiling, encrusted with black bodies of those which had gone to their doom. But plenty of their relatives were still alive and frisky. We each ate with one hand, and batted flies away with the other. Our meal was fetched more quickly than we could have thought possible at that afternoon hour. Fried catfish, home fried potatoes and onions, hot corn bread, bacon and bacon gravy, some sort of cooked greens, blackberries . . . it all tasted home-made or home-picked or home-caught or home-gathered.

The wispy little lady twisted her hands in a soiled apron. "Is everything all right?"

"Everything is divine," Irene said. "Did you make these pickles yourself?"

Proudly. "My sister makes em. They're right good."

"Everything is right good," we chorused again, flapping at flies.

Through a smeared window we watched the people of Mack's Creek and visitors from surrounding hills. Almost to a man the males wore black hats and the overalls which were next to being uniform. Older women had their sunbonnets, but younger ones strolled bare-headed, pleasantly aware of the shine of their hair. Yes, more and more were wearing it bobbed . . . only a few girls left with long hair now.

Across the way stood the local bank. On its window was printed the bank's name and– *Capital and Surplus, $15,000.*

That's the Ozarks for you.

Ha, what am I saying? That *was* the Ozarks.

Forty years ago.

Forty years ago we had never heard of a Nazi, or anyone named Adolf Hitler, or anyone named Joseph Stalin. No one had ever seen a picture of FDR in the White House. No one had ever heard of a Bank Holiday or anything called The Depression. If you'd said "Battle of Britain," folks would have thought you referred to the year 1066 and the Norman Conquest. . . . Where were such places as Tarawa, Iwo Jima, St. Lô, Bastogne, Remagen? On the moon, maybe. . . . The Japanese were a quaint people who raised silk-worms, sold fans, wore kimonos, and said, "So solly."

The execution of Ruth Snyder and Judd Gray was still fresh in the public mind. (They had beaten their victim to death with a sash-weight, so no anti-gun legislation was in the works. Navy wives were not heroically turning in the weapons which their husbands had awarded them for home protection while they–the husbands–were gone away on active duty; and the Boy Scouts of America were not about to sagely dispense with their merit badge for Marks-manship. No one had imbibed any cocktails of *psycho*delic hysteria. To stop and think for a moment, Robert F. Kennedy must have been playing with a toy pistol or two at the time; and, as a tiny tot in

Massachusetts, he was totally unaware that a brown baby named Martin Luther King had recently been born in Atlanta.)

We went back to Mack's Creek last year.

The Basket King of the Ozarks was advertising with a tumult of signs as we approached from the north on U.S. 54. DAVIS BASKETS. They had not only baskets; they proffered everything from hickory nuts to T-shirts—fireworks, huckleberry honey, sweaters, sassafras candy, jams and jellies, hand-blown glass. And Concho Belts, whatever those are.

When at last we came to the Basket King's lair, we took it to be one of the ghastly tourist traps to end ghastly tourist traps. Gas pumps out in front, of course; a few cars parked; and all sorts of wares strung along walls. Same thing you see in the Great Smokies, where avaricious descendants of the once-significant Cherokee stand out in the middle of the streets of adjacent towns, offering articles for sale, and wearing costumes which would have made their noble ancestors throw up: war-bonnets modeled after supposed style of the Sioux or Pawnee, but fashioned entirely of pink and green feathers. (The Cherokee didn't wear those spreading war-bonnets. None of the Eastern tribes did.)

Not only were the Davises vending T-shirts and Concho Belts along Route 54; they were selling bird baths too. And ceramics . . . ceramics designed, we decided, by inmates of a State Hospital at Fulton or Farmington. The bird baths would have frightened any self-respecting bird out of his wits.

Mack's Creek. Population 123.

Anyone care for recent statistics on the Bank of Mack's Creek? *Capital, $25,000. Surplus, $50,000. Undivided profits, $65,768.* Course, the dollar hain't war hit wore in 1929. . . .

We sat parked a while in shade, watching two little girls and an orange-colored kitten a-skirmishing in play. Some elder buildings still wore their sloping canopies of wood or corrugated iron, supported by posts or by brackets sticking out from the fronts of the stores. Barns and woodsheds beyond . . . a dozen cannas in bloom, and modest display of dahlias and roses brightening a stucco wall. The populace moved in thin parade, entering or emerging from the Missouri Farmers Association grocery store.

On a hill northwest of the village proper, stood the Mack's Creek Clinic. It had a canduceus, somewhat modernized in design, on the side of the building. . . . Go back. Oh, go back, far into brush beyond the Little Niangua . . . go back forty years, and gather up that lamentable dwarf who squatted beside her crutches on the shanty stoop. Fetch her along to this fine new clinic.

Can they do her any good?

Nay.

But today's little boy who steps on a rusty nail—

No longer need there be resort to a poultice of sour dock leaves and spittle, bound against his dirty foot. They load him into the new Falcon, and rush him to the Mack's Creek Clinic where he receives the proper shots, and everything is taken care of. No need for his parents to complain that "Alfie's got an awful misery. His leg is all swoll up. Reckon we better send for Granny Langford?" Granny could not have helped, either, back yonder then. Alfie would have perished, and in agony, and would have been toted to that lorn burying-ground alongside the barren one-room church, to tenant pebbly soil adjacent perhaps to that occupied by our old man with the long beard and the bell-tone voice.

But in this decade the caduceus offers its promise, as it afforded appeal to myth-dwellers who watched Mercury bearing it hither and yon. Alfie gets his shots; he lives, plays basketball, goes up to the Lake of the Ozarks to work all summer, and earn enough money to buy himself a used Chevy II.

A new brick schoolhouse on the extreme hilltop behind and above the clinic, and rows of yellow buses parked in their season. The Camden County young are exposed to intermediate education not much different from that supplied in Maplewood, Willow Springs, Poplar Bluff . . . name the tree, name the town.

If Alfie remains in his home community, he may become a partner in possession of a Laundromat. His slim wife, with flaxen Saxon hair and cheekbones of the tie-whackers who bred her line, will go out in stretch pants to manicure their lawn with a power-mower. At night they'll eat TV dinners and watch whatever's on their favorite channel. And they will have a boy, Sean, named after a favorite actor. And a little girl named Sheri or Kim.

An indigo bunting adorned the air in front of us, iridescent as his remote ancestors we'd glimpsed long before . . . like the "changeable" taffeta of that age . . . Persian blue, indigo again, black as he flashed into shade.

Then a hideous dump: papers, cans, cartons, an old stove, flung heedlessly on the border of once-pristine woodland. . . . New ranch-style homes dotting the region . . . twin jet contrails bending high and far across the blue, above clouds to the south.

"It must have been somewhere down this way. The bearded man with the magnificent voice–"

"Probably within a mile or two, one direction or another. But we'd better turn around, get off this side road, go back to the main grade again. We don't want to try to ford any streams in this here contraption. General Motors would be perfectly furious."

I pulled into a lane beside a small house. Young fellow out in the yard, working on his motorcycle . . . aye, a *Japanese* motorcycle. Backed around, returned up the steep hill, and across a ridge, and down to Mack's Creek.

We went into the restaurant to eat. On the window they advertised *Home-made Biscuits* and that sounded beguiling. This was not the restaurant of yore; no flies, Ma; the place was well ventilated and cooled. The jook-box was sacred at the moment to a demoniacal chant, but Elvis Presley was probably standing by to take over. Noisy teen-agers grouped along the counter . . . a thirtyish mother and her two daughters came in. All had their hair done up on plastic rollers, and there wasn't a skirt in the lot . . . girls in abbreviated shorts, mother in toreador pants. They called back and forth shrilly, talking with the long-hairs at the counter.

Our lunch arrived: fish sticks, obviously of the frozen variety, for Irene; a so-called steak for me, pounded thin as a sheet of paper, and with a clammy bandage of batter wrapping it. They did have some delicious green beans, however, and mashed potatoes and gravy fit to eat.

Same old Super-Mart formaldehyde biscuits which had been set before us in scores of Missouri towns.

"Miss, it says, there in front, 'Home-made biscuits–' "

"You didn't ask for em. Ought to have asked."

"Can't we have them now?"

"Haven't got any today, anyway. Got home-made pie."

I tried a piece . . . home-made by whom? Engelbert Humperdinck? He was occupying the amplifiers now, bawling and blatting. Last time we'd encountered Engelbert Humperdinck he was infesting the Palladium in London.

Irene said, after we left the cafe, "Do you suppose there's any place where we might rent a jeep?"

"What would we do with a jeep?"

"I thought it might be possible, if we could rent one, to drive along some of those trails where we once went, and–"

"See things as they once were?"

She mused for a while . . . laughed sadly. "I don't suppose there's ever been a jeep invented which could take us back that far."

19. Of Jooks and Linguistics

Menu looked attractive. Air-conditioning was quiet and well balanced, kitchen odors beguiling, waitress neat and prompt and polite. In this tiny restaurant we settled ourselves for another noontime hour of rest, review of the morning's drive, appreciation of the good Little Things in Life—

Then four disheveled tramps, male and female, came in up front, ordered beer, slid money into a slot, and the honeymoon was over. Gangrene set in instead. One could believe that the resultant pop music polluting the atmosphere was recorded in a Nigerian slum by a combo of half-witted baboons, each of whom had just swallowed a mixture of Chlorox and Drano by mistake.

Music? Why, that jook-box was loaded with—

Did I say jook-box?

Ah. The word was mentioned a while back.

The ensuing information is drawn from *A New English Dictionary*, Volume 5, Part 2, edited by Sir J. A. H. Murray, Henry Bradley, W. A. Craigie, and C. T. Onions. More commonly known as the Unabridged Oxford. The first volume appeared in 1888, and the last in 1928—twenty tomes in all, published over a period of forty years. What you might call a philological labor of love.

"JOUK, JOOK: A sudden elusive movement, a quick turn out of the way."

Also, in modern Scottish, "A place into which one may dart for shelter."

As a verb the word is spelled variously iouk, iouck, iuke, iowk, jowk, juck, jeuk, jook, juik, and jouk. (There is no *juke* listed as a variant.) "To dodge, to duck, to swerve for a moment; to dart or spring with an adroit elusive movement out of the way or out of sight; to hide one's self by such action, to skulk."

In the Highlands of Scotland, *jook* is sometimes used to designate a grouse which has stolen away from feathered kin, and hides in heather by itself.

We learned of the existence of jooks when first we moved down to Florida, in 1936. We became acquainted that year with many natives—some who called themselves Crackers, some who spoke of themselves pridefully as Conchs—and others of various degrees of sophistication, education, accomplishment. But one and all they referred to jooks, pronounced to rhyme with *looks, books, crooks.*

I'm thinking of our friend Iris Huguenin, born Iris Bassett in the Gulf Coast town of Punta Gorda. We'd be talking about plans for an evening. If we just wanted to go out and drink—perhaps do a little dancing, eat a sandwich—Iris or one of her friends might say, "Why don't we go jooking?"

"What's that?"

"Oh, go out where you can get a drink, maybe play some music. You know—some of those places along the road—"

"Why do you call this jooking?"

"That's because of what these cafes are called. Jooks. Or jook joints."

"In England they'd call it pub-crawling. But I never heard of a jook before."

"Everybody calls them that, here in Florida. Folks always have, I guess."

"How do you spell it, Iris?"

"I don't know. I suppose j-o-o-k?" She appealed to her husband. "Phil, how do you spell jook?"

Phil said, "Well, now, I'm just a transplanted Illinoisan, but one who's been here for a long time. I swear I never saw the name in print. But everybody calls a little roadside cafe—one where you can buy drinks and play a nickel-in-the-slot phonograph— They're called jooks." And he rhymed it with *nooks* and *brooks.*

This interested me very much as a piece of Americana. When back North again I lost no time in proceeding with the research indicated above.

The application of this meaning to a remote cafe was obvious. So often they were on lonely roads. Natives knew where they were, if the outlanders didn't. (And the only impressive tourist invasions were then centered in Miami territory or similar areas.) Such nondescript places often sold liquor contrary to local laws. Thus the illicit or elusive connotation would be apparent.

Jook joints were often indeed skulkers. Also, like the grouse, they were loners.

. . . Wish that I had the mental capability to be a linguist. Oh, when abroad I try to use the proper words for requests, greetings, thank yous, goodbyes— And for designation of various articles. But more often than not, except in rural places, the people with whom I'm conversing—or *attempting* to converse—will smile politely and then begin speaking in English.

An appallingly small supply of French, a few words of German, now and then a word of Swedish, Danish, Japanese, Gaelic . . . smattering of hotel Italian comes back to me in Italy. I astonished both Irene and myself in Switzerland last winter by asking road directions of a German-speaking Swiss who apparently believed my Swiss-German to be fluent. He replied with what seemed a lengthy geographical or topographical discourse, accompanying himself with appropriate gestures. I said, *Ja. Danke schön*, and we went on through Zermatt and actually found the place we were seeking.

But that doesn't happen often to a dunce like myself, who just doesn't have a linguistic spot in his mentality. Spanish and Dakota (Sioux) are the only languages I've ever studied (had six lessons in Spanish). We've lived in Spain a total of two or three years, but I can employ only the present tense, and that haltingly. I've got a fair vocabulary and can manage an acceptable accent, and can get my meaning across in most Spanish provinces. But I'm lost when they come volleying at me in reply.

As for the Dakota study: that was done solely while preparing—and writing—*Spirit Lake*. I've forgotten the greater share of it now, as will all other *Waśićun* (whites) who don't speak the language constantly.

Śni wéksuya! (I remember not.)

Regional idiom in English is stimulating. It would be magnificent to have enough intimacy with other languages to be able to relish their variations as well. Sectional speech in the United States was delight and mystery and perpetual discovery until that, too, went out of style. Nowadays the radio announcer in New London sounds just like the one in Colorado Springs or Nashville. They read weather reports (about all I ever listen to on the radio anyway) with the identical self-conscious pompous phony graciousness and good cheer which New York City speakers employ. Some of us typify this as a tragedy, but I suppose the majority of Americans don't. Not in this day and age. They not only want everyone to speak alike; they want them to dress alike, act alike, think alike, feel alike, be born alike, love alike, live alike, die alike.

One time during World War II I found myself flying with an RAF crew which included the following: a runaway Hollander who had eluded the Nazis; an Australian, a Scotsman, a Lancashireman, an Irishman; and a pink-cheeked Flight Lieutenant with Public School accent a mile high. You should have listened in on our interphone. People who were at the scene when the Tower of Babel achieved its vexatious distinction must have sounded like that. It cannot be denied that such provincial differences could make for inferior communication at some crucial moment. But, leaving out that unpleasant notion, to the Etonian about one of his "mooters rooning haught." Or to hear the gunner from Galway explaining to the gunner from Glasgow that *he* had never fouled up the feed on those .303s when he was last on duty in that mid-upper turret.

Best of all was one afternoon when my job was merely sky-search, with head thrust into an astrodome. I could look down from time to time and observe the activities of others. . . . Our Public-School-type First Pilot was drinking his tea. He had been relieved at the controls by the Second Pilot, and was sitting on the deck. The aircraft gave a sudden lurch, and Armstrong's tea was spilled all over and around him. He called on the interphone, requesting a rag with which he might repair the damage. Finally a hand extended through a hatch, with fist closed on a wad of cloth. (Every lowly article such as grease-rags, dust-rags and all such, came from Salvage. Salvage was the big British wartime plan through which nothing was wasted. Everything served, up to its last final bit: paper, cloth, cardboard, cast-off clothing of all kinds.)

The rag offered in this instance was extended between our Skipper's hands as he gazed upon it in abiding disgust. It consisted of a pair of panties. Or rather, bloomers—bulky—and made out of pink flannel.

With a shudder close to convulsion, he sat with curling lip, regarding the offensive garment. His words came softly through buzz of the phone, but with all the clarity of a Noël Coward character—

or an Oscar Wilde character, say, in *The Importance of Being Earnest*.

"My word! How did such an object ever come to be aboard my aircraft?"

All personnel who were in nearby positions viewed the scene with appreciation, and spoke of it in their own accents. Finally the deep voice of Tonny, our Dutchman, overrode the others.

"Ve neffer haff nudding like dot until dot American gums aboard."

Little good it did me to cry indignantly that no woman in America would have been caught dead wearing such a bifurcated monstrosity. No, the crew had it their way. Those pink flannel panties were my doing—or undoing, if you like.

It's a long leap from jooks to ugly underwear, or is it? But a discursive writer such as this author will carry you over the course. Or try to.

In 1936 I was planning a modern (then) book about Florida. Scene: lower West Coast and the Ten Thousand Islands. I latched onto this new word *jook*, since it was used in conversation by natives so liberally. Thus, on page 149 of *The Noise of Their Wings*, you find little Dora explaining, "My ma's gone jooking with my old man, and Ivy and Mary done gone with them."

And on the next page:

> The girl blew out a first draught of smoke. "Where have they gone?"
>
> "Jooking," said Hansen. "That's local terminology—you must have heard it before. They go to the little roadside places, and drink beer, and raise hell generally."
>
> Caraway said, "Jook-joints. I know. . . ."

To my belief this is the first time that *jook* or any mutation of it ever appeared in an American book. But, shortly after *The Noise of Their Wings* came out as a serial in the *Post*, I noticed a column by Westbrook Pegler. Included therein was something to the following effect: "Here on the edge of the Miami district there are little cafes and liquor places out along the highway, which the natives call juke joints." After that, Pegler, who seemed as interested in the word as I had been, referred to *jukes* on several other occasions. That wasn't the way Floridians pronounced the word. As I said before, they made it rhyme with *cook* or *look*. But that was the way Peg spelled it.

I can't tell you what Westbrook Pegler's reading public numbered in those days, but he was syndicated in a great many papers. Many more thousands read his *juke* than read my *jook*, I'll warrant you that. My guess is that Peg thought it had something to do with the Juke family. As stated in *The New International Encyclopedia* (used to be published by Dodd, Mead & Company) the name Jukes was "a pseudonym used to protect certain worthy members of a family in New York State whose history displays unique conditions of crime, disease, and pauperism."

Very often in the 1930s you'd come across a Florida jook which displayed "unique conditions of crime, disease, and pauperism." So let's not blame Pegler too much.

Another few years elapsed, then appeared a novel (can't remember the author) called *Juke Girl*, and the harm was done. The word came into use all over the country. Juke-boxes figured prominently in the social life of our population, and have continued to do so.

But I'm damned if I'll spell the word j-u-k-e. It wasn't pronounced that way, and it still galls me to hear it or see it employed.

The walls of my library are lined with the shrunken heads of a number of copy editors who have tried to overrule me in this decision.

20. Arrow Rock

JOHN

Maggie, you forget yourself. There couldn't be another woman, once I was a married man.

MAGGIE

One has heard of such things.

JOHN

Not in Scotsmen, Maggie; not in Scotsmen.

MAGGIE

I've sometimes thought, John, that the Scotch are hard in all other respects, but soft with women, and the English are hard with women, but soft in all other respects.

Meanwhile, back at the cemetery, dead-and-buried Baptists were turning over in their graves. For this was *What Every Woman Knows,* presented in the Baptist Church at Arrow Rock.

To a Barrie lover, and to an Arrow Rock lover, this suggested an impish incongruity. First time I sat in that church it was to suffer through a colorless sermon—preached by some visiting divine, however—and to hear hymns sung lustily and well. Even as a strictly *former* Baptist, I couldn't forget that there must be a baptistry underneath boards and carpeting behind the pulpit. I wondered whether that baptistry was as clammily odoriferous as the one wherein I was immersed and had my sins washed away, in 1913.

At the risk of once more being dubbed a tiresome raconteur who delights in quoting from Own Works, let me insert a paragraph from *But Look, the Morn:*

And in all the symbolism, in all the words spoken, in all the organ notes and the smells of the tank itself, there came no semblance of worship, no beauty of release, no recollection or feeling of those other outdoor waters in a faraway land where, once upon a time, a brave and sensitive young Man was led down into the ripple of the Jordan by His friend.

The parson who effected my own purification—a generally good-natured soul named J. O. Staples—was inflexibly and volubly opposed to The Moving Picture, The Dance (Dawnce), Card-Playing (Gaming), and, above and beyond all else, The Stage. There is little reason to suppose that Arrow Rock Baptists were any more liberal than he. Thus arose the speculation about all that turning-over in certain local graves.

One time some brothers named Krimsky took over an abandoned church on the Upper East Side in New York City, and wowed the populace with a several-years-long presentation of *The Drunkard* and suchlike plays. But that was in New York—not in a cobwebby village where a sagging tavern, restored and administered under auspices of the DAR, might come close to being entitled *What Every Missourian Knows.*

Frequently we had dined, slept, breakfasted at the Arrow Rock inn, and poked among a store of curios which filled cases in the old tap room, or hung upon its walls. Though the tavern, and indeed the entire village, had undergone a face-lifting since last we were there, it was rewarding to examine again the stock of memorabilia.

Here you can read the allegedly original copy of Governor Claiborne Fox Jackson's historic reply to Simon Cameron, when the Secretary of War requested the Missouri governor to mobilize troops for the defense of the Federal Government.

Executive Department,
Jefferson City, Mo.,
April 17, 1861.

Honorable Simon Cameron,
Secretary, Washington, D.C.

Sir:

Your requisition is illegal, unconstitutional and revolutionary; in its object inhuman & diabolical. Not one man will Missouri furnish to carry on any such unholy crusade against her Southern sisters.

Respectfully,
C. F. Jackson.

There exists another version of this communication, somewhere around. Can't think just where. I read it years ago, and remember distinctly that it included the phrase, "and cannot be complied with." Well, either that bit of scratched paper now exhibited in Arrow Rock is not valid, or else the representation which I saw was a fake. Doesn't matter too much. . . . Death was a-waiting old Claib, just a whoop and a holler ahead. He galloped off with the Secessionists, sure enough; and had barely time to be named a general officer before he was struck down by that same dastardly foeman who wielded his weapon yesterday and today. And will wield it, I fear, tomorrow as well.

Cancer.

It is pleasanter to recall Jackson before the Civil War, when he was handsome and vigorous . . . vigorous enough to make a habit of marrying Sappington girls.

Fortunes of the Sappingtons, Marmadukes and Jacksons, and their blood as well, were commingled. No account of the life of Dr. John Sappington can be found in most encyclopaedias, but no review of early American medicine would be complete without reference to him.

His birth coincided with the birth of this Republic, in 1776. He became a man of widely varied talent and activity—doctor, manufacturer, salesman, farmer, trader, politician. After John Sappington removed to Missouri, when he was in his forties, the charm of his lovely daughters became traditional. One girl was married to Meredith Miles Marmaduke, who momentarily served as Acting Governor in 1844, between the Reynolds and Edwards administrations. But it was Claib Jackson who hung up the record for Sappington marriages. He was wedded to three of those girls, one after the other. (None of the history books I've read has ever advanced such distasteful theory, but it seems to me that Claib must have been pretty hard on *wives.*)

Anyway, after the first Sappington girl died—as Mrs. Jackson—her relict husband revisited the worthy doctor, and secured permission to take to wife a second Sappington girl. But when he came back the third time, with a plea for Daughter Number Three, Dr. John is supposed to have replied, "All right, Claib, take her. But don't come back for the old lady, cause she's all I've got left."

They're buried together in the Sappington family graveyard a few miles from Arrow Rock.

It's a pity that the public at large doesn't know more about Dr. John. Some very exciting fluid coursed through that old gentleman's veins— I say *old*, because he lived to be eighty, and that was rather unusual in 1856. *Reader's Digest* ran a piece about him in its June 1944 issue; but that was a quarter-century ago.

Fever scourged the frontier even more savagely than resistant Indians. Dr. Sappington was the scourge of fever. The moment quinine came into being in this country (as an extract of Peruvian bark. It had not been isolated as a drug until 1820, and that occurred in France) he began to employ it. The prevailing attitude of the medical profession during that period was, of course, calamitous: they were all anti-quinine. Dr. Sappington was fiercely abused, and accused of malpractice.

So old Sly-Boots rolled some quinine pills along with a mixture of licorice, sassafras, myrrh and God knows what else, and the public gobbled them voraciously. He had as many as two dozen salesmen out on the road at a given moment, selling those pills. Dollar-and-a-half a box. A dollar-and-a-half was heavy dough in those days, and any profit you made was yours, yours, yours; and any profit Dr. Sappington made was his, his, *his*. Some of the original pills are displayed in the tavern museum, along with the doctor's account book. I reckon his bank account was hefty enough, what with all those salesmen raking in the shekels.

He wrote a book, *Sappington on Fevers*, said to have been published right there in Arrow Rock, though the town never seemed large enough to hold a job press, let alone a book-bindery. This work may have been an early presentation of his *The Theory and Treatment of Fevers*, published in Philadelphia later on. Sappington revealed exactly what was in his pills, and stressed that it was quinine which was banishing "the febrile humors."

History should take more than a second glance at this remarkable gentleman. History should take a third glance, and a fourth and fifth, at Sappington and the line he led. His grandson was John Sappington Marmaduke, that dashing officer—and duelist—who rose from lieutenant to major-general in the Confederate Army in three years; and afterward cut a swathe in the commission and insurance business, and in the newspaper field; Secretary of the State Board of Agriculture, Railroad Commissioner . . . in 1884 he followed his father into the gubernatorial chair, exactly forty years after M. M.

Marmaduke held that position. General—or rather, Governor—Marmaduke died in office when he was a little past fifty.

Sitting in the Baptist Church—parm me, the Arrow Rock Lyceum Theater—later that same evening, we were considering actors and actresses. We thought again of Dr. Sappington; and held it unlikely that he might, among other crafts and abilities, have possessed a crystal ball. Therefore he could not know that he would have a great-great-great-granddaughter named Ginger Rogers. But that's just what he did have.

. . . Ah, lovely character. Like Daniel Boone, he stored his coffin under the bed. But he added a fillip of his own: he kept apples and nuts in that casket, and doled them out to visiting grandchildren. Reckon the children didn't mind. . . . One story says that he kept candy there, too. We've all heard of cough drops, but these may well have been the only *coffin* drops in history.

History . . . history . . . antiquity.

Charles Lamb:

> Antiquity! thou wondrous charm,
> what art thou? . . .
> What were thy *dark ages?*

Sometimes it appears that every articulate person from Napoleon to Henry Ford and back again all the way to Sir Walter Raleigh, has had his say on this subject. It is both stimulating and baffling to discover that the same thought has been in so many minds: i.e., that people, rather than events, as such, shape the record.

Carlyle wrote, "The history of the world is but the biography of great men." And Emerson, "There is probably no History; only Biography." Which one said it first? I know not. The two men were contemporaneous, but it is doubtful that one drew his notions from the other's works. Then along came Tolstoy, a generation later, with, "The subject of history is the life of peoples and of humanity." And forever Shakespeare reminds us, in *King Henry IV:* "There is a history in all men's lives."

Sappingtons, Jacksons and Marmadukes contributed their share. You become aware of that in the Arrow Rock tavern if nowhere else. . . . And the Coopers also. An intimate corner of Howard County, directly across the river and encompassed in the bend of the stream flowing south and turning east, is mounded with their graves. A breeze still whispers their names to sensitive ears.

. . . Boonesboro, Boonville (spelled without the *e*, apparently from the very start), Old Franklin, New Franklin, the Boonslick Springs or the Boon's Lick Forts– The *e* is gone also from Boon's Lick, whether rendered in one word or two words. And did this stem from some original ignorance of how to spell correctly Daniel's family name? No one can tell us, any more than anyone has ever been able to describe to me—any professional historian or layman—why Missouri is called the Show-Me State, or how it came to be known as Old Mizzou. Oh yes, one school declares that *Old Mizzou* refers solely to the University, not the State. Then how come that California gold miners talked tenderly of "going back to Old Mizzou" when they couldn't even read or write? The sycamores may know, or some of the oaks. They remain mute.

. . . Coopers everywhere. Colonel Benjamin A. Cooper, referred to as a "patriarchial leader," and Captain Braxton Cooper, and his daughter Mildred. Or was Mildred the daughter of old Colonel Benjamin? Granddaughter, I judge. The anecdotes are confused, and confusing. Is it possible that, one way or another, the traditive story of Betty Zane's heroism was somehow transferred from Ohio to Missouri?

MAG reports:

. . . Fort Cooper was attacked by a large number of Indians. Captain Braxton Cooper and a few men who were in the fort at the time debated the possibility of sending to Fort Hempstead, some six miles to the east, for help. Since none of the men could be spared, Mildred Cooper asked her father if she could go. He consented, although the circle of Indians seemed impregnable, and lifting her to the saddle, asked if there was anything she wanted. "Only a spur, father," was her reply. The spur was produced, the gate of the fort drawn open, and "like the arrow-strung bow, Milly and her good steed flew beyond its portals, and away in the deep and intricate forest she sped on her mission." Her sudden appearance surprised the Indians; the shrill war whoop "rang from a hundred savage throats, the sharp, clear report of as many rifles." Hours passed. That Mildred had been killed seemed certain. Then "the shout of friends was heard above the din of strife, the firing rapidly ceased," and the rescue party appeared before the fort, with Mildred at their head.

So the usual sacred junk clutters the place. Dr. Sappington's old black hat, and curry-combs and smoothing-planes, and little folks' shoes, and rolling pins. Dried-out saddle-bags filled with drugs; a set of surgeon's instruments; and General James Shields' pistols. (Well, that's what they call them, but actually they're revolvers: a matched pair in a case.) Ask the next ten people you meet, ask the next hundred, and it's dollars to doughnuts that not one will know anything about General James Shields. "Governor of two States, General in two wars, Senator from three States: Illinois, Minnesota, Missouri. Judge of the Supreme Court of Illinois." An Irish boy immigrant who came to the United States when he was sixteen . . . three times wounded in those two wars mentioned above. . . . A real square. Or would demonstrators nowadays say *Pig?*

One springtime Saturday in 1814, Captain Sarshall Cooper drew on his plaid vest over his shirt . . . that was at Cooper's Fort, across the river from Arrow Rock. The captain had no notion that a piece of that same vest, still showing the rust of his blood, would be on exhibition at Arrow Rock a century and a half later. . . . Interesting date, that April 14th, 1814. It was exactly fifty-one years, to the night, before Abraham Lincoln was shot.

Poor Sarshall Cooper.

"With his wife by his side and his child on his knee he sat by the open fire, talking with a visitor from Fort Hempstead. The raging storm prevented them from hearing an Indian as he picked a hole through the mud chinking, through which the fatal shot was fired. To prevent others from being shot from the light in the room, his last words to his wife were, 'Put out the fire, I'm a dead man.'"

Irene and I entertained vivid—and romantic, if you like—recollection of low-ceiled bedrooms upstairs in the tavern . . . chambers with big four-poster beds in them, and chintz curtains at the windows. Alas, these were no longer available to guests. Also we found that the dining room had been remodeled since last time. The new (to us) hostess told the truth, however, when she said that every effort had been expended to maintain the cuisine at its high level. Country ham was just as tasty as ever, so were the home-baked beans. So was baked chicken and stuffing. Our handsome silver-haired hostess came to sit with us for a few minutes as we finished the meal, though she is a busy woman, and conducting the old tavern is a demanding task. Her name: Mrs. Claudia Mapes. Her husband was one of that same Mapes family which included Mary Mapes Dodge, author of *Hans Brinker, or, The Silver Skates.* That book came near to being Required Reading for several generations of young Americans. The same Mary Mapes Dodge, as editor of *St. Nicholas*, propelled the magazine from obscurity to a position of importance. How many writers, I wonder, who later achieved international fame in their chosen profession, saw their first printed words appear under the auspices of the St. Nicholas League? Stephen Vincent Benét told me, back in 1935, that his first printed poem brought him a three-dollar check from *St. Nicholas.*

Said Steve, "It was entitled *The Regret of Dives.* Fortunately for me, the name appeared only in the title, for I was under the distinct impression that *Dives* rhymed with *hives.*"

Thus the fabric of the Past. One goes to Arrow Rock to revisit the tavern, and he encounters Mrs. Mapes; and then he starts thinking about Mary Mapes Dodge and *St. Nicholas;* and then he starts thinking about Steve Benét and– The Past is a combination of such bewildering richness, such intermingled prosperity of human birth and living and dying, that it would seem no modern beings except the fiercest of barbarians would wish to trample it. But they do, they do.

The performance at the Arrow Rock Lyceum Repertory Theater was not scheduled to begin until eight-fifteen. We had time to stroll down to the area of the old jail. Maybe some who read this book will have heard Burl Ives singing a ballad which I wrote long ago.

> . . . Here in this room, it is my tomb,
> I can't take the Sante Fe Trail.
> Until I die, here I must lie,
> Locked in the Arrow Rock jail.
>
> And early in the morning,
> The drivers will go by,
> And they will see me hanging
> Against the lonely sky.

Probably it would be best to confess that there never was any such prisoner. *MAG* goes so far as to state, of the jail, "Legend says the only prisoner kept in it 'hollered and raised such a racket they just had to let him out.'" But when I wrote the ballad I was youthful and fanciful and– Carl Sandburg liked this song, and chanted it enthusiastically until he happened to inquire as to the source. I said, "I wrote it myself. Words *and* music." Then he was miffed.

JOHN

You've forgotten the grandest moral attribute of a Scotsman, Maggie. That he'll do nothing which might damage his career.

MAGGIE

Ah, but John, whatever you do, you do it so tremendously; and if you were to love, what a passion it would be. . . .

The performance, directed by one Henry Swanson, was satisfying from start to finish, whether any grim Baptists were turning over in their graves or no. Maggie was a treasure, played by Alice Swanson– Wife of the director? Maybe so.

John Shand, the lead, was played by Michael Doyle. He reminded us of a young Chris Plummer or a young Barry Sullivan: a very good boy, with an easy air of confidence (which so many actors try to manage, especially in earlier seasons of their careers, and yet achieve only smugness). Indeed the whole company was infectious in their expression and excitement.

We looked over the list of patrons and sponsors and donors. Folks from Marshall, Boonville, Fayette, Sedalia, Columbia and other places, eagerly assisting in the project. This is a non-profit organization, chartered as a corporation by the State of Missouri, and dedicated to "the advancement, promotion and furtherance of literary, artistic, civic and social culture among its members," and the general public. That's a large order. We felt honored at being permitted to witness one moment, at least, of its fulfillment.

During an entr'acte we had strolled out to the steps and sidewalk in front of the church (excuse: Lyceum Theater) and stood breathing medicinal night air (had the revenant of Dr. Sappington just ridden by?) and watching lightning hustle along the clouds. We wondered whether another storm might be tumbling toward us, violent as one experienced during the afternoon when tornado-warning sirens sounded far and wide.

. . . Heard Irene say, "Well, hel*lo*. How are *you?*" and turned to see what acquaintance she was greeting. A brand new acquaintance. He sauntered at a leisurely pace up the steps, glanced in at the open door, then turned and curled himself in a manner of comfort, not caring how many people would have to step over or around him. Mostly beagle, with a few tick and Spaulding types numbered amid his ancestry. We bent to stroke his ears, and wisely stopped there: he had been exploring some mighty muddy territory. Maybe he'd been in the nearby Missouri River. Remember how Senator Tom Benton announced that it was "a little too thick to swim in, but not quite thick enough to walk on."

Irene said, "The Old Arrow Rock comes calling on the New."

"Reno, get a load of this little folder. They're going to have a special production, from August 29th to September 4th, of Arthur Miller's *Death of a Salesman*."

She said, "I trust that Snoopy will still be in attendance."

Evening storms did not develop, at least in that area. It was an easy drive, after the play ended, down to Interstate 70, and thence to our motel in the suburbs of Columbia. Irene was sound asleep five minutes after we took off, so my musings were solitary as I drove. Having observed once more a rendition of that sound and enduring play (golly, how Helen Hayes did Maggie, years and years ago!) I fell to evaluating Barrie and the inheritance he left us.

Combination of the tavern's relics, together with the aspect of an elder village where people are working to preserve respect for ancient as well as for modern cultural activity, was evocative of a consideration of Sir James M. Barrie, and what he stood for, and how he felt. I recalled Stevenson's comment in a letter to Henry James —an almost offensively patronizing evaluation of one Scot by another. "There was genius in him, but there was a journalist on his elbow." What Stevenson did not envision, and what he would never live to see, was the First World War. That war brought out the steel which previously lay unperceived within the nature of Sir James. Even now, when people think of him, *if* they think of him at all, they see him surrounded by a host of Sentimental Tommies, Little Ministers, Peter Pans, and Alices-Sitting-By-the-Fire. They are unaware of the hardiness generated by this aging philosopher through his last years.

Among the few books I'd brought along for mere reading pleasure was a copy of *Courage*. It's a small volume containing the Rectorial Address which Sir James delivered at St. Andrews University, his *alma mater*, in 1922.

Late as it was, I shopped through the book that night before going to sleep. Didn't want to read the damn newspaper; I cast it from me. Just glanced at the front page—that was all, and enough. Some more tramps being publicized to their profit and joy, and to the encouragement of the vile cause they represented. More riff-raff permitted to burn draft cards in public; another mob defiling our Flag; more "liberal" members of college faculties—more doctors, and members of the clergy—excusing them, apologizing for them. And thus exhorting them to fresh harlotry.

Then, in another few minutes, these words of Barrie's leaped from the page. Pray that all men might read them and recognize their bitter sanity.

"There is a form of anemia that is more rotting than even an unjust war. The end will indeed have come to our courage and to us when we are afraid in dire mischance to refer the final appeal you could listen with pure glee to the Lancashireman trying to explain to the arbitrament of arms."

21. Of Corncobs and Offset

The corncobs harmonized with wine and roses. They gave forth a branny breath reminiscent of reliable soil and reliable toil, and honesty, and hard work and the exhilaration found in that work. (I can just visualize the shock-haired way-out book reviewers sneering at *that* sentence.) Glaring days, and hot damp nights when people muttered, "Listen. You can hear the corn growing." So you could hear it . . . minute snap and rustle, as long leaves stretched themselves and unfolded, uncoiling firm slick surfaces in darkness.

These cobs were seasoning in bins, in the basement of the Missouri Meerschaum Company, in the town of Washington. That's where the cob pipe business began. Strangely enough—for people of German descent have long since assumed command of this industry—the first pipe manufacturer, in 1868, was a Hollander named Henry Tibbe.

In earlier times if you wished to have a cob pipe, you manufactured it yourself. It wasn't much trouble. You'd cut off a section of corncob, dig out the pith in the middle—but leave plenty at the bottom for a base—and with a sharp nail you could ream a hole at the side. Then insert any hollow stem which struck your fancy.

Corncobs constituted my very first chore, before I was old enough to go to school. Even a little boy could hoist a coal-scuttle full of cobs without straining himself. They made the best kindling for the Great Magestic range, so every autumn my grandparents would order in a load. The farmer came driving, his lumber-wagon piled high with shelled cobs, and dumped them in the old buggy shed next to our barn, which had come to be called the Cob House. The maroon pile lay offering its munificence, sloping up two-thirds of the way to the roof.

Reed's Yellow Dent was the corn most commonly grown in our county. In such yellow corn—that is, field corn—the cobs were red. It was a choring any child might enjoy, although there ruled consistently the fear of an occasional rat which went scooting over the pile when disturbed at his searching for stray corn kernels which might have been missed in the shelling.

I'd tote the bucket of cobs to the kitchen, realizing as instructed that I must place two or three cobs in a tin can kept at a safe distance from the stove, half-filled with kerosene. These soaked cobs were the lighters. A match to flare in the firebox on an icy winter morning, more dry cobs to be placed on top of the kerosene-soaked one; wedges of soft coal to follow. In no time at all the range moaned and clicked with its ascending blaze, and you could see brilliant orange through every crack around the lids. . . .

I told the Otto brothers, who own the Missouri Meerschaum Company, "I haven't smelled cobs, like this, in years."

"Smell good, don't they?"

"Wonderful."

"We season them two to five years before they're ready to be worked on."

Carl Otto, the more slender and younger of the two, related genealogy of the corn. He said that white cobs made the best pipes by far, for a variety of reasons. They'd started with the old Boone County White. But modern corn used in this trade is not a pollinated corn, as was the Boone County White. It's a hybrid, discreetly developed for this purpose. Has its own name now.

"That's how it's known in the trade: Missouri Pipe Number 4. Just the way you have Pioneer 317, or 245, or any other of the regular market hybrids."

Long ago, farmers used to bring their cobs to the factory, but today the factory contracts for an entire crop of corn. They shell it and sell the corn, out at the farms; then truck the cobs into Washington to be stored.

They use between two and three thousand acres of cornfields to supply this factory, in the course of a single year.

"How many pipes do you produce per day?"

"Anywhere from thirty-five to thirty-eight thousand."

"In one *day?*"

"That's about average, for us."

We'd started with the raw cobs in the basement, progressing upstairs through two stories of smoothing, sorting, sawing, scraping, searing, shellacking.

We asked the Ottos how it came about that this town, boasting perhaps nine thousand inhabitants, had come to be the cob pipe capital of the world, with three companies manufacturing there.

"This is certainly a lucrative business, and an interesting and a clean kind of business. Why is it that more people haven't tried to emulate you, in other places?"

Carl Otto explained, "There used to be a factory at Union. And then there was one at Owensville— The biggest competitor we had was up at Boonville, but we've gradually absorbed these people. You must remember that, years ago, the demand for corncob pipes, like all other pipes, was down. But for the last fifteen or twenty years it's gradually increased. Then the demand spurted in 1964, when the main conversational topic concerned the disastrous effects of cigarette smoking. After the impact of the Surgeon-General's report had worn off, briar people went back down to normal. But cob pipes have stayed right up on top, ever since."

Edmund Otto, the elder and plumper brother, said that when the cigarette scare was going on, a lot of people tried pipes for the first time in their lives.

"The majority weren't rolling in dough, so they selected inexpensive pipes to start with. Many of those picked out a cob, and then they stayed with it. Remember, this product isn't consumed solely in America. We ship all over the world. You'd be surprised if you knew some of the strange little distant countries—and big distant countries too—which are steady customers. And we're proud to be the oldest manufacturers in the industry."

The brothers had a picture they wanted to show us, in their private office. I was glad they asked us in, because of the safe, with its door standing open . . . though I didn't want to steal anything out of it. Just wanted to look—hadn't seen one of those in a long time. A permanent part of the building structure, like a high-ceilinged tomb lined with shelves and strongboxes, and with gold-and-pink-and-blue forget-me-nots and roses—a garden of flowers and curlicues traced out on the black door. It brought along as many memories as the odor of cobs.

"Right over here on the wall. Recognize him?"

The photograph was of General Douglas MacArthur, cob pipe stem between his jaws. It hung with a framed letter, one which Ed Otto had sent to the general when MacArthur was still commanding in the Far East . . . the general preferred cob pipes. So, if it wasn't against all rule and regulation, might not the Missouri Meerschaum Company be allowed to send him a small supply?

He had written in the margin, "Thanks. Send them along," or some such brief note of acceptance. But I wasn't a very accurate reporter at the moment.

. . . Because on glimpsing that face a distant panorama came unreeling . . . late afternoon, Tokyo sunlight, and Japanese swarming opposite the Dai Ichi building. It was as if they had him confused with their own Emperor on the white horse. And those MP's: spit-and-polish to the hilt. Suddenly the holding to Attention, and the little party emerged. Down to the car he would come . . . crushed battered cap, the cob pipe, the characteristic but still military slouch . . . and all that crowd giving forth their applause, their squeals of approval and admiration.

Mac-san, Mac-san! Banzai! Mac-san!

A few months later, President Truman—known fondly as Uncle Harry to the bulk of Missourians—cut off Mac-san's head, and our face was lost in Asia. Oh, yes, in 1950 my jeep driver used to leer and jeer, and point at a shabby building which was the headquarters of the Japanese Communist Party, and passing pedestrians jeered as well. *Ah so desska.* Communists were a joke.

But in another year, after the Old Soldier had been ordered to fade away, they were upsetting American cars in the Ginza.

"What about stems—or rather I mean bits? The part that you bite on—"

"Nylon and C-11 Bakelite."

"What about bones? Most of the old cob pipes used to have a bone bit—"

"We can't get them any more. Those were made from the shinbone of a very heavy steer, but they're just not in supply. It's more economical, and more satisfying to most of our customers, to use the other materials."

It seemed a little sad that they couldn't have the bones back in the act. But that didn't distress me as much as the varying processes for making cob pipes look like non-cob pipes—making them look like briar pipes or leather-covered pipes or white meerschaums. Seemed kind of immoral. Why should anyone wish a cob pipe to look like anything other than what it was? A ruling cowardice, that's what: people afraid to stand up for their own rights; people afraid they'd be ruled eccentric if they went around puffing on a cob; but who loved that rare gentle taste which cannot be duplicated. Well, whatever their motives, there was an hypocrisy here.

But I couldn't be impolite to the Otto brothers when they urged samples on me. To be perfectly frank, I'll accept cob pipes as long as anyone will offer them. They make nice casual gifts, too, and other smokers appreciate them. Those generous Otto brothers really loaded me down.

Then we went up the street to visit George H. Buescher, president of Buescher's Manufacturing Company. There it was some more of the same: machines going around and up and down and in and out; belts whirring, men and women pushing levers. It appeared that one woman made a single identical motion all day long, like Charlie Chaplin in *Modern Times*.

But the employees seemed sedately undisturbed by the repetitious nature of their tasks. Many had been working in one factory or another (there's a third company in town) through most of their workaday lives. They have all the calm detachment of true German artisans, whether they be male or female, old or young. The visitor is willing to bet that many of the bald or gray-headed ones started in the jobs when they were kids. You think of toy-makers in Germany, clock-makers in Switzerland. And the local names shown in signs, advertisements, social or professional or political activities, as reported in the local paper . . . Kuenzel, Stemme, Wesselschmidt, Ziegler, Hemker. You go into Liggett's drugstore and find picture magazines printed in Stuttgart prominently displayed, along with every *Zeitung* printed in any American city large enough to sustain a German language press. Come to think of it, when you examine the terrain around Washington—or Herman, the next good-sized town to the west—you think of Westphalia or the Rhine Palatinate, or central Bavaria.

George Buescher said, "Washington is the only true cob pipe manufacturing center in the world. We ship anywhere from ten to fourteen million, every year."

"Is that your top capacity?"

"Well"—easily—"I rather guess not. But that's a lot of pipes."

That was what I came out of his factory with, too: a lot of pipes. With combined largesse from the Ottos and from George Buescher and his staff, I entertained visions of becoming a man of prominence among pipe-smoking friends, once I got home. A man to be courted, wooed, favored . . . a man, in short, whom it might be hoped would show the same philanthrophy which generous Missourians had displayed.

Buescher's young promotion manager even gave Irene some pipes—little bitty ones with slightly curved stems. About the size of thimbles.

"Thank you, but I don't smoke a pipe."

"Well, then, Mrs. Kantor, you can use em for cigarette holders. See, like this—"

"But I don't smoke cigarettes. Don't smoke at all. Haven't smoked since the spring of Nineteen-sixty-three, and never expect to smoke again, and am I happy about it!"

"Oh, take em along anyway. For marijuana."

It was Jim Miller who'd guided us to the factories. He publishes the *Washington Missourian*, which won annual awards as Missouri's best weekly newspaper all the way from 1955 through 1967, except for one year when some ringer slipped in and swiped the title away. Before we went to the factories, he took us to lunch. We had a little argument about that—had expected to take *him*—but, since we didn't know any place to go, it seemed rather foolish.

James Miller is a stocky man who looks like he'd fed on German cooking all his life. "There's a club outside town which has pretty good steaks. People like to go out there; but unfortunately this is a Monday, and they're closed on Monday."

"We don't need to go to any fancy place at all. Isn't there some old German restaurant where they have *sauerbraten* or *klops?* Or ham hocks and—"

"No, no, nothing like that any more. We haven't got a one in town. Anyhow, that's awfully heavy food. Who wants that stuff, anyway?"

We said, "*We* do," and then all of us were laughing. Jim advised us to go to St. Louis if that was what we sought. He took us to a very pleasant un-*sauerbraten*ish place, and we had a light lunch. . . . Jim said that most of the picturesque old ways had gone by the board. No more *Turnverein*. They'd organized one in Washington, away back before Civil War times; before that, even, there was a *Theaterverein*. But modern days and ways had taken their toll.

"Even thirty years ago or so, some of the old families were still dishing out the herring salad which you had on Christmas Eve. The idea was that if you ate that dish on Christmas Eve—I guess if you even ate herring at all—it would be promising for your future. Some of the old folks said that you would have good luck every day of the year; others said if you taste herring on Christmas Eve, you'll never be needy. Practically all the old customs have vanished now. It's mainly the linguistic shreds which are left."

It made one a little unhappy, when you saw those names in the paper again . . . Shelich, Allebach, Kroeger, Niederhelm— Well, let's not talk about it. This may be a good thing, for a lot of reasons, but I'm just sentimental enough to feel regretful.

Jim showed us through his newspaper plant. The place was beaming, shining. But— What? No clinking of linotype machines, no dies dropping, no smell of hot lead.

"Offset," he said. "All the new automatic offset process. No more of the old rolling presses. Everything done with tape now."

I shuddered, but had to admit that they were putting out a beautiful paper.

"Why, one girl can set more type in an hour on her machine, using this tape, than three Linotype operators used to be able to do in the same time!"

Still it didn't seem like a newspaper office . . . didn't *feel* like a newspaper office. You missed it even when they turned over the offset printing apparatus to run between its rollers. Didn't sound like a press. This would wound anyone who was ever sent over to the *other* newspaper office and told to bring back some type lice.

A moment later, however, my eyebrows went up, and I pointed like a Weimaraner. There was a boy about fourteen years old, running around back there in the case—if they still *called* it the case—

"Well, you haven't been able to dispense with one thing."

"What's that?"

"The devil. Printer's devil."

James Miller chuckled. "Yes, we've still got him. But I can't send the devil out for a left-handed line-gauge nowadays, because we don't use that sort of line-gauge."

We thanked the publisher for his hospitality, apologized for the trouble we'd put him to—

"No, no, don't say that. I was in need of taking a few hours off. Just got my current Amazon story put to bed this morning."

"Your– Beg your pardon. Your *Amazon* story?"

"Sure. I travel a lot. I've been down to the Amazon, checking on activities at missions in the wilds. Took a lot of pictures, too, to use along with the articles. I'll send you some of the stories. Just finished one about Mujui dos Compos. A couple of the missioners–not mission*ar*ies, but missioners–took me up there in the jungle. You ought to see those neat little Indian girls in their school uniforms! And nobody starves in the jungle. There are plenty of bananas, wild fruits; and fish to be had for the taking.

"There was one man in Mujui who lived with two women, and had had thirty children from the two. Oh, the two women don't live in the same little house, but they know about one another. Their man spends an equal amount of time with each one– One night in this hut, next night in that one. He works on a farm for less than a dollar a day. How he can support two families on that, with a total of thirty children, is beyond understanding–"

This from a small-town newspaper man. But, as made plain by Leonard Fetchley, active Missourians do have hobbies and they do get around. No telling where Jim Miller's next trip will take him. But he'll be writing about it, and photographing it, and then publishing the whole thing in his paper.

In offset.

Irene had taken her farewell some time before. I found her completing a health stroll, which she had confined to a half-block sentry beat in front of the newspaper office, for fear I mightn't discover her.

She was laughing. She stepped over into the shade and folded her blue parasol. "See that old colored man, going down the block there?"

I did see him. He was waving back at Irene.

"He's the cutest little old thing. But he seems to be gravely disturbed at hearing all this talk about picketing and demonstrations. He stopped and looked at me a while, walking back and forth. Then he said, 'What you walking for? You on strike? You on *strike?*' I said, 'Oh, I'm just walking up and down–' 'But you got an umbrella. You got an *umbrella*. What you walking for?' I said, 'Well, it's awfully hot, and I like to use a sunshade.' He shook his head and smacked his lips knowingly. 'You sure on strike. You must be on strike! You just *picketing*, that's what!' "

"Goodness sake," I said. "Let's get out of here before a rumor spreads all over town that employees of the *Washington Missourian* have walked out on Jim Miller."

"Nonsense. I don't think he'd be much alarmed. But did you know that it's after five o'clock, your official time for smoking?"

"Why, so I *can* smoke."

"Do light up one of those corncobs, and let me learn secondhand how it smells."

No Dunhill or Barling ever smelled better.

22. Young Man in a Hurry

First time the boy passed us, he was coming like a bat out of hell. I edged over to the right as far as I could, and slowed down, although I'd been driving at only about 35 mph. A lot of hazard piled along there in the shape of coarse gravel.

He shot around us, free as a hummingbird, fast as a hummingbird—gaunt angular white-shirted kid astride a shiny blue-and-silver motorcycle—elbows stuck out, bare feet splayed, crash-helmet white as a hemisphere of vanilla ice cream . . . chin-straps flying high and wide. By the time we crested the next low hill, our boy was completely out of sight.

Irene said, "At least he's wearing a helmet."

"With the chin-straps unfastened," and I thought of GIs with their straps dangling.

Three miles distant, our county road ran blind against U. S. Route 63. I turned north, and soon passed a truck stop and restaurant. We saw the barefoot boy with the luscious new motorcycle again. Cycle was parked in front of the restaurant, and the boy stood swinging that pristine helmet as he confabulated with two little mini-skirted brunettes who pranced before him. *Boy meets girls.* . . . " 'How often, oh! how often,' " Irene quoted, and we laughed, and kept going north.

Six or eight miles beyond, there rose that same accelerating roar from behind. The kid swept by, swung in ahead, waited for a car to pass from the opposite direction, then accelerated again, and creased around a black Chrysler. I didn't notice whether or not he'd fastened his chin-straps this time. He was just a blur, going by.

Next thing—

Dust-devil. A fog of tan whirling dirt beyond the other car.

Instantly red lights blazed on the Chrysler's rear end, and our seat-belts cut into us as I slammed on my own brakes.

Irene. "Oh, my *God.*"

The Chrysler skidded to a halt well beyond the crumpled motorcycle. I managed to stop just short of it. A big white truck was slowing, on the opposite side of the road.

As I knelt beside the boy, I could hear feet thump-thumping rapidly on the pavement, and other brakes and wheels were screeching.

He'd been flung a considerable distance before he hit the hard-baked ground (though we didn't see him flying through the air: too much dust. That was the reason for the *Dust-devil* notion). He lay doubled on his right side, with a crash-helmet— Oh, maybe fifteen feet beyond, in a wide shallow ditch. I had a hunch that it was all over, even before I squatted down.

He was not staring, the way men so often do after they've been hit by enemy fire. He had his left eye squeezed shut . . . thick and yet delicate, those eyelashes, even under grime.

I held the limp wrist . . . couldn't find any pulse. There appeared to be a lot of cranial fluid mingling with hemorrhage . . . changes the color, you see. The boy's shirt had been half ripped from his body; his chest was bare now, and I leaned over, and put my ear between the ribs. That smooth tough skin— Warm and sweaty against my ear—

By this time a young man in Bermuda shorts was crouched on the other side of the sprawled figure.

"Any heart?" he asked.

"Try it. I can't get any."

He tried . . . finally lifted his sunburnt face, tossed out his hands in a helpless gesture.

People clustered around, fairly on top of us. In the background sounded that intermittent scream of brakes, and tremble of more feet coming. A woman lifted her defiant voice. "Well, can't they even pick him *up?* Can't they even take him to the *hospital?*"

I spoke to a disordered array of faces. "Look, has anyone called the Highway Patrol? If not, please get to the nearest telephone." Either someone went, right then, or else someone had already done so. It wasn't too long before the trooper arrived.

Fellow on the other side of the boy said, "Well, we've done Number One, which is pulse, and Number Two, which is heart. How's about Number Three?"

"Let's pull up an eyelid and take a look."

We did: left eye only, because the right side of the face was a mess. The young man applied his fingers, and the lid came back, and we both saw the same thing. No contraction.

"What do you say?"

"Killed instantly."

"Right. Take a look at this." He pointed down to the right side of the boy's head, which I hadn't been able to see from my position. Scalp was scraped off where he'd hit the ground or skidded along it, and there was an actual line of demarcation–splintered velvety bone where the skull was split open.

We got up slowly, and automatically dusted off our knees. I saw Irene leaning against the fender of our car. She was crying.

"Aren't you going to take him to the *hospital?*" Mrs. Tiresome was still demanding.

Mr. Bermuda Shorts addressed the whole crowd. "Listen, people. This boy is dead. There's nothing any of you can do for him. And you, lady, ought to forget that idea about hauling off seriously injured people to the hospital. You might cripple them for life! When there's a serious accident, let the person lie right where he is. Just keep him warm, that's all. And try to stop any hemorrhage."

A big man in white dairy coveralls said, "That guy is right. I've seen plenty of dead ones, and this here one is dead, too. I just took a look at him."

By this time there were about twenty cars parked along both sides of Route 63, and of course the usual idiots not parked at all, but just sitting there, blocking the road, staring.

The dairy truck driver said, "What we need is to keep the traffic moving, and get these people out of here." He walked out across the pavement, making brisk gestures with his left arm. "All right, Uncle, on your way! Come on, get a-rolling. You're blocking traffic–"

I went back to our car and took the keys from the ignition. Opened the trunk, and pulled out our tartan blanket.

Irene came. "You're sure he's dead?"

I said, "Johnny doesn't live here any more."

"One man says that he saw him, just before he went into that spin. He said the machine was shimmying. The front wheel–"

. . . Motorcycle seemed obscene in its spread-out posture, twisted but still gleaming. There was the name in chrome, *Yamaha,* and I wanted to kick it. I had the feeling that it had let Johnny down, when as a matter of fact it was probably Johnny who had let Yamaha down.

A number of loose laths were scattered along the roadside; apparently they'd blown off from a truckload. I made a little tripod of laths, tied together with my handkerchief, and arranged it above the dead boy's head. Then we unfolded the blanket and spread it over him and over the tripod. No point in having that treasured blanket soaked with blood.

Big Mr. White Dairy Coveralls was doing a right capable job as traffic cop. I looked back down the road . . . thought I heard a siren. Yes . . . a remote flashing red light, whirling above the Highway Patrol car.

I kept thinking, "Witnesses." Inquired of Bermuda Shorts, "Did you see this actually happen?"

"I saw it, I saw it," others were crying.

"If anyone saw more than a column of dust—which was all I saw—please stay here a minute, and give the details to the officer. He's coming now."

In a few more seconds the big blue vehicle halted as far off the road as the driver could get, with all that jam of cars. Some people had already left the scene, but others had taken their place. Just as the trooper stopped, I heard two women exclaiming, "Why, isn't that dead youngster the Wannett boy?" One said, "I didn't get too good a look, because that man"—resentfully—"put a blanket over him. But I think it may be. That oldest Wannett boy."

Trooper got out of his car, reaching back in for a first-aid kit. I had crossed the pavement. "You won't need that."

"How do you know? You a doctor?"

"Used to be with the cops." I opened my wallet and displayed a miniature gold-and-blue badge with the arms of the City of New York.

He put the first-aid kit back into the car. "Was it a collision with another vehicle?"

"No, apparently he lost control, and went off the road. He was going like hell."

The trooper said, "They do. Man, they do! Were you a witness?"

"All I could see was a dust explosion. But I pulled up just behind him, and found that he was dead."

The officer crossed the road. "Anybody see this? Who saw it?" A number of voices responded. But actually I don't think that anyone got a clear view, unless it was the folks in that first southbound car.

The officer lifted up our blanket, and I removed it and the tripod. In the distance another siren was moaning . . . probably an ambulance.

Kneeling beside the boy, our trooper made the same checks which had already been made, and then, as we had done, he got up and dusted himself.

"Would you folks mind– The ones who saw this–" He opened his notebook.

Irene and I shook out our blanket together, and folded it, and I put it back in the trunk. We drove away.

. . . Rear vision mirror. The ambulance had arrived, and they were hauling out their stretcher cart.

Irene said, "Think of his family. They don't even know it's happened. . . . Gad. He was going so *fast.*"

"He surely was traveling."

After a while she asked, "What is that old Air Force expression, about climbing–?"

"'Climbing like a homesick angel?'"

"Oh, poor little tall thin homesick angel!"

23. Just Driving Around

As we came into Marceline from the south on State 5, appropriately we observed an assemblage of ponies and pony colts. There ought to be a tablet or a sign on the highway, informing the casual visitor that this was Walt Disney's birthplace.

Last time we drove through they hadn't gotten around to honoring him. All they'd set forth was a sign stating that the population numbered 2,872. Walt didn't grow up here; his schooldays were spent in Kansas City and Chicago.

Besides the equine contingent on the outskirts, there was nothing reminiscent of Walt Disney in Marceline. No companies of deer or woodchucks or rabbits; no squadrons of embattled mosquitoes, hummingbirds, hawks, wolves, wombats. Never a sorcerer, never a witch. . . .

Stumps of big trees lined Missouri Street, running north and south through town. I fear that they were once elms, and that the Dutch curse came this way. . . . Not a bunny, not a beaver, not a bear. No fairies, no pirates. . . . It seems a weary village. In the middle of a clear August day, there were very few people about.

Ah, give em time! Resourceful souls will get together, and invest, and build and contrive; then the place will be booming. They'll have a Minnie Mouse Cafe and a Donald Duck Swimming Pool. And without doubt the Walt Dizz-Nee Motel. If enough people come, as certainly they will (once the attractions are built) there might be room for a Beaver Valley Fact-O-Ree Out-Let, a Three Little Pigs Bar-Bee-Kew, a Seven Dwarfs Fross-Tee-Dare-Ee Kitch-Inn.

. . . What's that, Irene?

"And out here on the north edge of town, there'll be one of those play places for children: rides and swings and a little car-bumping arena, and a merry-go-round. Maybe a choo-choo train, and a ferris wheel. And— Guess what? They'll call it *Disneyland*."

I could come up with only one more suggestion. "And the town prostitute—"

Irene, primly. "How do you know that all the twenty-eight hundred and seventy-two inhabitants of Marceline aren't God-fearing, well-behaved, chaste? How do you know there *is* a town prostitute?"

I told her that a great many people in my own home town had embraced those virtues and attitudes. But, despite widespread rivalry offered by amateurs, there were still several professionals in operation.

"So Marceline might have one. If so, when the great day comes, she should carry a sign on her back reading, *Follow Me, Boys*."

Hugo and Liza are husband and wife, and had been entertaining for eight weeks at the Pony Express Motor Lodge on the outskirts of St. Joseph, by the time we arrived. Hugo plays the squeeze-box with one hand, the organ with his other hand; Liza manages traps and drums; and they both vocalize, in solo or duet.

Entertainers who truly believe in themselves, and know their business, and know their instruments, and know what to do with their voices— It's remarkable how so many of them turn out to have bright warm natures. So it is with Hugo and Liza. The manager told us that they'd been back year after year at that same resort. No wonder: customers come flocking from downtown St. Jo; they drive over from Cameron, or even up from Atchison and Leavenworth, Kansas. Plenty from Kansas City too.

Once again, the triumph of the motel. There wasn't anything like the Pony Express in St. Jo years ago. Well, there weren't any entertainers around like Hugo and Liza, either.

She's a blonde; he's rather fair-haired also—one of those blondish Italians. Born in Salerno, but hasn't been back since boyhood. That was— Well, a spell ago. He says the first time they can get loose from their work, Salerno's where they're going.

"You can understand," says Hugo, having concluded *Torna a Surriento* with a flourish, "why I like to do so many of these wop numbers."

The regulars pack the place, night after night, and beaming Liza spots them every time, and knows their preferences. "Hugo, there's Mr. and Mrs. Galland. They just came in with that party."

"Let's do *Whispering*, then," says Hugo. "It's her favorite."

"And there's Colonel Casey with his wife. What's their special number—?"

"*Some of These Days*."

"Oh, yes. And then, *Begin the Beguine* and *Cielito Lindo* for Dr. Palma—"

The room is dimly lighted, but not too dimly . . . you can see people, but don't have to watch them through a glare. Nor do you stumble blindly to your table as if you were a coal miner.

Trim waitresses are friendly and efficient. Smell of charred steak gratifies the air, along with that grainy odor of beer. Beer and hot meat . . . what witchery when you are both hungry and relaxed. In pleasance you look back on the day you've just spent . . . foretell the contentment of rest so soon to come . . . yet anticipate, with animation, the day ahead.

> Aura Lee! Aura Lee! Maid of golden hair!
> Sunshine came along with thee, and swallows in the air.

"Hugo and Liza, you said your home is in Vero Beach. But you didn't give your family name. Please tell it now, so I can include it in my book."

"Oh, don't bother. Just say Hugo and Liza. That's the way everybody knows us."

Most people, even those well informed on geographical details of our United States, believe that the Missouri River forms a permanent boundary between Missouri and part of Nebraska, and between Missouri and part of Kansas. Also they will inform you that the Mississippi River flows between Illinois and Missouri, between Missouri and Kentucky, and between Missouri and Tennessee.

These folks don't get no cigar.

At St. Joseph a portion of Missouri occupies the west bank of the river, embracing the city airport. Up in Atchison County a lump of Nebraska roosts along the east margin of the Missouri River. The vagaries of this stream are legion; the same is true of the Mississippi. One can scrutinize a large-scale map intently, and observe to his astonishment exactly where these rivers *used to run*.

Across the State in Mississippi County, a couple of wafers of Kentucky land exist on the west bank of the Mississippi River. But the most extensive phenomenon of this sort occurs a few miles downstream from Ste. Genevieve, adjacent to the little town of Saint Marys. Here a good-sized wad of Illinois, containing perhaps twenty-five square miles of bottomland, has the Mississippi River running widely between it and the rest of the State of Illinois.

We drive downhill, east from Saint Marys, through a soft storm of blowing cottonwood fuzz. Yes, you can see how it happened. An ancient bed of the Mississippi lies at the foot of the hill, just beyond the railroad tracks. It has degenerated into a series of bayous, bridged by an iron structure and by low wooden trestles. The Illinois State Line is directly ahead: here's the big blue sign announcing it. Sure enough, we're *still west of the Mississippi,* but entering the State of Illinois.

Banks of solid underbrush, cottonwood trees, grapevines, trumpet flowers. It is somewhat reminiscent of the Winneshiek Bottoms, hundreds of miles upstream along the Iowa-Wisconsin border. Likely enough this entire area has disappeared beneath floods more times than the weather historians could count. But at last the river tore a fresh hole and made a new passage for itself, miles to the east.

. . . Drive past a village, past a tavern . . . a few farms where corn is standing valiant and green. (A mighty levee protected this pocket from high waters earlier in the year.) Then we turn and go back into Missouri, a little saddened by considering how many families' trust and plans and hopes have been swept to extinction, drowned under desperate oily swirling tides . . . a stubbornly repeated tragedy, until there was nothing to pick up and go on with, nothing but exhaustion and a numbness more cruel than exhaustion.

. . . Past the bayous again. They are dyed to a yellow-green chartreuse by algae clustering thickly.

. . . Once more into smoke of blowing cottonwood froth. Often warblers line their nests with it. May there be many warblers around to take advantage of this fragile gift from the Great Giver.

Ste. Genevieve is proud of its Jean Baptiste Vallé house—its Amoureux House, Bolduc House, Mammy Shaw house—its Museum and Green Tree Tavern, its Jour de Fête with a revival of the La Guignolée singers— One of the old French river towns doing its level best to attract tourists, but not yet possessing sufficient comfortable accommodations to care for many sightseers at the same time.

We departed from its self-conscious antiquity, and in a few minutes had identified the Big Boss of Ste. Genevieve.

The Big Boss of Ste. Genevieve is the Mississippi Lime Company. Down in a valley beside the town a horrid complex squats and sprawls and reeks. You blink your eyes through burning gray haze, and make out an immense sign reading, SAFETY IS EVERYBODY'S BUSINESS. Gradually you discern angles, lines, gradations of structures, sharp steepness of roofs. . . . Ah, it is a monstrous thing! Looks like a movie-set maker's dream of what a lime or cement plant might be if situated on the planet Mars.

Blink again, rub dry venom out of your eyes, and try to count how many smoke-stacks are belching. *One, two* . . . try to count. . . . Sixteen or eighteen stacks at the very least. Some exude thick smoke, some puff with dust or steam.

Dust, dust, dust. Flour-white at one end, gradually shading off into gray powder at the other. The pulverulence covers poles, fences, markers, signs . . . drifts on across the landscape.

Aye, people are breathing this.

On the hillside beyond is a mountain of— Whatever their waste is. Reminds one of phosphate companies down South.

Want to venture into the valley and learn what this stuff smells like? Let's go.

. . . It's smog across the roadway and— Pitiful thought!—directly in the path of blowing fumes and dry residue, held against the ground by atmospheric conditions on this day, here's a herd of cattle, forced to make their living off the herbage of a pasture which is mantled with this stuff.

A monster emerges like one of the Legion of the Damned, from out the drift. Is he a robot? . . . No, no. (Why can't they have robots performing these tasks, if indeed they must be performed, and not *men*—not men who started out with pure bodies, but were sentenced to this hell-hole.) Is he wearing a mask? . . . No, just one of those hard hats. And he's wearing spectacles—not even goggles.

What are the lungs like, inside that maltreated chest? (Oldtimers in Missouri mining regions used to talk about "miners' con," a form of silicosis which in its later stages ran into tuberculosis.)

Our throats are dry, our lungs parched. . . .

All hail, promoters and erectors and proprietors of The Hideous and Exasperating and Menacing! We award you the Order of Destruction, First Class. You have not yet wrecked totally our American life as it was once known, but you're getting on with the job. Getting on very nicely.

. . . Playing back a band on the Dictaphone.

"Let us note the custom of county road departments, which demands the piling up of gravel for mile after mile along narrow roads—Along *one side* of the narrow roads. And long before it's to be used. As a result, heedless motorists drive in the middle. We came up over a hill yesterday, clinging desperately to the right-hand side, and here was another car hurtling at us, head on. Had to go into the ditch on that one. The other driver went into the gravel which was piled on his side. A sublime conception of road maintenance. They do it in county after county."

(N.B. More than three weeks after I'd encountered a specific five miles of this idiotic condition, I had occasion to return into the same area. Through a mistake in navigation, I found myself on that identical C road again. The five-mile-long heap of gravel was still there—unused, unspread—but forming a severe traffic hazard through all that time.)

Hours after we'd left Ste. Genevieve, we met up with segments where gravel *mingled with tar* had been bountifully dumped.

"That's a favorite rural sport hereabouts. Get a few thousand tons of tar and a few thousand tons of gravel or crushed rock, then spread them, and let people attempt to travel on the mixture. You can't go over ten miles an hour or you'll get a heavy undercoating of this concoction. Every now and then some lunatic approaches at a higher speed, and he's throwing up a storm as he comes. I just had to hit my horn like crazy, and turn on my bright lights, to discourage one truck which would have covered us with the stuff. Thank the Lord, he got the hint and slowed down, and we slid and wavered past each other."

They wait until midsummer, when tourist traffic is at its height. Then— Fetch out the machines, fetch the rollers! Sometimes these latter beasts creep in echelon formation, and the only way you can pass is to drive down a ditch. And there may be a culvert or a pipe, waiting just ahead.

Missouri ain't all roses.

And I was about to declare that Missouri abounds in delinquent dogs, but thought better just in time. The notion arose solely because we had been traveling several thousand miles through the State; and it is on our treasured back roads that dogs populate dooryards. Though there isn't much traffic on State or U.S. highways in certain regions. In some places, a great deal less traffic than a generation ago, before express arteries came to rip and roar.

In examining notes, I learn that, in a summer noontime, I drove twelve miles on U.S. 40, somewhere between New Franklin and Midway, without overtaking a car, meeting a car, or seeing a motor vehicle of any kind except those parked in farmyards. Drove on wide smooth pavement with every excuse for at least local traffic between towns.

The answer: Interstate 70 runs parallel a few miles to the south, crammed and moaning.

Nevertheless if only one car were to pass in a day, car-chasing is a grievous fault, and grievously do some dogs answer it. I came near to clouding the reputation of decorous Missouri dogs only because I have traveled there more extensively in recent years than in any other State. (In 1966 our hearts were in our mouths just as many times up in Maine—say, between South Jefferson and Augusta—as during the next year in Missouri.)

. . . They have an evil habit of lying in wait, then springing out with a bellow. In Harrison County one pair used to work together. The black-and-tan shepherd type would be crouched in his nest among weeds; when you slowed down for that curve, he bounced out and *woof*ed and snapped his jaws. His pal, a handsome female collie, sat at a distance where she could watch the entertainment with that smug air which collies adopt when they wish to appear aloof and unsinning. Next time you'd come past the place, the collie would be in ambush, and the shepherd would retire to let her take over. Twice I felt impelled to stop and lecture them, but they outshouted me.

I wouldn't say that Harrison County dogs are generally more sinful than Shannon County dogs or Jasper County dogs. It is merely that dogs have felt the internationally pervading sense of moral decay, and are making their own demonstrations about . . . ?

Fiddlesticks. Naughty dogs chase cars, and always have, ever since automobiles were invented. Before that they chased other vehicles. Lord God of Hosts!—when Jehu and Joram went tearing out in their chariots, there must have been dogs scrambling volubly after them.

Uncle Jas Bell kept a collie as companion through all the Best Years of His Life, which terminated in his eighty-second year. I don't say it was the same collie, but forever he did have a collie—little resembling modern long-nosed types developed by Albert Payson Terhune and others (one time before his death Bert Terhune told me that he regretted ever breeding in that Russian wolfhound strain. It flattened the head, and there was a definite loss of cranial capacity). No, sir: big broad-shouldered blunt-nosed congenial farm types. The collie's name was always Jack. Uncle Jas had a dog named Jack, first off when he was a boy. It didn't seem right to him not to have a Jack around the place.

The particular Jack I'm talking about gladdened Uncle Jas's last days half a century ago. Jack had a melodious bark, a pink tongue which would have looked good in a sandwich, and plenty of burrs in his tail. A matted bundle of canine virtues and conceits— Brave, clean, and reverent.

But Jack owned one hideous weakness. Cars. Uncle Jas agreed with psychologists who hold it important in child-rearing that the punishment follow as quickly as possible on the commission of the crime itself. Trouble was, although spry enough when described in general terms, Uncle Jas was not up to catching and thrashing a recalcitrant dog who refused to respond to his orders to come immediately and get switched. Having chased a car, Jack would retreat cagily to a distance, and then sit on his haunches to be scolded at safe range.

Said Jack, "To hell with the scolding. What I like is to chase cars, and growl, and try to bite their tires, and have a good time generally. Scolding is *as nothing* to me."

But a day of reckoning came, and I wish that I might have been present.

Uncle Jas held benign court (he was known as the Tall Hickory of the Boone, and he had served in the Northern Border Brigade, and was the beau ideal of the pioneer. Bryant Baker might have sculpted him, complete in every detail). He would sit outside for hours of each fair day, puffing on that great pipe of his (cf. *Story Teller*, p. 215) ready to wave at all comers, and conduct conversation with them if they chose to halt at his gate. The concrete stoop served as dais; the chunky white house was only about thirty feet away from a winding graveled road. Uncle Jas had ample opportunity to observe Jack, the collie, in transgression. Usually Jack would lie beside Uncle Jas's chair or at his feet, but he could hear a car coming long before anyone else could. Therefore, detecting the approach, Jack would rise, amble down the path as if bent on no evil intent, and disappear among ragweed and sunflowers which grew along the verge. After a while Jack's master would himself hear the car. Knowing what was about to happen, he would call loudly for Jack to return and take up his proper position on the stoop or alongside it. But Jack's ears were plugged with the cotton of his own villainy.

. . . So along came this car, and it was driven by Mr. Neese, a good friend and family connection, who had business in the village beyond, and wasn't prepared to linger for any conversation. He jolted past in his Model-T, and all he did was cry, "Hey, Jas!" and flap his hand, and be saluted by Jas in return.

And be attacked by Jack, who leaped from his covert like a Madhupur man-eater pursuing a lame child.

On this day Jack was not content with merely snapping at dusty tires. He held another desire, a vaulting ambition which perhaps few other collies had ever owned. He, Jack Bell, would show the way, and light the path for car-chasing dogs to follow. Nay, he would not waste aimless yaps alongside those blurred wheels—

(There were no hub-plates on Fords of fifty years agone. They had hub-*caps*. Each cap was cylindrical, and protruded several inches from the wheel itself.)

And Jack— Yes, he would *do it*.

His jaws closed tightly on a whirling hub-cap.

It might be overly presumptuous to consider Jack as the first airborne collie. Balloonists of other centuries were known to carry animals aloft with them . . . who knows but what some primitive collie may have soared? And early pilots of heavier-than-air machines have confessed to the eccentricity of toting pets along with them. Some Laddie or Lassie of yore may have accompanied a flyer in some old Taube or Farman Shorthorn. It matters not.

A great gold-and-white furry flopping object sailed high and far. Uncle Jas said afterward, "Looked like it throwed him fifty foot. I figured he was killed, for sure." Then the law of gravity prevailed, and Jack dropped into a patch of burdock and thistles.

Mr. Neese, unaware of what had happened, continued merrily on his twenty-mile-an-hour course. Uncle Jas arose, grasped his cane, and went out through the gate, fearing the worst. As he poked apprehensively into one end of the brake, he lifted his glance in time to see an abject Jack emerge from the other end. The collie, pausing only to shake each leg in turn, and to give himself a general spasmodic shaking, disappeared around the corner of the house with plumed tail squeezed between his hind legs.

"He went down cellar," Uncle Jas told me, when I arrived for a visit two days later. "He's still down there. Won't move."

"He may be hurt after all."

"No, he ain't hurt. I went down there, and so did Aunt Jen. We felt him over; didn't seem like no bones was broken. But he just won't come out. Won't go in his kennel, won't go to the barn, won't come in the house. Aunt Jen took him down a pan of leavings—lot of things he specially fancies, like left-over apple fritters and scraps of pot roast. But— Not he. Wouldn't touch it.

"You see, Jack has always felt that he had cars on the run. He was chasing em out of the yard, so to speak, time and time again. So this was just too much for him. If a car can do that to Jack, why— He ain't going to give a car another chance."

I descended into the cellar, and tried to persuade and cajole. Got nowhere. All I could see were a pair of green eyes glaring balefully.

He did emerge the next morning. By that time we felt it wise not to make an issue of the matter. Casually we accepted Jack—didn't congratulate him effusively on his return to society. We acted as if he'd been there all along.

He stretched, yawned, gave a feeble wag or two, and then visited the kitchen door for a modest repast. When he'd finished that, he came around to the front and lay down at Uncle Jas's feet.

Pretty soon a car came downhill from the southwest. It was a Stanley Steamer, hissing and puffing in a manner fit to attract attention of the most lethargic dog. . . . What sort of pale monster was this, breathing out threat and menace? One to be attended to by every Shep or Rover along the route!

But not by Jack Bell.

Uncle Jas said, "I guess that's Claude Richeson," and lifted his hand in response to children's waves from the car.

Jack didn't alter his position. The only muscles he moved were those in his neck and shoulders. He turned away as the Steamer approached, and seemed studiously counting pansies which Aunt Jen kept growing along the edge of the concrete stoop . . . pansies were interesting. All dogs should be capable of studying pansies. He regarded them intently. That Stanley Steamer could have been on the other side of the world, far as Jack Bell was concerned.

Only when it had gone snuffing across the river bridge and up the opposite hill, did he return to any contemplation of the general landscape.

Uncle Jas was still talking about it at the Old Settlers' Picnic next year. "You couldn't get that dog to look at a car, not if you took a horsewhip to him. And when folks *drive into the barnyard*— He goes down cellar again. Won't come out till the car is gone."

Bill Rogers started his Bill Rogers Float Service thirty-odd years ago, when *he* was in his thirties. But he'd done a lot of fishing and a lot of guiding before that. Big of frame, bald of head, smooth-shaven, with lines of laughter all over his face— And yet very shrewd eyes looking out through spectacles—

Bill came to greet us, the instant we stopped in his driveway, even before I could get the car door open.

He uttered two words. They were good to hear . . . you like to listen to those words . . . savor them, when you've been driving here, there, everywhere.

A moment later, Bill's wife, Addis, came hastening. She, too, spoke the words. (Are there any better in the language?)

Welcome home.

They told us to drive straight down to the end of their line of little apartments . . . right ahead . . . that was the one they were saving. It was all ready. . . .

I got the trunk open, to remove essential bags before fishermen began returning from the James River, before trucks came banging in with johnboats towed behind them on trailers. Necessarily there would be a lot of backing and filling . . . johnboats are unwieldy, unless they're floating on the streams for which they were created.

I asked Bill why they called them johnboats.

He studied the matter. "Well, there seem to be a lot of theories about that, and I don't know which one is correct. Some say that the first ones were built by a man named John: hence the name. Others believe that it's because they're so *long*. You know how people speak of winter underwear as 'long johns'? So these folks say the name derived from that. But I think it seems mighty far-fetched."

I told him that the Seminoles had boats which looked a good deal like these, hollowed out of cypress logs. "And one time, up the Toro

River in Panama, we went out with a native in a similar boat. I think they called them *cayugas,* down there."

"Oh, you find a lot of mention of johnboats in publications which deal with the White River, and even the Red, and the Mississippi." He led toward the door of our apartment. "Come on—I want to show you about the switch on this air-conditioning. It's kind of tricky—"

Addis and Irene were already inside, talking a mile a minute. The American Indians can be thanked for many things; but all who ever knew the Rogerses will thank the Indians especially for giving some of their blood to Addis. She's one of the loveliest hostesses you ever met in your life. And then some.

For one thing, she remembers a man's weaknesses.

"Mack, guess what we're having tonight?"

"Not— Not *roast pork?*"

"Yes."

"Oh God. And not— Not with—?"

"Yes. With dressing." She giggled. And then said it again, with a different intonation. "Welcome *home*. To Galena, Missouri."

Bill cried, "Hey, take a look. See who's coming along out there—"

I saw a squat diminutive figure, and hurried across the yard. "Hoss!" Hoss Jennings, our former camp cook.

"Heard you was a-coming in." He squinted all over his face while we shook hands. "Thought I'd come over and say Hello."

"Hoss, tell me. Are you still going on the float trips, cooking?"

. . . To tell the truth, he was more or less retired from that field. He was getting pretty old, and found it pretty wearing. "Course, sometimes I go, when special friends are coming along. You going to float?"

"Just can't do it. Got to get down to Florida."

"Well, maybe we'll try it some other time. Hey—" As a red truck swung into the yard. "Know that fellow, standing up there in back?"

I looked. Randy Layton, with his old straw hat on the back of his head.

"Randy!"

He dropped to the ground, wiping a hand against his shirt. "Golly, I don't know whether I ought to shake hands or not. Got fish all over my hands."

"What's a little fish between friends?"

"You know, I've been saving a book for you. Guess you'd call it a booklet. It's just printed on paper; but it belongs to my wife, and it tells all about the old Bald-Knobber gang. I'll bring it over tonight or in the morning. Say, Jerry Hunt says he's coming down from Springfield tonight. To say Hello."

Jerry had been another of our guides. "You mean to say Jerry and his wife and kids are living up in *Springfield?*"

"Yep. He's building himself a new house, too. Guess it's near to completion by this time."

Another truck was grunting in, hauling boats, and Hoss and Randy and I moved out of the way. Thus standing closer to the kitchen door. Thus being able to scent an elysian combination of sage, onion, pork gravy.

Oh boy.

That night I dined on you-know-what, but the diet-wise Irene partook of fare more suited to her appetite and general inclination: dainty pink-fleshed trout. (Long ago there were no trout in the Ozarks, but there are now. Here's one of the few occasions where Man has intruded upon Nature with a salubrious result.)

These trout were the gift of Major-General Tom Yancey (Ret.), who had been whipping a mean fly-rod that afternoon.

Said Tom Yancey, "In your search for those qualities so typical of the Native Missourian, please don't neglect to mention that he likes to fish. And is usually damn good at it!"

Irene's mouth was too full of trout for her to venture a comment. All she could do was nod her head vigorously, and wave a finger in adjuration.

That night she woke me up, gasping, "Oh, those doggone *dogs!*"

I listened sleepily. "There's just two or three. They must have got on a fox"—meaning a fox's trail—"down there by the river."

"Those aren't the ones. Wait a minute. You'll hear them."

I did hear. Much closer at hand. *Owoooooooooo.*

"*That's* what I mean."

I sat up in bed. "*Those* dogs aren't chasing any fox. They're just howling."

"Indeed they are howling!"

Owoooooooooo.

"Two of em."

"But what's the *matter* with them?"

"Well, for one thing, they're not full grown. Their main objection is that they're penned up, and can't get out and work that fox, along with those other hounds. That's why they're complaining."

Owoooooooooo.

"Can't somebody make them *stop?*"

"Nobody could make them stop. They're mourning, and consider that they have a perfect right to mourn. They want to do what the other dogs do. *You* think it's unreasonable for them to howl like that; and so, probably, does everyone else within range of their voices. But the hounds: *they* think it's *reasonable*. You couldn't make them believe any differently if you used a rack and an Iron Maiden."

. . . In the morning I inquired of Bill, "Were those your pups, howling last night?"

"Heavens, no." Bill held up his hand in a manner of prayer, and lifted a pious glance to the sky. "I think those pups belong to Randy Layton."

When Randy came into the yard, I asked him. "Were those your pups, Randy, a-howling early this morning?"

Randy grinned. "No, they weren't mine. I think," he said, lowering his voice, "twas some of Bill's dogs."

The final paragraphs are difficult to write. In fact, I'd rather write about anything else in the world.

. . . Maybe the sensitive gliding of current, or a chuckling over rocks at a rapids . . . murmur and music of rapids in the James River, or over on Flat Creek. Or—in the old days—talkative waters of the White River . . . or certain dreamy pools under willows and cottonwoods where bass were waiting, ready to spring. Or where, if you chose to dabble a worm in the water, yellow catfish came obligingly to seize it—and to sizzle eventually in Hoss Jennings' deep charred frying-pan.

. . . Or a fire on a ridge. And Bill and Addis and Irene and I there beside the neighbors, waiting . . . listening . . . smelling our fire in the night.

"*There* they come. They got him up out of that holler!"

Pure music welling thinly through trees, and then stronger and more clear and melodious as hounds loped up to higher ground.

. . . Or to think of times when we just sat in a booth at Bill's restaurant, having coffee or Cokes, and yakking away on whatever topic suggested itself.

So it pains, to write these paragraphs. Last August– One day I received one of those messages which none of us likes to receive. And now I have to think of Bill buried in his native soil at Drake's Creek, near Japton.

I cannot imagine him thus, though reason tells me that he is lying so. . . . Can't believe it. He's walking through Ozark woods, or drifting on Ozark waters.

Two long-time friends, Dick Glendinning and Wyatt Blassingame, wrote of Jim Bridger in their book, *The Mountain Men.*

> When he died in 1881 at the age of seventy-seven, his daughter took the youngsters aside. "Children," she told them, "your grandfather has gone to heaven."
>
> "No, he hasn't," one of them said. "He's gone back to the mountains."

24. Silver Dollar City

Sun punished the main street of Silver Dollar City in the Ozarks . . . sun seemed trying to make it into Silver City, New Mexico, or a similar southwestern place.

> When Billy the Kid was a very young lad,
> In old Silver City he went to the bad. . . .
> Way out in the West, with a gun in his hand,
> At the age of twelve years that he killed his first man.

It was more than hot sunshine which made us think of the ballad about Silver City and Billy the Kid. A taut feeling of suspense ruled the town square. Men, women and children were rimmed thickly—watching, waiting.

Irene asked, "What was it that the town marshal said? He seemed to be making a public announcement—"

"He said Curly Wolf was rumored to be coming into town. I don't know who Curly Wolf is. Why don't we go over and ask that blacksmith?"

So we did.

. . . Blacksmith was a very good ad for the place, if Curly Wolf wasn't. His name was Lloyd Heller, and he came originally from Stroudsburg, Pennsylvania, but he'd lived out in the Ozarks long enough to acquire the nickname of Shad. *The smith, a mighty man is he.* Shad Heller was gray-bearded, and through his metal-rimmed spectacles he looked out impassively at any suggestion of approaching strife. While he spoke, his powerful fingers toyed fondly with a bit of iron which he intended to hammer into a new shape, once he'd heated it at the glowing hot-perfumed forge.

"I guess there's going to be trouble all right. You see, it was our local marshal's testimony which sent Curly up to the penitentiary, some years ago. Curly shot a man—shot him in the back, which was his usual habit. But now he's escaped from Jeff City, and they do say that he's sworn to shoot the marshal on sight. We've heard he was headed this way. Shouldn't wonder but what he'd show up most any time."

We went back to join the crowd—a crowd considerably thicker by the minute. The cool handsome marshal kept a hand on his revolver holster while his eyes roved rooftops of the low buildings. We guessed that Curly had a habit of crawling over those roofs when he was going to shoot somebody. . . . But, before we could ask, Curly's wife appeared.

She pranced, screaming, gesticulating—a termagant if you ever saw one. She wore yellow calico and an old-fashioned sunbonnet, and she howled like a she-wolf. . . . Marshal tried to hush her up, but that was like trying to put out an oil-well fire in Oklahoma. One minute she'd insult the marshal, next minute she was turning around to the crowd and screaming imprecations at everyone. Curly should have considered himself to be pretty well off, up there at Jefferson City, rather than in the company of this slut.

But just about the time we had this figured out— *Bang! Bang!* Two revolver shots, fired from the roof of the Silver Dollar City General Store. It was Curly, all right . . . mean-looking young man . . . we could see him creeping around up there. The marshal fired at him twice, but Curly dodged back, and he must have dropped to the ground, unhurt, behind the building. For he came charging out at the street intersection a moment later, bursting into the town square right through that crowd. He halted, out in front of everybody, challenging the marshal to pull his gun again, and they'd settle matters then and there.

Trouble was, the wife was still dancing between the two men, shrieking invective at both. . . . Give Curly and the marshal credit: they were angling to get out of the way, so's they could finish their feud, but they didn't have a chance, long as that harridan waved her arms and hollered and whirled between them.

. . . Boys and girls, if there ever was a vixen, it was that woman!

I almost used a worse word than vixen . . . female of the canine species, rather than the vulpine.

But what really brought about the finish was something she said, herself. She was asking for it, believe me.

She brayed at Curly, "Why can't you quit being such a nasty man, and come home, and take care of our thirteen kids?"

Curly froze. Distinctly we heard him call to her, "What do you mean—thirteen kids at home? When I was sent up to the pen, there was only *nine*."

I reckon that wild woman became more resentful than ever, but by this time she was giving up in sheer exhaustion.

She swung away from Curly and the marshal. She said, "Oh, well, settle it between yourselves," or something like that. "I can't boss you, anyhow," or something to that effect. She turned and started off with purposeful strides.

Again, this was a thing you had to see in order to believe it. And happening right there on the main street, too! And right in these Uncanny Nineteen-sixties.

Curly and that marshal took a long look at each other. Then simultaneously they turned their revolvers on that witch. She absorbed plenty of lead . . . let's see: they each had four live rounds left in their revolvers. So the lady—*Ha!*—must have been hit eight times. Fairly riddled. She fell dead at the side of the street, with her skirts almost up to her waist as she kicked her last kick.

Curly seemed to feel an obligation to good manners. He went over and pulled down the dead woman's petticoats. "Couldn't even die decent," he said. Then he and the marshal shook hands over the prostrate corpse.

You could see that everyone in that town square favored what Curly and the marshal had done. They clapped, whistled, yelled their approval. This was good riddance of some mighty bad rubbish.

We discovered that there was a steam engine with cars attached, downhill at the station. Irene said, "Why, we haven't ridden on a steam train in goodness knows how long. Why not get this taste of sudden death out of our mouths? A nice little jaunt, riding in an open car behind an antique locomotive, looking out at peaceful forests and hills— That's just what we need."

So we got aboard. But, Good Lord Alive, as Queen Mab would

say, it seemed that there was nothing but crime in the Ozarks any more. First off came a railroad detective, prying around, asking whether anyone had seen a young man of such-and-such description. And the moment his back was turned, by golly if that young man didn't jump aboard the train. . . . Also we heard that there was a valuable mail pouch—or a lot of express money, I forget which—being carried on that train. They were pretty apprehensive about a possible hold-up.

Held up we were, too, in no time at all. Held up by a gang of brothers, sort of like the James boys or the Youngers. But I wouldn't advise any other modern badmen to fool around with those railroad people in the Silver Dollar City area. For there sounded a lot more gun-play, and even shotguns were booming. Soon those robber brothers lay stretched on the ground, dead as that termagant wife back yonder in the village. The train passengers approved of this, too. They applauded fiercely, except for two or three tots who were howling their heads off in fright.

(I'd better make apology to those psychologists mentioned in Chapter 10. This *is* truly a violent world and we are surely a violent Nation. Especially at Silver Dollar City. They don't care how many people get knocked off.)

After we'd returned to the station, Irene wanted to go and watch some glass-blowers and wood-workers, but I went to watch Lloyd Heller. He was doing a very simple thing for any master smith: demonstrating how one welds a link for a chain. . . . How delightful to hear the clang of hammer-on-anvil once more. *And children, coming home from school, look in at the open door.*

Old children and young children, we gathered along a rustic fence which separated the smithy from the crowd. Shad Heller explained in a clear even voice exactly what he was doing, and why, at each step of the game. It was good to observe how the Little People of today were mesmerized by this primitive performance. Reckon they enjoyed it more than any of their favorite television programs.

Before the act was concluded, I felt impelled to find a shady place nearby, to do a little dictating on my portable machine. But I noticed that, when Heller finished his stint, there came a spontaneous roar of applause from the watchers. Why, maybe they applauded even louder than they did when Curly Wolf and the town marshal made an angel out of that harpy. I looked back up the street . . .

no, she wasn't a-laying there no longer. Guess some folks had took pity, and toted her away.

In May, 1968, they honored Mary Herschend by making her Missouri's "Small Business Man for the Year." But she's still all woman, and looks it. She was born at the turn of the century; but throngs of gals, ten or fifteen years younger than she, might envy her poise and posture, her radiant face and eyes and, above all, her accomplishments.

"When you and your husband decided to take a ninety-nine-year lease on Marvel Cave, back in 1950, how many people did you employ?"

"Three."

"And now, in operating the twin attractions of Marvel Cave and Silver Dollar City, how many do you employ?"

Mary explained, "It's well over three hundred, during the March-to-December season. In winter we average about a hundred and twenty employees, just taking care of things, servicing equipment and premises. Naturally it's in wintertime that we do the most of our building expansion."

Hugo Herschend died of a heart attack in 1956, and it was up to his widow to take over. She admits now that she suffered a few qualms. Her two sons were still very young, but she held hope that they could work capably along with her. That they did, and in successful harmony, is evidenced today by the fact that Silver Dollar City, with its enormous adjoining cavern, attracts several million visitors yearly.

Jack, the elder son, occupies himself mostly with the finances of the establishment, and long-term planning. Son Peter handles the operational end, chiefly, and deals with day-to-day problems. Governor Hearnes recently named Pete to be a Missouri State Commissioner of Tourism.

Then there's the promotion manager, Don Richardson, Sr., who fairly bounces with youthful energy. It makes you wonder . . . if this is Don Richardson, *Senior*, how old might Don Richardson, *Junior*, be? About two, I reckoned. Later I found out that the boy was entering his teens. They must have a fountain of youth down in that Marvel Cave.

Silver Dollar City, or as some like to term it, "The Williamsburg of the Ozarks," occupies two thousand acres on hills above Table

Rock Lake, a few miles west of Branson. This was once the White River country, but now, after damming, there are also Bull Shoals Lake and Lake Taneycomo. . . . *The Shepherd of the Hills Country* is plastered all over the place. Proprietors of such enterprises make a great thing of pointing out Jim Lane's Cabin and Old Matt's Homestead and the Wash Gibbs Museum. I didn't know that there were any Harold Bell Wright addicts left alive, but apparently there are. I first read that lurid and driveling novel at the age of nine or so, and thought it perfectly marvelous. Next time I read it, I could discern that it was tailored for the nine-year-old mind. However, sixty years after its publication, there is no way to restrain a few people from making a fast buck out of a long-dead novelist who achieved far wider circulation than he merited. But there's none of this Shepherd of the Hills guff in Silver Dollar City.

First time we ever went there, the parking problem was excruciating. Had to park at a vast distance from the Visitor Center, and walk all the way up there under a blazing sky. Very cleverly the Herschends have now improved on that situation. They've got open cars—as many as three cars can be pulled by one engine—and visitors throng aboard the cars as they did at the New York World's Fair in the late Nineteen-thirties. It made us recall those dollies, with horns playing melodiously that boys-and-girls-together phrase from *The Sidewalks of New York,* and pedestrians dodging out of the way.

We told Mary that once we'd mentioned this to Gregory Peck . . . Greg said, "Maybe you dodged *me* in 1939. Because I was piloting one of those things at the Fair."

Mary smiled. "Well, perhaps one of our drivers may some day turn out to be as famous an actor as Peck." Then she became very serious when I remarked that already she had some excellent actors playing the roles of Curly Wolf and the town marshal. And, above all, that vicious wife of Curly's.

"Some visitors seem to have the idea that all we're running is a kind of shoot-em-up procedure. Certainly we do have these attractions, and people consider them enjoyable. The Hatfields and McCoys, for instance, do a little banging of their own at a different hour. And then there's Retreat, with soldiers in old-fashioned uniforms participating in military ceremony, and firing a cannon, and all. But what I'm proudest of is our presentation of Ozark life as it was really lived in the Eighteen-eighties, and our revival of manual skills. Shad Heller, with his blacksmith's shop, isn't the only thing of that sort which we have. What about our General Store and Post Office, just the way they used to be? And there is no other place in the land where you can secure a custom-made cigar-store Indian! How about our candle-makers and our pottery work? And the water-mill? And the flooded mine? And, above all, our Root-Digging Weekends in spring, and the Festival of Craftsmen in autumn! Tourism has become a bigger business in this State than most people realize. We are trying to approach it intelligently."

She passed over a clipping from the Kansas City *Times*.

. . . Almost 5½ million tourist cars entered Missouri last year, bringing in more than 20 million visitors. In all, a total of 71.8 million cars entered the State. These travelers, along with the tourists who arrived by bus, plane and train, spent an estimated 527 million dollars. Missourians themselves invested another 194 million on State-wide travel, bringing total tourist revenues to 721 million dollars. . . .

Where do all of the visitors come from? Eight States in this region account for 46 per cent of the crowds. Illinois and Kansas top the list. Surprisingly California is third, followed by Texas, Iowa and Oklahoma. . . .

We went out and explored some more, and grew dizzy after another hour or two, and had to give up from sheer exhaustion. Basketry, mountain music, Butterfield stage, spinners, weavers. A flour mill (the millers in our family, and they were many, always spoke of *flouring* mills) where yellow meal oozed from under the dressed burrs. And a pottery works and a candy factory, and a printing shop. And a homestead where you can see how Ozark people used to dwell in a homestead . . . the Wilderness Church, where you can see how and where Ozark people used to worship. They still hold services in that church, too. But unhappily we weren't going to be there at ten o'clock next Sunday morning.

Wish we could have gone into the flooded mine. Don Richardson spoke of this with enthusiasm, but we just didn't have the time. You travel in miniature ore barges which hold six people apiece. They're not propelled by oars or engines—just drift along with the current, like those gondolas at a fair, wherein you explore the Tunnel of Love. All sorts of adventures ensue . . . queer figures are illuminated along the dark channels . . . workmen doing things: digging, drilling, blasting. Just about the time you're accustomed to so many imitation miners, you encounter some live ones. Reminds you of that fellow in Madame Tussaud's Museum, in London, who stood motionless among all the static wax images, and suddenly would address some dame who was passing by, and almost send her into hysterics.

Indeed, in two visits, we found but one Silver Dollar City item to kick about. That was the snack bar, down a path behind the place where Shad Heller does his blacksmithing. The scenery there was as slimy and paper-strewn as at any of those wretched greasy-spoons compressed into temporary quarters at airport terminals which haven't yet been completed. We had to buck a chow line where unappetizing scraps were dished out by a corporal's guard of sullen slatterns who had never been near the Howard Johnson Training School and didn't need to go. In fact, any Howard Johnson's would look like Prunier's, in contrast to that dump. Uncounted relays of lunchers had preceded us at a foul table where at last we managed to put down our sandwiches and milk-cups. That table looked like the Yippies had been having a sit-in and a cook-out. Here was the only slum in Silver City, but it was a ripe one.

Maybe by this time Curly Wolf and the marshal have gone in there and shot up the whole joint.

Point is, I suppose, that the Herschends can't be everywhere at once. (This is true of all enormous projects. Every so often a corner sags.) For one thing, they're too busy making plans for the autumnal National Festival of Craftsmen. That comes in October, and is beginning to receive the wide attention it deserves. It's put on by the National Crafts Foundation, a nonprofit organization headed by General Mark Clark. In this Uncanny Decade—when we are beset by assembly lines in every direction, when we realize that such grotesqueries as TV dinners and Instant Breakfasts are here to stay—it's remarkable how many folks still appreciate donkey-powered sorghum grinding; or rope making, yarn dyeing, china painting, fiddle making, quilting, meat smoking, rail splitting. Frank Farmer, our newspaper friend, says that hotels and motels are filled to overflowing when that sixteen-day festival is on, all the way up to Springfield and past. That's forty or fifty miles away.

For families who take autumnal holidays, this couldn't be better. When one thinks of how Mary has labored to bring such activity about—in October, too, when the Ozarks are a glory—he's more than willing to forgive her . . . forgive Mary and Pete and Jack

Herschend, and Don Richardson, Sr., the memory of the snack bar.

Anyway, as stated, it's entirely possible that Curly Wolf and the marshal have dealt with that repulsive situation by this time.

For information, good people, send your carrier pigeons to Don Richardson, Sr., Silver Dollar City, Missouri, 65616.

(When Don, Jr. gets married and has a little boy of his own, his father will have to become Don Richardson, Sr. *Emeritus*.)

25. Green Memorial

Faint oh faint the chicken cry. It rises as thin eerie wailing, first from neighbors' roosters, and a boy listens in waking . . . momentarily reluctant to rise, he will admit to himself neither that he wakes nor listens. On on over the dark damp world a piping sound advances, multiplies, and soon nearest roosters are calling their report on the wide pink light scaling higher higher; verdure is banked solidly against it, the country world blushes again as on a day before and on a day to come, as country herbage will hold dampness and pastel colors until no growing things are left or needed, until tubes and crucibles contain the only blossoms.

Sleep falls from the boy like abandoned sheeting, he pushes his spindly frame out of bed, adorns himself with drawers, shirt and pantaloons (the robing of a century agone). Quietly he opens the door and goes into miraculous tints, clear unsullied air, and sees those charming patches of soft silver spread upon gleaming grass here, there, all over everywhere. Aunt Sue, the only maternal creature whom he can remember, has told him many times about those fairy tablecloths . . . almost from the start he held suspicion concerning such magical origin and design . . . wondered about the fairies, thought some variety of condensation or spiders might be assisting. In heading for the spring in his first task of the day he walks amid these delicacies, but is careful not to blunder and destroy . . . let the sun dry them up later.

He winces and makes a face during the initial bathing as his big-toed bare feet go into cold greenness (but grass is softer than the hard-trodden path, it's more fun to travel in. More rewarding too . . . what have we here? Toadstools? Why are some of these fungi called mushrooms, and others merely toadstools? Aunt Sue knows which but not why . . . and never yet has he seen a toad sitting on one of those stools, nor even putting its pointed feet thereon).

Our lad wears the harness of his momentary trade: a wooden yoke spread far wider than his bony shoulders, with buckets depending. Products of native cooper's art, the buckets are staved and hooped of red cedar; filled many times each day, they are never quite dry; sometimes when empty they *clock-clock-clock* together and make a sound like dull melodious soaked wooden bells.

In a gentle secret region below an elm and walnut ridge the spring is waiting. Also it is a cubby unexplored by the sun, and there was fear in the boy's heart when first he went choring there in tinier years. But now he's grown into lanky philosophy and understanding —fears have been supplanted by a love for the little ghost-flowers which grow in perpetual shadow and have no verdant pigment in their frail tissues . . . photosynthesis? Chlorophyll? No one has yet spoken such words within his hearing, he does not yet need to know the litany of angiosperm and cotyledon. . . . The yoke is slipped from him, buckets make their hollow protest at this interruption of an appointed task, and then are silent. And the boy sits, a plant held in his lean hand, and it is as if he were praying over it for long, for long; the sun climbs hot, a shirt is discarded, boy and plant are motionless, no water is being carried for the needs of pigs or people, the boy sits through the years.

That treasure-house which is to become his life cannot be opened as yet. No Presidents and Vice-Presidents of the United States come a-calling, no educators cry their need for him, no industrialists seek to flatter this child with whispers of enrichment to be had. The Congressional committee room is empty of his presence, his paintings are not yet exhibited, the laboratory waits still for the stimulus which he alone can provide. His name (in far future to become a household word) has not rung beyond the borders of this rough small farm.

Decades swarm before him, packed with labor, treacherous with undreamed wars and other terrors and emergencies . . . *he is sitting with his plant* . . . in time the Government acquires this soil and all growth and waters therein, to keep the farm inviolate *In Memoriam Perpetuam.* A sympathetic sculptor named Robert Amendola comes to find the boy in such primitive concentration; he sees him with the eye of the mind; he goes back to his clay and, eventually, to his bronze. Thus the youth is captured at this rustic study and in this rustic chapel. He has sat so, half-naked to all winds and weathers, will sit there until the final missile is aimed at Omaha, and someone fouls the missile up, and it explodes instead above Diamond, Missouri, and the George Washington Carver National Monument.

I'd tried to refresh my memory about Dr. Carver, the day before we drove to Diamond. The *Encyclopaedia Britannica* said, "U. S. Negro chemurgist and agricultural experimenter, devoted his life to agricultural research for the betterment of the south and his people." This was the first time I ever knew that he was a chemurgist, and wasn't quite sure what meaning was conveyed. I would have called him a noteworthy chemist and agronomist and botanist, but that "chemurgist" knocked me for a loop. After coming home I looked it up in both my Webster's and my Short Oxford, and the twenty-volume Oxford as well. No "chemurgist." Which brings to mind the fact that I don't have much faith in the *Britannica* anyway. (For instance, in the above quotation, it would be proper usage to capitalize *south* and make it *South.*) They asked me to write for them once upon a time or twice upon a time. They suggested as a topic, "The Negro in the United States." That is a subject in which, let us say, I have never specialized. No. Thanks.

Chemurgist or no, Dr. Carver was, within himself, as Carl Van Doren said of Ben Franklin, "a harmonious human multitude." He did not own or need the Philosopher's Stone; already he had, intrinsic and undiluted, that reverent humble poetry of the philosopher's spirit.

"One of the things that have helped me as much as any other is not how long I'm going to live, but how much I can do while living." He scribbled that in a scrapbook only a few months before he died, and you can see it when you go to the museum in the Visitor Center at the Memorial.

They'll offer a folder with a photograph of Amendola's statue on the cover. It gives a summary of Carver's life, and a list of his formal achievements: the Theodore Roosevelt Medal for Distinctive Service to Science; the Spingarn Medal for Distinguished Achievement by an American Negro; appointment as Fellow of the Royal Society of Arts, London; Honorary Doctor of Science degrees from Simpson College and the University of Rochester; the Honorary Birthday Award, Thomas A. Edison Foundation; and appointment as a collaborator in the Bureau of Plant Industries of the U. S. Department of Agriculture. . . .

You'll find a capable sympathetic staff, and a superintendent named David L. Hieb, a veteran of over thirty years with the National Park Service, whom you promptly want to promote to be Secretary of the Interior. These people act as if they held, as in a sacristy, this relic of eternal importance. So they do.

I don't know who designed the static exhibits at the Visitor Center. Probably they've been here since the start, and that was long before the current superintendent appeared on the scene. There are a few little antiquities: mementoes, notebooks, college publications, old photographs. Later photos also, taken at the height of his fame with Franklin D. Roosevelt, Henry Wallace, Henry Ford. Over in another corner is the bed in which he slept when he lived with Aunt Mariah and Uncle Andy Watkins at Neosho, with George's trunk at the foot of the bed and Aunt Mariah's Bible on a table.

Considerable space, however, is devoted to fancy presentations—a little too commercially styled and rather garish, some may feel. It reminded me of things the Air Force used to get together when I was on duty at the Pentagon, when we in Psych-Air were trying to sell a bunch of people on a new program. Or perhaps when we went out to the HQ of one of the field commands, and sought to win their coöperation. We set up elaborate charts, pictures, quotes and symbols, assembled in a style suggestive of Madison Avenue. And at the Carver National Monument you can almost hear someone saying fervently, "I tell you, boys, we're going to *sell* George Washington Carver to the public!"

What the hell? Maybe they're doing just that, and succeeding.

Superintendent Hieb explains dryly, "I've only been here since 1965. Hence I can claim no credit for the manner in which the area and its facilities have been developed."

Behind me could be overheard the conversation of a man and his wife, people we'd noticed getting out of a car with a Colorado license.

The woman asked abruptly, "Isn't that Dr. Carver over there in that picture?"

"Yeh."

"Well, who is *this*, in *this* picture?"

"That's Moses Carver, his owner during slavery days. I mean, he owned Dr. Carver's mother—"

"Well, who was his father?"

"I don't know."

I turned and offered help. "Here's this folder—didn't you get one? It reads, 'George's father was said to have been a slave from a neighboring plantation, who died from an accident.' "

They thanked me, and I moved on to look at something else, but could still hear the couple talking.

"So that man was his *owner?*"

"That's what it says. Moses Carver."

"Well, all I can say is, they look a lot alike."

"Yeh."

North of the Visitor Center where The Boy Carver Nature Trail (they call it that) begins, we halted at the Hanging Tree. There exists a legendary tale about Uncle Moses Carver's being pulled up by his thumbs, tortured by a gang of bushwhackers who were trying to find out where he'd hidden his gold. Same way in all such stories: it's either gold or the family silver, it isn't just plain money. Though it seems that good Federal banknotes might have been welcomed by any bushwhackers, any time. . . . Nope. Had to be gold.

This old black walnut has been dead for a long while. Stripped of its bark, it stands skeletal—Rockwell Kent tree, Salvador Dali tree—in contrast to stately beauties still foliated, spaced round about and through the woods beyond . . . walnuts, oaks, elms. The Dutch elm disease has not as yet swept this area, though there are indeed a few stumps which look painfully fresh.

In elm shade of the Carver Monument, picnic parties still continue. Two were in progress as we went toward the Trail: a colored picnic and a white picnic. Nice-looking folks in both cases, families and friends gathered around long tables . . . the sight made one entertain affectionate consideration of cold baked ham and perfection salad and cucumber pickles. Also it would have broken the hearts of rabid integrationists. Those two contented picnic parties should have been busted up immediately, and a white-colored group made at one table, and a colored-white group at the other. If Dr. Carver had devoted himself to such worthy works, instead of teaching poor Negro farmers to increase their sweet potato yield from thirty-seven bushels per acre to two hundred and sixty-six bushels per acre, he might really have amounted to something.

"Birthplace Cabin. On this site stood the simple log cabin in which George Washington Carver was born."

Shade thickens as the lawn blends down into a ravine at the north. Wisely they have not attempted to rebuild dilapidated barns or sheds. Farther on stands the Carver house where Uncle Moses lived after George had left the place, but that's all. The rest is sacred to forest and bushes and ferns and flowers growing as they always grew.

Each variety is labeled unobtrusively. You bend close to read tiny signs. Frost Grape, Day Flower, Red-bud Tree . . . even Poison Ivy duly noted. Black Cherry Tree . . . Wild Rose. . . .

Pause before the Amendola statue and give thanks for its rapture and dignity. There's an identical statue at the George Washington Carver Housing Project in New York City. It makes you wonder about the denizens of that Project. . . . Do they study Carver? Do they read his words, accept any sermon found therein? "Look about you. Take hold of the things that are here. Let them talk to you. You learn to talk to them." Or do the Project-Dwellers sit around waiting for the Federal Government to extend a new program which will pay them a premium for being incompetent or for being pure damn old-fashioned lazy?

. . . Irene said to M.C.–last year, down home in Florida: "M.C., that date palm must be moved. It's going to be too much of a job for you to handle by yourself, so bring another man to help you when you come tomorrow."

Next day he showed up alone.

"What happened? Where's the man you were to bring?"

"I couldn't get no man. I go down to that place where they spose to go, on Twenty-seventh Street. They wait there if they wants to work, and people come pick em up. They ask me, 'What these folks pay?' I say you pay regular wage. They just laugh. One of em he say, 'I come help you move that tree if he pay me twenty dollars a day.' All they wants to do is get that free money."

Condemnation of a common attitude among his own people, spoken by a black man.

It was another black man who said, "I like to think of nature as an unlimited broadcasting system, through which God speaks to us every hour, if we will only tune in."

Correct. Carver.

You can push a button on the wall near the statue and from some hidden amplifier there issues the vocal portion of a ceremony, or series of ceremonies. We made the mistake of pushing that button. Lord knows what came spewing from the amplifier. It may have been an address delivered when the Monument was dedicated in 1953. Or perhaps it had something to do with unveiling the Amendola statue (which didn't occur until seven years later). There should have been some easy way to turn the thing off if you didn't want to hear any more, but I could find no such switch. Aphorisms poured in a stream—"youthful hands," "fervent ambition," and such. We fled through red cedars, weeping willows, honey locust trees, among yellow wood-sorrel and buck-brush. A good five minutes later, distant voices were still importuning from that amplifier. Maybe the mechanism was stuck.

To quote David L. Hieb again, "Those of us who come along in later years to administer these areas simply do our best to see that the basic Master Plan is followed, and occasionally updated and refined in minor ways."

I have a suggestion for a minor refinement. Get rid of those speeches, and have Mahalia Jackson sing *His Eye Is on the Sparrow* instead. But gently, Mahalia, gently, pray.

The human inventive capacity can take a benefit and transform it into a monstrosity. We were forcibly reminded of this when, in the Lot Valley of France, we went to visit an ancient castle which had been wasting and sagging for centuries but was now being *restored.* We were eager to see the place before the *restorers* had screwed it up entirely. The owner of the establishment was resolved to lure the sightseeing public with a cultural bonus. A young man who greeted us at the crumbling gates promptly pulled a switch, and instantly the Fifth Symphony was roaring and banging from every ledge and pinnacle. God knew that that castle had been a wreck, with birds flying through flower-grown apertures for at least a hundred years before Beethoven was born.

"*Pourquoi la musique?*" asked Irene.

The manager drew himself up proudly. "It is music appropriate to the occasion, madame."

"Please, monsieur. It is too loud."

. . . Young Man said that he had been instructed to start the tape the first moment any visitors appeared.

My own spoken French is only taxicab French and bar French, so I asked Young Man if he spoke English. He said he did. I delivered a brief lecture on the Fifth. . . . We realized that it was a theme tune of the *Résistance* so active in that region. *Vive la France!* We were honored to recognize the historic composition. We realized also that Lawrence Gilman typified the Fifth Symphony when he wrote, "This is music pregnant with the greatness of the indomitable human soul." (I had to raise my voice and repeat slowly, because of the noise.) But– I suggested that if they had an alternate and somewhat more muted recording–say, Debussy's *Nuages*–why, put it on. Failing that, please to plug the orchestra into oblivion. You couldn't hear larks or hawks soaring toward drifting cumulus, and you couldn't smell the ghosts, nor could you feel the castle.

Nice Young Man. He turned it off.

Past buzzing locusts and past a massive green ash tree and past cat-briar vines, we found a walnut hedgerow leading on toward the cemetery. The burial plot is bordered by a stone wall of recent manufacture but shaded still by a few tall elms. The inscription says merely, "Here are the graves of Moses Carver, his wife, and many other members of the Carver family. The cemetery has been restored to its historic appearance."

According to Rackham Holt's biography of George Washington Carver, neighbors were buried in this graveyard as well. The author draws a picture of George attending the buryings.

> The little group of mourners stood on fence rails laid about the fresh grave to keep their feet dry, but he had been born to stand apart. A little way off from the others and alone, his feet in the mud, he watched with solemn eyes the earth reclaim its own.

Dr. Carver lies in far-off Tuskegee beside Booker Washington, so we paid our respects instead to Moses Carver's grave. "Born August 29th, 1812, and died December 20th, 1910." Ninety-eight years, babe, is a mighty long time.

The gravestone bore one version of the familiar hackneyed rhyme about, "O stranger passing by," etc. Crows kept cackling about it over in the woods, talking in Nervous Nellie voices. Sounded like a flock of critics from *The New Yorker*.

We went diagonally across a field toward the Visitor Center. Serene midday sun disclosed tiny flowers amid truant hay and rougher weeds. We slowed to admire and relish them. These were unlabeled and we could identify only two or three species.

"He would have known."

"Yes, oh yes. Would have taken them apart to see whether he could make a salve, fertilizer, condiment, God knows what."

Irene asked, "He never married? Not once? Had no sweethearts?"

"None recorded. As the books and articles point out, he was shy, opinionated, often choosing to be withdrawn from all mankind and womankind. His voice was congenitally high-pitched–"

"Do you think he was homosexual?"

The idea had often crossed my mind, yet I'd heard or read no evidence sufficient to bring a conclusion. "Perhaps devoid of sex, as such. What's the term: asexual? . . . Remember how Grant was?"

(I spoke of Grant Wood, our intimate from the day we first met in early 1927 until his death fifteen years later. He married, suddenly and unexpectedly, in middle age. Marriage, he said after this union had foundered, was not for him. "Why, I never went out with girls, not even in school days. Never had what might be called a sweetheart in my life, until I met Sara. Actually I resented the sexual act in practice, was afraid of it, it seemed to be robbing me of some vitality which I needed in my work. And–" Grant's meticulous voice continued in its inveterate honesty–soft, rounded, but never employed as an instrument to betray a fact. He owned the courage of several grizzly bears compressed into one stubby pink body. "There were bound to be people who mistook my attitude. When I went into the Camouflage Corps, in the First World War– And later, when painting in France again– I encountered girls who thought that they, and only they, might instill the spark of lusty desire. A number of experiments were performed which at best might be termed unsuccessful. . . . Would you like another scotch? I would." The peeling forehead ashine, pale blue eyes mischievous within their thick-lensed cage. "Following futile campaigning by the females, I endured from time to time the attentions of gentlemen, newly entered upon my small scene, whose preliminary advances might easily be mistaken as an expression of warm friendship, but whose subsequent demonstrations had necessarily to be repulsed. On one or two occasions– By force of arms, I regret to say." I shook my head, and wondered how those characters looked, afterward. Grant Wood's arms were as muscular as abbreviated pythons, and his freckled fists looked like knobs of granite from his native prairies.

"Male or female, I was forever compelled to explain to all comers that I would rather go home to my studio and paint." He's been vanished for a long generation as these lines are written, and there is more, much more—relevant and pitying and praising—which could be written. Sometimes I wonder: Are Irene and I the only people now living who know the whole story? It goes back into Grant's boyhood and— But no more. We return to another genius of a different age and color. We contemplate no *American Gothic*, no *Daughters of Revolution* amid this particular holy landscape. We see before us instead, and soon: love apples.)

"It's strange, though. Dr. Carver's years were all an embodiment of the life force."

"Yes. Dust from the stamen going to the pistil—"

"He found his sex vicariously. In plants—"

"This we suppose. We don't *know*."

"I think it's true. So everyone should be glad."

"They should. And never puzzle longer."

As we came close to the Visitor Center and a row of functional structures opposite, here were tomatoes turning entrancing red cheeks to the ripening light. Their vines crawled among weeds in none-too-well-kept gardening, but that didn't matter. We were delighted to be thieves devoid of all conscience. Who had planted this knotted treasure-trove and for what purpose? Did the pretty fruit (so erroneously termed to be vegetables, in a decision handed down by the U. S. Supreme Court, no less) belong to Superintendent Hieb? Had seeds been injected, or plants set out, by other men whose function it was to care for lawns, paths, signs, footbridges? When the pungent things were ready for the plucking, did folks take them home at night, or munch them as accompaniment to lunches their wives—or maybe Heloise—had put up for them?

To none of these questions did we hold answer. Any moral consideration as to property rights was intolerable. We'd been strolling, exploring, musing for long, and our throats were arid. We were and are tomato fiends, as previously emphasized. Neither of us had picked and eaten a Midwestern tomato, warm off the vine, in what the English call "donkey's years." And these were sprung from the precious soil of George Washington Carver. . . .

"How's yours, hon?"

"Oh, gad." With her mouth full. "*Mar*velous."

"So's mine. Think anyone saw us?"

Irene said, "I looked all around—not like a guilty child, but like a guilty grandmother, and that's much worse. And I never saw a single soul."

"Neither did I. Too bad we haven't got a little salt—"

"No one," said Irene firmly, "should ever require salt on a Carver love apple."

Presently she asked, "Suppose we'd been apprehended. What do you think happens to people who steal such blessings from the Department of the Interior?"

I knew, or at least thought I did. "*Leav*enworth, darling."

About two o'clock in the morning I suffered an excruciating nightmare in which a youthful George Washington Carver stood listening to an oration uttered by one H. Rap Brown or one Stokeley Carmichael. Carver's wounds were thus discovered unto him, and he went home licking them. Look here, he told himself, you were born in slavery. Was that being underprivileged? Goodness Gracious: the understatement of the century! . . . Look here, he told himself. Legend has it that when you were an infant, and the bushwhackers carried both your mother and you down into Arkansas, you were ransomed on payment of one mule colt offered by John Bentley. Do you call that an insult or do you not? Probably, had you been a *white* infant, it would have taken *two* mule colts to ransom you from the guerrillas. Discrimination! . . . Look here. When first you tried to enter college out at Highland, Kansas, they said, "We don't take niggers here." Nobody offered to drive you around to a white school in a bus. Segregation at its worst. . . . You met people like the Milhollands and the Robbinses, and they took you into their homes, awarded hospitality and encouragement and affection. But why were they so interested in you? Because you were black, that's why. In their hearts they called you a nigger, and probably told all their friends how unusual it was to see a nigger work himself to death and half starve himself to death in order to secure higher education. Man, you didn't even have sense enough to stay cool, man, cool! You play it cool, and Whitey will pay you for being a school drop-out. . . . And Dr. Pammel gave you all sorts of encouragement, and even made you his assistant, and put you in touch with leading botanists and agronomists— Tama Jim Wilson and the Wallaces made out that you were just about the smartest mule colt that ever came down the pike. But what did those honkies have up their sleeve? . . . And as for Booker T. Washington, did he ever try to *integrate* Tuskegee? No, man, no! He was a real Uncle Tom—just sucking up to Teddy Roosevelt so's he'd get invited to the White House. You cat, hear me? I said *White* House. You don't hear no Whiteys calling it *Black* House, do you? Listen, souls—

Then George Washington Carver leaped into the air, yelling *Black Power!* at the top of his lungs. He ran through the streets with an increasing mob at his heels, and in his left hand he had a home-made Molotov cocktail (made it himself, at the kitchen sink, instead of fooling around with cowpeas and peanut oil and such trivialities) and in his right hand he brandished a carbine stolen from the local National Guard Armory. *Black Power!* The mob grew and grew. First they caved in the windows of a TV shop and stole all the television sets which could be easily carried away, and they smashed the larger sets; and by that time another mob had crashed into the J. C. Penney store across the street, and they were singing, *We Shall Overcome*, and it seemed in this nightmare that a lot of white Leftists were with them; and part of the mob waved Viet Cong flags, and others waved the shirts and jackets they'd just stolen from Penney's; and by that time the cops and State Patrolmen and soldiers had arrived; and George Washington Carver barricaded himself in a plundered apartment, and you could hear him calling above the explosions of his carbine cartridges, "Come on, you cats, and let's get ourselves some honkies!"

In the capriciousness of such delusions and delirium, you change hats and uniforms and attitude in a crackling instant.

Next moment, Dr. George Washington Carver—

(Did you know? He was just plain George as a boy; but during pre-college years, when he operated a one-youth-powered laundry in Minneapolis, his mail kept getting mixed up with that of another person named George Carver. He inserted a *W* in his name, and folks turned that into *Washington* as a natural result.)

Next moment George Washington Carver and Booker T. Washington were riding in a car down in Macon County, Alabama. It wasn't back in Dr. Carver's lifetime, either, or in Washington's: it was nowadays, because I had my own current car, a 1966 Cadillac. I was driving, in the role of chauffeur, and Carver and Booker Washington were in the back seat. Night . . . we moved not far from the Tuskegee campus . . . somehow we could see college buildings in the background . . . see the institution where Carver spent the last forty-seven years of his life.

Where he grew the largest onions anyone had ever grown.

Where, according to Rackham Holt, "From leaf, root, stem, and fruit of twenty-eight plants he squeezed 536 dyes which could be used on leather, cotton, wool, silk and linen, and which would not fade in washing or in light."

Where "from the bare skeletons of cotton stalks left standing in the fields . . . he made paper and rope and fiber rugs."

Where, out of *Arachis hypogaea*, commonly fed to elephants and cocktail imbibers, he made a list of products which defies the imagination and captures it in the same breath. Everything from axle-grease to rubber, paper, wallboard, pickles, a dozen beverages, and, miracle above all, milk. Milk to save the lives of babies half a world away.

Tuskegee Institute. Where his accomplishments would fetch statesmen and scientists, to assemble in a manner of worship.

. . . But here was another car coming up behind us, overtaking rapidly, car without lights. It swerved and hovered alongside, and was filled with white men, and they looked like those sweet characters who were attacking the colored cop from Philadelphia in that fine movie, *The Heat of the Night.*

(Oho. Fine it was, with Rod Steiger and Sidney Poitier and all, but the rest of the whites portrayed were a bunch of lugs. Couldn't there have been one or two decent whites living in that little town? I never knew a Southern town which had only bad whites in it. Never knew a tenement block in New York City which had only bad Negroes, either. And I knew plenty of tenement blocks when working in the 23rd Precinct.)

The people looked over from that car, and they grinned, and the muzzles of guns were directed. They ordered me to pull over to the side of the road.

"What you doing with those niggers in your car?"

"None of your damn business."

"What are you? Some kind of Freedom Rider or something?"

"No, I don't like Freedom Riders or Freedom Marchers or Poverty Marchers or—"

"What are you? A Communist?"

"No. I hate Communists."

"You a Yankee Liberal from up North?"

"No. I don't get along well with Yankee Liberals, either."

They asked in whiny voices, "Know what happened the other day?"

"What happened the other day?"

"A bunch of nigger students back there at Tuskegee locked up the trustees of the college, and held em prisoner."

I said, "Oh yes, I read about that. But that happened in 1968. You see, Washington and Carver are right here in this car. It couldn't have happened when they were at Tuskegee: they taught folks to stick to their work. So we can't be in the *Now.* We must still be in the *Then.*"

I said, "Booker Washington believes that it's better for people to work hard for an education than to agitate for Civil Rights. Have I quoted you correctly, Dr. Washington?" and I turned around to emphasize my point. Booker Washington nodded gravely.

"And as for Dr. Carver, his biographer says that he never made a public speech on the race problem in his life."

They said, "Well, Martin Luther King sure did."

"Look. I wouldn't give Martin Luther King a ride, living or dead. It got to the point where, if you didn't agree with press and pulpit that he was an unmitigated saint, you automatically became one of the red-necked Kluxers which you fellows probably are. There went a man who made a career out of stirring up the most evil elements of our society, white and Negro alike—stirring them up, setting them at each other's throats, and then coolly withdrawing as if he were walking on eggs, shaking his finger coyly, and saying in effect, 'Now, don't you folks get violent.' When asked if he intended to obey the Law of our land, he said with sanctimony, 'I'll have to consult my conscience about that.' He was brave enough—perfectly willing to stick his neck out—but he caused untold destruction and agony. How he lived as long as he did I'll never quite understand, not with people like you around.

"Or take that precious brother of his, the Godly Reverend Mr. A. D. King. He stood up at a rally and said, 'We're not here to *destroy* St. Petersburg, but we mean to scare hell out of it!' That's a lovely non-violent preachment, isn't it? And all I did in Sarasota—maybe twenty years ago—was to urge that our county buy a beach for the colored folks. Promptly the Klan announced that they were going to burn a cross on my front lawn. I had to sit out there with a Winchester .348 in order to discourage them."

Somebody said softly, "You nigger-loving son of a bitch." Guns began to blast, they riddled the car and us three in it.

Later in dawn we strolled a peaceful woodland place. Why, it was the Nature Trail at the Carver Memorial, back in his boyhood Missouri. Dr. Carver got down on his knees and showed us some fresh green shoots. "Look at this . . . look at that . . . everything which grows is so wonderful."

Then he arose, wiping his hands carelessly against baggy trousers, and said in his falsetto voice, "Now I'd better go away from you all." He went off down the path. I looked around for Dr. Washington, and he was nowhere in sight. I stood alone until overcome by frantic desire to follow George Carver. I ran and ran, and when I got down the slope, there he was, turned into a boy again, sitting in bronze with his plant.

26. Little Brown Jug

. . . Some rite in which we must participate, some pleasantness to be effected . . . a ceremony demanded.

Then a liquor store slid into view on the left side of the road, and in that moment I knew the answer.

. . . Stopped, got out, went into the store and bought something. I asked the proprietor to put the jug in a paper sack, so that I might surprise my traveling companion.

She did express curiosity, but I observed Security until we were only a few rods from the Arkansas-Missouri line. Then I pulled off into a shady spot under trees.

"Why, you've bought a jug. A real *jug*."

"'Little brown jug, how I love thee.' Let's open up the fridge, and get out some water and ice. I won't need any ice, but you will. You always want lots of ice."

"What under the sun is in this *brown jug?*"

"Sweet essence of Missouri."

Irene was reading aloud the inscription. "'Aged in the Hills. Platte Valley Straight Corn Whiskey.' But, darling, you prefer vodka, and I always drink scotch—"

"Woman, we're departing from Missouri. And in this glossy container is, to the best of my belief, the only legally distilled *aged* corn whiskey in America."

She mused, "Platte Valley. The Platte is in Nebraska. The two rivers—North Platte and South Platte—out there where your great-grandfather served at that fort in the Indian days—"

"The Missouri Platte is a Platte of another Platteness. Daniel Boone went that far in his solitary trapping journeys, when he was past eighty. The stream rises away up in Worth County, just short of the Iowa line. It flows down through Nodaway, Andrew, Buchanan, and the county which bears its name, and finally meets the Missouri River practically on the edge of Kansas City."

"It says *Weston* on this jug."

"That's the old tobacco-market town where this distillery is located. You remember my speaking of Ben Holladay, father of the stagecoach lines? His brother, Major David Holladay, is credited with discovering some ideal limestone springs, and thereupon initiating the first distillery at Weston. Nowadays there's a big plant owned by the Cray family."

The Crays don't mention it in their publicity, but I cling to the notion that their ingredients are not merely attar of corn and rye, and barley malt . . . ah, no. There may be juneberries, and sap of maples, and possum grease; and a dust of shiny coal from the mines, and flavor of lead and tin? And a few scorched grains of powder scraped from the barrel of Wild Bill Hickok's gun, after he shot Dave Tutt in 1865 at Springfield? Yea—and ash of Daniel Boone's campfire, seasoned with drippings from the venison he jerked there when he was an old man, oh so very old, but leathery to the last. . . . Ink from the printing press which Mark Twain first served when he was a boy at Hannibal . . . and dandelion heads like butter on hillsides. And moisture of slippery elm's inner bark. And pussywillows. And the juice of a hot-dog purchased at a roadside stand, or of a hamburger munched at a ball game in St. Louis.

I told my wife that, although the distillers neglected to emphasize the fact, obviously this whiskey was concocted with assistance from a host of Missourians living and dead. Henry LaCossitt and George McManus together fetched in the corn after frost had touched it. George Caleb Bingham performed the actual grinding, with maybe Roy P. Basler helping out, while Belle Starr stood guard in case somebody came a-bothering. T. S. Eliot and O. O. McIntyre toted limestone water from that spring first used by Holladay; and Tex Rickard added the barley malt, and cooled the mash when it had cooked sufficiently. And didn't Ginger Rogers get into the act? The woman's touch. . . .

"And, for the poet's touch, Sara Teasdale could come forward with the secret yeast those people use. General John J. Pershing might be delegated to take charge of the first run, and General Maxwell D. Taylor the second run, once the mash was fully fermented. The Crays claim to use one of those old-fashioned pot stills; you'll believe that when you taste the dear stuff. And maybe Belle Starr has grown weary, so Martha Canary—'Calamity Jane' to the entire Western historical world—takes over on sentry duty. And through the years while aging continues in charred oak barrels, Marion Talley sings soothing songs to the liquor. And Mary Margaret McBride will broadcast the news, the moment J. C. Penney is ready to offer any of this celebrity-endowed nectar for sale."

Irene inquired, "What about Eugene Field?"

"Gene Field has been standing by all this time, waiting for the finished product. Appropriately he would be selected as Official Taster."

"Where, pray, did you yourself first taste the finished product?"

"At Leonard Fetchley's bar. I was sticking to vodka that night, principally, but I did want to learn what was in a Platte River bottle which Fetch handled with such Tender Loving Care."

We lifted our cups, and spoke in unison. "To Missouri." We sipped its warmth, bite, spicy gold.

Beside us we felt and heard the shudder of constant traffic. A boxcar-sized oil truck howled past . . . far through our windshield in sky beyond, a pair of Upstairs Boys were at work . . . contrails told the story as they made a long 90° to the right . . . scream of those blazing engines was nullified by distance, by yawning altitude.

Sun had fallen below whatever ridges lay beyond trees to the west. The whole side of our valley was in shadow.

Traffic lulled for a few minutes. Irene held up one finger and sat listening; I listened too. It was faraway and faint, but could be detected: the cry of dogs who'd found a scent that suited them in some darkening ravine.

We finished drinking our toast with those chopping hounds' voices still remote and a-flutter, and drove into Arkansas.

Irene looked back at the realm we had left (left with a new affection, and still an awareness of essential mystery). She quoted words of the long ago.

"'Missouri is spooky.'"

Yes. It still is.